The Reality of Aid
2004

The Reality of Aid 2004

An Independent Review of Poverty Reduction and Development Assistance

Focus on Governance and Human Rights

The Reality of Aid Project

Edited By Judith Randel, Tony German
and Deborah Ewing
Development Initiatives

IBON Books
Manila

Zed Books
London

The Reality of Aid 2004, An Independent Review of Poverty Reduction and Development Assistance was first published in the Philippines in 2004 by IBON Books, 3rd Floor, Social Communication Center Building, 4427 Interior Old Sta. Mesa, 1008 Manila, editors@ibon.org, www.ibon.org

This edition is published outside of the Philippines in cased edition only by Zed Books Ltd, 7 Cynthia Street, London N1 9JF, UK, and Room 400, 175 Fifth Ave., New York, NY 10010, USA, www.zedbooks.co.uk

Copyright © 2004 by The Reality of Aid Management Committee

Layout by Rosalie D. Santos and Benjie C. Aquino
Cover design by Benedict Deldoc
Photo credits: Torben Ulrik Nissen
Printed and bound in Great Britain by Antony Rowe Ltd, Chippenham, Wiltshire

Distributed in the USA exclusively by Palgrave Macmillan, a division of St Martin's Press, LLC, 175 Fifth Avenue, New York, NY 10010

US Cataloging-in-Publication Data is available from the Library of Congress

ISBN 971-0325-25-6 (IBON Books)
ISBN 1 84277 588 X (Zed Books)

Contents

Contents

Contents

Reality of Aid Project

The Reality of Aid Project exists to promote national and international policies that will contribute to new and effective strategies for poverty eradication, built on solidarity and equity.

Established in 1993, the Reality of Aid is a collaborative, not-for-profit initiative, involving non-governmental organisations from North and South.

The Reality of Aid publishes regular, reliable reports on international development cooperation and the extent to which governments, North and South, address the extreme inequalities of income and the structural, social and political injustices that entrench people in poverty.

From 1993 to date, the project has published a series of reports and Reality Checks on aid and development cooperation.

These reports provide a critical analysis of how governments address the issues of poverty – and whether aid and development cooperation policies are put into practice.

The Reality of Aid Project Management Committee is made up of regional representatives of all participating agencies:

Chair	Antonio Tujan Jr, IBON
Vice Chair and OECD (outside Europe):	Brian Tomlinson, Canadian Council for International Cooperation (Canada)
Asia:	Gopal Siwakoti 'Chintan', Nepal Policy Institute
Europe:	Gunnar Aegisson, BOND, UK
Africa:	Moreblessings Chidaushe, AFRODAD
Latin America:	Jorge Balbis, La Asociacion Latinoamericana de Organizaciones de Promocion (ALOP)

Reality of Aid Secretariat: Jazminda Lumang-Buncan, IBON
Email: roasecretariat@ibon.org
Web: www.realityofaid.org

Acknowledgements

The Reality of Aid is written by authors from NGOs worldwide, whose research draws on knowledge and expertise from aid agencies, academia, community-based organisations and governments. We would like to thank those who have generously contributed their knowledge and advice.

Overall editorial control of the *Reality of Aid 2004* lies with the Reality of Aid Management Committee, but the views expressed in the report do not necessarily reflect the views of the Management Committee or IBON.

Participating agencies

If you have any problems contacting people, please email roasecretariat@ibon.org

AFRICA

ZIMBABWE
African Forum & Network on Debt & Development AFRODAD
31 Atkinson Drive Hillside
P.O. Box CY 1517
Causeway, Harare
Zimbabwe
Tel 23-4-778531
     23-4-747767

ASIA, PACIFIC and the MIDDLE EAST

FIJI
ECREA
5 Bau Street
GPO Box 15473
Suva
Republic of Fiji Islands
Tel (679) 3307 588
Fax (679) 3311 248
Email kjbarr@ecrea.org.fj
Web http://www.ecrea.org.fj/

INDONESIA
International NGO Forum on Indonesia Development (INFID)
Jalan Mampang Prapatan XI/23
Jakarta 12790
Tel + 62 21 7919 6721 2
Fax + 62 21 794 1577
Email infid@infid.org
Web www.infid.org

JAPAN
Pacific Asia Resource Center
Toyo Building 3F, 1-7-11
Kanda Awaji-cho
Chiyoda-ku
Tokyo
Japan 101-0063
Tel +81-3-5209-3455
Fax +81-3-5209-3453
Email office@parc-jp.org
Web http://www.parc-jp.org/parc

PHILIPPINES
IBON Foundation, Inc.
Rm. 303 SCC Bldg.
4427 Int. Old Sta. Mesa,
Manila
Fax + 632 7160108
Tel + 632 7132729
Email ibonred@info.com.ph
Web www.ibon.org

NEPAL
Nepal Policy Institute
60 New Plaza Marga, Putalisadak
Kathmandu
Nepal
Telefax 0977-1-4419610
Email npi@ntc.net.np

MIDDLE EAST
Arab NGO Network for Development (ANND)
P.O Box 14/5792 1
105 2070 Beirut
Lebanon
Tel +961 1 319 366
Fax +961 1 815 636,
Email annd@cyberia.lb.net
Web http://www.annd.org

LATIN AMERICA

COSTA RICA
ALOP
Apartado Postal 265 1350
San Jose de Costa Rica
Tel (506) 280 8609/225 8935
Fax + 506 283 5898
Email info@alop.or.cr
Web http://www.alop.or.cr

Participating agencies

PERU
Centro Peruano de Estudios Sociales, (CEPES)
Av. Salaverry 818 Jesus Maria
Lima 11
Fax + 51 44 331744
Tel + 51 14 336610
Email cepes@cepes.pe

OECD

AUSTRALIA
Australian Council for International
Development (ACFID)
Private Bag 3
Deakin Act 2600
Tel+ 61 2 6285 1816
Fax+ 61 2 6285 1720
Email sspillane@acfid.asn.au
Web www.acfid.asn.au.

AUSTRIA
Arbeitsgemeinschaft
Entwicklungszusammenarbeit (AGEZ)
Bergasse 7
A -1090 Wien
Fax+ 43 1 317 4016
Tel+ 43 1 317 4016/4020
Email agez-office@utanet.at
Web www.oneworld.at/agez

and

Osterreichische Forschungsstiftung fur
Entwicklungshilfe (OEFSE)
Bergasse 7
A -1090 Wien
Fax+ 43 1 317 4015
Tel+ 43 1 317 4010
Email office@oefse.at
Web www.oefse.at

BELGIUM
11.11.11 *(formerly Nationaal Centrum voor
Ontwikkelingssamenwerking NCOS)*
Vlasfabriekstraat 11
B-1060 Brussels
Tel+ 32 2 536 1150
Fax+32 2 536 19 06
Email Han.Verleyen@11.be
Web www.11.be

CANADA
Canadian Council for International
Cooperation/Conseil canadien pour la
cooperation internationale (CCIC/CCCI)
1 Nicholas Street
Suite 300
Ottawa
Ontario K1N 7B7
Fax+ 1 613 241 5302
Tel+ 1 613 241 7007
Email btomlinson@ccic.ca
Web www.incommon.web.net www.net/ccic
ccci

DENMARK
Mellemfolkeligt Samvirke
Borgergade 14,
DK-1300 Copenhagen K
Tel+ 45 7731 0000
Fax+ 45 7731 0101
Email ms@ms.dk
Web http://www.ms.dk

EUROPE
BOND
Regent's Wharf
8 All Saint's Street
London N1 9RL
Tel + 44 (0) 20 7837 8344
Fax + (0) 20 7837 4220
Email bond@bond.org.uk
Web http://www.bond.org.uk

Participating agencies

FINLAND
Kehitysyhteistyoen Palvelukeskus ry /
Servicecentralen foer Utuccklingssamarbete
(KEPA)
Soernaeisten Rantatie 25
FIN-00500 Helsinki
Tel+ 358 9 584 233
Fax+ 358 9 584 23200
Email kepa@kepa.fi
Web http://www.kepa.fi

FRANCE
Centre de Recherche et d'Information pour le
Developpement (CRID)
14, passage Dubail,
75010 Paris
Tel+ 331 4472 0771
Fax+ 331 4472 0684
Email info@crid.asso.fr
Web http://www.crid.asso.fr

GERMANY
Terre des hommes
Postfach 4126
D-49031 Osnabrueck
Tel +49 (0)541/71010
Fax +49 (0)541/707233
Email terre@t-online.de
Web http://www.tdh.de

IRELAND
Concern Worldwide
52 - 55 Lower Camden Street,
Dublin 2
Tel +353 1 4754162
Fax +353 1 4757362
Email info@concern.ie
Web http://www.concern.net

ITALY
Movimondo
Via di Vigna Fabbri39
00179 Rome

Tel.+ 39 06 7844211
Fax +39 06 78851280
Email Info@movimondo.org
Or marco.zupi@cespi.it
Web http://www.movimondo.org

JAPAN
Japanese NGO Center for International
Cooperation (JANIC)
5F, Saito Bldg
2-9-1 Kanda Nishiki-cho
Chiyoda-ku
Tokyo 101-0054
Tel+ 81 3 3294 5370
Fax+ 81 3 3294 5398
Email global-citizen@janic.org
Web http://www.janic.org

NETHERLANDS
Novib - Oxfam Netherlands
PO Box 30919
2500 GX The Hague,
visiting address: Mauritskade 9
Tel +31 70 3421777
Fax +31 70 3614461
Email admin@novib.nl
Web http://www.novib.nl

NEW ZEALAND
Council for International Development/
Kaunihera mö te Whakapakari Ao Whänui
(CID)
P.O. Box 12-470 Wellington
Tel+ 64 4 472 6375
Fax+ 64 4 472 6374
Email cid@clear.net.nz
Web http://www.cid.org.nz

NORWAY
Norwegian Church Aid
Sandakerveien 74
Postboks 4544
Nydalen
0404 OSLO

Participating agencies

Tel + 47 22 09 27 00
Fax + 47 22 09 27 20
Email nca-oslo@nca.no
Web http://www.nca.no

and

Norwegian Forum for Environment and
Development (ForUM)
Storgata 11
N-0155 Oslo
Tel + 47 23 01 03 00
Fax + 47 23 01 03 03
Email forumfor@forumfor.no
Web http://www.forumfor.no

PORTUGAL
OIKOS Cooperação e Desenvolvimento
Rua de Santiago 9
1100 – 493 Lisboa
Fax+ 351 21 882 3638
Tel+ 351 21 882 3630
Email edu.oikos@oikos.pt
Web http://www.oikos.pt

SPAIN
Intermón Oxfam
Alberto Aguilera 15,
28015 Madrid
Tel + 34 93 482 0700
Fax + 34 93 482 0707
Email marias@IntermonOxfam.org
Web http://www.IntermonOxfam.org

SWEDEN
Diakonia
172 99 Sundbyberg
Tel 08 453 69 00
Fax 08 453 69 29
Email diakonia@diakonia.se
Web http://www.diakonia.se

Forum Syd
Box 15407
S-104 65
Stockholm
Sweden
Tel + 46 8 506 370 00
Fax + 46 8 506 370 99
Email forum.syd@forumsyd.se
Web http://www.forumsyd.se/

SWITZERLAND
Swiss Coalition of Development Organisations
Swissaid/Fastenopfer/Brot für alle/Helvetas/
Caritas/Heks
Monbijoustrasse 31
CH-3001 Bern
Tel + 41 31 390 9330
Fax+ 41 31 390 9331
Email mail@swisscoalition.ch
Web www.swisscoalition.ch

UNITED KINGDOM
BOND
Regent's Wharf
8 All Saint's Street
London N1 9RL
Tel + 44 (0) 20 7837 8344
Fax + (0) 20 7837 4220
Email bond@bond.org.uk
Web http://www.bond.org.uk

UNITED STATES
American Council for Voluntary International
Action (InterAction)
1717 Massachusetts Avenue NW,
Suite 801,
Washington DC 20036
Fax + 1 202 667 8236
Tel + 1 202 667 8227
Email ia@interaction.org
Web http://www.interaction.org

Part I
Introduction

Introduction

Reports from NGOs in this *Reality of Aid* present a very diverse picture of governance and human rights in international cooperation. At one end of the scale we see donors and developing country governments focusing on the very practical questions of how aid can be better managed and coordinated. At the other end, we see how selective interpretation of 'good governance' may be used, consciously or unconsciously, to reinforce long-standing patterns of economic and political domination, and the new hegemony of wealth and power concentrated in the hands of a very privileged élite in a uni-polar world.

But despite this diverse picture — a few clear messages come through loud and very clear.

- the risk that aid is being diverted from the overriding necessity of eliminating poverty for the many to the narrow, and very probably illusory end, of promoting security for the few;
- the continued domination and maladministration of global political and economic mechanisms by OECD countries, especially G8 donors and very particularly, the United States;
- the Alice in Wonderland interpretation of governance and human rights by OECD donors - so that these terms mean whatever OECD countries want them to mean.

Less than five years after they were endorsed by world leaders, the Millennium Development Goals are off track. The goal of halving the proportion of people living in absolute poverty, who still number 1.3 billion people today, is being put at risk, by donor countries who again are failing to live up to their commitments on aid and policies needed to achieve a more equitable world order.

The judgement of history on those who, despite having wealth and power at their disposal, opt for narrow national interest rather than poverty elimination and the promotion of human rights of ordinary people, will be harsh.

Antonio Tujan Jr, IBON
Chair, Reality of Aid

Governance: reclaiming the concept from a human rights perspective

Reality of Aid Networks

'Donors are playing a dangerous game. You come with inadequate amounts that are highly conditioned and fundamentally unreliable, then you insist on negotiating as though you are a valuable partner, then you are surprised that these governments don't trust you. Put some real money on the table. Then you can start negotiating'.

This comment, from a senior aid official in a meeting on development cooperation in Addis Ababa in February 2004, captures the tone of much of the analysis in this latest edition of the *Reality of Aid*.

In Sept 2000, World Leaders at the UN General Assembly endorsed a vision of global justice for the 21st Century in the Millennium Declaration. Central to this, was a commitment to the Millennium Development Goals, which aim to halve the proportion of people living in poverty by the year 2015 (see page 164). Subsequently, donors have made much of a stronger focus on poverty and increased efforts to improve aid effectiveness and strengthen North/South partnerships in pursuit of the MDGs.

But just three years later, in October 2003, the Development Assistance Committee (DAC) of the OECD released a controversial policy statement, endorsed at the highest level by OECD aid ministers, on development cooperation and the prevention of terrorism.[1] This policy asserts that 'development cooperation ... [has] an important role to play in helping to deprive terrorists of popular support and addressing the conditions that terrorist leaders feed on and exploit'. (OECD, DAC, 11) These conditions include the poverty, marginalisation and disaffection of people whose 'frustrations and educated energy can make them useful foot soldiers and supporters for terrorism'. States with 'weak, ineffectual or non-existent governance systems' are considered 'more likely to provide the environment in which terrorists are recruited and supported' (OECD, DAC, 13, 16). In the face of profound crises of poverty, growing inequality and conflict in Asia, Latin America, the Middle East and Africa, the lens through which donors now wish to assess their priorities appears to be their own security interests and the 'war on terrorism'.

Only two years ago, in its 2002 Report, the Reality of Aid drew attention to the critical failure of the international community

Political Overview

to meet its obligations and commit the necessary resources and policies for deep global and national reform to reach even modest Millennium Development Goals (MDGs). To achieve these goals, global leaders adopted the Monterrey Consensus at the 2002 UN Conference on Financing for Development (FfD). This promised 'a new partnership between developed and developing countries'— albeit one that continued largely with the foundation of now clearly bankrupt donor-imposed policies of integration into a global economy (at any cost), privatisation of state capacities and a single-minded focus on economic growth as essential ingredients to addressing poverty.

But by 2003 the United States and its allies had instead unilaterally committed hundreds of billions of dollars to destructive wars and reconstruction efforts in Afghanistan and Iraq, expanding a global 'anti-terrorism' state and military security apparatus across many countries throughout the South. In the name of a 'whole-of-government' approach to global security, some donors are seeking to 'expand' the criteria for official development assistance (ODA) as they merge military, political and humanitarian responses to countries experiencing protracted crises, in the name of the 'war on terrorism'.

In Australia for instance, NGOs are concerned about an overt shift to a new agenda that conflates the combating of terrorism and combating of poverty, as if they were the same thing. Australian aid now includes several initiatives for counter-terrorism capacity building, including bilateral counter-terrorism programmes with Indonesia and the Philippines, a 'Peace and Security Fund' for the Pacific Island Countries, and a contribution to an Asia-Pacific Economic Cooperation (APEC) fund for counter-terrorism capacity building. While it is necessary and legitimate for governments to support an effective programme to combat

terrorism, Australian NGOs have argued that the resources for these activities should come from national security budgets, not from the overstretched aid and development budget.

This trend towards the 'securitisation' of aid brings into sharp relief the notions of governance and the promotion of rights in international cooperation and aid, which is the theme of the *Reality of Aid 2004* report.

The current international rights framework covers a spectrum of rights embodied in various treaties, declarations and programmes of action, developed under the auspices of the United Nations, ILO and UNESCO. The two basic treaties that provide a foundation for human rights are the UN International Covenant on Civil and Political Rights (ICCPR) and the UN International Covenant on Economic, Social and Cultural Rights (ICESCR). The ICCPR covers rights that include the right to life, freedom from torture and slavery, and the right to freedom of conscience and religion. The ICESCR covers the right to work, to join a trade union, to education, to enjoy the highest attainable standard of health, the right to social security and to an adequate standard of living. The Rio Conventions and the Kyoto Protocol cover rights that affect the ownership of communities over resources, local people's livelihoods and the role of international cooperation in protecting the environment and promoting development.

The indivisibility of rights means that no right is more fundamental than another. Rights are supposed, except in times of dire emergency, to be applicable to every person at all times.[2]

The obligation to respect, protect and fulfil human rights rests with the State. But the extent to which individual governments recognise and discharge human rights obligations varies widely. In principle, development cooperation could and should play a key role in enabling the international

Political Overview

community to work together to promote a legally binding international human rights framework. Article 2 Paragraph 1 of the ICESCR urges States to take steps 'individually and through international assistance and cooperation, especially economic and technical, to the maximum of available resources, with a view to achieving progressively the full realization of rights'.

The UN has also developed a conceptual framework and content for the right to development, also known as the collective rights of peoples, communities and nations, mainly through the adoption of the Declaration on the Right to Development in 1986. However, efforts to make this document a binding legal instrument have not been successful due to the lack of support and cooperation from the developed countries and international financial institutions.

The selective way that donors interpret ideas of governance and human rights is not consistent with a genuine rights approach to development and poverty. Japan for example is said to have applied its human rights criteria more harshly on small countries than on larger and more resource-rich countries such as China and Myanmar.

The United Nations human rights bodies have criticised the International Financial Institutions for not paying sufficient attention to the adverse effects that Structural Adjustment Programmes (SAPs) and other economic and trade policies can have on the realisation of economic and social rights. In some cases, developing country governments have had to balance competing obligations: to pursue the realisation of social and economic rights by undertaking necessary measures for poverty eradication or to comply with narrow economic conditionalities. There may be conflicts between international obligations to comply with UN treaty obligations and IFIs conditions or WTO

agreements. In such a situation, governments may be left with no choice but simply to ignore the human rights treaty obligations, as the pressure from largely donor-imposed conditionality is stronger. Countries may be punished for violating IFIs and WTO conditions, but not those of the UN.

Achieving the Millennium Development Goals within a human rights framework
At the UN General Assembly in September 2000, the international community brought a different, a more hopeful, universal vision to the challenges of the 21st century. In the Millennium Declaration, they articulated a global consensus focusing on global justice, and in particular committed to the achievement of the Millennium Development Goals by 2015. For all donors, these Goals, combined with strategies to improve aid effectiveness and renewed North/South partnership, were to become the defining paradigm of international cooperation for the next 15 years. Adopted by both developed and developing countries, the MDGs, without question, respond to clear humanitarian and ethical imperatives to end global poverty and place an unequivocal responsibility on all development actors — official donors, multilateral institutions, civil society organisations (CSOs) and the private sector — to contribute to their realisation.

The imperatives to act, and the costs of inaction, are morally shocking, with catastrophic human consequences for hundreds of millions of people around the world. One third of all human deaths — some 18 million people a year or 50,000 daily — are due to poverty-related causes (such as starvation, diarrhoea, pneumonia, tuberculosis, measles, malaria, perinatal and maternal conditions), which could be prevented or cured easily, and increasingly HIV/AIDS, which is still largely untreated among people in poverty. This death toll

Political Overview

since the end of the Cold War in 1990 is about 270 million people, a majority women and children, roughly the population of the United States.[3] How many more will die, as the world turns away from even modest targets in order to finance its 'war on terrorism'? The UNDP's 2003 *Human Development Report* has demonstrated that the era of globalisation has accompanied such levels of poverty with a widening inequality gap, where the richest 5% of the world's people receive 114 times the income of the poorest 5%.[4] Nearly half the world's population lives on less than US$2 a day and command a mere 1.25% of the world's global social product, while a third as many people in rich countries command 64 times the income and 81% of the global social product.[5]

The MDGs are clear and committed benchmarks for donor and developing country governments, as they assess their priorities in international cooperation and social development policy. Yet they are also exceptionally modest in their reach. For example, the first goal to reduce the proportion of people living on less than US$1 a day by 2015, if it is achieved, will still leave an estimated 900 million people living in absolute poverty in 2015, a mere reduction of about 230 million or less than 20% in the *numbers* of people living in poverty between 2000 and 2015.[6]

While now adopted by the UN General Assembly, the Goals had a less than democratic birth; they were proposed and agreed in 1996 by developed country aid ministers operating within their exclusive 'donor club' at the OECD DAC, unencumbered by developing country 'partners'. Many civil society commentators at the time, including the Reality of Aid network, were highly critical of donor ministers who thereby avoided commitments to, and drew attention away from, the critical structural issues for global economic

justice. Among these were debt cancellation, fair trade and equitable participation in global institutions, which had been raised repeatedly in the 1990s global UN conferences by both developing country governments and many participating CSOs.

Despite their rhetorical expressions of support, several years later the Goals at best inform the discourse of multilateral organisations, government ministries and development specialists. Despite coordinated campaigns by the UNDP and some CSOs, ordinary citizens have little sense of ownership of the MDGs, or of their role in holding their governments accountable for national strategies to tackle social dimensions of poverty based on the MDGs.[7] Indeed, the Goals are silent on basic issues of citizens' rights, empowerment and improved equality, and thus ignore the politics inherent in working for their achievement in many countries. Even the World Bank recognises, at least intellectually that empowerment and equality are essential social conditions for overcoming poverty.[8]

Ending poverty is inherently a political process, specific to local economic, social, cultural, ecological and gender equality circumstances in each country. As the work of Amartya Sen demonstrates, people-centred development for poverty eradication is ultimately about recognising the rights of the vulnerable and transforming the power relations, and cultural and social interests, that sustain inequality. Development is therefore a political process that engages people, particularly people who are poor and powerless, in negotiating with each other, with their governments, and with the world community for policies and rights that advance their livelihood and secure their future in their world. But as the *Reality of Aid* commentary on the Middle East points out, the focus of discussions on governance in the Arab world has been on procedures

Political Overview

and has ignored political and economic forces, both internal and external.

People in poverty are not subjects to be acted upon by 'development' but rather central actors in sometimes conflictual politics seeking pro-poor development strategies. Consequently, finding avenues to address unequal power, capacity, and access to resources for those whose rights are beyond reach — due to poverty and marginalisation — is a fundamental challenge to development actors wanting to link poverty reduction to democratic governance and participation. The UN system, the Charter, and its various Declarations and Covenants on Human Rights, provides a normative framework within which these issues can be addressed.

While based on international legal codes and covenants developed over the past century, the rights framework is a dynamic one that continues to evolve through intense national and multilateral political processes. It has been the result of many decades of struggles by peoples' organisations — women's movement, indigenous nations, gay and lesbian networks, workers and labour organisations, fishers' and farmers' organisations, human rights defenders. Human rights are essentially active and should not merely be 'promoted' or 'protected', but are to be practiced and experienced. They have implications for the actions of all donors, governments, and non-state actors in development. In the words of John Foster, 'participation is central to a human rights approach to development as a right, an *entitlement guaranteed by international law, rather than an optional extra or tool for the delivery of aid'* Nevertheless the challenge for development practitioners, civil society and official aid agencies alike, is to make the language and analysis of rights accessible to citizens and organisations working to overcome the

conditions of poverty, from community to national levels.[9]

In this context, the MDGs are *one* expression of economic, social and cultural rights, to which all governments are bound and must be accountable. Achieving these goals would be a positive though insufficient step towards the eradication of poverty. The MDGs are minimal but very useful targets, which can serve as a political framework for leveraging political commitment to poverty-focused development. This must not undermine existing broader obligations on the part of governments to international human rights law. Some members of the Reality of Aid network, particularly in the North, focus on the MDGs in their advocacy for accountability with their governments and multilateral institutions, with strong support from the UNDP leading a global campaign. Others, understanding the importance of a holistic approach to poverty, point to their limitations noted above. But irrespective of the emphasis on the Goals, all members of the Reality of Aid network stress that the MDGs can only be achieved within a rights framework whereby citizens and governments are engaged in restructuring global and national power relations in order to transform the root causes of poverty. Hence democratic governance and citizens' rights, at all levels, with full local ownership of development initiatives, are fundamental.

The Reality of Aid 2004 calls for all actors in the global aid regime (including multilateral organisations, the international financial institutions, bilateral donors and civil society organisations) to entrench the discourse of human rights, not only the in their policies, but also in their practices for international cooperation to achieve the Millennium Development Goals and the eradication of poverty. Respect for human rights is the foundation for effective governance to achieve these goals.

Competing Notions of Governance and Citizenship in the Aid Regime

The question of democratic governance is at the heart of effective strategies to end global poverty. Concern for governance has a long pedigree for both donors and civil society. In 1989 the World Bank explicitly identified 'a crisis of governance' behind the 'litany of Africa's development problems': it defined governance as the 'exercise of political power to manage a nation's affairs'.[10] Since then the policies and interventions to promote 'good governance' have become a central preoccupation in the official donor community. But reports from NGOs in *The Reality of Aid 2004*, represent a serious critique of the way that donors are currently approaching governance. The first charge, is that donors often have strong pre-conceived notions of what constitutes 'good' governance. This often results in local traditions and accountabilities being undervalued and undermined. INFID's detailed description of Consultative Group processes in Indonesia illustrates a wider point on how de facto alliances between very powerful international institutions and local élites can leave very little room for alternative perspectives, let alone policies, despite stated commitment to participatory approaches and 'good' governance.

Linked to this criticism is the fact that donors take an 'Alice in Wonderland' approach to governance, so that the term means whatever a donor wants it to mean.[11] NGO reports from France highlight how a bewildering variety of interventions are explained away on the basis that they will improve governance.

But perhaps more serious is the way that some donors seem to be using good governance like a can-opener, to prise open markets and dismantle national regulatory frameworks. When the result of changes to promote 'good' governance is poor people having to pay for privatised water, international companies extracting new profit streams from fragile southern economies and the most vulnerable people having to bear the risks of unemployment in a capricious global market, the relationship between governance policies and poverty reduction has to be questioned. The AGILE project in the Philippines and the Melamchi River diversion project in Nepal, both show how external donors' pressure and corporate interest can combine to negate genuine participation and jeopardise the long-term interests of poor countries and poor people.

According to Bank President, James Wolfensohn, a comprehensive 'bargain' was spelled out at Monterrey in 2002 whereby the 'developing countries promised to strengthen governance, create a positive investment climate, build transparent legal and financial systems, and fight corruption'. The 'developed countries agreed to support these efforts by enhancing capacity building, increase aid, and open their markets for trade'.[12] While Wolfensohn takes the developed countries to task for failing to live up to their end of this bargain, particularly evident in the breakdown in WTO trade negotiations at Cancun, what is remarkable is what is missing from Wolfensohn's discourse.

A few months earlier, Kumi Naidoo, addressing the President and officials of the World Bank, suggested that the 'old notion of governance is breaking down in an era of globalisation with the emergence of a devastating 'democratic deficit" in several local and national contexts, and certainly at the global level'. He went on to challenge the Bank 'to be willing to bring its own decision-making processes into line with those it is encouraging its [government] clients [in participatory PRSPs] to use'.[13] For

Political Overview

more than a decade the developed countries, which clearly control the operations of the Bank and the Fund, and in practice the WTO, have ignored repeated demands and proposals for reform.

The UN Financing for Development (FfD) conference brought reinvigorated attention to governance/democratic deficits in the international economic, financial and trading system.[14] The Monterrey Consensus calls explicitly for 'broadening and strengthening of participation of developing countries with economies in transition in international economic decision-making and norm-setting', and in particular invites the World Bank and the IMF to respond to these concerns (para 56 and 57). These institutions have been at the forefront of major systemic crises in developing countries (for example, Argentina, Indonesia, Ghana among many others) with devastating social and economic consequences for citizens in these countries, particularly people who are poor and vulnerable. After 30 years, they have largely failed to deliver promised opportunities for poverty reduction from structural adjustment policy and loan conditionalities based on the primacy of deregulated market-led growth. Instead, as we shall demonstrate below, globalisation has undermined the policy alternatives and the capacity for effective governance for many of the poorest countries. This situation is reinforced by donor priorities such as the German good governance conditionalities, which require adherence to market friendly economic orthodoxy and preclude freedom to explore alternatives.

The fostering of a different model of global governance is of critical importance, because the current model, designed for the post-war 1945 world, is no longer relevant or sustainable for the 21st century. A . strengthened coordinating and agenda-setting role for the United Nations is at the very

core of a democratic vision for the management of urgent global social, environmental and economic issues. But some major developed countries, with their controlling shares in decision making at the Bank and the IMF, are reluctant to see more democratic processes determining these issues. In assessing the results to date of the comprehensive 'bargain' of Monterrey, Roberto Bissio, founding Coordinator of Social Watch, representing NGOs at the October 2003 UN High Level Financing for Development Dialogue, put it to the delegates: 'The spirit of Monterrey that we all praise, needs to find a body to live in. Otherwise it will remain a ghost.'[15]

Issues of governance permeate the discourse of the official donors and the Bank, the IMF and official donors, but focus almost entirely on the need for reform in the South. There is little doubt that issues of governance in developing countries are important conditions for empowering citizens and people living in poverty. But how do official donors understand developing countries' Monterrey promise to strengthen governance? In general, 'good governance' for donors has some if not all of the following effective dimensions:

- public accountability and transparency;
- the rule of law;
- anti-corruption measures;
- decentralisation and local government reform;
- democratic performance;
- juridical reform;
- social safety nets;
- a regulatory but lean state apparatus for efficient private markets;
- civil society participation in development; and
- overall respect for human rights.

Political Overview

In practice, however, donors have focused on governance largely through a much more restricted lens of 'good governance' in the technical management of government resources and effective implementation of (often donor-directed) macroeconomic and anti-poverty sector policies.[16]

Many in the South, including authors for *The Reality of Aid 2004*, are asking whether donor concerns for 'good governance', now referred to as the 'Post-Washington Consensus' are no more than repackaged structural adjustment programmes that were highly contested in many countries in which they were imposed in the 1980s and 1990s, now with a supposed human face for demonstrable 'country ownership'?

Civil society networks in the Reality of Aid, by contrast, focus their policy and advocacy attention on issues in *democratic governance*. As such, governance is not an end in itself, to be engineered through technical assistance and policy interventions by donors. Rather it is fundamentally about politics, power and the exercise of rights in society, and is therefore an evolving and particular process that may take decades. In the words of Kavaljit Singh:

'A good governance system is the one under which all public policy affairs are managed through broad consensus in a transparent, accountable, participatory and equitable manner. However, such an ideal system of good governance remains a far cry in the developed world, leave alone the poor and the developing world. Hence, governance cannot be an end in itself. It is an evolving process and has the potential to become a potent instrument for radical transformation provided it is

applied in all spheres of social life. Like democracy, good governance cannot be implanted or imposed by the donor community, it has to be imbibed, nurtured and cherished from within. That is why recent efforts to impose universal blueprints have not yielded positive results.'[17]

The Reality of Aid network shares with the UNDP the identity of 'effective governance' with democratic governance. In its 2002 *Human Development Report*, the UNDP defines governance as a culturally and country-specific democratic means, both process and institutions, for the exercise of peoples' rights, which ensure equity, promote social solidarity and sustainable livelihoods. Unlike the technocratic approach of the World Bank and many donors, focusing on administrative efficiency, processes of governance within a rights framework takes account of unequal power relations within society and globally, including gender relations. For the UNDP advancing democratic governance has several implications:

- The links between democracy and equity are essential for human development, which is not automatic when a small elite dominates economic and political decisions;
- Democracy that empowers people must be built — it cannot be imported — and will take many forms in a given context;
- Establishing democratic control over security forces is an essential priority — otherwise, far from ensuring personal security and peace, security forces may actively undermine them; and
- Global interdependence also calls for more participation and accountability in global decision-making.[18]

Political Overview

These normative issues surrounding governance are strongly contested in national and global political realms between government, socio-economic élites and CSOs representing the interests of people living in poverty. Internationally, CSOs are contributing to critical policy discussions and promoting democratic process in the Bank, the IMF, the WTO and within the United Nations, as well as regional bodies such as the Africa Union. Nationally, civil society often acts to promote citizens' rights as representative organisations that articulate different ideas and values, and serve to negotiate and peacefully accommodate various social forces. Civil society can be a space to constitute processes that encourage the conditions for democratic governance — tolerance in the context of pluralism, diversity and mediation of social and economic conflict.

Drawing on the contributions of Reality of Aid global partners, this report offers some analysis and lessons with regard to governance and rights in the context of the urgent need to bring deep-seated democratic reform to the multilateral system. In this light, we also ask how might official donors (including northern CSOs) construct real democratic partnerships in international cooperation, in their practices for effective aid and collaboration to realize a shared goal of poverty eradication?

Governance and rights in the aid regime: reforming multilateral institutions

In this uncertain and volatile period in world history, with new threats to peace and their impact especially on poor and vulnerable people, the international community must respond, not through threats of violence and war, but by reinventing democracy for the 21st century (See Box 1, below). But this option is not apparently the one being pursued by powerful countries.

Box 1: A Challenge to the Global Community
Secretary General Kofi Annan, Addressing the General Assembly, 23 September 2003

'Three years ago, when you came here for the Millennium Summit, we shared a vision, a vision of global solidarity and collective security, expressed in the Millennium Declaration.

But recent events have called that consensus in question.

All of us know there are new threats that must be faced - or, perhaps, old threats in new and dangerous combinations: new forms of terrorism, and the proliferation of weapons of mass destruction.

But, while some consider these threats as self-evidently the main challenge to world peace and security, others feel more immediately menaced by small arms employed in civil conflict, or by so-called 'soft threats' such as the persistence of extreme poverty, the disparity of income between and within societies, and the spread of infectious diseases, or climate change and environmental degradation.

In truth, we do not have to choose. The United Nations must confront all these threats and challenges — new and old, 'hard' and 'soft'. It must be fully engaged in the struggle for development and poverty eradication, starting with the achievement of the Millennium Development Goals; in the common struggle to protect our common environment; and in the struggle for human rights, democracy and good governance....

Political Overview

Excellencies, we have come to a fork in the road. This may be a moment no less decisive than 1945 itself, when the United Nations was founded.

At that time, a group of far-sighted leaders, led and inspired by President Franklin D. Roosevelt, were determined to make the second half of the twentieth century different from the first half. They saw that the human race had only one world to live in, and that unless it managed its affairs prudently, all human beings may perish.

So they drew up rules to govern international behaviour, and founded a network of institutions, with the United Nations at its centre, in which the peoples of the world could work together for the common good.

Now we must decide whether it is possible to continue on the basis agreed then, or whether radical changes are needed...'

The consolidation by the United States of a unipolar world order, dangerously based on economic and military might, with few checks and balances, has instead weakened multilateral institutions and values. NGOs in Switzerland, for instance, report growing concern that the role of the US and its allies in the fight against terrorism is increasingly influencing the World Bank's donor coordination role in PRSPs. These multilateral institutions, with a potential for building global democratic consensus on priority global public goods issues, such as fair trade or combating curable diseases, are being sidelined by the United States and several other developed countries, when they do not serve the US administration's immediate and expressed strategic interests.

At the same time, key international financial institutions (IFIs), including the WTO, while a part of the multilateral system, are largely controlled by these same powerful countries. IFIs have a long history of structuring policy choices for developing countries. In doing so, as we have seen above, these institutions have been widely challenged for their lack of democracy and their rigid defence and promotion of the interests of industrial countries in the management of global crises and the expansion of global economic opportunities,

often in the interests of unaccountable global corporations.

Recently, Kofi Annan warned that the United Nations, which is at the centre of multilateralism, was at a 'fork in the road' and called for 'radical reform' of the organisation that must consider 'the adequacy and effectiveness, of the rules and instruments at our disposal'. He urges member countries to reinvigorate the UN by 'demonstrating its ability to deal effectively with the most difficult issues, and by becoming more broadly representative of the international community as a whole, as well as the geopolitical realities of today'[19] A strengthened United Nations, and particularly its Security Council and Economic and Social Council (ECOSOC), built on the foundation of a system of norms and standards arising from its Charter and Universal Declaration of Human Rights, could be a critical counter-weight to the competing normative framework of corporate and private property rights in a market economy, long promoted aggressively by the IFIs and their allies among the corporate and government élites. What are the challenges and opportunities for reform of these international financial institutions within a framework of democratic governance and human rights?

Political Overview

There is little doubt that the IFIs, the Basel Committee (of the ten most powerful Central Bankers) and the WTO, along with regional development banks, are the central pillars in global economic governance. The IFIs are also the apex institutions in the international aid regime, with an almost unquestioned role to define for all donors the legitimate terms of policy discourse with developing countries and effective strategies for the delivery of aid in relation to poverty reduction. The pervasive influence of the World Bank's *Assessing Aid: What Works, What Doesn't and Why*[20], adopted now by almost all donor agencies for improving their aid effectiveness, is but one example. World Bank assumptions about aid effectiveness in this and subsequent reports set out the intellectual foundations and the 'right' policies in developing countries for coordinated donor initiatives in budget support and harmonised sector programming for 'effective' poverty reduction strategies (PRSPs). As a result many donors, notably the European Commission among others, now focus their aid with a high degree of country selectivity based on country 'owned' but Bank/IMF endorsed PRSPs and on Bank/IMF 'certification' of compliance with Bank/Fund policies for economic reform and 'good governance'. Governance reform makes up increasing levels of multilateral and bilateral aid packages; and some countries have been suspended based on donor perceptions of governance issues.

What reforms in the multilateral system, and particularly with the International Financial Institutions, would enhance democratic governance within a human rights framework?

1. The International Financial Institutions must no longer be the exclusive intellectual and authoritative 'gatekeeper' for policy advice on governance reform and resource transfers in the aid regime. These institutions must take on board the substantial critique of their past and current practices, which exposes the fallacies and undermines their credibility as source for definitive development discourse and practice for the donor community.

Northern donors have become both the judge and the jury of 'good' governance in high aid-dependent poor countries, with all donors closely integrating into their own aid policies a Bank-defined 'Post-Washington Consensus' As noted earlier, this Consensus links Bank-inspired macroeconomic policies for growth with institutional reform to assure political 'ownership' and governance capacity in the poorest countries to implement these policies. The donors have adopted this Post-Washington Consensus with the explicit working assumption, rooted intellectually in the Bank, that, on the whole, the development agenda is indisputably known and only the details need attention.[21] By gaining a near monopoly on official donor development analysis and the extension of its assumptions to the donor community as a whole, the Bank is able to validate its ideology and essentially discount the emergence of alternatives outside its paradigm.[22]

In assuming this mandate on behalf of all donors, the IFIs in effect serve to protect national donors from the political risks associated with what would be seen to be inappropriate and intrusive policy interventions in the sovereignty of recipient countries, that is, with respect to their right to choose democratically the policy options that best meet the needs of their citizens. Governments of the poorest countries, in the face of the overwhelming capacities of the Bank, the Fund and major donors acting in concert, in practice, have few options to challenge this policy advice (although even in

Political Overview

the most aid-dependent countries' governing élites have often been effective in protecting their own interests and avoiding the worst impacts). The Reality of Aid networks suggest that the governance agenda for donors has more to do with the exercise of their power as aid donors to achieve a given policy agenda in the poorest countries than it has to do with their concerns for the democratic rights of citizens affected by the exercise of this power. Few donors publicly question the sometimes serious limitations of governance in China, India or Mexico, for example.

The World Bank and IMF adopted their focus on governance in the 1990s in the context of a widely recognised failure of their neoliberal economic policies to address growing poverty and inequality. In exercising their power as donors, rather than question the integrity of the policies or their own responsibility for inappropriate neo-liberal 'advice' (the earlier 'Washington Consensus'), the Bank and the Fund were quick to blame poor implementation and poor institutions in borrowing countries for this policy failure. So, for example, the Bank argued that inefficient financial systems, excessive political interference and widespread corruption required more attention as the institutional preconditions for market economies and successful reform efforts.[23] The IFIs have shown little restraint in using their designated role on behalf of all donors as a 'gatekeeper' that may choose whether to open the door to substantial resource transfers from all donors, in order to continue to push these same policies of economic liberalisation or privatisation of essential social services. Bank hegemony has also been reinforced by actions of other donors. New research by the UK NGO network BOND, suggests that EC Country Strategy Papers in Bolivia, India, Kenya and Senegal have replicated and enhanced the World Bank and IMF country analysis and

remit for development assistance.[24] This has resulted in World Bank macroeconomic policy prescriptions being imposed without proper consultation.

Recent focus on developing country 'ownership' of strategies to tackle poverty in Poverty Reduction Strategy Papers (PRSPs) further consolidates the power of the Bank and the Fund over development options. With intense pressures to cancel debt for the poorest countries, the Bank and the Fund were able to condition debt cancellation on the presentation of effective strategies for using these resources for poverty reduction through the PRSP. Needing ultimate approval and considerable support from the Bank and the Fund to develop PRSPs, the IFIs have been able to position themselves as *the* arbiter of the content of such strategies, thus sidelining the UNDP, which had more than a decade of experience working with developing countries on country planning frameworks.[25]

In contrast to governance of the IFIs, the EU Cotonou Agreement opens up a formal political space for Southern governments and activists in its institutional architecture. NGO commentators argue that this moves the donor-recipient relationship towards a model of rights and obligation, rather than beneficence and paternalism. And while negotiations on trade under Cotonou have been flawed, some incremental improvements, such as the 'Everything But Arms' agreement, have been achieved.[26]

Civil society join with donors and developing country governments who insist that aid must focus on the core elements of effective strategies to address poverty. However, as *Reality of Aid 2002* pointed out, authentic ownership of such national poverty strategies, to guide donor collaboration, depends on the quality of national efforts to consult those most affected, often with very limited capacities to participate, and to

15

Political Overview

reach often difficult social consensus on appropriate poverty reduction goals and socio-economic policy.

While some in civil society have been able to take advantage of the often-limited 'consultations' afforded by the IFI-mandated PRSPs, it is clear that PRSPs to date have not been able to provide the independent political space in which authentic national efforts can evolve. As the Norwegian report asks, will donor promotion of PRSP processes that strengthen the role of the executive but marginalise elected representatives, strengthen or weaken a system of governance that is accountable to the people. The latter, as demonstrated by Uganda's experience developing their own poverty strategies, occurs over several years and with different degrees of government coordination of civil processes with *invited* support from outside donors. Humility is a critical ingredient on the part of donors, civil society and governments, in the face of the immense challenges of poverty eradication — from structural reform to assuring gender equality. Well-targeted and effective country-designed poverty reduction strategies will require a diversity of approaches and policy mixes that may often challenge the policy prescriptions emanating from the Bank and the Fund that currently seem to define the overarching content of PRSPs.

There is also emerging evidence that PRSPs may serve to *depoliticise* the politics of poverty eradication. As one field-based study concluded, 'the social and ideological foundations of the [Tanzania] Poverty Reduction Strategy are narrow, representing the views of a small, homogeneous 'iron triangle' of transnational professionals based in key government ministries and donor agencies in Dar es Salaam. The content and process of the PRSP thus reflects a depoliticized mode of technocratic governance'. Indeed the authors point to

'signs of domestic [civil society] advocacy groups being 'crowded out' of policy debates due to the superior resources and readiness of transnational [private] agencies, which are becoming surrogate representatives of Tanzanian civil society in the state-donor partnership.[27]

These reflections on the Tanzania process reinforce a more general observation on the impact of aid's technocratic and bureaucratic approaches to governance, in which 'in the guise of a neutral, technical mission to which no one can object, it depoliticizes both poverty and the state.' The process is one of 're-engineering' government to insulate, in effect, government power from popular demands and to shift power away from parliaments into an elite public service.[28]

The Post-Washington Consensus is an overwhelming agenda for institutional reform that is premised on optimism about the relevance of northern models of governance and pessimism about local southern governance capacities and structures.[29] It is a model that many would argue is ill-suited to the real conditions of governance facing the poorest countries to which it is directed. These countries are being overwhelmed not only by deep institutional reforms imposed by the IFIs, but also by a host of rules and regulations arising from their compliance with the Uruguay Round GATT trade agreements. The expectations for the breadth of public sector reform within very close time horizons to make progress would tax the most committed government in the North, with far greater institutional capacities to respond.

Not unexpected, the evidence to date is of very limited success. By the Bank's own reckoning, in the late 1990s fewer than 40% of projects with institutional development goals showed 'substantial impact'. Less than a third of civil service reform projects achieved satisfactory results and many of

Political Overview

these proved unsustainable. Another study suggested that juridical reform has paid exclusive attention to putting in place the institutional context for the rule of law (to strengthen a formal market economy) and has often undermined informal mechanisms to resolve disputes on which people in poverty depend. This study concluded that the IFIs have approached governance issues with 'a combination of impatience and a readiness to use borrowers as guinea pigs'.[30]

Despite a significant critique of the governance agenda promoted by the Bank and the Fund, which is largely substantiated in independent research and participant observation by southern CSOs, the monopoly weight of this Bank agenda can have profound consequences for the eligibility of borrowing countries for all donors. Significantly, the Bank has recently determined each borrowing country's aid allocation against a 'Country Policy and Institutional Assessment' (CPIA) tool, for which there is evidence that the Bank allocated five times more resources to countries that received an 'A' rating than those that received an 'F'. An analysis of this system concluded that 'developing country governments are not given the same flexibility that industrial countries claim for themselves when determining whether or when to liberalize, privatize or exercise greater budgetary discipline. By modulating a government's access to credits, the Bank rewards or punishes governments depending on their performance relative to CPIA standards....A government will not gain access to its full allocation of credits... unless it accomplishes specific policy actions, or 'trigger' derived from the CPIA.'[31]

Currently the Bank is adjusting the CPIA to align it more closely with the views of the US government and its allies with respect to 'good policies', which is also an approach that the United States has taken to determine eligibility for its Millennium

Challenge Account, announced with great fanfare at the Monterrey Conference.

Sogge concludes that the problem with the IFIs is 'not know-it-all arrogance, but an unchecked power to define truth and falsehood. The net effect is to intimidate, cut off debate and close off alternatives.' He suggests that people living in poverty are better served by 'breaking up the aid industry monopoly practices and, above all, the closing of gaps between citizens at the receiving end and those who take aid decisions on their behalf'.[32]

2. In establishing new and equitable partnerships with developing countries, the International Financial Institutions must abandon the practice of externally imposed policy conditionalities and policy undertakings, enforced through their roles in negotiation of multilateral aid loans and in their facilitation of donor coordination in the international aid regime. World Bank-led dialogue with developing countries should adopt a rights-based approach.

The *Reality of Aid 2002*, with its focus on conditionality and ownership, suggested that donors and developing country partners needed to negotiate resource transfer within a framework of *reciprocal obligations* based on shared values and a commitment to direct these resources to benefit those who are socially and economically excluded. In the words of Opa Kapijimpanga from AFRODAD, a Reality of Aid member network, 'Donors must stop dictating what they think African countries must do. Conditionalities must stop.'[33] Donors must instead give support and priority to *national political processes* for determining appropriate strategies in relation to local economic, social, cultural, ecological and gender equality circumstances for poverty reduction.

Our 2002 Report asserts that 'fundamental to determining a fair and

Political Overview

equitable process for such negotiations is who decides, shifting the highly unequal power relations in current aid decision making.'[34]

Governance reform now makes up a significant and growing proportion of multilateral and bilateral aid agreements for structural adjustment loans, as well as budget support and sector programs in health or education, particularly for the aid dependent poorest countries or countries facing insurmountable economic crises. In a review of conditionalities found in IMF agreements, Kapur and Webb counted an average of 82 governance-related conditions out of a total of 114 conditions per agreement for Sub-Saharan Africa (or 72% of all conditions). In Asia and Latin America such conditions made up 58% and 53% of total conditions respectively. Moreover they point out that for aid dependent countries, some of the most important conditions do not make it into the formal agreements, but are subject to 'side letters' and 'pre-programme' conditions.[35] These do not include any comparable conditions and undertakings attached to World Bank loans to the same countries, which are also likely to be substantial, given a process of streamlining IFI conditions that was initiated in 2000.

The World Bank itself is quite categorical about the perverse effects of conditionality. Paul Collier, Director of Research in the World Bank, has written:

'The extension of the practice of conditionality from occasional circumstances of crisis management to the continuous process of general economic policy-making has implied a transfer of sovereignty which is not only unprecedented but is often dysfunctional'.

Joseph Stiglitz, former Chief Economist at the Bank, has argued:

'There is increasing evidence that [conditionality] was not [effective] — good policy cannot be bought, at least in a sustainable way. Equally critically, there is a concern that the way changes were effected undermined democratic process.'[36] Quoted in Ibid., 7-8.

Nevertheless the practice of conditionality in the loan programmes of the Bank and the Fund persists. Southern civil society commentators in the pages of *The Reality of Aid 2004,* and in response to the impact of structural adjustment programming in their own countries, confirm the significant distortions imposed by these programmes on both democratic process and on the livelihoods for a growing number of poor people.[37]

A great deal of research has demonstrated that governance is in fact a product of complex and inevitable political processes in which different groups in society compete and benefit differently from alternative governance agendas. Therefore, 'sorting out priorities [for governance reform] from the perspective of different interests is a political process, and one that cannot be short-circuited by technical analysis or donor [conditionality] fiat.' Grindle goes on to assert that 'an important incentive for organizations and officials alike is the capacity of citizens and groups to demand fair treatment, to have information about their rights vis-à-vis government and be able to hold officials and government accountable for their actions.'[38]

Externally-imposed conditionality, by focusing broad-based policy dialogue in often secret negotiations between select government officials and those from the Bank and the Fund, clearly undermines democratic accountability by removing significant policy options from public processes for citizen and parliamentary oversight. A rights approach puts people, particularly those living in poverty, the vulnerable and the marginalized, at the centre of local and national political processes. In rejecting conditionality, The Reality of Aid proposes that the World Bank provide policy space for a rights-based approach as an alternative to policy conditionalities. In this approach, donors would work to assist developing countries to move towards the realisation of their UN treaty obligations and international human rights law. The framework for such dialogue with donors is the mutual obligations and requirements, arising from these treaties and Covenants, for all countries to progressively realise economic, social and cultural rights of their citizens.[39]

3. The decision making processes at the World Bank, the International Monetary Fund and the WTO must be reformed and democratised and brought within a new framework led by the United Nations, with limited mandates subject to the United Nations legally binding international human rights framework and the social values embodied in the Millennium Development Goals.
As noted earlier the renewed partnership and spirit of the Monterrey Consensus included a commitment to 'broadening and strengthening of participation of developing countries with economies in transition in international economic decision-making and norm-setting' (para 56). Civil society has long challenged the legitimacy of the IFIs in terms of their impact on governance and democratic accountability in the poorest developing countries. Two decades of secret negotiations for structural reforms have removed the political locus for national decision making away from domestic political checks and balances where citizens have a potential influence on public policy. In the 1990s as the IFIs became more deeply

involved in issues of national governance, the focus on the governance of these institutions themselves has intensified.

Like Christian Aid and many other CSOs around the world, the Reality of Aid believes that better representation of the poorest countries at the IMF and the World Bank, and improved transparency and accountability in these institutions, would lead to more appropriate, and better informed, decision making and country-led ownership of strategies to combat poverty.[40] But Reality of Aid NGOs also assert that democratic reform of governance within the institutions must also go in tandem with a strengthened role for the United Nations in the social and economic areas.[41] The IFIs have assumed a commanding role in the international aid regime that goes into areas far beyond their original mandate, in areas that were originally deemed the prerogative of the UN and its agencies or never before addressed on a global level.[42]

With respect to the IFIs, changes in their systems of governance must include changes in voting structures and quotas to more effectively reflect the principle of one country one vote, with possible use of double majorities (weighted by financial contribution and by constituencies, similar to the current practices of the Global Environment Fund). They must include changes in the constituencies of Executive Directors. Currently two Directors for Africa have the daunting task of representing 44 Sub-Saharan African countries and their interests on the Board. An improved balance is needed in the composition of the Executive Board between industrialised, middle income and low income countries. Greater Board transparency and accountability to all member countries is also important.

At the October 2003 UN General Assembly special high level follow-up to the financial for development conference, CSOs sought a

Political Overview

new relationship between the IMF, World Bank and the jurisdiction of the United Nations. CSOs supported proposals from the Secretary General to upgrade and reform the positioning of the ECOSOC as a forum for dynamic interactive dialogue on crucial issues relating to global economic governance. It is also proposed that an Executive or Steering Committee, representative of country groups within its membership, would provide greater direction for its work promoting policy coherence and follow-up to the Monterrey Conference, including preparations for more substantive high-level dialogue with the Bretton Woods Institutions and the WTO.[43]

CSOs, monitoring the impact of the WTO on development options for poverty reduction in developing countries, also seek to bring current rounds of global trade and investment negotiations at the WTO and in regional forums within the overarching normative framework of the UN system. The collapse of WTO negotiations at The Ministerial Meeting in Cancun Mexico in September 2003 was seen by some as a setback to the continued extension of a Northern-driven trade and investment liberalization agenda. For others, the emergence of effective coalitions among developing countries was seen as an important accomplishment upon which to build. These countries were able for the first time in many decades to collectively raise substantial issues affecting the development agenda as a counter-weight to the authoritarian practices of the Quad[44] in the WTO.

The WTO processes have been characterised as secretive and opaque in which developing countries, particularly the poorest, have little opportunity to influence outcomes. In recent years, leading members of the WTO have organised highly undemocratic Mini-Ministerials, by invitation only, to 'advance' the negotiating agenda. In the words of a global coalition of CSOs

involved in WTO issues, 'the lack of internal transparency, participation and democracy is appalling in such an important organization whose decisions and actions have such far reaching effects on the lives of billions of people...in an organization that prides itself for being a 'rules-based organization' and for championing the 'principles of transparency, non-discrimination and procedural fairness'.[45]

Governance and rights in the aid regime: reforming bilateral donor practices

The Reality of Aid networks have noted and critically welcomed over the past several years an improved focus of bilateral aid donors on poverty and social sectors that most affect those living in poverty, improved attention to issues of donor coordination and commitment to harmonisation, greater attention to programmatic mechanisms (budget support and sector wide programmes) that intend to support recipient country priorities and reduce recipient transaction costs, greater untying of aid commitments by some donors, and commitments to increase aid resources by some donors.[46] A few donors, such as DFID in the UK, have set out 'a rights-based approach' to development and the achievement of the MDGs, which includes 'incorporating the empowerment of poor people into our approach to tackling poverty' and 'making sure that citizens can hold governments to account for their human rights obligations'.[47] But what are the realities of these new donor commitments and practices? What are the implications of these practices for more effective aid delivery for improved governance and citizens' rights in the recipient countries?

1. Effective strategies for official bilateral aid that focus exclusively on ending global

Political Overview

poverty, and achieving the targets contained in the MDGs, must be grounded in a rights framework, with an expanding and equitable contribution of untied financial resources to enable effective international cooperation to realise these goals.

The *Reality of Aid 2002* highlighted the centrality of 'local ownership' in the conceptual framework, first set out by aid ministers in the DAC's 1996 policy statement *Shaping the 21st Century*, for donor efforts to improve the effectiveness of their aid relationships. 'Ownership' is not an absolute condition, but rather a definition of relationship and the power and influence of different stakeholders to negotiate the content of this relationship. Local ownership, for example, cannot be understood without understanding gender equality—do women have equal access to society's resources and power? Are women's experiences and capabilities an integral part of development strategies, or are they excluded? Donor commitments to ownership in the context of North/South aid relationships is not just about strengthening the state to take up its responsibilities, but it is also fundamentally about citizenship and building capacity for the exercise of people's rights in the context of exclusion, marginalisation and poverty.

Our 2002 *Report* called on donors to move beyond a rhetorical respect for local ownership with real change, evidenced in institutional practice and donor commitments to expanding the resource base for international cooperation. *The Reality of Aid 2004* suggests that these changes can bring positive capacity for a strengthened rights approach in several key areas:

♦ Donors must strengthen ownership and local accountability by reducing their reliance on donor country technical assistance. Despite the rhetoric on ownership, reliance on technical assis-

tance to increase the capacity of sectoral ministries in developing countries to manage donor project relationships has not diminished. In 2002, US$15 billion or 38% of bilateral ODA, worth US$39 billion, was in the form of technical cooperation. From a rights perspective, technical assistance might make a positive contribution, if it were to be provided *on request* to build the capacities of governments and other constituencies of the poor to achieve rights commitments and engage in policy dialogue on rights obligations. The experience in Tanzania explained in this report shows that with commitment from developing country government and external donors, the principles embodied in the DAC Task Force on Donor Practices can be translated into 'real benefits for the poor in terms of increased aid effectiveness'.

♦ The unconditional untying of aid, including food aid and technical assistance, is an acknowledged pre-condition for the contribution of aid to strengthening local productive capacities and livelihoods of poor people through small and medium scale enterprises. The Reality of Aid notes the donor commitment made at the LCD III Conference to 'enhance the value of their development assistance by increasing the proportion of goods and services sourced in the recipient LDC or from other LDCs or developing countries to help boost poor-poor economic growth.'[48]

♦ The unconditional cancellation of all debts of the world's poorest countries is an acid test of donors' commitment to the right of all people to economic justice and the elimination of poverty. Despite a promising beginning in 2000, the HIPC II programme is bogged down in delays and inadequacy and is unlikely to deliver a 'permanent exit' from debt rescheduling. Since 2000 only eight

21

Political Overview

countries have received debt stock reductions, with 19 others waiting their completion point when debt stock is finally cancelled. Countries are being delayed in the HIPC initiative by conditionalities unrelated to the rationale for debt relief, including overly stringent fiscal criteria and a range of governance conditionalities that require privatisation of important sectors of their economies, resulting in 9 of 19 countries significantly off-track in reaching their completion point. HIPC countries have been highly vulnerable to external shocks from declining global commodity prices and the internal impact of HIV/AIDS.

As a group, 27 countries that have already entered into a HIPC II programme cannot afford to meet the MDGs and provide other basic services even with currently promised increases in aid. Achieving existing donor commitments to even the minimal MDGs by 2015 will require full debt cancellation for the poorest countries and consideration of international mechanisms for fair arbitration of unsustainable debts owned by middle income highly indebted countries.[49]

♦ All donors must establish and be accountable to a realistic timetable to achieve their long-standing commitment to reach 0.7% of their GNI for Official Development Assistance.

As noted in the Trends in Aid chapter of this report, global aid increased by 7.2% in real terms between 2001 and 2002 — marginally up to reach 0.23% of donor GNI.

But whilst this may be a reversal in the decline of global aid, the increases fall far short of the additional US$50 billion estimated by the World Bank as required each year to reach the Millennium Development Goals. These are appalling statistics when seen in the context of more than US$565 billion requested from Congress by the American Administration for Defense and other spending in its so-called 'pre-emptive' wars on terrorism.[50] The WHO Commission on Macroeconomics and Health estimate that a donor investment of US$27 billion a year, on TB, HIV/AIDS, malaria, and other infectious diseases and nutritional deficiencies, could save up to eight million lives a year. The UNDP estimates that the additional cost of providing basic education for all is only US$6 billion a year.[51]

Alternative proposals for financing the MDGs have been put forward by both NGOs and the UK government. UK Chancellor Gordon Brown is proposing an International Finance Facility that would use aid increases pledged at Monterrey to back the issue of bonds, the revenue from which would allow aid spending to be frontloaded. If all of the US$16 billion in increased aid is devoted to the IFF, this would generate the additional US$50 billion needed now to meet the 2015 MDGs.[52] While clearly a creative idea which merits further study, the proposal depends on donors achieving their committed 0.7% of GNI by 2015, at which time money owed to the bond holders will come due. Otherwise, the interests of the more than 900 million people still living in absolute poverty in 2015, not to mention many more living with highly vulnerable livelihoods, will be potentially compromised by dramatically reduced aid allocations in the post-2015 years. CSOs continue to demonstrate the feasibility of a Tobin Tax on foreign exchange transactions, or a Carbon Tax as significant sources of revenue for the multilateral system, while clearly contributing to a more stable international financial system and the Kyoto Protocol. Goran Hyden proposes the creation of 'autonomous development funds', managed jointly by government, civil society and donors, based on global reallocation mechanisms along the lines of the European Union equalisation funds.[53]

Political Overview

While aid allocations may be increasing, we note below deepening concerns for the integrity of aid allocations., with its overarching goal ending poverty in tension with foreign policy interests of donor countries. Equally concerning is the trend among donors to select countries for concentration of aid efforts based on Bank-sanctioned notions of 'good policies' noted above. Pakistan has moved from being 14th on the list of aid recipient countries in 1999/2000 to being top of the in 2001 and 2002. Donors frequently talk about the need to concentrate their aid in order to make it more effective in tackling poverty; but the danger is that in practice, considerations such as security, migration and governance crowds aid into countries who are for the time being 'popular', whilst strategically less important, but just as poor countries are often overlooked.

As 11.11.11 point out in their report on Belgium, 'With each new government, the list of partner countries changes, and the criteria used are not very clear'. NGOs in Belgium favour more concentration, but stress the need for continuity, and especially the need to avoid aid being diverted to priorities such as deterring asylum seekers.

The Reality of Aid strongly urges donors to avoid triage of poor people by developing inclusive, coordinated, approaches in their international assistance programmes, which support the rights of people living in poverty no matter where they may live. Such an approach requires that donors fulfil commitments to aid increases made at Monterrey, make specific commitments to reach the 0.7% target within a reasonable timeframe, and provide predictable levels of funding adequate for governments and societies to make medium term plans for sustainable progress on economic and social rights.

2. Donors are to be commended for bringing new support for strengthening government as an effective development actor and for coordinating their focus on key social sectors and poverty reduction plans through Sector Wide Approaches (SWAps) and Programme Budget Support initiatives in the poorest developing countries. These positive approaches, however, must be complemented by donor action to eliminate Bank/Fund conditionalities associated with these programmes and by efforts to strengthen domestic participation and effective accountable to CSOs and people living in poverty for their results.

Donor pooled resources and policy dialogue in support of Sector Wide Approaches for basic education or primary health programming, including a focus on HIV/AIDS, implicitly recognises the primary responsibility and obligations of government, within the Covenant on Economic, Social and Cultural Rights, to deliver universally accessible social programmes. However, as noted earlier, the World Bank often coordinates these programmes, usually directed to the poorest, most aid dependent countries in Sub-Saharan Africa. They include large numbers of governance conditionalities and a range of largely donor-imposed undertakings on recipient ministries and governments in exchange for the regular release of pooled financing.

While the product of donor dialogue with government officials, sector programmes and poverty reduction strategies often reflect what Sogge terms 'the politics of the mirror' — addressing potential aid donors 'in the language that is most congenial, and crucially, most easily reinforces the belief that they (outsiders) understand what [the recipient] needs.'[54] The terms of these conditions undermine not only national accountability for effectively tackling

Political Overview

poverty, they also promote approaches, such as privatisation or public/private partnerships, for the delivery of services that have had serious impact on the rights of the poor to access essential services.[55]

SWAps and Budget Support are accompanied almost universally by conditionalities that insist upon a decentralised local government model for the delivery of poverty-reducing programming and essential social services. Governance at the grass-roots level is often a critical foundation for effective strategies to reduce poverty that can be inclusive of people living in poverty. However, there are a number of critical factors that determine the local politics of development for poverty reduction — the resources available to local government, the parallel roles of traditional / local economic power structures in communities, the influence of local CSOs and community associations, open avenues for participation by those living in poverty and the vulnerable in decisions that affect their lives, and the impact of gender relations on the distribution of local benefits from development. Unfortunately many donors conflate these issues within simplistic notions of decentralisation and deal exclusively with administrative capacity, budgetary and corruption issues associated with programme delivery, while strongly encouraging private/ local government partnerships to overcome capacity problems. They seldom manage to engage local communities, who require substantial roles (and support) in the planning and delivery processes.[56]

In both Africa and Latin America, pressures by donors for decentralisation are accompanied by profound citizen distrust at all levels as government ministries use these resources to re-establish local clientist relationships often based on corruption. Goran Hyden argues that in much of Africa a long legacy of authoritarian politics and abuse of public positions for personal gain by politicians leave citizens deeply cynical about government and its role as guardian of the public good. He concludes pessimistically that

> *'Efforts by the international community to preach and impose principles of what they perceive as good governance have left few, if any traces in everyday politics...The idea that some one elected to office should treat it as a public trust does not register in these societies. Instead, holding office is viewed as giving the incumbent the right to use it discretionally for his own interest or those of his clients/ supporters...[P]ublic accountability as understood in the context of current conceptions of good governance will be very hard, if not impossible to achieve.'.[57]*

While recognising the limits of many CSOs in terms of their professed roles of representation and accountability to people living in poverty, political mobilisation of poor constituencies particularly in rural and local community is essential to hold officials accountable. Often the poor organise themselves to seek influence on specific local concerns, while CSOs — NGOs, labour unions, autonomous research centres, independent media — represent by proxy differing interests of the poor in society. Despite these potential limitations, Grindle suggests that less attention on government on the part of donors and more on 'the mobilization of the poor into political parties, interest groups, unions and NGOs may be a condition under which judicial reform, civil service reform, decentralization and other kinds of change are most likely to have a significant impact on poverty and on the poor.'[58]

Political Overview

The sole focus of new programme approaches by donors on the mechanisms of government in SWAps and Budget Support, and their reliance on national and local government to partner with civil society, is seemingly having a deleterious impact on the capacities of local civil society to play these roles. For some donors, such as DFID and CIDA, new approaches have been accompanied by a marked decline in the support of local civil society as development actors, whether directly or through international NGOs.

Based on local interviews in Uganda, Lister and Nyamugasira demonstrate the impact of the reduction in such project funding on a narrowing of 'political space' for local and national NGOs to hold governments at all levels accountable, and to direct resources to communities they represent. As DFID, along with other donors, has moved significant funding for local civil society projects to government Budget Support and SWAps, these community-based organisations are obliged to seek funding as contracting agents from local government and thereby become tied into local clientist politics and corruption. The study concludes that such organisations, often vital to local service delivery and grass-roots accountability, are in a quandary: 'They are unsure whether to abandon long-standing activities in which they have expertise and through which they provide vital service, or become sub-contracting agents of authorities they do not trust, and thus risk loosing the freedom to speak out'. They go on to find that donors, where they do support national NGO participation in development or monitoring of Uganda's poverty strategy do so on a highly selective basis, one which sees participation as an 'instrumental' value-added requirement for government management of services, rather than based on principled notions of citizens'

empowerment and the right to participate, which seemingly defines DFID's rights-based approach noted above.[59]

Bilateral donor support for programme approaches through SWAps and Budget Support would be greatly strengthened if they were to pay equal attention to assuring the continued engagement of local civil society accountability structures, which should also include continued piloting of innovation in service delivery at the community level. Processes of decentralisation in the context of extreme conditions of poverty are highly complex for which there is no easy 'one-size-fits-all' approach. Donors, government ministries and CSOs must approach comprehensive strategies for poverty reduction with both humility and the dedication of resources to strengthen the advocates for poverty eradication at all levels.

Reducing direct support for CSOs by donors may also prove a significant barrier for making progress on donor pre-occupations with high levels of corruption within ill-functioning governments and political processes. Corruption (including notably high levels of private sector corruption in several developed countries) concerns everyone who seeks socio-economic justice. Donors must also accept their own responsibility for corruption that has resulted from donor-imposed demands and policy advice for rapid privatisation and downsizing of civil services. By many accounts, CSOs can be effective in putting in place 'social accountability mechanisms' to monitor government action as well as in leading significant anti-corruption campaigns. A few examples

Many grassroots organisations, supported by national NGOs, have developed capacities to monitor official development budgets, have developed alternative budgets based on people's

Political Overview

priorities for poverty reduction, and analysed budgets from a gender perspective or a government's respect for human rights commitments to indigenous and vulnerable populations.[60]

- The development of community-based, convenient, internet centres to access basic government services, such as document retrieval and certifications, may be effective in cutting out petty corruption that affect poor people most dramatically in their dealings with government.
- Local organisations work with local communities to expose corruption through informal vigilance committees to monitor expected delivery of services or to assess the quality of publicly funded infrastructure.
- CSOs work to strengthen the capacities and roles of parliamentarians, as well as official auditors, as a key oversight institution, with recent examples of parliamentary action in Kenya and South Africa's Legislatures' Office for Public Participation' as outreach to those with grievances who are unable to access parliaments directly.
- CSOs mobilise grassroots groups broadly against corruption through district level monitoring committees and dialogues, acting on specific complaints and raising public awareness through plays, songs and poetry about the impoverishment effects of corruption.[61]

Civil society is a critical resource to tackle corruption, but it is often weak, disorganised, and lacking in the capacity and financial resources to expand these and other interventions. Donors can help create a favourable environment not only by demonstrating transparency and accountability in their own relationships with governments concerned, but also by

supporting country-level capacities to analyse human rights claims and obligations, and the capacity of autonomous civil society to hold stakeholders accountable to these obligations in the day-to-day working of governments.

As donors assess the complex issues in moving from donor project financing to coordinated support for sector programming that strengthen the roles of government in key areas of poverty eradication, they need to urgently review the roles of civil society organisations as development actors within the context of politics at all levels to promote effective approaches to poverty reduction.[62]

3. Bilateral donors must maintain the integrity of official development assistance (ODA) with an exclusive focus on poverty reduction. An effective contribution to improved governance through a rights-based approach will be significantly undermined by the seeming convergence of the global security agenda with priorities for international cooperation.

The promotion of the post-September 11th anti-terrorist global security agenda, whose terms and courses of action are defined by the United States government and its allies, but actively pursued by all governments, challenge the universal legal framework of human rights and the multilateral institutions established to guarantee these rights. The security agenda has profound implications for the promotion of effective structures of governance at all levels, not least being the unilateral declaration of war on countries that by-pass the authority of the (democratically-challenged) UN Security Council. Reality of Aid members have pointed to important examples of unilateral foreign militarised interventions, often lead by the United States, in countries beyond Iraq and Afghanistan, in Colombia, in military

Political Overview

repression of people in Aceh (Indonesia) and the denial of the human rights of the people of West Papua, in the Democratic Republic of the Congo (DRC), in Mindanao (Philippines) and in Palestine.[63]

Development aid and global security agendas are converging. Most clearly, the United States adopted the September 2002 National Security Strategy, giving the government the right of pre-emptive military action 'against ... terrorists, to prevent them from doing harm against our people and our country; and denying further sponsorship, support, and sanctuary to terrorists by convincing or compelling states to accept their sovereign responsibilities'. This Strategy was subsequently supported with a foreign aid policy statement, *Foreign Aid in the*

National Interest, which substantially linked national security and foreign assistance.[64]

This strategic posture has also affected the independence of American NGOs working in zones of conflict. In June 2003, Andrew Natsios, Administrator of USAID, provocatively challenged US NGOs working internationally to demonstrate and link their humanitarian assistance in Afghanistan and Iraq to US foreign policy and made it clear that they are considered an 'arm of the US government'[65]. InterAction, Reality of Aid's US partner, points to the increasing role of the Pentagon and private contractors in carrying out humanitarian and reconstruction missions for which they may be ill-suited, undercutting efforts to lay the foundation for long-term development.[66]

Box 2: Reality of Aid Statement in support of the independence of US NGOs

Reality of Aid affirms that NGOs are a key part of the independent voice of civil society. Their role in a democratic society is to ensure that the views of all of the people, including minority and other ethnic groups and those who are marginalised for discriminatory reasons, are heard by the decision makers.

Non-government organisations are, by definition, not an arm of any government. If they receive Government funding, it should be given on the merits of the application and in recognition of the NGO's ability to work in partnership with the grassroots people in developing countries, to promote basic human rights and assist towards poverty eradication. Through funding NGOs, governments contribute to meeting their commitments to reach the Millennium Development Goals as a first step in this process.

A society where there is no freedom of speech for civil society and no right to use the media as an outlet for its concerns cannot be called democratic and free. These are the very issues on which the US and their allies said that they went to war in Iraq and Afghanistan. The US Government should practice at home that which it preaches abroad.

There is growing evidence that donors are to a greater extent shaping their development cooperation priorities through the lens of the 'war on terrorism'.

Terrorism, as random deadly violence against unprotected civilians for the purpose of creating fear and insecurity among

surrounding populations, clearly constitutes illegal criminal action. Such acts are unambiguously and morally reprehensible and devoid of any political rationale. But September 11th notwithstanding, terrorism is not a pervasive tactic undertaken by significant numbers of groups and individuals

Political Overview

seeking change. Far more people and societies continue to be affected by persistent internal conflict and violence, which impact on large civilian populations and have had incalculable human and material costs over the past decade.

There can be little if any synergy between donor strategies to promote peace, prevent conflict and encourage social and political cohesion, and strategies and practices to prevent/combat terrorism.

The former emphasise the creation of viable and broadly responsive state and civil institutions, the promotion of social cohesion based on justice, and tackling the backdrop of socio-economic conditions that underlie endemic poverty and exclusion. In contrast, current actions by governments (North and South) to prevent and counter terrorism are oriented to the restriction of people's rights, deepening repression of communities in conflict with their government (whether peaceful or otherwise), strengthening within government the military /the police / agencies for covert action and the creation of a climate of fear among its citizens. These proactive anti-terrorism measures do little to nourish climates for peace and development in the interests of people living in poverty. There is a great deal of evidence that donors have compromised their attention to human rights in their 'war on terrorism' in countries such as Pakistan, seen to be on the front line with the Taliban and Al Qaeda in Afghanistan. The DAC policy insofar as it emphasises support for 'improved' security legislation and military/police capacities may further undermine an already weak focus by donors on a comprehensive approach to human rights in development cooperation

Donors acting through the OECD DAC propose to review the ODA eligibility criteria in the context of its policy statement on international cooperation and the prevention of terrorism. Opening ODA criteria will only

dilute the purpose of aid for poverty eradication, further reduce public support, and effectively divert scarce ODA resources away from its core goal. Reality of Aid members also argue that many current actions (police, security and military strengthening) to prevent terrorism, linked by some governments to a 'war on terrorism', clearly fall outside the boundaries of effective strategies for conflict prevention.

The integrity of the notion of ODA is already deeply compromised by the inclusion of financial support for refugees, as well as tied aid and the inclusion of economic and foreign policy considerations in its allocation. The DAC rules are already subject to abuse. Australia was able to count as ODA support for refugees in Australia and the costs of recent Pacific Island internment of boat people seeking refuge in Australia! The use of ODA for domestically inspired priorities, such as those noted in the Danish chapter of deterring or repatriating refugees and asylum seekers and offsetting obligations under the Kyoto Protocol, is not consistent with the DAC line that poverty reduction must be the overriding priority for aid.

A Call for Fundamental Reform:

> 'The poor should be considered as full citizens and not simply victims, as full citizens and not simply recipients, as full citizens and not merely beneficiaries or charity cases....Unless we put people, and particularly those that have been historically excluded, at the centre of public life, our development goals will continue to evade us.'

Kumi Naidoo, Secretary General, Civicus

Political Overview

As the UN Secretary General, Kofi Annan has recently highlighted, we live at a critical juncture in world history. It is one that urgently calls for both a return to processes of multilateralism and the international legal framework of human rights, and their reform to meet the challenges of peace and international cooperation. Aid alone plays a minor role in restructuring such an effective multilateral system for the 21st century; nevertheless aid is also a critical resource through which donors have structured a relationship with developing countries for more than four decades. But will the global community, both nations and citizens' organisations, find the creativity and building blocks for dialogue on the democratisation of governance and the promotion of rights through the aid regime?

The Reality of Aid network has set out some proposals for such reforms, in both the multilateral and national realms, and is committed to pursue them vigorously. They are:

1. Donor countries must carry out their development cooperation programmes so that governance reflects their binding obligations under human rights law and the rights based approach in line with internationally agreed human rights instruments, including the right to development.

Governance has been given a wide range of interpretations, but what it must mean is a framework based on democratic governance and human rights, which leads to a national political process that is democratic and based on the principles of law and human rights.

In practice, the ill-defined governance sector provides for the most part a space for pursuing a range of donor interests with aid money.

The principles of good governance apply to the management of international

cooperation and aid institutions as much as to developing countries.

2. Imposed conditions are incompatible with democratic governance. Any terms must be fairly and transparently negotiated with participation of and accountability to people living in poverty and in line with the principles of international human rights and a rights based approach.

Good governance should not be a vehicle for imposing market based approaches.

Conditionality cannot even be justified on the basis of effectiveness.

PRSPs that simply embody International Financial Institution prescriptions, leave little room for authentic local and national debate. Where accountability is essentially to the IFIs, rather than local stakeholders, these plans are not consistent with the principles of democratic governance and human rights, which are essential preconditions for effective strategies to eradicate poverty.

3. The MDGs are an expression of commitment to economic social and cultural rights and define a set of steps to enable those rights to be realised. If MDGs are to contribute to international goal of poverty eradication, efforts to achieve them must be founded on strategies that empower and recognise the rights of all people, including all the poor no matter where they live.

Donors must comply with their obligation contained in Goal 8 specifically increasing ODA to the UN target of 0.7% of GNI, improving the quality of their aid for poverty reduction and achieving debt cancellation for the poorest countries.

The emphasis on a global partnership in Millennium Goal 8 is welcome. But in promoting 'an open, rule-based trading and financial system', envisaging cooperation with the private sector and encouraging competition in the global economy, there

Political Overview

are real dangers that the poverty imperative will in practice be overwhelmed by corporate and donor national interests and that the rules adopted will be no different to current rules which reinforce unequal power relations.

4. The International Financial Institutions that are mandated to support the fight against poverty embody entrenched inequalities or power and wealth in their systems of governance. The IFIs must not remain the monopoly providers of policy advice on governance reform or the gatekeepers on resource transfers. Aid should support governments, representative institutions and legislatures, in formulating national poverty reduction strategies. Aid should not determine the process.

5. Aid should be treated as money held in trust for people in poverty. Current attempts to divert resources for poverty reduction to pay for donors' security interests are the most serious expression of the endemic problem of aid resources being hijacked to fund rich country priorities.

6. The imperatives of poverty eradication and democratic governance underline the obligations to reinvigorate multilateralism, in the current context of the adverse global impact of unilateralism, especially the practices of the US government and its allies.

The subsequent chapters take up this shared commitment to reform and its unique application in the particular contexts of Africa, the Middle East Asia, the Americas and the OECD donor countries. In pursuing governance and rights, clearly politics

matters. While we may fear that counter-terrorism measures may have subsumed the spirit of Monterrey and dashed hopes for international cooperation on financing for development[67], we must never lose the dream that continues to inspire millions of marginalised and poor people to struggle to secure their rights in their daily lives and in the politics of their particular locale. Indeed it is our obligation as citizens and governments to accompany and sustain people in their efforts to eradicate poverty.

The selective way that donors interpret ideas of governance and human rights is not consistent with a genuine rights approach to development and poverty.

There may be conflicts between international obligations to comply with UN treaty obligations and IFIs conditions or WTO agreements. In such a situation, governments may be left with no choice but simply to ignore the human rights treaty obligations, as the pressure from largely donor-imposed conditionality is stronger. Countries may be punished for violating IFIs and WTO conditions, but not those of the UN.

Civil society networks in the Reality of Aid... focus their policy and advocacy attention on issues in *democratic governance*. As such, governance is not an end in itself, to be engineered through technical assistance and policy interventions by donors. Rather it is fundamentally about politics, power and the exercise of rights in society, and is therefore an evolving and particular process that may take decades.

Two decades of secret negotiations for structural reforms have removed the political locus for national decision making away from domestic political checks and balances where citizens have a potential influence on public policy.

Political Overview

Notes

1. OECD, Development Assistance Committee (DAC), *A Development Cooperation Lens on Terrorism Prevention: Key Entry Points of Action* is available on the OECD DAC website at http://www.oecd.org/dataoecd/17/4/16085708.pdf. A joint statement of concern about the implications of this policy, signed by many members of the Reality of Aid network, is available on the web site of BOND, ww.bond.org.uk. An analysis of the DAC policy statement can be found on the web site of the Canadian Council for International Cooperation, www.ccic.ca.

2. States can take measures that derogate from their obligations under the Covenant on Civil and Political Rights, only in times of 'public emergency that threatens the life of the nation'.

3. Thomas Pogge, 'The First Millennium Development Goal', first Oslo Lecture in Moral Philosophy at the University of Oslo, September 11, 2003, ww.etikk.no/globaljustice/, 9

4. UNDP, *Human Development Report* 2003, New York: Oxford University Press, 2003, 38-39. The 25 million richest Americans have as much income as almost 2 billion of the world's poorest people.

5. World Bank, *World Development Report*, New York: Oxford University Press, 2003, 235 (quoted in Pogge, 2003, 11)

6. Pogge, 2003, p. 3

7. See for example, Kumi Naidoo, 'Civil Society, Governance and Globalization', World Bank Presidential Fellows Lecture, Washington DC, February 2003, pp. 7-8, accessed from the World Bank web site, www.worldbank.org.

8. Simon Maxwell, Heaven or Hubris: Reflections on the 'New Poverty Agenda', *Development Policy Review*, 2003, 21 (1), p. 13-14.

9. John Foster (North South Institute, Canada),'Crisis time: Repossessing Democratic Space, Governance and the Promotion of Rights in International Cooperation and Aid, A Discussion Paper for The Reality of Aid', April 2003, accessed from the Reality of Aid website, www.realityofaid.org., p. 8.

10. World Bank, Sub-Saharan Africa: From Crisis to Sustainable Growth, Oxford: Oxford University Press, 1989, 60.

11. Lewis Carroll's children's novel Alice in Wonderland, has the following exchange: *'When I use a word,' Humpty Dumpty said in rather a scornful tone, 'it means just what I choose it to mean — neither more or less.' 'The question is,' said Alice, 'whether you can make words mean different things.' 'The question is,' said Humpty Dumpty, which is to be master— that's all.''* A thorough discussion of the governance discourse can be found in a background paper prepared for the Reality of Aid International Advisory Council by Kavaljit Singh (Public Interest Research Group (India), 'Aid and Good Governance: A Discussion Paper for Reality of Aid', January 2003, accessible at www.realityofaid.org.

12. James Wolfensohn, 'A New Global Balance: The Challenge of Leadership', Address to the Board of Governors of the World Bank Group, Dubai, September 23, 2003, 6.

13. Kumi Naidoo, 2003, 7, 10.

14. For a review of the FfD process in relation to global governance, see Aduba, G., Caliari, A., Foster, J., Hanfstaengl, E., Schroeder, F., 'A Political Agenda for the Reform of Global Governance', October 2003, prepared as a background paper for the UN Financing for Development High Level Dialogue, October 29-30, 2003, by members of the civil society International Facilitating Group, accessed on the UN Financial for Development web site at http://www.un.org/esa/ffd/14April03-NGO-Statement-Plenary.pdf.

15. Quoted in Martin Khor, 'Report on UN Financing for Development Interactive Dialogue', TWN Info Service, November 5, 2003, page 2, accessed at http://www.twnside.org.sg/title/twninfo89.htm.

16. See background paper prepared for the Reality of Aid International Advisory Council by Kavaljit Singh (Public Interest Research Group (India), 'Aid and Good Governance: A Discussion Paper for Reality of Aid', January 2003, accessible at www.realityofaid.org.

17. Ibid., 7

18. UNDP, *Human Development Report 2002, Deepening democracy in a fragmented world*, New York: Oxford University Press, 2002, 'Overview', 1 - 9.

19. Secretary General Kofi Annan, 'Address to the General Assembly', September 23, 2003.

20. David Dollar et al, *Assessing Aid, What Works, What Doesn't and Why*, New York: Oxford University Press, 1998.

21. Alex Wilks, Fabien Lefrancois, 'Blinding with Science or Encouraging Debate? How World Bank Analysis Determined PRSP Policies', Bretton Woods Project, World Vision, 2002, available on www.brettonwoodsproject.org.

Political Overview

[22] Concern (Ireland) [no author], 'Is the PRSP Consolidating the World Bank's Dominant Position in the Development Process?' [no date] (approximately 2002), 2.

[23] Collingwood, V. (editor), 'Good Governance and the World Bank', University of Oxford, mimeo, 2002, 7.

[24] BOND research paper 'Civil society participation in European Community Country Strategy Paper processes', to be published in March 2004

[25] Concern (Ireland), 1.

[26] For analysis of Cotonou trade negotiations: www.actsa.org

[27] Jeremy Gould and Julia Ojanen, 'Merging the Circle, the Politics of Tanzania's Poverty Reduction Strategy', Institute of Development Studies, University of Helsinki, Policy Paper 2/2003. See also AFRODAD, 'Comparative Analysis of Five African Countries with Completed PRSPs', 2002, accessed from www.afrodad.org and Warren Nyamugasira and Rick Rowden, 'New Strategies, Old Loan Conditions, Do the New IMF and World Bank Loans Support Countries' Poverty Reduction Strategies, The Case of Uganda, April 2002.

[28] Sogge, D., *Give and Take: What's the Matter with Foreign Aid?* Reading, UK: Z Books, 2002. 122 - 131.

[29] Ibid., 150-1.

[30] Kapur and Webb, 7-11.

[31] Nancy Alexander, 'World Bank Judges Performance of Low-Income Countries', Citizens Network for Essential Services, 2003, accessed at www.servicesforall.org. Countries are rated overall for economic management, structural policies, social inclusion, public sector performance and loan portfolio performance.

[32] Sogge, 2002. 153, 107.

[33] Quoted in CAFOD, 'Summary of CAFOD's E-Consultation on NEPAD', June 2002, accessed from www.cafod.org.uk/policy/africa_nepad_consultation.shtml.

[34] Randel, J., German, T., (editors). *The Reality of Aid 2002, an independent review of poverty reduction and development assistance.* Manila: IBON, 2002, available electronically at www.realityofaid.org.

[35] Kapur, D., and Webb, R., 'Governance-related Conditionalities of the International Financial Institutions', G-24 Discussion Paper Series, No. 6, UNTAD, August 2000, 3-7.

[36] Quoted in Ibid., 7-8.

[37] See for example, the Structural Adjustment Participatory Review Network (SAPRIN) at http://www.saprin.org/.

[38] M. S. Grindle.'Good Enough Governance: Poverty Reduction and Reform in Developing Countries', Boston, Harvard University, Kennedy School of Government, prepared for the Poverty Reduction Group of the World Bank, November 2002, 18 and 23.

[39] See Ken Currah, Haidy Ear-Dupuy, Ruth Kahurananga, Melanie Gow, Alan Waites, 'Doing the Right Thing? The World Bank and the Human Rights of People Living in Poverty', World Vision International, 2003, accessible at www.wvi.org.

[40] Christian Aid, 'Options for democratizing the World Bank and IMF', February 2003, accessed from www.christianaid.org.uk. See also 'Open statement on steps to democratize the World Bank and IMF' supported by civil society organisations prior to the April 2003 meetings of the Governors of the Bank and the Fund, accessible at www.brettonwoodsproject.org/topic/reform.

[41] See the recommendations in 'The Summary of the Informal Hearings of Civil Society (New York, 28 October 2003)', UN General Assembly Follow-up to the International Conference on Financing for Development, accessible at http://www.un.org/esa/ffd/.

[42] Sabrina Varma, 'Improved Global Economic Governance', Trade-Related Agenda, Development and Equity, Occasional Papers, #8, South Centre, August 2002, 18.

[43] Adaba, G., et. al, 'A Political Agenda for the Reform of Global Governance', op. cit., for more details. The policy statement also supports initiatives to create Expert Working Groups that would support this Executive or Steering Committee, as proposed by the Secretary General, to allow for a wide range of stakeholders — governments, civil society, business, academics and multilateral institutions — to address the implementation of agreements coming out of the FfD Conference and follow-up. The annual ECOSOC meeting with the Bretton Woods Institutions and the WTO would become a major forum ensuring the coherence of monetary, financial and trading systems in support of development and the overarching goal of poverty eradication. In the medium term, member countries should pursue proposals to establish a more permanent global Economic and Social Security

Political Overview

Council within the structure of the UN, as originally proposed by Carlsson and Ramphal's 1995 Commission on Global Governance in its report, Our Global Neighbourhood.

44 The European Union, Canada, Japan and the United States.

45 Third World Network, OXFAM International, Focus on the Global South et. al., 'Memorandum on the Need to Improve Internal Transparency and Participation in the WTO', July 2003, accessible at http://www.twnside.org.sg/title/memo2.doc. The Memorandum sets out a range of specific proposals for reforming these undemocratic practices in the preparation and conduct of Ministerial Conferences.

46 See DAC, International Cooperation 2002 Report, DAC Journal, Volume 4, No. 1, 2003 for a donor perspective on these achievements to date and a projection of increased aid resources up to 2006. Reality of Aid analysis notes that the commitment to increased aid resources by the United States for example may not be fully realized [and any other qualifications that we put on these increases in our trends chapter] See the Trends chapter, pages X to Y..

47 DFID, 'Realizing human rights for poor people: Strategies for achieving the international development targets', October 2000, accessed at www.dfid.gov.uk. 7

48 LDC III final recommendation, para 84 (e) quoted in Actionaid, 'ODA and Aid Effectiveness in FfD', July 2001.

49 For details see Jubilee Research at the New Economics Foundation, Real Progress Report on HIPC, in cooperation with CAFOD, Christian Aid, EURODAD and Oxfam, September 2003 at www.jubilee2000uk.org/analysis/reports/realprogressHIPC.pdf.

50 Bridget Moix, 'Counting the Cost of War - A View from Capital Hill', Legislative Secretary on Iraq Issues, Friends Committee on National Legislation, Conflict in Iraq Bulletin, No 25, November 2003.

51 Russell Mokhiber and Robert Weissman, 'Other Things You Might Do with $87 billion', Focus on the Corporation, September 10, 2003, http://lists.essential.org/pipermail/corp-focus/2003/000160.html.

52 The International Finance Facility Briefing Note, Development Initiatives, UK September 2003.

53 Goran Hyden, 'How Can Civil Society be Rebuild in Africa?', University of Florida, paper prepared for the

'Langano Encounter', organized by Oxfam Canada, March 2002, 16.

54 Sogge, 2002, 48. He goes on to say that 'such behaviour renders the aid encounter closed, manipulated and unaccountable'.

55 For an analysis of the recent World Bank World Development Report 2004 on the delivery of essential services see Tom Kessler, 'Review of the 2004 World Development Report (WDR), Making Services Work for Poor People', Citizens' Network on Essential Services, September 2003.

56 Gould and Ojanen in 'Merging the Circle' (2003) found that social relations of governance at the local level in Tanzania precluded effective implementation of the Poverty Reduction Strategy. Policy implementation was often based on clientist relations and procedures and was abused by local politico-administrative elites who distribute resources among themselves via weakly regulated mechanisms of direct expenditure and sub-contracting. See also similar concerns in Uganda in Oxford Policy Management and ODI, 'General Budget Support Evaluability Study Phase I, Final Synthesis Report', prepared for DFID, December 2002.

57 Goran Hyden, 2002, 13.

58 Grindle (2002), 14.

59 Lister, S. and Nyamugasira, W., 'Design Contradictions in the New Architecture of Aid'? Reflections from Uganda on the Roles of Civil Society Organizations', Development Policy Review, 2003, 21 (1) 104.

60 See for example, John Samuel (editor), Understanding the Budget: As if people mattered, Pune: National Centre for Advocacy Studies, 1998. 'Gender and Budgets', Bridge Bulletin, #12, March 2003 (www.ids.ac.uk/bridge/) provides a number of examples from Tanzania and Recife Brazil.

61 Catholic Relief Services, 'Social Accountability Mechanisms: Citizen Engagement for Pro-Poor Policies and Reduced Corruption', January 2003 accessible at http://www.catholicrelief.org/publications/social_accountability.pdf

62 An example of such an initiative is Stein-Erik Kruse, 'SWAps and Civil Society: The Role of Civil Society Organization in Sector Programmes', A report prepared for the Norwegian Development Cooperation (NORAD) by the Centre for Health and Social Development, Oslo, December 2002. See also DANIDA (Danish Int'l Development Agency). 'Strategy for

Political Overview

Danish support to civil society in developing countries — including co-operation with the Danish NGOs.' Copenhagen: Draft analysis & strategy document, June/2000 and DANIDA, Partnership 2000, accessible at www.um.dk/danida/partnership2000/.

[63] See the political statement 'Stop Military Aid to Repressive Regimes' and 'Stop all aid to Burma' adopted by the International Advisory Council of members of the Reality of Aid network, meeting in the Philippines, June 24 - 28, 2003, accessible at www.realityofaid.org. See also IBON Foundation and BOND, 'Development and the 'War on Terror'', November 2003 (www.bond.org.uk/advocacy/globalsecurity.htm) for examples from Indonesia and the Philippines.

[64] President of the United States, The National Security Strategy of the United States of America, September 2002 and USAID, Foreign Aid in the National Interest, Promoting Freedom, Security and Opportunity, 2002, www.usaid.gov/fani/.

[65] Tracy Hukill, 'AID Chief Outlines Change in Strategy since 2001 Terrorist Attacks', UN Wire, June 2, 2003.

[66] InterAction, 'Foreign Aid in Focus: Emerging Trends', an Interaction Policy Paper, November 2003, www.interaction.org.

[67] Saradha Iyer of the Malaysia-based Third World Network, as told to IPS at the UN High Level Session on Follow-up to Financing for Development, October 27, 2003.

Part II
Africa

Governance and promotion of human rights in international cooperation

Opa Kapijimpanga, African Forum and Network on Debt and Development, Zimbabwe[1]

The hope for a developed Africa was first shattered by the decline in economic growth during the period 1975 to 1980.[2] Unable to be independently economically viable, Sub-Saharan Africa's relationship with the international community began increasingly to be shaped by development aid.

Despite efforts by the African community to define an economic paradigm and development strategy based on African individual and collective self-reliance, the development agenda for Africa has been dominated by the Bretton Woods institutions — the World Bank and the IMF — and now also by the World Trade Organisation. The structural adjustment programmes (SAPs) that were started in 1980s are still effectively in place today. All the 33 HIPC countries in Africa are subjected to the same conditiona-lities in securing development aid, which includes debt relief. While bilateral donor development assistance is important, its real impact is determined by the IFIs that essentially decide who gets bilateral donor assistance.[3]

This chapter examines international cooperation in relation to issues of governance and the promotion of human rights. Here, the definition of governance assumes that the state has a responsibility assigned to it (or delegated to it) by the electorate. Accordingly, the state and states are responsible for meeting the needs of people individually and collectively. In its relationships with other states, any state has to safeguard the interests of its people without violating the interests of the citizens of other states. Violations of rights are assumed to constitute bad governance at the national and global level.

Key conclusions of this analysis are:
- that the stated commitments of northern states (especially the USA) to democracy and harmony are belied by the way in which they use the IFIs, particularly the WTO, to dominate smaller nations;
- that continued aid conditionality is not only a sign of bad governance, but can also reduce the true impact of aid by undermining governance and people's rights;
- the need for all to focus on achieving the Millennium Development Goals, as a means of promoting human development and respect for human rights, and consolidating good governance norms within international cooperation.

Africa

Definitions

Definitions of governance, and especially good governance, vary widely according to the philosophy and ideology underlying the value system of those defining it. For Africa it is imperative to argue that the State is, and must be, a delegated authority that is expected to act in the interests of the people rather than its own.[4] The inclusion of stakeholders in decision-making processes is a fundamental aspect of good governance. In Africa, basic forms of governance begin from the village level, up to the chieftaincy, and through the district and provincial levels to the national level. Beyond the national level are the sub-regional groupings that form the building blocks of the African Union and are also structures of governance. The most important issue is the extent to which these structures represent and secure, rather than undermine or violate, people's interests.

International cooperation assumes a framework in which states are acting and interacting as equal partners. Where there is inequality, as is the case between the poor and rich nations, some level of good global governance is necessary to maintain equity and to safeguard of the interests of the weaker nations. Good global governance implies a fully functioning multilateral system. The current crisis in multilateralism is exhibited by the dominance of bilateralism — especially the hegemonic behaviour of the United States the negative and undemocratic processes in the WTO, and the disproportionate power of the Washington-based IFIs, which all constitute a source of bad governance at the global level. This also has negative impacts at sub-regional and national level governance where the same patterns reproduce themselves.

Any intention or practice that diminishes the role of state, in its representation of people's interests, would cause tension at the national level and even in international relations. Such tensions can only undermine sustainable development, peace, and security, which are the basis for good governance.

Since the United Nations General Assembly adopted the Universal Declaration of Human Rights in 1948, a series of declarations and covenants have moved beyond the first generation of civil and political rights to broader conception of rights, which assert and protect the inherent dignity of all members of the human family — equal, inalienable rights for all, the right to life, liberty, security of person, health, education, food, clothing, housing, livelihood, self determination, the individual's obligation to all humanity — and provide for agreement that nothing shall justify domination of one people by another. Human beings are at the centre of concerns for sustainable development; all states and all people shall cooperate in the essential task of eradicating poverty. States should cooperate to promote supportive systems leading to sustainable development.

At the Vienna Conference of 1993, the international community established a consensus on the right to development as universal, inalienable and an integral part of fundamental human rights.[5]

The declaration states that, 'Human rights and fundamental freedoms are the birthright of all human beings; their protection and promotion is the first responsibility of government.' Some argue that it is the immediate responsibility of African governments to secure development for their people and that any support for development provided by other states is 'philanthropic' or based on a 'kindness' and welfare approach. But as recognised in the International Covenant on Economic, Social and Cultural Rights (ICESCR), which

Africa

was adopted in 1966 and entered into force in 1976, every state in the world has a responsibility to support the development of peoples of other states in order to realise their rights. This must be interpreted to mean responsibility beyond borders. This is the essence of development cooperation, which should be defined as 'helping each other to secure the development that is a right for all'.

The 1997 Maastricht Guidelines on violation of Economic, Social and Cultural Rights,[6] are an important indicator of the evolution of the promotion of rights. Some key aspects relevant to the responsibility and the role of the state (and of states in international cooperation) include the following:

a) The State(s) has an obligation to respect, protect and fulfil human rights. Failure to perform any of these obligations constitutes a violation of such rights. Thus, the failure of States to provide for essential primary health care, basic education, essential foodstuffs, basic shelter and housing (to its citizens) may amount to a violation.

b) The scarcity of financial resources does not relieve States of certain minimum obligations in respect of the implementation of economic, social and cultural rights.

c) Rights are violated when a State pursues, or fails to protect its people from, policies that have a negative impact on them.

d) Violations of economic, social and cultural rights can occur through the direct action of States or other entities that are insufficiently regulated by States. Examples of such violations include active support for measures adopted by third parties that are inconsistent with economic, social and cultural rights (SAPs by World Bank and the IMF and the liberalisation Policies under the WTO).

e) The obligation of the state to protect its people includes its responsibility to ensure that private entities or individuals, including transnational corporations over which they must exercise jurisdiction, do not deprive individuals of their economic, social and cultural rights. States are responsible for violations of rights that result from their failure to exercise due diligence in controlling the behaviour of such non-state actors.

f) The State should ensure that violations do not result from the programmes and policies of international organisations of which the State is a member (e.g. The WTO and the International Financial Institutions).

The above considerations show that a rights-based approach to development goes beyond charity and welfare and raises the question of the state's responsibility to its citizens. International human rights law assumes that international cooperation will promote human rights, especially economic, social and cultural rights, including the right to development. The reality of under-development in Africa poses questions about the relationship between development, governance and promotion of human rights as key aspects of international cooperation in a global context.

Aid and the real resource gap

Current estimates put the financial gap between what African countries can raise and what they need to spend on development at some US$64 billion per year.[7] The gap could easily be filled by closing the leakages of financial outflows from Africa. These are estimated at more than US$75 billion, which includes terms of trade losses of over US$60 billion, unpayable illegitimate debt of US$10 billion and barriers to markets of US$5billion

Africa

per year.[8] But the 'gap' continues to provide the rationale for development aid.

Despite the amount of aid coming into Africa, poverty has continued to deepen. As noted in the World Bank World Development report of 2000,[9] 'if all the aid that went to Zambia between 1961 and 1994 had gone into productive investment, and if investment had been as important to growth as initially predicted, the country's per capita income would have been more than $20,000 in 1994, not $600.' The fact is that a majority of the Zambian people have become increasingly poor (per capita income in 1964 was US$1, 000). So the reason for development aid cooperation not being more effective in reducing widespread poverty in Africa remains an important area of investigation.

The desperate need for development aid leads key players in the aid industry to define how such aid is used and what approach is required for poverty eradication. The World Bank and the IMF remain the dominant drivers and gatekeepers of donor policy in Africa. Their assigned position gives them an added role as instruments of governance at the global level, even when this has no legitimacy. They continue to put pressure on African development through their conditionalities, using development aid as a lever to impose the neoliberal paradigm of privatisation, liberalisation and the markets. Under the poverty reduction strategy (PRSP) framework, they impose the same neoliberal framework as under the Poverty Reduction and Growth Facility PRGF). This undermines both people's rights and the sovereignty of the African state – and herefore governance.

Added to the family of the World Bank, the IMF and the OECD donors is the WTO. As innocent as the WTO may be seen in terms of trade, the power relations in the WTO suggest that this intergovernmental institution plays an important role in global

governance. Trade has a very strong link to development and therefore development aid. The resource gap that exists is largely due to problems that African countries face in the trade arena. Pressure from the United States on some countries, using development aid as a lever to secure agreement with the WTO, is a clear linkage between the trade agenda and development aid.

Conditionality, rights and governance

Aid conditionality has been widely discussed. Perhaps the best civil society exposure of the conditionality problem is that undertaken by the Structural Adjustment Participatory Review Initiative (SAPRI).[10] Some of the underlying policy impositions that have contributed to African poverty have been identified in the SAPRI process as follows:

a) Trade liberalisation is based on the neoclassical notion that competition from imports leads to specialisation, efficient allocation of resources and the elimination of inefficient producers, thus removing the burden on society of sustaining such entities. In the absence of institutions in Africa to deal with a world trading environment that is grossly uneven, the manipulation of prices by large international monopolies and imperfect competition have substantially contributed to increased poverty. In Zimbabwe, the manufacturing sector was the biggest victim of trade liberalisation. The manufacturing production index showed a decline of more than 20% between 1992 and 1997, resulting in retrenchment of employees and bankruptcy of enterprises. The Zimbabwe Congress of Trade Unions estimated a loss of 20,000 jobs, mainly in the textile sector, which could not compete with cheaper imports.[11] A similar fate befell the workers in the electronics industry. It is important to remind ourselves that retrenchment and loss of jobs is a violation of rights. The state has

Africa

not intervened, thus directly contributing to loss of a right. The creators of the policy — the World Bank and especially the IMF — do not take responsibility but, in reality, they are the fundamental cause of the loss of the right to work!

b) Financial sector liberalisation continues to have the following consequences:

The withdrawal of the state from the financial sector has reinforced structural weaknesses in many African states and regions. In Zimbabwe, liberalisation of interest rates caused an upswing in interest rates throughout the 1990s, increasing fivefold to 50% and making it impossible for small producers to access finance. The increase also led, among other things, to diversion of investments from productive sectors to speculative activities where returns were more than 30%. This has worked against employment creation.

Removal of government controls has been interpreted to mean a weakening of the state itself as an institution. As noted under governance, a weakened state generally plays a negative role as a delegated authority for ensuring that the interests of its citizens are met. In this regard, one can see the existence of a liberalisation policy that stifles increased job creation as bad practice in governance!

But despite the many arguments against conditionality, the conditions attached to multilateral lending and development assistance from bilateral donors have intensified. It becomes increasingly possible that there is a hidden agenda for those who propagate the conditionalities. The so-called economic reforms that are the key elements of the conditionality regime are designed to meet the interests of those that propagate them. Judged by the governance and human rights criteria, international cooperation based on conditionality does not meet the

minimum standards for governance and promotion of human rights.

As is already well known, the Bank and the Fund started to impose structural adjustment policies on countries in 1980 following the World Bank Berg Report[12]; these were further intensified following the 1989 Report, 'Sub-Sahara Africa; from crisis to sustainable development'[13]. Under the current environment of HIPC and poverty reduction strategies, policy conditionalities continue to be imposed. The Bank and the Fund continue to propagate their notion that strengthening the use of policy conditionality in lending is an important element in the efforts to improve aid effectiveness.[14]

c) Impact on labour:

The impact of adjustment on labour market policy springs from the notion that employment will be attracted by fewer regulations concerning labour stability and firing practices, greater flexibility in labour conditions, lower labour costs and reduced ability of the workers to organise. Labour liberalisation in Zimbabwe actually resulted in a violation of rights, because labour no longer had the right to organise into a strong trade union. Employers resorted to short contracts to lower the costs of labour by not paying various benefits associated with permanent labour. After signing its first stabilisation agreement with the IMF in 1983, the Zimbabwean government immediately abandoned the relatively high minimum wage established soon after independence in 1980. By 1995, the Labour Relations Act had been reformed, making the workers vulnerable, reducing the real wages and minimising rights to safe and secure employment.

In 2000, the failure of the Zambian government to pay a minimum monthly wage of K200, 000 (well below the poverty line) was largely because the IMF did not approve it![15]

41

Africa

d)   Civil society in Nigeria has openly complained that privatisation actually leads to 'giving away' African assets.[16] While it is true that in many African countries, state enterprises do not perform well, this is due to problems for which privatisation is now seen as the answer. In Uganda, for example, past performance had been due to the country's violent political reality. In more recent times, the reasons have included the lack of foreign currency and political interference.[17] Perhaps the most important political reason for privatisation being disliked in Africa is that, generally, the beneficiaries of privatisation are foreigners. In Uganda, foreigners took over 75% of the privatised assets, thus enriching a few transnational and large companies and not the people of Uganda. This is seen as 'legalised robbery'[18]. This explains the resistance to the privatisation of the electricity and telecommunications companies in Zambia. The Zambian government has argued that Zambian society has invested far more that they will regain through privatisation of these assets. The IMF will most likely be persuaded to accept partial commercialisation of these enterprises, in the ongoing negotiations for Zambia reaching the HIPC completion point. The Zambian government's resilience over the issue was because they found out that the World Bank's insistence on the privatisation of the telephone company was to safeguard the interests of its sister institution, the International Finance Company (IFC) in Celtel, which was interested in taking a major stake in the local telephone company.[19]

In order to bridge the gap between what the Bank and the Fund purport to support and what they do in reality, their work should be assessed in accordance with human rights criteria in the field of economic rights, since they are economic institutions.

This will then address the contradiction that is shown in their call for pro-poor policies. Pro-poor policies must fulfil the human rights criteria and enhance good governance.

Poverty Reduction Strategies and the conditionality regime

Poverty reduction has correctly taken centre stage in the development discourse because getting rid of poverty is good practice in governance and promotion of human rights. From the experiences of ten African countries studied by AFRODAD,[20] key issues emerged related to governance and rights:

- In line with the African Charter for Popular Participation,[21] PRSPs provide an opportunity for civil society to bring up microeconomic issues and good practices for effective poverty reduction. These microeconomic realities should be used by governments to inform macro-economic policies that will enhance economic development, which is a human right.
- Concepts of participation were notably different for the civil society and government led consultation processes. While government appointed people who spoke on behalf of 'the poor' countrywide, civil society organisations provided space for people in poverty to speak for themselves. The two approaches need to be integrated because they are strategically important for giving people in poverty real opportunities to participate in policy formulation for poverty reduction. This is good practice for good governance.
- After local representative or governance structures (village headmen and chiefs), parliaments are the first institutionalised forms of popular representation or governance. Parliamentarians must

Africa

of necessity participate in the whole PRSP process. Only in Burkina Faso and Mauritania did parliamentarians really participate effectively in the process. Their exclusion in most other African countries is an indicator of centralised power and decision making, which undermine national ownership of the PRSP process.

People's participation means that governments should not ignore the reality they bring up for discussion. For most African countries in the study, PRSP documents do not reflect civil society perspectives and inputs in any meaningful way. Not taking civil society views seriously can only make civil society 'participation' a deceitful act on the part of those who ignore civil society inputs.

While PRSPs appear to be rather innocuous documents, they are potentially instruments for strengthening civil society participation in policy analysis and strengthening the linkage between on-going government planning (national plans and visions) and implementation processes such as budgetary systems. PRSPs should orient policies and activities towards poverty reduction. They should offer a framework for coordinating development assistance and most of all, strengthening national ownership of processes and planning towards eradicating poverty.

Experience has shown, however, that PRSP linkage with development aid and debt relief poses a serious problem for Africa. AFRODAD studies show examples of how the macroeconomic framework of the IMF and the World Bank were imposed on the PRSPs. When these issues are actually excluded from debate and analysis, PRSPs cannot be reshaped at the level of macroeconomic policy. Thus the link between PRSPs and SAPs is through the

imposition of the SAP neoliberal macro-economic framework. A few examples:

In Tanzania, the enhanced HIPC matrix has about 30 neoliberal conditionalities. Of these 25 are from the IMF's Poverty Reduction and Growth Facility (PRGF) document and only 5 from the PRSP. Given that PRGF arrangement had been reached in January 2000, while the PRSP was only endorsed by the IMF and World Bank Boards in October 2000, the implementation of neoliberal policies obviously takes precedence over implementation and monitoring of poverty reduction policies. Furthermore, some bilateral donors cancelled Tanzania's debt on condition that Tanzania did not go off track on its obligations to the PRGF.

Donor resumption of development assistance for Kenya's PRSP was based on conditionalities outside of the PRSP process. Critical assessment and criticisms of neoliberal policies, which were raised at national and district level consultations with civil society, were excluded from the final PRSP document. This confirms that the PRGF and its framework have been imposed on poverty reduction efforts in Kenya. But, more importantly, it is the PRGF, and not the PRSP, document that defines support.

In spite of civil society submissions, the macroeconomic focus of the Malawi PRSP was on the so-called macroeconomic stability through reduction of budget deficits, deregulation, and privatisation. All of these measures cause contraction of the economy and job losses, thereby increasing poverty. The macroeconomic language in the PRSP is the same as that of the conventional IMF SAP prescriptions.

Two conclusions emerge. The first is that the PRGF and the donor conditionalities based on PRGF conditionalities must be delinked from HIPC and Development

Africa

Cooperation. The second is that PRGFs must be shown to bring about good governance and the promotion of human rights.

Institutional linkages: The WTO example

African countries have a keen interest in fully participating in the multilateral global trading system. They see the potential of trade as an engine of growth that will increase incomes and accordingly liberate them from dependency on development aid, whose conditionalities have undermined their governance by failing to provide development.

However, when the South Africans point out that '...thousands of workers lose their jobs as textile and clothing factories close down because of massive tariff cuts; three million South Africans infected with HIV/AIDS continue to die because they cannot afford treatment; disease and violence spiral in Paarl communities after a fruit canning factory closes down because it can no longer compete with subsidised European canned fruit...', one begins to understand that the role of the WTO, and its impact on people's rights and governance can be substantial.[22]

It seems that the WTO works in league with the IFIs. Both the World Bank and the IMF ensure that African countries observe conditions in line with the ideological thrust of the WTO. While trade liberalisation is the agenda of the WTO, it is the World Bank and the IMF conditionalities that are the forerunners. Many African countries have experienced this. Under the poverty reduction strategies, for example, the World Bank insisted that Uganda privatise and liberalise. Uganda 'agreed' on the understanding that regulations would follow. But the reality is that, under the WTO, liberalisation and privatisation must come without any form of regulation![23].

Within the WTO, powerful countries have pushed developed countries to provide for unregulated capital flows, unregulated privatisation, reduction of tariff barriers and import duties. But the developed countries maintain their protection against product and capital movement into their countries from the developing countries. On the one hand, they urge developing countries to reduce and remove their subsidies on agricultural products and to remove any barriers for developed countries' products. On the other hand, the developed countries heavily subsidise their agriculture and impose limits to the import of agricultural products from the developing countries.

The marginalisation of African developing countries in the WTO is an area of serious concern that goes beyond global governance and amounts to domination, which violates the African Charter on Human and People's Rights and undermines African governance. Undemocratic behaviour by the governments of powerful members of the WTO, mainly the G7 countries, is at odds with the rhetoric on enhancing good governance in developing countries. More importantly, it does not build trust, peace and harmony between peoples of the developed countries and those of the developing countries. This reality undermines global peace and security, which is an important human right for all.

Rights and the implementation of the Millennium Development Goals

In 1995, the Copenhagen World Social Summit resulted in commitments to:

- eradicate poverty;
- promote social integration by fostering societies based on promotion and protection of human rights;
- accelerate the economic, social and human resource development of Africa and the least developed countries.

Africa

The 2000 Millennium Declaration reaffirmed the collective responsibility of all governments to uphold human dignity, equality and equity at the global level. Governments, individually and collectively, endorsed the Millennium Development Goals (MDGs).[24]

The 2002 United Nations International Conference on Financing for Development, held in Monterrey, Mexico,[25] saw financing for development as a global challenge. The Monterrey Consensus spoke, among other things, of the need to enhance the coherence and consistency of international monetary, financial and trading systems, in support of development. The Conference resolved to promote the democratisation of global governance. It said that development assistance should support recipient countries' national strategies and should be untied.

The MDGs and Monterrey Consensus are consistent with meeting all aspects of human rights, particularly the right to development and to all economic, cultural, social, civil and political rights. The MDGs form the most critical pillar on which to build international relationships. But meeting the MDGs may require a very clear 'post neoliberalism' era, in which policies that work for eradicating poverty will be an integral part of global reality.[26] Neoliberal policies, on which the current reality hinges and which define current international cooperation, have failed to spur economic growth and to reduce poverty. Thus a set of new policies is required. These include:

- A move towards multilateralism as a form of governance at the global level.
- With respect to Africa: the immediate establishment of the Development Forum suggested in the NEPAD, as a basis for common positioning and as a framework in which the African Union and the OECD DAC could engage in meaningful negotiations on development aid.
- Bringing IMF, World Bank and the WTO increasingly under more democratic control — accountable to the United Nations.
- The power of the WTO must be reduced.[27] UNCTAD must be made to play a key role, especially on behalf of the developing countries, as has been suggested in the follow-up to the Monterrey process. Furthermore, there is a need to bring the WTO into the United Nations system to improve coherence.[28] This should stop the bad governance practices we see in the WTO in the form of powerful governments twisting the arms of poorer nations.[29]
- The Maastricht Guidelines on Rights could again be put on the development agenda, as a framework within which to cast development aid and international relationships.

Africa

Notes

1. **Opa** Kapijimpanga is Chairman of the African Forum **and** Network on Debt and Development, based in **Harare**, Zimbabwe.

2. **UN ECA** African Alternative Framework to Structural Adjustment and Transformation

3. Zambia's failure to meet IFI conditionalities always results in bilateral donors withholding assistance. There is an effort by some progressive donors such as Denmark to move away from this practice.

4. See Opa Kapijimpanga, 2001; may be obtained from opa@zamtel.zm

5. **The Vienna** Declaration and Programme of Action, **adopted** by the UN World Conference on Human **Rights**, 1993.

6. **On the** 10th anniversary of the Limburg Principles on **the** implementation of the International Covenant on Economic, Social and Cultural Rights a group of more **that** thirty six experts met in Maastricht from 22 to 26 **January** 1997 at the invitation of the International Commission of Jurists and others to elaborate further on the nature and scope of violations of rights and appropriate remedies. Details on the Limburg Principles can be found at http://ww.uu.nl/content/20-10.pdf

7. African Union NEPAD Implementation Committee estimate presented to the G8 Kananaskas meeting of 2002.

8. Unpublished AFRODAD 2003 research.

9. World Bank (2000) World Development Report 2000/2001 'Attacking Poverty', World Bank, pg.192.

10. See www.saprin.org in particular the Report: The Policy Roots of Economic crisis and Poverty. Country specific reports are themselves interesting material.

11. SAPRIN, The Policy Roots of Economic crisis and Poverty page. 50

12. **Long** term Development in Sub-Sahara Africa; World Bank 1979.

13. As a counter to the African Alternative Framework to Structural Adjustment. See also Opa Kapijimpanga Background material for the Public Hearing inn the European parliament, Brussels, October 1999.

14. See Global Development Finance, Financing the Poorest countries, The World Bank, 2002 (Analysis and Summary of Tables p. 101

15. See Pete Henriot, *Does Zambia need the IMF?* JCTR, Lusaka, 2000.

16. AFRODAD Reality of Aid West Africa Report, 2003.

17. ibid

18. ibid, p101

19. Unfortunately it is not possible to disclose the credible source of this information.

20. Burkina Faso, Ghana, Kenya, Malawi, Mauritania, Mozambique, Rwanda, Tanzania, Uganda and Zambia

21. "...at the heart of Africa's development must lie the ultimate and overriding goal of human centered development that ensures the overall well-being of the people through sustained improvement in their living standards and the full and effective participation of the people in charting their development policies, programmes and processes and contributing to their realization." African Charter for Popular Participation (UN-ECA, 1990 p.18),

22. See the brochure produced on the WTO by Campaign Against Neoliberalism, Group for Environmental Monitoring, Treatment Action Campaign, International Labour Resource Information group, Institute for Global Dialogue, Moteho Integrity Consultants Representing Africa Trade Network, Alternative Information and Development Center, South African Municipal Workers Union, and the Oxfam GB South Africa Policy and Communications Office, This pamphlet was produced before the Third Ministerial Meeting in Seattle in 1998

23. Warren Nyamugasira

24. UN General Assembly resolution of 18 September 2000.

25. See the report at www.un/esa/ffd/aconf198-11.pdf

26. See various arguments presented in "After Neoliberalism: Economic Policies that Work for the Poor" A collection of papers presented at a Conference on Alternatives to Neoliberalism, May 23-24 in Washington DC. See www.new-rules.org

27. See also arguments by Didier Jacobs in Democratizing Global Economic Governance, in After Neoliberalism, Economic Policies that work for the Poor.

28. Paragraph 16, page 68 of Monterrey report — trade must be an engine of development and not otherwise.

29. Aleen Kwa

Re-thinking aid: development cooperation in a multilateral crisis

Edward Oyugi, African Forum and Network on Debt and Development (AFRODAD)

To understand development cooperation in Africa, we have to address a number of questions:

What are the roots of the suffering and disadvantage that have turned the entire African continent into an object of worldwide sympathy and sometimes philanthropy, in the form of development cooperation?

Does Africa need aid? If it does, where should the aid come from?

Which aspects of our distress should such aid address?

In what modalities should such aid be delivered?

What development policy environment is appropriate for what kind of assistance?

Who should determine what assistance is needed — and in what quantities?

A content analysis of public discourses in the African media and other channels of communication reveal that the use of development cooperation-related expressions is disturbingly frequent. Development assistance, donors, aid, FDI, debt — you name it — appear more frequently in discourses than sovereignty or self-transformation-related expressions such as: patriotism, self-reliance, autonomy. And even when such purportedly neutral concepts as globalisation, good governance, development and trade appear, behind them seem to lurk connotations of development assistance relationships.

Why? Because, for many years now, little has been done in the way of addressing any aspect of economic development in Africa, beyond its ineluctable relationship with foreign aid, and many other forms of involvement by external forces.

Development assistance is treated here as a relationship between those offering assistance in some form or another — the 'aid givers' — and those receiving assistance — the 'recipients'. The donors may be individuals, NGOs or official bilateral or multilateral development agencies. In this relationship, the assumed goal is transformation towards autonomous and self-driven development — whatever development may mean for each of the above actors — on the part of the receiving party. But at the heart of this relationship is a paradox, which presents an intractable challenge, with far-reaching implications for the future of Africa's economic development.

This paradox can be traced to point four of President Truman's 1949 'Bold New Program', which is generally acknowledged as the starting point of modern development cooperation. In this declaration, Truman pledged, in the spirit of the Truman Doctrine of the 'struggle between democracy and dictatorship', to make the benefits of US

Africa

scientific advances and industrial progress available for the improvement and economic growth of underdeveloped areas of the world.[1]

Whereas this declaration may not have marked the beginning of many forms of bi- and multilateral development cooperation, it does illustrate the considerations that informed their origins, theory and practice. Common to the Cold War strategic justifications for aid, and neo-colonial hegemonic schemes, is the primacy of a political notion that old and new ties could be sustained and rearticulated in new strategic frameworks and operational modalities of domination in the guise of development cooperation. The Commonwealth, EU-ACP, and NEPAD to some degree, fit this analysis.

Historical and motivational context of aid

In the post Second World War era of the 1960s, 1970s, and a large part of 1980s, much assistance was given to the developing economies in order to maintain politically acceptable regimes and to ensure the continued supply of the natural resources that many underdeveloped economies produced or were capable of producing. The mortal fear of the emerging hegemonic forces in America and, to a lesser extent Europe, was of some developing countries ideologically gravitating to the Soviet Union and thereby swelling the *dangerous* ranks of the socialist nations and the communist threat. This motivated considerable foreign aid from the West. In the same manner, but more particularly in a bid to expand its ideological influence in the newly independent countries, the Soviet Union also provided development assistance.

This was the initial ideological and, therefore, motivational context, within which aid began to distort the natural

development and ideological orientation of African economies and societies.

Following the collapse of the Soviet Union and the emergence of the United States as the hegemonic centre of world capitalism, the theory and practice of development cooperation have experienced a significant strategic shift within a new world order, structured around triumphant capitalism.

Under the reign of the Washington Consensus, as driven by fundamentalist market forces, particularly during the unchallenged ascendancy of neoliberal orthodoxy, development aid became aggressively conditional upon good governance, as defined by the Washington-based multilateral financial institutions. Structural Adjustment Programmes (SAPs) provided the mould into which foreign aid transactions had to fit. Many developing economies not only stagnated, but even regressed as a result of subjecting the planning and management of their economies to the conditionalities of SAPs.

Faced with mounting intellectual revolt (from within and outside the West) and the negative economic signals from poorly performing Third World economies, a post-Washington consensus strategic retreat became necessary. Its necessity largely rested on the growing intellectual resolve to question and challenge some of the underlying theoretical assumptions and their practical implications. With stealth and tact, a new strategic framework for development cooperation was designed to accommodate new patterns of capitalist domination of the African economies. Poverty Reduction Strategy Papers (PRSP), the New Partnership for African Development (NEPAD), EU-ACP frameworks, the Multilateral Agreement on Investment (MAI), and a handful of strategically complementary bilateral and multilateral development cooperation frameworks have been designed to address the steady erosion of confidence in Western development assistance modalities. Central to the Post-Washington consensus is the purported devolution of ownership of the development agenda to recipients, based on the elusive imperative of *subsidiarity*. The reality is, however, different. Subsidiarity principles, as far as development cooperation is concerned, have remained a clever feint, if not dishonest rhetoric, the practical result of which has been to confer on local actors a false feeling of domestic control over development policy. In reality, these actors have absolutely nothing to do with the thinking and direction of economic development. They have a long way to go before reclaiming their stake in influencing what development should mean to them.

Development cooperation, like any encounter between social systems, is a complex phenomenon. It is also problematic. The fact that it brings local actors and their institutions together with outsiders and their understanding of development, and the very problematic notion that outsiders may pretend to plan a community's future, is more than indicative of the differential power relation in the encounter. The imbalance in power relations cannot provide a basis for the resolution of conflicts between the goals, rationales and conditionalities of outsiders, and the destiny and culture of the communities.

The tension between development cooperation and economic development in recipient economies remains a reality that is difficult to tackle. The beginning of what may turn out to be a solution is radical politics, which aim to challenge the characteristics of power distribution among the principal actors. The onus is on the politically conscious actors in recipient economies to stand up and keep their political-economic interest alive. The

strategic objective should be to work towards transforming the sites of encounter into democratic spaces, or assemblages of institutions[2] and actors, with the real capacity to decide and intervene, particularly if it happens that the outcomes of decision making fall outside the interests of some powerful groups in the encounter.

Multilateral crisis: a challenge for development cooperation or an anathema?

Multilateralism has had its ups and downs in the long history of international and intergovernmental relations. This is normal, particularly given the wide range of national and ideological interests — some contradictory and others congruent — that are supposed to be subordinated to a multilateral process. With the Washington Consensus, as the chief architect of a new world order, multilateralism became the first institutional casualty.

Assaults on multilateralism were unleashed from several angles. The UN was downgraded in respect of its capacity to regulate international relations in the interest of sustainable peace. The Washington-based multilateral agencies had their milk teeth removed and much sharper and stronger ones allowed to grow in their places, (ready for biting into the delicate territories of national sovereignty through development aid conditionalities). The WTO got turned into a Trojan horse, through which weaker economies were to be re-colonised by Western corporate interests. The MAI was designed to tame and prime Southern economies for domination by Western private sector interests. And then came the terrorist attack on the citadel of finance capital, increasing potential for a multilateral crisis. The mothballing of the MAI process, the Iraq war, the Cancun stalemate, the 'Development Cooperation

Africa

Lens on Terrorism Prevention — Key entry Points and Actions'³ and a few other sites of international strife point to the beginnings of this multilateral crisis. From the perspective of the need for coherence and harmonisation regarding development cooperation, there is a real risk that development aid may soon become simply an instrument of geopolitical and military interests, addressing domestic security agendas with neither multilateral nor bilateral concerns.

The World Bank proposal for a Comprehensive Development Framework (CDF), intended to reform the entire development assistance system, has generated more discussion than solutions to the age-old challenges of coherence and harmonisation of development efforts. Initially, the proposal was greeted with a lot of enthusiasm, given that its ostensible aim was to ensure a coordinated response by donors and creditors to development priorities, as identified by borrowing governments and their citizens. Such priorities were to be enshrined in a single development framework for each borrower, to which donors and creditors would be accountable.

The multilateral processes intended to anchor the implementation of this proposal took off, under the debilitating shadow of globalisation and allied neoliberal strategies but have yet to fly. The MAI got spiked before it could be foisted onto the developing countries. That its ideological substance had already insinuated itself into other seemingly unconnected multilateral processes and agreements, such as WTO negotiations and the EU-ACP agreement, has not come as a surprise. Sooner rather than later, there will be no reason to fob it off on African governments. Its strategic functions will have been taken over by other multilateral agreements.

All that has been said seems to point to the cementing of the union between aid and politics. Rather than the authority of metropolitan states being eroded or marginalised by the apparent proliferation of private actors, it is prudent to remain alert to the possibility that such strategies are simply a reworking 'of international power and its projection through non-territorial networks and private systems calculation.'⁴ This is why development aid, including humanitarian assistance, can no longer be left to bilateral 'anarchy'. It must not only be coherent and targeted, first and foremost it has be effective. The question still remains: effective for whom?

Aid effectiveness: what has not been, but ought to be, done

Issues concerning the effectiveness of aid in promoting development in Africa are moving to the centre of development discourse. At the same time, they are beginning to crowd out the optimism that greeted and justified external aid for the better part of the last century.

There are two major reasons for the recent apparent prominence of the aid effectiveness problematic. In the first place, the end of the Cold War era has removed one of the most important justifications for development cooperation: there is no ideological popularity contest in the era of a uni-polar world order. Second, foreign aid and development assistance are gaining a bad reputation, on account of their not showing any capacity to reduce poverty, even in economies that have attracted the largest share of foreign assistance. A few face-saving caveats have been put forward to dilute the impact of the misgivings about aid. The first caveat argues that it is unfair to judge foreign aid on its developmental effectiveness, where the post-Cold War aid environment and motivation are still not in

Africa

favour of real economic development, but are serving other interests.

The truth of the matter is that the African economies are worse off now, than before they began to attract foreign aid. Poverty is increasing everywhere in Africa, despite increased inflows of external resources.

Do we really need to waste paper and ink recounting the many observations that have confirmed that foreign aid — the way it is being delivered and managed — has not had any positive effect on the African economies? No. But we must not only know what is wrong with foreign aid, we must also begin to say what to do about it.

If foreign aid had had any anti-poverty effect on recipient economies, the level of budget support to Uganda and Tanzania would have put these two countries among not only the fastest growing economies,[5] but also those with the highest per capita income[6]. Despite all the plutocracy to which Moi's government subjected the Kenyan economy, Kenya was able to withstand donor withdrawal of multilateral assistance for close on two decades, without bringing the economy to its knees. Instead, the Kenyan economy was turned into an agitated oyster, whose capacity to produce pearls — not high quality ones but pearls all the same — was ironically enhanced. This lesson from Kenya should be a good one for the rest of Africa. The lesson is that real development can only come from local efforts and resources, put to prudent use by an effective government, with the effective participation of local subjects. The practice of donors throwing money, projects, and external know-how at problems in the South will not bring the desired changes in the lives of the affected populations.

Development assistance based on solidarity, and not on spurious notion of vaguely defined partnership, must build on

a country's historical and cultural circumstances, and must involve a fundamental societal transformation process that money and projects alone can neither stimulate nor sustain. Hence it is of critical importance that development aid, if it is needed at all, must be seen as enhancing the ability of countries and local institutions. In summary: countries need social capital to manage development on their own and in a sustainable way.

Foreign aid to Africa has acted like a storm gathering away from the rains. In many cases, the storm has ended up destroying social infrastructure, without boosting the economy. The theory and practice of foreign aid points to a power system that is not keen to provide the people of Africa with practical tools for mastering basic life challenges and innovative ways to navigate the road of life, on the basis of their capacity to control their own destiny, regardless of its global worth.

This is not to belittle the importance of external assistance. The point to underscore is that development aid can only make a difference to the lives of recipients, when it is made to stimulate local capacities within a policy framework negotiated between the local social groups. Development must not be taken out of the hands of power sites in the global North merely to be directed to locations of mimicry and mediocrity in the South. Macroeconomic policy that creates development policy frameworks needs to be anchored in social dialogue among the local stakeholders, not dictated by aid givers.

Instead of the present practice of foreign development assistance that has left continental economies worse off than before, Africa needs a strong, democratic and affirmative state sector that can effectively restore government sponsorship of labour as the source of all forms of wealth and development. Africa needs a New Deal with

Africa

its people and their labour-intensive capacities, which are required to lay the foundations of an economic take-off. Donor 'replacement therapies', such as free trade relations, promoting Foreign Direct Investment (FDI), and private sector leadership in the economy, can only be effective when matched to an economy that has available power, adequate road length per capita, and clean water for everybody. A growth accounting system that emphasises the well-being of a few people in the urban centres is not enough. Just linking aid to increased FDI inflows misses the point. The direct benefits of FDI are mainly intended for the parent economy. Relying on FDI flows as an aspect of aid, particularly in the era of mobile, speculative capital, hunting for captive labour in the global economy (where 'democratisation' has severely hampered the capacity of nation states, and where the purported allocative efficiency of the market has been severely compromised by wanton deregulation) is beginning to prove unworkable.

The pattern of foreign aid disbursement has clearly shown that more aid flows into economies where aid itself has caused the heaviest debt burden — thus increasing the need for economic relief.

Before aid became the basis of economic planning in Africa, it had been theoretically designed merely to help cover any shortfalls in the earning sectors of the receiving economies. It thus helped the growing economies of the newly independent African countries acquire the necessary scarce, but badly needed, foreign exchange. At that time there was an appreciable and logical relationship, between local resource gaps and foreign aid. Since aid has become the most critical input in our public expenditure, the level of distortion it generates in the African national economies is increasingly spiralling out of control and can, therefore, no longer

be wished away. When sponsors of NEPAD, for instance, came up with US$ 64 billion [7] as the amount required to finance its implementation, it was not, and has not since been, clarified whether the figure reflects a continental resource gap, against which foreign aid needs to be sought, or is just an arbitrary figure that should enable African economies to make a difference in the lives of the African people. This magic figure is yet to be disaggregated against specific development needs of the continent, as prioritised by its own people. But even if that were to be done, many questions would remain.

Some of the critical questions would be: What is NEPAD's agenda on debt relief? Unlike the Marshal Plan, the implementation of which was placed under the coordination of a multilateral agency — the Organization for European Economic Cooperation (OEEC), NEPAD's connection with the African Union is still problematic. Given that the proposed regional planning and management approach has yet to determine a definite strategic and institutional framework, many Africans are left wondering which multilateral African platform will be used to negotiate with either the OECD or the G8! Is NEPAD's vision of democracy defined by the people's need for social development, or by the requirements of creating a functional market as a space and mechanism for misallocation of national resources? Does neoliberal economic policy provide the framework within which NEPAD-generated resources will be put to use?

Mobilising domestic financial and human resources

The question of mobilising and retaining domestic financial resources has been on the agenda for some time. Increased liberalisation in the financial sector has made the discussion of the necessary challenges

Africa

even more urgent. Responses to the challenges have been heavily influenced by donor conditionalities, which have demanded more and more liberalisation. Alternative responses have been excluded from any discourse aimed at finding solutions, owing to the heavy hand of an increasingly manipulative, and occasionally totalitarian, multilateral environment.

The open nature, and excessive external dependency of African economies, has led to the disproportionate outflow of resources from the African continent. This has happened in varying degrees on the basis of:

- unfavourable terms of trade
- debt repayment burden
- capital flight
- profit repatriation and corruption
- transfer account procedures.

For example, capital flight from highly indebted poor economies of sub-Saharan Africa amounted to nearly half of the estimated external resource requirement.[8]

A significant proportion of domestic savings, which should be the primary source of investment financing, has been lost through capital flight, adversely affecting even some promising economies, such as Kenya, that have enjoyed high savings/GDP ratios.

With the adoption of free market policies, which have exposed African economies to the vagaries of liberalisation, and with African governments abandoning their traditional role of controlling interest rates, regulating credit and capital flows, and putting in place relevant institutional practices, African economies have been subjected to competition for which they are ill-equipped.

Against this unfavourable background, we need to engage in the affirmative action necessary to build domestic economies, particularly where globalisation is breaking down the defence mechanism required for building strategic frameworks for national economic agendas. Above all, this means that we, in Africa, must increasingly engage in selective liberalisation of the economy and push our 'wheelbarrows upside-down'[9] if our economies are to grow. Globalisation must be more of a choice than an inevitability.

Africa

Notes

1. Quoted in: Ruttan, V.W 1996, *United States Development of Assistance Policy: The Domestic Politics of Economic Aid*, Baltimore, John Hopkins University Press.

2. Riberio G Lins, 2002, in *Capacity for Development — New Solutions Old Problems*, edited by Sakiko Fukuda Parr, CARLOS lopes and Khalid Malik, UNDP.

3. Refers to Development Assistance Committee's policy statement and reference document released by a high level meeting of the DAC in April 2003 and endorsed by the Organisation for Economic Cooperation and Development (OECD).

4. Duffield Mark, 2001, Governing the Borderlands: Decoding the Power of Aid, in a paper presented at a Seminar on: Politics and Humanitarian Aid: Debates, Dilemmas and Discussions, Commonwealth Institute, London.

5. Measured by dubious statistics that hardly translate into poverty reduction.

6. Measured in terms of how many Ugandans are graduating from object poverty to better conditions of life.

7. The New Partnership for African Development 2002, Pretoria, South Africa.

8. Ajayi, S.I (1997), 'An Analysis of External Debt and Capital Flight in the Heavily Indebted poor countries of Sub-Saharan Africa'; in Zubair Iqbal and Ravi Kanbur, 1997, *External Finance for Law Income Countries*. IMF.

9. Referring to a legendary Londoner who, because of mental illness, had made a fetish of pushing a wheelbarrow along the London Street. At the end of day he would be trundling his wheelbarrow home, extremely tired, his wheelbarrow full of all sorts of rubbish that Londoners had thrown into his vehicle on account of his mental condition. After many years of doing so he, one day, he regained a certain amount of sanity that caused him to reflect on how he had been used to collect and transport other peoples' waste. The following day Londoners were surprised to see him pushing his wheelbarrow upside down as away of protesting against being misused.

The Poverty Reduction Growth Facility, Poverty Reduction Strategies and development aid

Nelson Nyangu, African Forum and Network on Debt and Development

The purpose of this chapter is to provide a critical analysis of the Poverty Reduction Growth Facility (PRGF) within the context of development aid. As an instrument that has been laid down by the International Financial Institutions (IFIs) for developing countries, the PRGF has come under heavy criticism for its inability to address poverty and human well-being in developing countries. In fact, the PRGF is seen as a major obstacle to the success of Poverty Reduction Strategy Papers (PRSPs) and other development initiatives preceding its introduction, because of its technicality, disregard for low financial, human and institutional capacities to effectively implement PRGF programmes, unrealistic and unattainable conditionalities and the neo-liberal paradigm that underpins the programme.

There is also a new dimension to the operations of two Bretton Woods institutions. They have ventured into private sector investment through entities such as the International Finance Corporation (IFC) of the World Bank. Shamelessly they even bid for state owned enterprise, putting pressure on adjusting governments to sell, offer concessions or commercialise. This casts serious doubts on IFI objectivity as being genuine official interlocutors between donors and recipients of development aid.

Background

The Poverty Reduction Growth Facility (PRGF) is the IMF's low-interest lending facility for poor countries. The PRGF was embraced by the IMF in September 1999, as a new antipoverty instrument for its work in low-income countries. Resulting from this, the IMF abandoned its Enhanced Structural Adjustment Facility (ESAF). This move was an apparent response to pressure from NGOs such as Jubilee 2000, a critical external evaluation of ESAF and a fundamental review of the Highly Indebted Poor Countries (HIPC) initiative. These processes showed that ESAF and HIPC were not working, and had actually increased poverty and hardship in adjusting countries. Looked at from an external perspective, policy changes effected on HIPC and PRGF were externally driven. They do not represent a substantive policy shift by the Fund, towards poverty reduction.

PRGF programmes are underpinned by comprehensive, country-owned poverty reduction strategies. Poverty Reduction Strategy Papers (PRSPs) are supposed to be prepared by governments in low-income countries through a participatory process

Africa

involving domestic stakeholders and external development partners including the IMF and the World Bank. The PRSP describes the macroeconomic, structural and social policies and programmes that a country intends to pursue to promote broad-based growth and reduce poverty. The link between the PRSP and development aid, is that the PRSP document stipulates external financing needs, including direct annual budget support from external partners and their associated sources. PRSPs are therefore important milestones in developing countries' efforts to mobilise development aid for poverty reduction and human well-being. PRSPs also provide a forum for external development partners and domestic stakeholders to contribute to policy design and dialogue with adjusting countries on economic governance issues.

The PRGF is strongly linked to the Initiative for Heavily Indebted Poor Countries (HIPC), first launched in 1996 by the Bank and the Fund. The aim of HIPC was to ensure that poor countries pursuing IMF and World Bank-supported adjustment and reform programmes did not face unmanageable debt burdens. At the time that PRGFs were put in place, the HIPC initiative was modified to provide faster, deeper, and broader debt relief and to strengthen the links between debt relief, poverty reduction and social policies.

The enhanced HIPC Initiative is now focused on macroeconomic adjustment, structural and social policy reforms with an emphasis on higher spending for health and education. Despite its recent reform, the HIPC initiative still poses difficulties for adjusting countries, in that certain conditions have to be fulfilled before countries can access debt relief. The adjusting country must have reached 'Decision Point', 'Interim Relief' and 'Completion Point'.

The main thrust of the PRGF, associated PRSPs and the enhanced HIPC is to have clear policies that are focused on economic growth and poverty reduction. This should come about due to better national ownership. Implementation should be consistent. According to the IMF, the new facility brings about a number of innovations, designed to ensure that lending programmes are pro-poor and in line with each country's own strategy for reducing poverty. These innovations are complemented by a stronger partnership with the World Bank, to increase the effectiveness and sustained impact of IFI efforts to reduce poverty.

Unlike the ESAF, the PRGF raised expectations about the role of the IMF in the struggle against poverty in the world's poorest countries. The most important innovation has been the PRSP process. PRSPs are prepared in all low-income countries intending to borrow from the IMF or World Bank, or to access debt relief under HIPC. National authorities base PRSPs on extensive consultation with stakeholders, including civil society and donors, rather than on negotiations with IMF or World Bank staff. The aim is to integrate the authorities' macroeconomic framework with an assessment of the poverty situation and plans to reduce poverty. Because this can be time-consuming, countries are producing Interim PRSPs covering existing policies and plans, and explaining how the more participatory, full PRSP will be developed. PRGF programmes can therefore incorporate some of the improvements in the new process, even before full PRSPs are completed.

The PRGF and development aid

To achieve clear policies focused on economic growth and poverty reduction, the PRGF-supported programmes are derived

Africa

from PRSPs, in contrast to ESAF-supported programmes. Within the context of development aid, PRGF loan arrangements are derived from the Poverty Reduction Strategy described in the adjusting country's PRSP. This is also the basis for all other official creditor support. Under ESAF, Policy Framework Papers (PFPs), which were a basis for loan arrangements, were prepared jointly by country officials, IMF and the World Bank staff without broader consultations.

In theory, the PRGF process incorporates contributions to policy design from across society. PRGF-related documents are extensively distributed and emphasise country leadership and enhanced collaboration with the World Bank. This makes the PRGF programmes more transparent, enabling other donors to use PRSPs as the basis for their own development aid. So the PRGF is viewed as a more coherent and country-led approach to poverty reduction policies. The World Bank and IMF jointly assess the PRSP, which then serves as the basis for concessional lending by both institutions. That way, the two institutions can tailor assistance to fit their respective areas of responsibility in supporting the PRSP strategy.

PRGF-supported programmes have a number of distinctive features. These are: public participation, economic aspects of governance and conditionality. The key feature of broad public participation and increased national ownership is to ensure that civil society has been involved in the formulation of the PRSP, that the country authorities are the clear leaders of the process, and that the programme is properly embedded in the overall strategy for growth and poverty reduction.

Economic aspects of governance place emphasis on effective and efficient management of public resources, strengthening fiscal governance to improve public services and ensuring proper use of HIPC debt relief and other government resources. Government budgets under PRGF-supported programmes need to be more pro-poor and pro-growth. Government spending should focus on activities that demonstrably benefit those in poverty, especially where debt relief under the HIPC Initiative, is releasing funds previously used for debt service.

The Bank helps adjusting countries to link their PRSPs and Medium-Term Economic Framework (MTEF) through an effective Public Expenditure Management (PEM) system. The focus of PEM is to emphasise the main functions of the budget: control of public resources, planning future resource allocation and management of resources. The MTEF is a three-year framework within which available resources (both government and donor) are divided between sectors, on the basis of agreed priorities. In short the MTEF is a medium term focus on resource planning. From the MTEF, annual national budgets are derived. In terms of development aid, civil society and donors should have participated in the PRSP process. Civil society's role is to increase public engagement on policies, coordination with Ministries, Provinces and other Spending Agencies (MPSAs) and monitoring and evaluation of PRSP implementation. The role of donors in the PRSP-MTEF process is to provide estimates of donor inflows for the three-year period, to provide input into sector priorities and programmes, and make comments on overall government priorities vis-à-vis the PRGF.

According to the IMF's April 2001 fact sheet, PRGF-supported programmes should pay more attention to the social impact of major reforms. Where there are expected to be major reforms, analysis of the impact on people in poverty has to be conducted (normally by the World Bank where governments lack the capacity to do this

Africa

Figure 1. Link between national priorities, PRSPs and MTEF

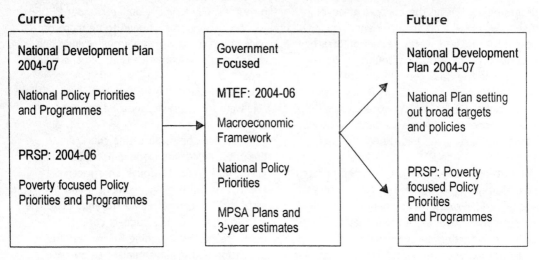

work themselves) and, where necessary, countervailing measures should be incorporated into the PRGF-supported programme.

At the same time, tax reforms should aim to improve both equity and efficiency. Appropriate flexibility in fiscal policy, including in targets for fiscal balances, is equally important. PRGF-supported programmes also have the scope to react to commonly experienced shocks, such as deteriorating terms of trade, poor harvests or conflicts. And when it is clear that funds could be used productively, new foreign aid may become available in the course of the fiscal year.

The conditionality feature stresses the importance of focusing on measures that are central to the success of the country strategy, particularly in the macroeconomic and financial spheres. Conditionality should focus on *reinforcing* the priorities set out in the country's strategy and should be applied sparingly. Almost all structural conditions in PRGF programmes are confined to four core IMF areas:

- fiscal management (expenditure control, accounting, auditing);
- tax reform;
- financial sector reform; and
- governance.

PRGF programmes in some countries have *no* structural conditions outside the fiscal management area but other countries such as Zambia, Kenya, Zimbabwe and Cameroon have more detailed conditionalities on governance. However, the number of conditions under PRGF is generally well below the average under ESAF.

The World Bank is also closely involved in PRGF countries, especially in the application of Bank conditionalities. Originally under the PRGF approach, World Bank and the IMF were meant to focus on their respective areas of expertise and responsibility. PRGF countries should, therefore, have a clear division in the conditionality applied by the Bank and the Fund. To this effect the Bank has established the Poverty Reduction Support Credit (PRSC) to enable it to link its own lending directly to the implementation of PRSPs.

Africa

Box 3. Terms of the PRGF

- As of September 2003, a total of 77 low-income member countries were eligible for PRGF assistance.
- Eligibility is based principally on a country's per capita income and eligibility under the International Development Association (IDA), the World Bank's concessional window (the current cut-off point for IDA eligibility is a 2001 per capita GDP level of $875).
- An eligible country may borrow up to a maximum of 140% of its IMF quota under a three-year arrangement, although this limit may be increased under exceptional circumstances to a maximum of 185% of quota. The maximum amounts do not constitute an entitlement and the amount lent will depend on the balance of payments need of the member, the strength of its adjustment programme, its outstanding use of Fund credit and its record on such use in the past.
- Loans under the PRGF carry an annual interest rate of 0.5%, with repayments made every six months, beginning five-and-a-half years and ending ten years after the disbursement.

Source: IMF Fact Sheet (Poverty Reduction Growth Facility) September 2003

Financing Mechanism for the PRGF

Concessional lending under the PRGF is administered by the IMF through the PRGF and PRGF-HIPC Trusts. The PRGF Trust borrows resources from central banks, governments and official institutions, generally at market-related interest rates. It lends them on a pass-through basis, to PRGF-eligible countries. The difference between the market-related interest rate paid to PRGF Trust lenders and the rate of interest of 0.5% per year paid by the PRGF eligible countries, is financed by contributions from bilateral donors and the IMF's own resources.

PRGF, development aid and development realities in low-income countries

Development realities or characteristics in the 77 low-income countries that are under the World Bank and IMF sponsored programmes are varied! The neo-liberal approach of the Fund's 'one-size-fits-all' remedy for 77 of the world's poorest nations is, like previous

policy interventions, not going to work! The following section reflects on the Fund and Bank's compatibility with pro-poor policy choices, as promised by the poverty reduction strategies.

The IMF's traditional neo-liberal stance is that *a sound macroeconomic policy environment will lead to external viability and economic growth, and that economic growth will lead to poverty reduction.* But this has been proven to be a simplistic and unworkable analysis for low-income countries.

An analysis of ESAF success stories shows that those countries that experienced significant per capita growth under ESAF, were also the largest beneficiaries of external aid. Very few showed that long-term sustained growth came through domestic savings, investment and human capital development. Flows of external aid are influenced by a number of factors, including geo-political considerations (Israel, South Korea), relations with the Group of Seven (G7), the presence of well-developed factor

Africa

markets, religious inclinations, and other bizarre motivations. Most countries in sub-Saharan Africa do not qualify under these criteria.

The Bank and Fund approaches, even under the PRGF, have emphasised economic stability and growth arising from economic liberalisation, as the main delivery mechanisms for poverty reduction. Economic liberalisation entails a number of changes to adjusting countries. Key among these are: trade liberalisation, tax reform, divesture of the state from direct participation in the economy, financial reforms and macroeconomic stabilisation.

Trade liberalisation

Most of the adjusting countries have not benefited from trade liberalisation. Although the 77 low-income countries currently under PRGF programmes have different development needs and characteristics, structural deficits in their economies leave them beset by chronic balance of payments (BOP) difficulties. The economies of low-income countries are highly dependent on a small cluster of raw commodity exports. It is estimated that the declining value of raw commodities relative to manufactured goods between the 1980s and 1990s was more than 30%. This resulted in declining terms of trade and significant losses in purchasing power.

Deteriorating terms of trade are further compounded by internal problems such as poor transport, communications, marketing infrastructures, limited domestic market, and a small and shrinking industrial sector. The education and health sectors of low-income countries have made very limited progress, thus affecting the lives and well-being of the people and undermining human capital formation. This situation according to CIDSE, sets a 'weak initial condition', that when coupled with crippling debt burden

amounts to a hostile and an unfavourable investment environment that affects the capacity of low income countries to respond to economic growth opportunities and challenges.

In view of the above, stabilisation and adjustment processes which are conditionalities under the PRGF and HIPC, have a negative effect on economic growth. Conditionalities regarding stability of exchange rates, avoidance of competitive devaluations and orderly correction of balance of payments problems, coupled with inherent and historical structural problems, make the stabilisation and adjustment programmes difficult. As most countries try to address foreign exchange inadequacies, by compressing the economy's aggregate demand, they actually depress economic growth.

A number of studies reveal that the costs of unilateral and rapid trade liberalisation fall most heavily on the poor. There has been a widespread failure of markets and institutions to create job opportunities, build human resources, create savings and provide micro finance services to poorer communities. The winners in SAPs have tended to be those with prior access to productive resources and assets, such as multinational companies.

Tax reform

As part of the rationalisation of the revenue and expenditure equation, IMF policies have aimed to shift the burden of taxation away from income tax, towards indirect taxation, sometimes including basic foodstuffs. There has also been a preference for shifting taxation from external trade to domestic consumption, as reflected in Value Added Tax (VAT). This has led to a number of changes in adjusting countries. In fact the guiding principle, especially on the expenditure side of the equation, is that you cannot spend what you do not have, thus the introduction of strict cash budgeting system. This has implications for those sections of society that depend on the state for their survival. Most states have been forced to spend less on non-economic sectors such as education, health and welfare. Such measures have led to cost shifting or cost sharing in the provision of public goods such as education and health. Under ESAF, education and health sectors performed very badly and the majority of people who are poor and vulnerable have been deprived of essential services. If the PRGF pursues this policy line, further deterioration can be expected.

The narrow view taken by the Fund, on how taxation should be pursued in adjusting countries, has been regressive in terms of the distribution of public services to the poor. It has diminished the capacity of governments to pursue re-distributive policies.

Divesture of state from economic activities

The Bank's Structural Adjustment thinking on the role of the state in economic activity is the same as that of the Fund. From the 1980s to date, the Bank's policy has been to remove the state from the market place, on the assumption that state intervention was inefficient, costly and affected free market wealth creation.

The impact of these policies was privatisation and commercialisation of state-owned enterprises. The consequence was redundancy and retrenchment. Rapid withdrawal of state participation in certain sectors, such as agriculture, transport and rural banking, had disastrous effects in a number of countries. In Zambia, the government's withdraw from crop marketing and running public transportation systems, led to a contraction of selling opportunities for poorer, remote farmers. This meant a redistribution of marketing opportunities, in favour of richer farmers, in locations

closer to the country's inadequate transport infrastructure.

The role of the state in economic activity is still one of the focuses of PRGFHIPC conditionality. Zambia in 2003 failed to have 50% (US$3.5 billion) of debt written off by creditor nations, because it failed to reach the HIPC Completion Point! Some of the benchmarks for reaching the HIPC completion point were the privatisation of the state-owned enterprises, among them a commercial bank, an electricity utility company and a telecommunications company. Others benchmarks stipulated no increment on the salaries of public workers, and failure to meet agreed releases/expenditure on education and health sectors. The argument of the Fund and Bank was that expenditures on the above were causing the Budget overrun.

The ability of low-income countries to participate in, and benefit from, 'open and freer' international and domestic markets, is clearly circumscribed by the degree of protectionism in industrial and regional markets. Equally, the opening up of local markets to international competition, has led to total collapse of local industries, because most of them are poorly capitalised, lack investment in human capital and are unable to compete with cheaply produced or subsidised imported goods. Zimbabwe and Zambia have experienced this problem, whereas South African exports were subsided by the state, and managed to land in these countries at below existing market prices.

Although investment in infrastructure, human and social capital is universally accepted as a stepping stone for economic growth, and vital for low-income countries, the Fund's policy position is that this should be a priority that comes after, rather than integrated with, adjustment and stabilisation frameworks!

Africa

Macroeconomic stability

The Fund's institutional priority is low inflation. It advises that this should be achieved through a tight anti-inflationary policy, managed exclusively by cutting fiscal deficits. This approach compresses demand, is anti-poor and undermines the sustainability of growth. However there has been no prescription for what would be the acceptable, or optimal level of inflation, to balance sustainable economic growth with government expenditures that protect both the vulnerable and support investment in poverty reduction. *To date the Fund's view is that adjusting countries must get the macros right!* Macro economic stability is still seen as the back-bone for sustained economic growth and, consequently, poverty reduction under the PRGF arrangement.

The Fund's paper setting out the institutional guidance on PRSP operational issues, asserts:

> *'Sacrificing low inflation to finance additional expenditures is not an effective means to reduce poverty, particularly in cases where inflation is above single digit levels.'*

Fiscal and financial liberalisation

The rapid and open liberalisation approach in the financial sector has certainly led to contraction of available credit stock on the market. If the law of supply and demand is followed, this policy prescription would lead to a restriction in the availability of credit to those living in or vulnerable to poverty. Zimbabwe's experience of simultaneous financial and fiscal liberalisation in 1991 was also based on IMF neo-liberal paradigm, rather than grounded in analysis of the specificities of the Zimbabwean economy. In 1991, Zimbabwe's ESAF programme opted

for the double whammy of overnight fiscal and financial openness. High levels of government domestically held debt were exposed to steep rises in interest rates. This in turn gave rise to increases in interest payments, a widening fiscal deficit and falls in investment, precipitating a financial crisis with political and economic reverberations that have almost destroyed Zimbabwe's financial markets.

It is clear that policies shaped around country specificities should be at the centre of poverty reduction strategies. It is also clear that macroeconomic policies should be aimed at raising aggregate supply, and developing pro-poor growth strategies.

Equity and equality considerations in the PRGF, HIPC and PRSPs

Almost all previous development interventions prescribed by the Fund and the Bank lacked any consideration of equity issues. The result was characterised by widening socio-economic inequalities. These compromised prospects for future long-term growth and poverty reduction. In addition, the social exclusion resulting from economic reform added to stresses between social groups at the macro and household levels, increasing the burden of poverty especially on women in their quest to meet the daily households needs. The net effects have been inequitable, irreversible and degrading to humanity.

De-institutionalisation of the provision of health care, especially in the wake of the HIV/AIDS pandemic, also failed to consider intra-household gender dynamics.

During the formulation, implementation, monitoring and evaluation of PRSPs, cross-cutting issues such as gender, age, governance, HIV/AIDS and others are referred to. But the Bank and the Fund do not make these issues a pre-condition for endorsing PRSPs, whereas they insist on macroeconomic issues. This shows their lukewarm commitment to issues of equality.

Conclusion

Development aid is critical for all low-income countries, whether through Bank or Fund-supported programmes. Aid should, however, be directed to areas such as raising overall investment in infrastructure and human capital formation in low-income countries.

Therefore if poverty reduction strategies are to succeed, it follows that policies must be changed to accommodate broader definitions of revenue, and to enable governments to maximise income and expenditure, without giving rise to excessive macroeconomic distortions.

In the new poverty reduction strategy landscape, the ability to maximise the inflow of resources to low-income country economies is vital, if the conditions for pro-poor growth are to be built. It is essential to raise aggregate supply and to build the capacity of economies to grow. This cannot be achieved within the current PRGF and HIPC conditions.

ESAF and other Fund and Bank-sponsored programmes have had devastating impacts on education, health care and welfare provision. In an effort to reduce government deficits, SAPs programmes have introduced cost-recovery measures or user fees for access to basic medicines and schooling. These have been disastrous. Mitigation measures for the vulnerable such as social safety nets have, by and large, failed to be accessed by those in poverty.

Meaningful participation of civil society in the PRSP process calls for a well-informed civil society group, with adequate mechanisms to lobby government on certain pertinent issues. But the capacity of most social movements in Africa to engage meaningfully in PRSP processes is still rather weak. Civil society must be involved right from the PRSP formulation stage, through to the last stages of the process. This is what should constitute 'meaningful' civil society participation.

Equally, national governments must prioritise the use of local resources and avoid unnecessary expenditures such as by – elections and excessive foreign travel.

The Bank and Fund's role as official interlocutor between donors and aid recipients is, in reality, a cost to administration of development aid. Their role must be revisited. The financing mechanism for the PRGF, where the Fund has to source money from donors for PRGF borrowers, is inefficient and should be revised. Direct aid flow from bilaterals to recipients is less bureaucratic, more efficient and the better option.

The social exclusion resulting from economic reform added to stresses between social groups at the macro and household levels, increasing the burden of poverty especially on women in their quest to meet the daily households needs. The net effects have been inequitable, irreversible and degrading to humanity.

Donor conditions aid increasing poverty

Leo Atakpu, Africa Network for Environment and Economic Justice (ANEEJ)

The influence of France and Britain in West Africa dates from the colonial era. Their interests have been both political and economic.

The West African sub-region was mainly agrarian; its economy depended largely on agriculture and mineral resources before the advent of colonial rule.

The French monetary economic and commercial system, as well as other forms of financial arrangements, was easy to operate and relatively trouble-free. This was because France guaranteed the convertibility of local currencies into metropolitan ones. This arrangement, according to Wilfred Ndongko (1986)[1] facilitated inter-state trade and payments, movement of capital and labour among the Francophone countries, and maintained the stability of the exchange rates between CFA Franc and other currencies.

These special advantages accounted for the creation of many regional groupings between the French-speaking African countries. The attainment of independence by many of these countries, in the early 1960s, led to the renegotiation of the cooperation agreements between France and its ex-colonies and a relaxation of the rigid rules that had hitherto governed the functioning of monetary and commercial relationships.

Francophone Africa is dotted with a multiplicity of regional economic groupings and institutions, designed to promote economic integration among the various African states. But this does not mean that cooperation in West Africa is limited to the Francophone states (Ndongko, 1986).

Superimposed on the various regional groupings in West Africa is the Economic community of West African States (ECOWAS), established on May 28, 1975. ECOWAS membership not only transcends linguistic barriers, but also comprises all of West Africa.

One of the oldest economic groupings was the West Africa Economic Community (Communauté Economique de l'Afrique de l'Ouest - CEAO), which was launched in 1970. In June 1972, the Treaty setting up the regional grouping was signed by six French-speaking West African States — Upper Volta (now Burkina Faso), Senegal, Niger, Mauritania, Mali and Ivory Coast (now Côte d'Ivoire).

There were more ambitious groupings, but both CEAO and ECOWAS recognised that, for the most part, the African countries depended on foreign capital, technology and technical skills for development. This invariably means that the foreign countries on which African countries depend will be able to influence their policies.

West Africa

Today, there is hunger, poverty and disease at critical levels across the length and breadth of West Africa.

Efforts to provide aid to West African countries have proved little more than a drop in the ocean. In fact, some aid, linked to conditionalities, has further impoverished the sub-region. Some of the conditionalities are the Structural Adjustment Programmes (SAPs) and the Enhanced Structural Adjustment Facility (ESAF). Countries like Mauritania, Senegal, Niger, Ghana, Nigeria and Sao Tome and Principe spend 20% of their export earnings on debt management.

Trade liberalisation and privatisation policies being pursued by the Bretton Woods Institutions, with the tacit support of France and Britain, have further increased poverty in the region.

Today, most West African States depend largely on external aid to manage their budgets. According to the ANEEJ Secretariat in Benin City, the percentages of aid as a share of government expenditure are: Nigeria 5%, Ghana 60%, Mali 73%, Sierra Leone 60% (recurrent) 90% (capital development), Senegal 70%, Burkina Faso 85%. Nevertheless, the budgets do not remotely address poverty reduction. Even Nigeria, considered an oil rich nation, budgeted only US$8 billion for its services in the 2004 fiscal year. This is a far cry from what the country needs to meet its development needs.

Even in the face of biting poverty, aid delivery to the sub-region has suffered some hiccups, owing either to the failings of weak institutions or the behind-the-scenes actions of some donors and the ex-colonial masters. Aid is either mismanaged or sometimes diverted. This explains why donors and some development workers are promoting 'good governance' and a rights-based approach to the delivery of development cooperation.

During colonial rule and before the mid-Eighties, when SAPs were introduced, the central motive of France and Britain was to keep the Francophone and Anglophone countries within their sphere of influence. Issues of good governance, human rights and other conditionalities did not arise.

Good governance, as a concept, provides the framework through which citizens and groups exercise their rights, meet their obligations, and articulate their interests. Abdalla Hamdok (2001) emphasises that while various types of governance systems have been developed at different times, the recent emphasis on governance as an essential ingredient of Africa's reform process is unique, in that it was initiated by donors and not by domestic leaders under pressure from their constituencies (Doornbos, 2001).[2]

Hamdok also notes that as a policy framework, 'good governance' imposes demands on policy makers in their exercise of power. It encompasses:

1. An effective state, i.e. one that provides an enabling political and legal environment for economic growth and equitable distribution.
2. Civil societies and communities that are represented in the policy making process, with the state facilitating political and social interaction, and fostering societal cohesion and stability.
3. A private sector that is allowed to play an independent and productive role in the economy.[3]

Globalisation is another source of pressure on West African governments to adopt 'good governance'. With developing countries competing with each other for international investment, experience has shown that funds tend to flow to countries that already have an economic environment that is considered amenable by domestic entrepreneurs.

West Africa

But what has been the experience in West Africa with governance and policy in Africa?

Multi-party democracy is considered one of the pillars of good governance. Hamdok (2001) notes that the major political change in the 1990s was the re-introduction of multiparty systems of government. This included the holding of multi-party elections, adoption of new pluralist constitutions and the legalisation of opposition party activities. In several countries, there have been big improvements in the rule of law and civil liberties have been gaining ground.

However, also in the course of the 1990s, some West African States seemed to disintegrate into civil war and collapse of the rule of law. Liberia experienced close to a decade of civil war (1989 - 1997), which seriously destabilised many neighbouring countries, notably Guinea-Bissau and Sierra-Leone. Since 1992, Sierra-Leone has undergone a bitter civil war, whose effects have spilled over into neighbouring countries.

In Ghana, since independence in 1957, the experience of democratisation leaves much to be desired, especially as it relates to economic reforms. Ghana's experience stands in contrast to the empirical findings of Dollar and Svensson (1998) that democratically elected governments are more likely to reform successfully. The relationship between democracy and reform in Ghana has been complex. Donors have expended much energy and resources pushing democratisation, in the belief that political and economic liberalisation will necessarily lead to good economic policy (Yvonne M. Tsikata. 2000). But Ghana's economy is characterised by fragility and vulnerability. In the 1990s, fiscal deficits escalated to 10% of GDP, putting a strain on the financial system.

Starting in 1991, democratisation in Mali somewhat modified the influence of vested interests on the role of aid in promoting reform. Democratisation should naturally promote the ownership and internalisation of reforms. The experience of Mali has shown, however, that the process is slowed down when certain irreconcilable interests are involved and there is not sufficient mediation capacity at the government level (Patrick Guillaumont et al. 2000).

Role of Britain in Western African economic management

Nigeria, Ghana and Sierra-Leone are Anglophone countries. As their colonial master, Britain was driven to provide aid, both to empower governments to provide essential services for their populations, and directly to the people.

During colonial rule and up till the mid-Eighties, when Nigeria's President Ibrahim Babangida (1985-1993) introduced the SAP, the first motive of British Aid was keeping Nigeria within its sphere of influence; the second was to keep up agricultural production, which serviced British industries. After Ghana's independence in 1957 and Nigeria's in 1960, aid was driven by the need to maintain Britain's neo-colonial hold, so as to always have cooperation in the Commonwealth, the United Nations and other World bodies. The British government still needed access to Nigeria's cultural resources. Also, Britain wanted to keep its foothold in Nigeria, from where it could continue to launch its Cold War against the Soviet Union and its Warsaw Pact countries on the African continent.

Between 1968 and 1969, during the civil war in Nigeria, Britain swung its development aid and support behind Biafra (the splinter Ibo group) because of the vast oil resources in the secessionist enclave. However, when it dawned on Britain that Nigeria would

West Africa

have the upper hand in the war, it re-established support for Nigeria. For its part, France provided development assistance for Biafra and put pressure on Cameroon and Gabon to allow their territory to be used for shipping in military, medical, food and other supplies. It was partly because of this problem that Nigeria's head of State, Yakubu Gowon, conceded the oil-rich Bakassi Peninsula to Cameroon, as a carrot to get it to close the air, sea and land corridor in the Peninsula, against Biafra.

The issue of good governance, human rights observance and other conditionality for aid did not arise. But these are central issues within aid today.

With the end of the Cold War in the late Eighties came the dominance in world politics of America and her allies, including Britain. Since then, British aid to Nigeria, Ghana and Sierra Leone has no longer been largely dictated by an attempt to keep the countries within its sphere of influence. Britain's support for Nigeria is now in line with that of America and the Bretton Woods Institutions, which are the leading voices in the promotion of good governance.

America had not considered Nigeria a priority area for development aid but recently recognised it as a regional force in Africa, which needs to be wooed. However, during the Iraqi war, the USA was not pleased by Nigeria's neutral posture. Hence it froze military aid to Nigeria, disingenuously citing the Zaki Biam Civilian massacre in Benue State by Nigerian soldiers, as an excuse for its action.

Nigeria does not seem to be a strategic ally of America in the war against terrorism and in its effort to find lasting peace (the American way) in the Middle East. However, America shows understanding for Nigeria's peacekeeping effort in the West Africa subregion. Hence, America's aid is propelled mainly by a desire to show appreciation for Nigeria's effort, as well as to encourage the empathy of Nigerians with America's new role as the most powerful nation on earth. It is largely for these reasons that Nigeria will be receiving a chunk of America's US$15 billion for combating HIV/AIDS in Africa, although South Africa and Botswana will be getting a much larger share.

One cannot ignore the fact that aid flows to Nigeria today are mainly for economic reasons. For instance, the general thinking in the North is that Africa cannot achieve the MDGs unless Nigeria, which constitutes 20% of its population and has one of the largest private sectors and domestic markets, is helped to develop. Thus, in spite of some reservations, aid is being provided for Nigeria, with the donors hoping to enjoy the multiplier effects of such investment.

Meanwhile, Ghana is a case study of an African country that has received massive aid from the early 1980s to date and yet is currently ranked as a Highly Indebted Poor Country (HIPC). The high level of commitment and prompt implementation of policy actions by the PNDC government, coupled with support from donor partners, resulted in the success of the early SAP programmes. Aid flows to Ghana increased in the early 1980s, because many donor countries were eager to support a 'winner'. Ghana and Uganda became the World Bank and IMF models in Africa. They were highly publicised 'success' stories of reform programmes under the HIPC initiative. But today, the people of Ghana are worse off than they were 30 years ago (Yakubu Zakaria, 2003). The country remains on the HIPC list, with GDP per capita of US$380 in 2003. External debt is equivalent to more than 75% of GDP. External debt stood at US$5.9 billion in 1998 (up from US$4.8 billion in 1993) though it did dip to an estimated US$4.6 billion in 1999 (IMF, 1999).

West Africa

The West African region was doing better when it was not taking loans and other development assistance. As from 2003, 60% of Ghana's budget has come from aid. Without development aid, the Ghanaian economy would collapse. To worsen matters, Ghana is neck deep in debt servicing.

One condition of aid to Ghana is to prevent the country from subsidising cocoa farming. At one time Ghana was the world's leading producer. But the ending of the cocoa subsidy because of aid resulted in the collapse of the cocoa industry. Subsidy removal is a key element in Ghana's eligibility for the Africa Growth and Opportunity Act (AGOA) — the window of opportunity for trade opened for Africa by America. This eligibility requirement went against the practice in western countries, which subsidise their own agricultural inputs with about US$350 billion annually.

The case of Ghana reinforces the need for a de-standardisation of economic recovery programmes in Africa, since different, unique conditions exist in various countries on the continent.

During his five-nation African tour in July 2003, President George W Bush said that America would increase its core development aid to poor nations. He also revealed that America had urged the World Bank to make available US$200 million in loans to ten African countries to support small business over a one-year period. President Bush explained that funds under the US Millennium Challenge Account would only be available to three categories of leaders in Africa: those who rule justly, those who invest in health and education; and those who implement policies for economic reform.

But these American conditionalities for aiding needy African countries do not stand alone. What will ultimately drive US aid to these countries is the political support they give America in the global institutions

where international issues are tabled for discussion.[4]

Globalisation is today the economic slogan of rich countries of the North, including Britain and America. The aid that Nigeria, Ghana and Sierra Leone are getting from their multilateral and bilateral donors is aimed at co-opting these countries into the global economy, an unequal playing field, where the interest of the developed nations predominate.

Agricultural raw materials, crude oil and gold from Nigeria and Ghana, continue to service British and American industries, to the detriment of both African countries.

The role of France in West African economic management

France and Britain, as has been noted, have similar interests in their role in Western Africa economic management. France however, exerts a very strong hold on its ex-colonies, as the Franc zone in Africa, established in colonial days, still exists. The only possible contenders with France in Francophone West Africa are possibly the United States and the Bretton Woods Institutions and the World Trade Organisation. There are several explanations for this.

Firstly, the monetary system in Francophone countries was organised so that the central bank in France held an unlimited amount of cash reserves from banks in these countries. The French authorities said this arrangement was to ensure that the Central Bank could guarantee the convertibility of the West African CFA currency. Under this arrangement, each Francophone country is allowed to keep a limited amount of money (aid) in their central bank and the West African Clearing House is also allowed a limited amount of money.

The implication of this arrangement is that it enables aid donors to earn an income for aid given, whether it was used or not. It

West Africa

does, however, deprive these West African Francophone countries of development funds (Agbokou Isidore, 2003).

Secondly, France wields its grip on Francophone Western African countries through the establishment of economic groupings and institutions. These groupings include CEOA — 1962, West Africa Monetary Union (WAMU) and the West Africa Economic and Monetary Union (WAEMU) — 1994. Although established by the Francophone countries, French influence is usually in the background, sometimes with the aim of using such organisations to counter British influence on the sub-region or to thwart Nigeria, which has more than half the population of the sub-region and the largest market.

Today, most Francophone countries' economies are in the woods. They are virtually dumping ground for goods made in France. They are all HIPC listed, with their budgets heavily dependent on external aid. Agriculture and pastoral farming, which used to be the mainstay of their economies, have collapsed, as farmers no longer enjoy subsidies in agriculture, because of aid conditionality. As expected, countries loyal to France get more of its attention.

The study carried out by Elliot Berg et al (2000), for Côte d'Ivoire explains: France is a major donor, the third-largest contributor of ODA to Côte d'Ivoire after the IMF and World Bank. France provided two thirds of bilateral aid in 1996, well ahead of Japan's 26% and Germany's 5%.

French financial assistance to Côte d'Ivoire is accounted for by history, commercial and financial interests and political strategy. Colonial history and cultural links, strengthened the ties with the former coloniser, as did the strong pro-French sentiments of the country's first, and long-time, head of state, President Felix Houphouet-Boigny. The President not only

maintained French influence in Côte d'Ivoire, but also championed it in other Francophone countries. France has commercial and financial interest in Côte d'Ivoire, which is its second largest West African market (after Nigeria). The equity capital of many Ivorian firms is largely French. Large-scale trading businesses are French or French controlled. Finally, Côte d'Ivoire was valued as a political asset, a heavyweight partner in the sub-region.

France provided financial support for the economic development of Côte d'Ivoire.[5] This assistance was vital, especially during the difficult years in the mid-1980s and between 1990 and 1993, when the country was trying to avoid bankruptcy. France cancelled its ex-colony's debts to save it from default.

In the year before the devaluation of the CFA franc, French influence on policy was diluted by the strong presence of Bretton Woods Institutions. Its influence by no means disappeared, however, not least because the French strategy of co-financing most reform programmes provided continuing opportunity. Co-financiers' consultation mechanisms were used by France to press its views, dissent from policies, and occasionally provide the political backing that Côte d'Ivoire needed in negotiations with these institutions. After the devaluation, the role of co-financier of Structural Adjustment Programmes was strengthened. Indeed, the Agence Francais de Development (AFD) spent 600 billon CFA francs in Côte d'Ivoire in the period 1994-98, of which more than half (315 billion CFA francs) was for structural adjustment loans. These resources financed external debt service and internal debt arrears to the private sector.

One major implication of the liberalisation reforms, was a wider opening of the local market to non-French businesses. This was foreseen by France, which released another 150 billion CFA francs in credits to

West Africa

the private sector — 25% of total AFD assistance between 1994 and 1998. Almost three quarters of this aid was in the form of loans to finance the participation of French-controlled firms in the provision of public services — electric power, gas, water, transport (rail and airport). seaport, and toll bridges. A French firm won the bid to privatise the National Telecommunications Network.

French firms engaged in the local market benefited from guarantees to facilitate borrowing. These amounted to CFAF 38 billion in 1994 - 1998, that is 25% of AFD assistance to the private sector. Thus, it can be argued that the French aid inflows associated with the liberalisation reform reinforced the already strong position of French firms in the economy, especially in key strategic sectors (Elliot Berg et al (2000).

The story is different today. The country is labouring under a huge debt burden and in 1999 the coup led by General Guei led to the stoppage of all development assistance. Aid flows resumed after the election in 2000. But in 2001, there was an army mutiny. This was followed by a period of instability, which contributed to a serious economic crisis in a country largely import dependent on its agricultural exports, namely, cocoa, cotton, and coffee, the prices of which collapsed due to unfair trade terms in the global market. France, which was expected to come to the rescue of Côte d'Ivoire, turned the other way (Kone Solange, 2003).[6]

Just as unfair trade relations hamper Côte d'Ivoire, so the trade relationship between Mali and donor countries, are at odds with principles of development cooperation.

Eighty per cent of Malians are engaged in agricultural and pastoral activities. Mali is the world's second largest producer of cotton after Egypt. But the price of cotton has been very low. In 1990, the price was US$3.4 per kilogram. In 2001 it had fallen to US$0.24 per kilogram, causing widespread poverty in the country.

The price of cotton is determined in Paris or Washington. As a condition for aid, the Malian government is not to subsidise cotton production, while America's annual subsidy to its cotton farmers is US$4 billion (World Bank Report, 2003). Mali's total GNI in 2002 was under US$2.8 billion. To worsen matters only 1% of Malian cotton was consumed locally, while 99% was exported.

Governance and quality of institutions

A rapidly growing literature documenting the relations between various indices of governance and economic performance notes that the legacy of a country, for instance its colonial history, is likely to be a major determinant of institutional quality. Evidence from studies suggests that cross-country variations in institutional quality are an important explanatory factor behind cross-country variations in economic growth[7].

But why does institutional quality differ so much between countries? One possibility is the legacy of history, such as religious or colonial heritage, or ethnic diversity[8]. Chong and Zanforlin (2000) suggest that the legal tradition affects the quality of institutions. In particular, they find that countries with a French civil code tradition have less bureaucracy, more corruption and lower credibility of government policies than do countries with a common law tradition. This in turn may lead to slower economic growth.

Conclusion

Francophone and Anglophone countries of West Africa are all categorised as HIPC. The combined GDP of ECOWAS is about US$105 billon. Nigeria's share of this is 51%. Thus, although a poor country in absolute terms, Nigeria remains a major economic player in the West Africa sub-region.

West Africa

Given the heavy weight of poverty in ECOWAS countries, aid has continued to flow to the sub-region from both multilateral and bilateral donors, to the extent that country budgets are now based on foreign aid. Despite this aid flow, poverty, disease and hunger have remained on the increase, which strongly suggests that something is wrong with the kind of aid flowing to the ECOWAS region. The chief problem is conditionality.

Britain and France have been major donors, but they have played a key role in the underdevelopment of the sub-region, using their influence to support conditionalities that have reinforced their ·own interests.

Up until the 1990s, the issue of governance and human rights was not much of a condition in international cooperation and aid delivery. But today the issue has

been placed on the front burner in international cooperation.

For both donors and recipients, the issue of governance and human rights is vital in addressing the development challenges in West African countries, particularly in the context of the MDGs.

The commitment to halve poverty can only be achieved if donors take responsibility to hold themselves accountable for their approach to governance and human rights. Currently, recipient countries are expected to hold their governments, ex-colonial governments, donors and all stakeholders accountable for their commitments on the Millennium Development Goals.

Donors must improve the quality of their aid for poverty reduction, and set out clear plans for increasing aid to the United Nations target of 0.7% of GNI.

West Africa

References

1. Wilfred Ndongko. *The West African Economic Community (CEAO): Its existence and the largest implications for the structuring of West African Inter-Governmental Organisations and the Evolution of the African Common Market.* 1986.

2. Aigbokan, Ben. *Debt, ESAF/HIPC Initiative and Economic Development in the West African subregion.*1998.

3. Doornbos, M. 'Good Governance: The Rise and Decline of a policy Metaphor', *Journal of Development Studies* Vol. 37, No.6. 2001

4. Hamdok, A. 'Governance and Policy in Africa', Discussion Paper No. 2001/126 of the World Institute of Development Economics and Research. 2001.

5. Hamdok, A. 'Good Governance and the policy Challenge: The African Development Bank Perspective', Presented at the workshop on Evaluation capacity Development in Africa, Johannesburg. 2000.

6. Hamdok, A. and H. Kifle 'Governance, Economic Reform, and Sustainable Growth: The Policy Challenge for International Development Organisations', presented at the First International Forum on African Perspective on Emerging Africa, Organised by the African Development Bank: Abidjan, and the OECD Development Centre: Paris. 2000.

7. Dollar, D, and J. Svensson. 1998. 'What Explains the Success or Failure of Structural Adjustment Programmes?' Policy Research Working Paper 1938. World Bank, Development Research Group, Washington D. C.

8. Tsikata, Y. M. *Aid and Economic Reform in Africa, a case study of Ghana,* A publication of the World Bank. 2000.

9. Guillaumont et al. *'Aid and Reform in Africa' a case study of Mali,* A publication of the World Bank. 2000,

10. Zakaria, Y. 'Aid flows and Economic Performance, A Ghanaian Experience'. A paper presented at the ECONDAD/AFRODAD Joint conference on Aid in Lagos, Nigeria, 8-9 September 2003.

11. Kamara, V. 'Sierra Leone: Report on Reality of Aid', a paper at the ECONDAD/AFRODAD Reality of Aid workshop, 8-9 September 2003.

12. Agbokou Isidore. 'Reality of Aid in Republic of Benin', a paper presented at the ECONDAD/AFRODAD Reality of Aid workshop, 8-9 September 2003, Lagos, Nigeria.

13. Elliot Berg et al. *Aid and Reform in Africa, a case study of Côte d'Ivoire.* 2000

14. Guillaumont Patrick et al. *Aid and Reform in Africa, A case study of Mali.* 2000.

15. Devarajan, S. Dollar, D. and Holmgren, T. *Aid and Reform in Africa: Lessons from Ten Case Studies* World Bank: Washington DC. 2000.

16. Anders, Danielson. *Economic and Institutional Reforms in French-Speaking West Africa, Impact on Efficiency and Growth.* 2001. http://swopec.hhs.se/lunewp/abs/lunewp2001_013.htm

Notes

[1] Wilfred A. Ndongko, Professor, of the Institute of Human Sciences, Younde, Cameroon.

[2] The United Kingdom's Department for International Development (DFID, 200:2) has, for example, listed seven key capabilities, which governments in developing countries need to develop in order to meet the international development targets, which revolve around the eradication of poverty. These touch on many of the governance issues including politics, political and financial accountability.

[3] See Hamdok, 2000; Hamdok and Kifle, 2000.

[4] A study by economist Albert Alesina (Harvard University) and David Dollar of the World Bank has revealed "friends" of the United States and Japan who vote "correctly" at the UN get their substantial aid, granted that major donors usually buy political support in the UN, etc.

[5] Elliot Berg et al (2000).

[6] Kone Solange of FNDP, presented this position at the ECONDAD Annual General Meeting held in Lagos, September 8 - 9, 2003.

[7] The possibility of reverse causation, i.e., that rapid growth leads to improved institutions is tested for and almost always rejected. Again, the stability of institutions as compared to rate of growth makes a causal link running from growth to institutions less plausible (Knack, 2000). However, Aron (2000:128), in a careful survey of the evidence, cautions that a definitive positive conclusion on the links between growth and institutions is difficult to pin down, suggesting that the claims for causality should be treated with caution.[8] Barro, 1996 a, b.

Partnership produces some best practice on aid management

B M Elikana and J K G Mapunjo

Tanzania's history of development cooperation dates back to the early 1960s when external financing policy was broadly derived from socio-economic policies spelt out in the ARUSHA Declaration of 1967 and from Tanzania's policy of Socialism and self-reliance. The main external finance guidelines were based on the fact that Tanzania recognised the role of external finance in bringing about the intended Socialist Development.

The external finance sector was said to have an important role in the economic development of Tanzania and to need proper management.

- Because of Tanzania's limited capacity to generate adequate domestic resources, external aid should be encouraged, in order to complement the country's own resources.
- Where external aid was to be offered, this should be on the best terms and on conditions acceptable to the Government of Tanzania: that is, grants and loans on concessional terms and without any political strings,
- In terms of Tanzania's policy of Non-Alignment, aid could come from any source regardless of the political leanings of the donor/lender.

- Overall, external aid had to help Tanzania to achieve its Socialist development goals.

However, for reasons beyond the scope of this paper, the intentions of the Arusha Declaration to make Tanzania self-reliant were not realised. As a result, the country continued to be sustained by foreign aid in order to meet development expenditure. Thus, foreign aid has played, and will continue to play, a big role in the Tanzanian economy. It is estimated that, since 1990, the annual aid flow to Tanzania has averaged around US$1 billion, at today's prices.[1]

Tanzania has received aid to support development in most sectors, with a changing emphasis over time from agriculture and transport in the 1960s to industry and energy in the 1970s. Currently, the focus is moving towards pro-poor expenditures, such as support to health and education, as well as development management. Despite the volume of aid received, Tanzania is still considered as one of the poorest aid dependent countries.

During the 1980s and early 1990s, aid became increasingly exposed to criticism for failing to bring the desired results. Since then, there have been a number of initiatives both at the national and international level with a view to making aid more effective and efficient.

Tanzania

The most important developments include the Helleiner study (1995), the New Nordic-Tanzania Development Partnership, OECD's DAC — shaping the 21st Century, the Tokyo International Conference on African Development (TICAD II), the Tokyo Agenda for Action, the Stockholm Workshop on Making Partnerships work on the ground, the New Partnership for African Development (NEPAD), Monterrey Consensus (2002), and the Rome Declaration (2003). The emphasis in all these initiatives is on:

- Promoting local ownership and leadership
- Promoting partnership
- Improving aid coordination and mechanisms
- Improving transparency, accountability and predictability of aid
- Strengthening capacity of aid recipient governments

- Capacity strengthening of external resource management
- Harmonising donor policies and procedures.

Aid/donor coordination and harmonisation in Tanzania

The Aid/Donor Coordination and Harmonisation process began in 1995, following a period of difficult relations between Tanzania and its Development Partners and the subsequent adoption of the recommendations of the Helleiner Report in 1997 (See Box 4).

Since the adoption of the Helleiner recommendations, there has been an increased focus on the identification and implementation of measures that can make development assistance more effective and efficient.

Box 4. The Helleiner Report

A group of independent advisers, led by Professor Gerald Helleiner, was commissioned to evaluate, and make proposals on how to improve, the aid relationship in Tanzania. The recommendations of the 'Helleiner Report', which was jointly adopted by the government and donors in 1997, included promoting the Government of Tanzania's ownership and leadership of the development process, the need for the government to set out a clear vision and set of national priorities for development' greater donor transparency, coordination of aid modalities; rationalisation of donor assistance, strengthening of government financial systems and improvements in accountability and enhanced effectiveness of the budget management process.

National Development Policy Framework

During the late 1990s, the Government of Tanzania, in consultation with other stakeholders, formulated the National Vision 2025, which provides the overall development framework. It sets out the national objectives for social and economic development and the vision of attaining a middle-income society by 2025.

The long-term poverty reduction targets are articulated in the National Poverty Eradication Strategy (NPES). In the short and medium term, the Poverty Reduction Strategy

Paper (PRSP) provides strategies for poverty reduction in those areas that are identified as priorities, as well as indicating financing needs and monitoring mechanisms.

The framework for strengthening aid/donor coordination, harmonisation of processes, partnership, national ownership of the development process and managing the external resources for development is provided in the Tanzania Assistance Strategy (TAS), launched in June 2002. The aims encapsulated in the TAS are also a reflection of the international consensus that has emerged since the early 1990s on aid management.

It is now widely agreed that, in order to improve the effectiveness of aid in support of poverty reduction goals, there is an urgent need to improve aid coordination, promote harmonisation of systems and strengthen government ownership of the development processes. Recently, the High Level Forum on Harmonisation (2003), the OECD DAC Task Force on Donor Practices (2003) and the New Partnership for Africa's Development (NEPAD), have all outlined the practical steps needed to bring about substantial improvements in aid/donor coordination and harmonisation. The TAS is Tanzania's guide to ensuring that these objectives are achieved on the ground and transformed into real benefits for people living in poverty, in terms of increased aid effectiveness.

Box 5. The TAS

TAS is a coherent national development framework for managing external resources to achieve the development strategies set out in the National Development Vision 2025, the National Poverty Eradication Strategy, and the Poverty Reduction Strategy. It is a Government initiative aimed at restoring local ownership and leadership by promoting partnership in the design and execution of development programmes. It seeks to promote good governance, transparency, accountability, capacity building and effectiveness in aid delivery. TAS is neither a programme nor a project, rather a process for change.

Current status on partnership, aid coordination and harmonisation

The Government of Tanzania, its development partners and civil society have come a long way in building successful partnerships and in improving aid management, donor/aid coordination and harmonisation. This was possible because, following the adoption of the Helleiner recommendations, both sides of the partnership played their role. The international community accepted the need for harmonisation and enhanced aid efficiency. For its part, the Government adopted a clearly articulated development policy framework (including the Vision 2025, NPES and the PRS), strengthened accountability, and improved financial management systems. Most importantly, both sides agreed to work together in mutual trust and renewed their focus on the common goal of poverty reduction.

Today, Tanzania is widely recognised as being at the forefront on issues of aid coordination, harmonisation and partnership. This has resulted in a store of knowledge of best practices that can be shared with other countries and institutions.

The TAS document articulates the national development agenda and policy

Tanzania

framework, as well as the best practices in development cooperation and a framework for monitoring progress towards achieving best practices in development partnership.

The TAS document lists 13 key best practices in aid coordination covering both government and development partner actions (See Box 6).

Box 6. *TAS Best practices in Development Cooperation*

- Government leadership in developing policy priorities, strategic frameworks and institutionalised cooperation mechanisms in various areas/sectors.
- Government involves civil society and the private sector in developing national policies, strategies, and priorities.
- Government prioritises and rationalises development expenditures in line with stated priorities and resource availability.
- Integration of external resources into the strategic expenditure framework.
- Integration of reporting and accountability systems.
- Adequacy in resource disbursements relative to prior commitments.
- Timing of resource disbursements is responsive to exogenous shocks to the Tanzanian economy.
- Donor policies complement domestic capacity building.
- Firm ODA commitments are made for longer time periods.
- Improvement in public financial management by government.
- Government creates an appropriate national accountability system for public expenditure.
- Ministries, regions and districts receive clean audit reports from the Controller and Auditor General.
- Transparency in reporting and accountability at the central, sectoral and local levels.

While the TAS provides a broad outline of best practices for Tanzania and her development partners in development cooperation, the TAS Action Plan, which was developed in FY 2002/03, sets out the practical steps that the government and development partners will follow in order to implement the TAS in the short and medium term. The TAS Action Plan highlights four areas requiring urgent attention and representing the greatest challenges in terms of reducing the burden of transaction costs and inefficiency, and promoting harmonisation over the three years of TAS' implementation.

These are: first, improving the predictability of external resources; second, increasing aid flows captured in the government budget system; third, promoting government leadership of the policy process and rationalising processes; and fourth, improving national capacities in aid coordination and external resource management.

Improving the predictability of external resource flows
Over recent years, there have been improvements in the predictability of external resources, particularly the direct

Tanzania

budget support. Improvements in predictability have resulted from greater transparency between government and development partners, better systems for gathering information on projections and changes in modalities of aid delivery. The formulation and adoption of the PRS, involving various stakeholders, including development partners, civil society, etc., has encouraged a more integrated approach to different sources of funding and hence a greater degree of information sharing. The greater degree of trust and cohesion in the development partnership in Tanzania has also led to a transformation in the way that commitment and projection data and shared. While previously, information on commitments and projections was provided in the form of confidential pledges made at the Annual Consultative Group Meeting, the government has now developed a mechanism for collecting full data on projections as part of the routine activities of the Public Expenditure Review process. This has facilitated prediction of resource flows by improving both the quality and availability of projections data.

The steady increase in budget support and pooled or basket funding and the decrease in project funding have also influenced the pattern of predictability of external resources. Efforts have been made to move away from rigid conditionalities towards the adoption of agreed actions that are jointly adopted and monitored and are an integral part of government's reform programme. In the FY 2002/03, the Policy Assessment Framework (PAF) of the Poverty Reduction Budget Support facility and the World Bank Poverty Reduction Support Credit (PRSC) were adopted. The PAF sets out a set of agreed actions on reform, which are monitored by development partners and the government on an annual basis. The broad assessment of progress in PAF targets

provides the trigger for release of budget support resources.

Integrating donor funds into the government budget system

Improvements have been made to integrate donor funding into the government budget system. This integration hinges on the on-going and significant reforms of the government's public financial management system. They include: the Integrated Financial Management System (IFMS), the Public Expenditure Review (PER), the Medium Term Expenditure Framework (MTEF), the Public Finance Act 2001, the Procurement Act, 2001 and the Public Financial Management Reform Programme (PFMRP).

The Integrated Financial Management System (IFMS), which has been adopted and implemented in all government ministries and agencies, has strengthened the capacity of the government to record, monitor and control expenditures. It has also allowed government to introduce standardised coding to facilitate monitoring and tracking of expenditure through the budget system.

The consultative forums with development partners and other stakeholders, including the Public Expenditure Review (PER), the Medium Term Expenditure Framework (MTEF) and the Consultative Group Meeting, have been very successful in establishing an open dialogue on budgetary issues, giving comfort to all partners and stakeholders. This in turn has led to greater transparency and trust in the government financial management system. The Secretariat, which was previously housed by the World Bank, has now been shifted to the Ministry of Finance, thereby enhancing llocal ownership.

In addition, the ongoing implementation of the Public Financial Management Reform Programme (PFMRP), together with the Public Finance Act and Public Procurement

Tanzania

Act of 2001, has enhanced confidence in the government's financial management capacity and control processes.

All these undertakings have resulted in increased donor trust in the government. This has encouraged them to provide direct support to the government budget, through the PRBS and PRSC facilities and to support sector-wide basket approaches in the Education and Health Sectors, as well as joint funding of the Poverty Monitoring System, the Legal Sector Reform Programme, and Local Government Reform Programme.

While budget support and basket funds are already integrated within the Government's exchequer system, the greatest challenge remains in capturing resources that flow directly to projects being implemented by sector ministries and local government.

Harmonisation and rationalisation of processes

Multiple and overlapping processes, missions, reviews, meetings, studies and parallel systems place undue burden on both the government and the development partners; they also increase transaction costs and reduce national ownership of the development process. In order to reduce transaction costs, there is now a strong move to rationalise these different processes within the National Budget and Poverty Reduction Strategy framework, as well as within the government systems and structures.

It has been agreed that one way of supporting this objective would be to produce a rationalised calendar of government-donor processes and to identify 'quiet times', — periods when government and development partners agree to minimise meetings/reviews/missions, in order to allow the government space to focus on the budget formulation and attend to the Parliamentary Budget Sessions.

During the FY 2002/03, a study to identify the scope for rationalisation and harmonisation in the cycle of processes and consultative mechanisms, including the 'quiet times' was carried out. Based on this study and discussions with various stakeholders, a 'proposal for the Rationalisation of the Cycle of Policy Mechanisms and Consultative Processes', including a period for quiet times, has been developed (see Table 1 at the end of the paper).

In addition, efforts are being made to reduce transaction costs by encouraging joint missions and reviews. In May 2003, the World Bank and the UN held a joint review of their development assistance to the country. Moreover, the bilateral donors and the World Bank, who are directly supporting the budget through PRBS/PRSC facilities, are increasingly carrying out joint reviews and using the same assessment framework.

Capacity building for aid coordination and external resource management

The TAS and the multiplicity of reforms that have been launched since the mid 1990s, all place government firmly in the lead of the development programme. It is widely accepted that government leadership and ownership is one of the key factors that will determine the success of these reform programmes.

In the past, donor support to capacity building tended to focus on strengthening capacity in relation to the requirements of specific projects or particular donor systems, rather than general on capacity building to support the system. This, coupled with the fact that government did not articulate an overall vision of capacity building, has led to a somewhat weak capacity for aid coordination and resource management.

In order to improve performance and strengthen the voice of Tanzanians in managing external resources, capacity is needed within the civil service and at all levels of government — as well as within civil society to act as a monitor on government performance on external resources — across a whole spectrum of activities, including financial management, project management, and negotiation skills.

Now the focus of both government and the development partners is on building capacity in sector ministries, in particular, the Policy and Planning Departments. These departments are supposed to play a leadership role in coordinating all processes and in promoting the effective ownership of budgeting processes, such as the PER/MTEF, as well as in aid coordination and resource management of their ministries.

Institutional set-up for promoting donor/aid coordination and harmonisation

In order to guide the government and development partners in moving forward on improving aid coordination and harmonisation, and in implementing the TAS, a TAS/Harmonisation Implementation Group, under the chair of the Ministry of Finance, has been established with joint membership of the government and the local Development Assistance Committee (DAC). The role of the group is to advise and oversee the implementation of TAS and harmonisation initiatives. In addition, a TAS Technical Secretariat, consisting of Government and DAC representatives, has been established to support the work of the TAS/Harmonisation Implementation Group by providing technical inputs. The secretariat is stationed at the Ministry of Finance.

Consensus has been reached between the government and development partners to institutionalise the process of independent monitoring of the development partnership in Tanzania. In early 2002, an Independent Monitoring Group, (IMG) under the leadership

of Prof. Samuel M. Wangwe of the Economic and Social Research Foundation, was assigned this task.

The IMG undertakes a medium term assessment of progress made towards the goals of the development partnership as jointly adopted by both the government and development partners, and as set out in the TAS. The group is involved in setting targets and recommending solutions to overcome any difficulties in attaining these targets. The first IMG report was submitted at the CG meeting held in December 2002. The report provided some important suggestions for improving aid coordination and harmonisation.

Constraints, challenges and the way forward

There are institutional constraints, with the donors' institutional set-up not being supportive. In most cases, decisions have to come from head offices rather than local offices. Commitment is required, both by the local DAC and by development partners' head offices, to make practical improvements in this area.

The government's capacity to manage the various processes, implement the TAS and harmonisation initiatives is also constrained. Although capacity building is being addressed across a wide range of programmes, including the Public Sector Reform Programme and the PFRMP, efforts are needed to develop a comprehensive capacity building programme.

Parallel systems and structures for implementing development projects and programmes are a major challenge both to the government and the development partners. Development assistance is badly needed in Tanzania to tackle the greatest enemy, namely, poverty. However, for this assistance to be effective, and in order for the government to be held accountable for these funds, they should be delivered in a

Tanzania

manner that supports national public financial management systems and structures. While it looks easier to integrate new development projects and programmes within the government systems and structures, the real challenge is to integrate those projects and programmes currently operating parallel to the government systems and structures.

As recognised by the OECD Task Force on Donor Practices and the Declaration on Harmonisation, made by development partners at the February 2003 High Level Forum on Harmonisation, development partners should provide opportunities to rationalise the various processes, systems and structures. Some joint initiatives have started to take place, such as the joint portfolio review of the UN System and World Bank held in May 2003. In the medium term, efforts should be made to consolidate donor interventions within a common Country Assistance Strategy with a single cycle of reviews. Such a strategy would indicate comparative advantages between donors in sector work and modality.

Table 1. Proposed Annual Process Cycle

Quiet Time shaded a)	July	August	September	October	November	December	January	February	March	Apri	May	June
PRS	National Poverty & Human Dev't Report	JSA (Joint Staff Assessment)	**PRS Annual Review/Progress Report**	Poverty Policy Week						Participatory Poverty Assessment field work	National Poverty Analysis published	
		On-going PER Meetings										
PER	Annual Work Plan Set	TOR Circulated	Sector PERs & Macro Studies conducted and finalized.	Deadline for Donor Submission of Projections Data			Cycle of PER Sector Reviews of PER Studies/BGs/Budget Inputs	External Review	PER Annual Meeting/External Review Report			PER workplan
GOT Budget & MTEF	Government Budget Session				Budget Guidelines Preparation			Sector Budget and MTEF Preparation	Tax Task Force	**Budget and MTEF Preparation**		Government Budget
PRBS/PRSC			Budget Review /2		Annual Review/Pre-Appraisal				Mid-Term Review/Appraisals and Negotiations			
PRGF 3			IMF PRGF Mission		IMF Staff PRGF Report issued			IMF PRGF Mission	IMF Staff PRGF Report issued			
Consultative Group	CG Meeting (date to be agreed based on need)											
TAS/Harmonisation Process		Annual Implementation Report Issued	Group Meeting			Group Meeting			Group Meeting			Group Meeting

81

Part III
Asia/Pacific and the Middle East

Competing paradigms of good governance, human rights and democracy

Kevin J. Barr MSC, Ecumenical Center for Research and Advocacy

Today almost every bilateral or multilateral donor agency says it seeks to reduce poverty, bring about development and achieve the Millennium Development Goals. To this end, donors are demanding that 'good governance', democracy and the enforcement of human rights become top priorities for recipient countries.

However, these terms are subject to different interpretations that give rise to two differing paradigms for development and poverty reduction.

One says that, to reduce poverty and bring about development, it is necessary to achieve strong economic growth. The way to do this is to follow policies based on neoliberalism, outlined in the Washington Consensus. Good governance, human rights and democracy must be promoted in the interests of trade, investment and furthering neo-liberal reforms. Bad governance, in the form of corruption, mismanagement of public funds and a biased judiciary is seen as being the main cause of the ills confronting developing countries — including their growing poverty.

The other says that the way to fight poverty and promote development is to build, not only strong processes and institutions of government, but also to encourage the participation of a strong civil society, which engages the power of the people. This will give rise to real democracy, the implementation of human rights, and will result in good governance.

Paradigm one: governance from the top-down to achieve economic growth

It seems that, until recently, development discourse has been dominated by those who declare that neoliberal economic policies are the only reliable way to achieve economic growth, which will, in turn, make the reduction of poverty possible. This has been the model outlined by the World Bank, the IMF and the Asian Development Bank. When it did not achieve its objective, these agencies diagnosed the reason as being lack of good governance. So, under the rubric of 'good governance' they (and other bilateral donors who followed their lead) demanded greater Western-style democracy and the enforcement of human rights, as a precondition for development aid.

However critics say that their interpretation of good governance, democracy and human rights is very selective, because it underlines only those areas of governance, democracy and human

Fiji and the Pacific

rights that support their neo-liberal economic policies. Thus, Kavaljit Singh (2003:10-11) writes:

> 'Governance reforms, as promoted by these institutions are actually oriented towards strengthening market reforms instead of genuine democratisation and attainment of human rights. Consequently, the promotion of good governance has become part of the emergent global economic order.'

Consequently, he sees the shift in the policies of the international aid community, making good governance a precondition for development aid as a 'disturbing phenomenon' that needs to be rigorously questioned, especially when these International Financial Institutions are blind to the need for good governance, democracy and human rights within their own institutions and within the wider corporate world of big business (Kavaljit Singh 2003:7 and also Stiglitz 2001:2 and 8).

The World Bank, in 1992, defined good governance as 'the means in which power is exercised in the management of a country's economic and social resources for development... good governance is synonymous with sound development management'. All the IFIs tend to equate good governance with those institutions and structures of government that control corruption, promote accountability and transparency, democracy, the rule of law and the protection of the interests of foreign investors. While these issues are important, this narrow 'top-down' approach does not address the issues of the people for whom governance really matters – a better quality of life, a more equitable distribution of wealth, just wages, full employment, access to education, housing and health care, controlling the privileges of

élites and dismantling the concentrated structures of property ownership.

It seems that good governance, democracy and human rights rhetoric is subtly being used to further the old neo-liberal economic agenda previously imposed on many developing countries as structural adjustment policies. These very acceptable expressions (promoted by the NGO community) are being used to provide a smoke screen of plausibility to justify and reinforce old economic policies whose success is seriously questionable. It is like putting a new cover on an old book to make it look new.

It would appear that 'developing' Third World countries are being required to mould themselves after the image of the 'developed' First World countries that are providing the aid. This is a new form of domination, being used by the new colonial masters of globalisation. Little account is taken of the fact that there can be other models of economic and political development. Kavaljit Singh (2003:17) writes:

> 'The implantation of Anglo-American institutions of governance is the overarching theme of the new agenda. It is based on the assumption that the developed countries have the best institutions, which should be embedded across the world irrespective of cultural and historical conditions.'

As an example let us take the Asian Development Bank – a dominant player in the Asian-Pacific economic scene. It states that, according to its mission, its 'overarching objective is to promote poverty reduction' (and to help Developing Member Countries achieve the Millennium Development Goals). So far, so good!

Fiji and the Pacific

However, the ADB paper of Ron Duncan and Steve Pollard, entitled *A Framework for Establishing Priorities in a Country Poverty Reduction Strategy*, outlines the process whereby poverty reduction is to be achieved. It stresses the need for economic growth as a prerequisite for poverty reduction. It states that the way to achieve economic growth is through the neo-liberal policies associated with an export-oriented, market-driven economy. Good governance is necessary for these policies to be effective. However good governance is seen very much in terms of 'strong government'. The aspects of good governance stressed are those associated with transparency and accountability of government, a good judiciary, the rule of law and the enforcement of human rights. Good governance is seen as important because it assists trade, investment and the furthering of neo-liberal policies. Consequently, contracts and rights to private property are stressed, while minimum wages, the right to a just wage, workers unions, and rights of association, are down-played, as being unhelpful for investment and employment. Also, the private ownership of land is given preference over communal ownership — the latter being seen as an obstacle for investors. If all this is implemented, then we are told that poverty will be reduced, because there will be more employment and the benefits of economic growth will provide revenue for governments to build schools, hospitals and roads for the benefit of the poor. It is the old 'trickle-down' theory in new dress.

It is interesting to note that in 2000 the Meltzer Commission of the US Congress reached a shattering conclusion about the effectiveness of the IFIs: 'Neither the World Bank nor the regional banks are pursuing the set of activities that could best help the world move rapidly toward a world without poverty or even the lesser, but more fully achievable goal of raising living standards and the quality of life, particularly for the people in the poorest nations in the world'. (United States *Report of the International Financial Institutions Advisory Commission, Alan H. Meltzer, Chairman*, Washington, D.C. 2000:5)

Paradigm one in the Fiji situation

The Fiji government rightly notes that good governance requires government and other key national institutions to perform their functions in a predictable, accountable, transparent and lawful manner. The institutions that it has established to reinforce the principles and practices of good governance are:

> The Office of the Ombudsman;
> The Fiji Human Rights Commission;
> The Office of the Auditor General;
> The Financial Intelligence Unit (to investigate money laundering, as well as criminal and terrorist funds).

Most of Fiji's Overseas Development Assistance (ODA) comes from Australia, Japan, the European Union (EU), New Zealand, China and UNDP. Loans are also negotiated with the World Bank and the Asian Development Bank. After the political upheaval of May 2000, various donor countries suspended all new aid programmes to Fiji, subject to the successful resolution of important constitutional issues. Only in November 2003 did the EU resume its funding for long-planned projects. This is a good example of the successful use of donor pressure to ensure good governance in terms of the rule of law and democratic principles.

Over the years, Fiji, under the influence of the World Bank, the IMF and the ADB, has pursued the export-oriented, market-driven economic agenda and all the policies associated with the Washington Consensus. Even though it had no debt to warrant the enforcement of structural adjustment

Fiji and the Pacific

policies, Fiji accepted the preaching of the World Bank. As Susan George said on a visit to Fiji: 'The World Bank sends out good missionaries and Fiji became a devoted convert'.

In order to achieve economic growth we have seen the following measures:

- The introduction of VAT (10% in July 1992 raised to 12.5% in January 2003). VAT was acknowledged as a regressive tax; however the benefits from it were to be used for poverty relief. In fact this did not happen. Instead, companies and those in the higher tax bracket had their taxes reduced. A capital gains tax was promised to bring about greater equity but this never materialised;
- Government attracted investors with the promise of 'keeping wages low' in order to be 'competitive'. A study based on the Census of 1996 showed that 47% of those in full-time employment were earning wages below the poverty line — two thirds of them being women. Labour unions were also forced to accept controlling 'reforms'.
- Policies directed towards increasing corporatisation/privatisation have often meant an increase in the cost of services, such as water.
- Support for private sector development in the 2004 Budget saw a decrease in personal and corporate taxation from 33% to 32%, no increase in social welfare spending and an increase of tariffs on food and other items affecting the lives of workers and the poor.

Government has said that greater economic growth is going to make it possible for it 'to devote more resources to tackling poverty and crucially important social services'. But in the years since these policies have been introduced, there has been a great increase in poverty and inequality — from 25% in 1990-91 to around 33% in 2002. Although other factors must also be taken into account, the economic policies prescribed by the IFIs must take a large share of the blame.

What use is it to say that government will use economic growth to assist the poor and needy, if that economic growth is achieved by actually creating more poverty and need? It is not surprising that people are sceptical when government says growth will lead to poverty reduction.

Two things need to be noted:

First it seems that economic growth has been achieved at the expense of people. If workers are exploited and paid low wages, then who benefits from the economic growth notched up by investors? Again if increases in VAT and tariffs impact negatively on ordinary people's ability to purchase proper food and clothing, and pay educational and health costs for their family, then who benefits from the economic growth brought in by increased government revenue? Further, if the economic policies pursued by government have demonstrated their ability to make the rich richer and the poor poorer in other parts of the world, why should Fiji be any different?

Secondly, economic growth must be shared so that all the people benefit — not just the few. But growing inequality in Fiji shows that, over the years, economic growth has not been shared despite all the nice words. As the *Fiji Poverty Report* (1997:45) notes: 'While the Fiji economy grew approx 25% between 1977 and 1990-91, the proportion of the Fiji population living in poverty grew by around two thirds. Most benefits of growth must have therefore gone to the well-off and little "trickle-down" to the poor has materialised, even in a period of relative prosperity.'

In 2003, a Participatory Poverty Assessment carried out by the Asian

Fiji and the Pacific

Development Bank and the government of Fiji, showed some sensitivity to the situation in Fiji. The ultimate remedy proposed for poverty and hardship, however, was the same old set of economic policies.

Paradigm two: responsive governments and empowered citizens

Recently, the Commonwealth Foundation (CF) and the United Nations Development Programme (UNDP) have stressed the need for a broader understanding of good governance, democracy and human rights principles. They say that good governance and democracy cannot be restricted to institutions within government itself, but must be applied more widely to include all areas of civil society. Both the CF and UNDP speak of governance in terms of strong government *and* strong civil society. *Both* are integral to good governance. While stressing transparency and accountability of government, a good judiciary, the application of the principles of human rights, the rule of law and so on, these organisations also give prominence and support to civil society organisations and to agendas that help to create democratic or 'people's governance'. The style of development they seek is people-centred and the type of economic growth they advocate is pro-poor.

In the Commonwealth Foundation's document, *Citizens and Governance: Civil Society in the New Millennium* (1999) we read:

> 'The new consensus for the new millennium is about responsible citizenship and responsive, participatory democracy. The two are mutually reinforcing and supportive: strong, aware, responsible, active and engaged citizens along with strong, caring, inclusive, listening, open and

> responsive democratic governments. This is the basis on which a good society can be built. ... Poverty, marginalisation and discrimination can only be overcome through responsive governments and active citizenship.'

Through civic education programmes, or the conscientisation methods of social analysis, people can be assisted to become more aware, so that they are empowered. Empowerment then leads to involvement and involvement leads to the transformation of society, in the interests of the needs of all the people — not just the few.

The human rights of *all* are stressed — the rights of investors to private property as well as the rights of workers to a just wage. The Commonwealth Foundation document, *Human Rights and Poverty Education*, (2001:25) notes with regret, that under the ideology of globalisation, 'market-oriented rights' are prioritised over social rights. Property, investment and trade rights are given priority over equality, mobility of labour, social justice and the rights of communities. Intellectual property rights, for example, are now accorded pre-eminence and give richer countries power over poorer countries.

In the Fancourt Declaration, (1999) the Commonwealth Heads of Government noted that while, in principle, democracy should be promoting the greater participation of all (including the poor) in decision-making processes, it sometimes goes only as far as holding elections periodically. In between elections, people remain removed from the processes of governing. They declared:

> 'If the poor and vulnerable are to be at the center of development, the process must be participatory

Fiji and the Pacific

in which they have a voice. ... Good governance requires inclusive and participatory processes at both national and international levels.'

We need not only *representative* democracy, but also *participatory* democracy.

In the document, *Reviving Democracy: Citizens at the Heart of Governance*, Knight, Chigudu and Tandon (2002:131), point out that governance involves 'collective decision-taking and action that leads to the common public good' but 'in which government is only one stakeholder among others'. Such an understanding of good governance involves a strong state with a strong civil society, a 'democratic culture' and an enlarged role for citizens.

As Foster (2003:5) notes, 'strong civil society' does not just refer to the number of NGOs, but rather to citizens' community-based and mass social movements. NGOs are important only insofar as they contribute to 'avenues and structures for citizen participation, building cohesion and solidarity, and facilitating partnerships (with the state) for progressive development outcomes'.

Knight, Chigudu and Tandon (2002:162) write:

'Citizens regard the state and civil society as equally important and, in their view, both need to be strong ... What kind of strong state do citizens want? Citizens want efficient and effective performance from their governments. They want public institutions to ensure that basic needs are met through the provision of essential services. They want the state to encourage associational life, so that citizens can play a full part in delivering public goods. They want the state to encourage political participation, and to take steps to ensure human rights, social justice and other requisites of a civilized state.'

Fiji - from a culture of silence to a more democratic culture

The Commonwealth Inquiry (2002) spoke about the need for a 'democratic culture'. Traditionally, Fiji was a hierarchically ordered, male dominated society. Decisions made by chiefs commanded unquestioned respect and obedience. Fathers alone made decisions for the family. This unquestioning respect for authority has carried over into modern times and applies also to church leaders, teachers, and government officials. It has given rise to what has been termed a 'culture of silence' where ordinary people do not ask questions or take initiatives, but wait for those in authority to act and decide. This makes for apathy and a reluctance to take responsibility.

However, the 'culture of silence' is slowly giving way to a 'democratic culture' as people become more educated, more exposed to the media, more class conscious, and more dissatisfied with corruption, growing poverty, inequality and government mismanagement. People today question the decisions of chiefs and government, become involved in public demonstrations and trade union disputes, and select the political party of their choice. The part played by NGOs in all this has been significant. Among Pacific Island Countries (PICs), Fiji has the largest grouping of NGOs outside of Papua New Guinea. They fall under a variety of umbrellas — charity organisations, groups that educate and empower youths, women and communities and organisations that advocate policy changes and challenge government.

Recent research by Steven Ratuva for UNDP analysed the extent to which people in Fiji were educated in civic awareness. His

Fiji and the Pacific

study revealed serious deficiencies and the need for better education at various levels of society.

More ordinary people — the workers and the poor — need to be empowered to speak up and speak out, to make the governments they elect more accountable to them, and not to the demands of the International Financial Institutions (IFIs). For this to happen, ordinary people need greater economic literacy and better information about the consequences of the economic policies foisted upon them. They also need better civic education and encouragement to form strong community groups, so that they can lobby government in the same way that business elites lobby effectively for their interests.

If this form of democratic or people's governance is operative, corruption will be seriously questioned, as will policies that are detrimental to the poor. Moreover, people will want to be consulted on the policies and projects that touch their lives. This will give donors an opportunity to tap into the concerns and priorities of local people, on the understanding that donors should comply with the priorities of both government and civil society.

In a recent report, entitled *Poverty in Indo-Fijian and Minority Communities in Fiji (2003)*, Professor Subramani said that the most imaginative and innovative practice in poverty reduction, sees the poor themselves as the main experts in poverty. He writes:

'Therefore they must be consulted on all aspects of poverty alleviation and must be included in decision making. However the poor are politically weak, geographically dispersed, lacking in networking, not well educated and do not have ready access to government departments.'

Subramani notes that a most important aspect of poverty alleviation should be strategies to mobilise the poor, so that they are equipped for collective action. The poor, he says, should be taught to make demands on the State and to uphold their rights to political recourse.

However, due to their poverty, people are often excluded from full participation in political, cultural and social life and from access to proper education and health care (as well as technological and scientific resources and advances such as information technology). They are often plagued by a sense of frustration, powerlessness and dependency.

International human rights conventions provide people with a legal framework for poverty reduction strategies, since they apply to all people regardless of social class, race, colour, sex or religion. However, for a rights-based approach to poverty reduction to be effective, people in poverty — and the general public — need:

- to *become aware* of these rights — guaranteed in the various UN Conventions (and often incorporated into their national constitutions). To this end, educational/awareness programmes need to be conducted.
- to *mobilise* themselves to demand their rights. To this end, there is a need for community empowerment programmes.
- Many funding agencies are happy to promote human rights as a means of overcoming poverty. Some are interested in educating people in their human rights; others provide civic education. Very few, however, see the need to help people in poverty to mobilise. In fact, some donors are wary of this because they associate it with demonstrations, rallies, uprisings — all of which they consider 'dangerous'.

Fiji and the Pacific

In Fiji today we are proud to have:
- regional and national UNDP programmes for good governance and civic education;
- ILO campaigns for 'decent work' for the workers of Fiji;
- organisations such as the Fiji Human Rights Commission (FHRC), the Regional Rights Resource Team (RRRT), the Fiji Women's Rights Movement (FWRM), the Citizens' Constitutional Forum (CCF) and the Ecumenical Centre for Research Education and Advocacy (ECREA). Most of these have programmes for grassroots empowerment and/or human rights education.

Government's recent *Strategic Development Plan 2000-2004* (nos 3.117 – 3.121) speaks positively about civil society:

'Civil society (which comprises non government organizations, churches, trade unions) is a powerful force for social and economic development and is an important partner in nation building ...'

and in par. 19 page viii:

'Government will encourage greater participation of civil society in formulation, implementation and monitoring of programmes, as well as enhancing coordination between government and civil society.

Despite these encouraging words, we have also seen strong government outbursts against some NGOs, the media, trade unions, and academics. Public protests have been prevented in the name of national security. A Media Bill, to control the media, has recently come under discussion. There is also a danger that 'counter-terrorism' legislation may be used to clampdown on the activities of NGOs.

One of the important roles that NGOs, academics, unions, students groups and women's movements play in society is to act as watchdogs on government. They provide a critical analysis of government's policies from the viewpoint of their particular interest group. As many have pointed out, the Christian churches, which are very influential in the Pacific, need the courage to act as the conscience of society.

Some success stories within this second paradigm have been the Chandrika Prasad court case whereby, with the assistance of the Citizens' Constitutional Forum (CCF), an ordinary Indo-Fijian farmer was able to successfully challenge government on constitutional issues. Also, a number of NGOs have submitted reports to the UN in Geneva to complement, contradict, or challenge government's own reports on the Convention on the Elimination of all Forms of Racial Discrimination (CERD) and the Convention on the Elimination of all Forms of Discrimination Against Women (CEDAW). Moreover, there has been a significant move on the part of NGOs – partially acknowledged by government – that civil society needs to be consulted on the annual national Budget. NGOs were also successful in preventing government's acceptance of a controversial Constitutional Review Report drawn up under the chairmanship of Professor Ravuvu. Further, some women's groups took the initiative to have a Family Law Bill drawn up and eventually passed by Parliament.

The Asian Development Bank and people's participation

Over the last few years, 2001-2003, the Asian Development Bank in conjunction with the governments of PICs has been sponsoring Participatory Assessments of Poverty. These assessments aim to find out 'the needs, views and hopes of communities throughout

Fiji and the Pacific

the country — especially the disadvantaged and poor themselves'. Studies have been done of the Marshall Islands, Samoa, Vanuatu, Fiji and Papua New Guinea.

While the concept of people's participation in identifying common perceptions of poverty is admirable and much good work has been done by the consultants responsible, the results are often carefully worded so as not to question ADB's economic policies. For example, the low wages paid to workers are not mentioned as a cause of poverty; instead. 'insufficient income' is listed as a reason for people saying they are poor. The word 'hardship' is preferred to poverty and the main reasons given for poverty/hardship are connected with lack of access. No specific mention is made of the policies of government (and the IFIs) that impact negatively on people's quality of life.

The Asian Development Bank is also funding a Pacific-wide project to help people understand how governments draw up their annual budgets, how people can influence these budgets, and how they can monitor government expenditure and thus keep government accountable. However, they carefully steer clear of helping people understand the economic policies behind the budgets, the effect of those policies on the lives of ordinary people, who has influenced government to follow these policies, and how people can be empowered to protest against policies that do not address their priorities.

While the ADB uses the right jargon and declares it is encouraging 'participation in the Budget process', the style of participation it encourages is very limited and very non-threatening to those very powerful forces that are pulling the strings behind the scenes. It does not encourage people's involvement to put pressure on government to make budgets truly

'people-centred'. Moreover, in this ADB process the voices of the people may be acknowledged but are not necessarily heard by government.

Conclusion

In the first paradigm, good governance, human rights and democracy have been hijacked or co-opted by the World Bank, the IMF, the WTO and the ADB to promote policies supporting the neo-liberal reforms associated with the Washington Consensus and so serve the over-riding economic interests of the G8 countries (especially G1) and their multi-national corporations.

The second paradigm reclaims these terms and uses them in the interests of strong, transparent and accountable government *as well as* people's power and people-centred development. It says that the roles of the state and of its citizens must be seen as complementary, if good governance is to be achieved. This paradigm aims to serve the interests of both government and people. It can be an important means of combating corruption and ensuring that local priorities (both of government and civil society) are addressed. It seeks to uphold the power of the state, not the power of the global masters. Unfortunately, there is a danger that, in the name of anti-terrorism legislation, the voices of civil society,. working for people-centred development, democratic governance and human rights, will be silenced.

There is a positive dimension to good governance, democracy and human rights. They are desirable goals that can help overcome corruption, instability and exploitation. However, people's organisations and NGOs must:

- Become aware of how IFIs and other donors misuse or twist the interpretation of these terms (a) to reinforce neo-liberal economic agenda and (b) to

Fiji and the Pacific

impose a new style of US/Eurocentric colonialism;

- Expose this misuse and twisted/limited interpretation through meetings with governments, NGOs, the media;
- Use these terms positively to justify serious efforts to empower people, so that they actively participate in society to bring about a people-centred style of development and ensure that globalisation benefits all. As Kofi Annan, UN General Secretary said: 'If globalisation is to succeed, it must succeed for poor and rich alike. It must deliver rights no less than riches. It must provide social justice and equity no less than economic prosperity and enhanced communication'.
- Make those who use good governance and human rights terminology focus more directly on the real issues of poverty that need to be addressed: not just property rights for investors, but just wages for workers; not the 'benefits' of privatising basic services, but the rights of all to basic services.
- Protest against the use of anti-terrorist rhetoric and legislation that demonises or compromises authentic people's struggles, trade unions and NGOs by restricting civil liberties and human rights.

As Aung San Suu Kyi stated in her address to the World Commission on Culture and Development in Manila (1994):

'People's participation in social and political transformation is the central issue of our time. This can only be achieved through the establishment of societies which place human worth above power, and liberation above control. In this paradigm, development requires democracy, the genuine empowerment of the people.'

Australia: big brother or pacific deputy for US imperialism

It is true that Australia spends millions of dollars every year on aid to PICs and is geographically very much a Pacific neighbour. Consequently, Australia does have an interest in seeing that good governance is observed across the region, that governments honour their obligations and that the region is as safe as possible. Nevertheless, Australia has always claimed that it does not wish to impinge on the sovereignty of the PICs. Even when asked by the Solomon Islands to intervene in their state of near civil war, Australia was hesitant to do so. Then came George Bush's war on terrorism. Almost overnight, Australia accepted the invitation to become involved – not only in the Solomons, but also by suggesting that a number of its neighbours were coming close to being 'failed states' and potential havens for terrorists. These included the Solomons, Papua New Guinea, East Timor, Fiji, Vanuatu and Nauru. Increased Chinese involvement in some PICs, as well as 'look North' policies seem also to have caused concern. Consequently the Howard Government is now pushing a policy of more direct government and perhaps military intervention in the south-west Pacific.

Recent papers from the Defence-funded Australian Strategic Policy Institute (ASPI) in Canberra manifest US-style security phobias and biases. They seek to justify a policy of more direct intervention in the Pacific. One paper suggested that the Solomons could become 'a petri dish in which transnational and non-state security threats can develop and breed' and that 'potentially hostile major powers could operate forces from bases in our immediate neighbourhood'. In view of these 'threats', some form of intervention is suggested. The question is asked: 'Is there a middle option between our present detachment and an attempt to

Fiji and the Pacific

reassert colonial rule?' This is answered by arguing that sovereignty is no longer an absolute, as the 'security challenges presented by failed states have forced international policymakers to overcome many post-colonial hang-ups'. The key to offsetting any accusations of re-colonialisation could be 'broad-based international or regional support' for any intervention, and 'if at all possible, the consent of the affected state'.

Seemingly, Australia's newly found concern for PICs stems not only from national self-interest (which was always present) but from its strong ties to the US and the Bush Administration's war on terrorism, together with its determination to push the neo-liberal economic agenda. On his recent visit to Australia, George Bush repeated and affirmed an earlier media observation that Australia's Prime Minister John Howard was his 'deputy sheriff' for the Pacific.

At the August 2003 Pacific Islands Forum Meeting in Auckland, Howard not only succeeded in having an Australian appointed as the Secretary General of the Forum but, in line with an Australian Senate Report, proposed a European-style common market for PICs, with a common currency based on the Australian dollar. As first steps, he proposed a Pacific-wide policing structure to be trained by Australia and the pooling of airline resources. This went under the name of 'pooled regional governance'.

A plan for a Pacific free trade agreement was successfully completed in 2001, when the Pacific Island Forum endorsed the Pacific Islands Countries Trade Agreement (PICTA) and the Pacific Agreement on Closer Economic Relations (PACER). These agreements are intended to provide stepping stones, to allow PICs to gradually become part of a single regional market and integrate into the international economy. Ultimately this free-market globalisation will occur under the domination of Australia and New

Zealand. Many fear that free trade will devastate Pacific economies that already suffer grossly unequal trading relations with Australia. Already many of the 'economic reform and governance' projects in AusAID programmes, seek to export Australia's own neo-liberal policies into the public institutions and economies of the Pacific countries.

Consequently, some have referred to Australia as the 'Pacific's free-trade bully' and have suggested that all this amounts to a plan to strengthen Australian domination over the countries of the Pacific Islands Forum (PIF) and open up their economies to Australian corporate domination and exploitation.

Of concern is that the governments of PICs have been urged to adopt the narrow definition of security propagated by the US and Australia. This definition can easily be used to silence the voice of civil society on issues such as human rights, corruption, transparency and accountability and thus impinge negatively on good governance from the 'bottom-up'. It is becoming clear that 'terrorism' and the perceived danger of 'failed states' are providing an excuse for political and economic interference by Australia (and ultimately the US).

The Solomon Islands

The Solomon Islands gained Independence from Britain in 1978, but have struggled to manage their own affairs. There have been many cases of serious culpability on the part of successive governments; the country's resources have been systematically depleted through corruption and mismanagement. Poverty levels and youth unemployment — especially in urban areas — began to grow alarmingly in the 1990s. This led to people's mistrust of politicians and consequent social disorder. In the latter part of 1998, ethnic tensions and rivalry over unequal

Fiji and the Pacific

development and wealth distribution eventually erupted in armed conflict between the Isatabu Freedom Movement (IFM), representing the Gwale people of Guadalcanal, and the Malaitan Eagle Force (MEF), representing the people of Malaita.

After years of unresolved civil conflict in the Solomons, the government's request for Australian assistance to restore civic order was undoubtedly necessary. In July 2003, Australia sent a large deployment of troops to the Solomons – setting a new precedent for involvement in the affairs of Pacific Island nations. Australia has brought peace and some degree of stability with its Regional Assistance Mission to the Solomon Islands (RAMSI) programme. While it is in process of bringing to justice those responsible for armed violence, many are critical that it has done little to bring to justice those corrupt politicians and businessmen whose actions provoked the turmoil in the first place.

But the aim was not just to quell the social conflict and provide security. Australia has also set out to bring the economic policies and structures of the Solomons in line with the neo-liberal paradigm it promotes in the rest of the Pacific, together with the World Bank, the International Monetary Fund and the Asian Development Bank. In September 2003, Australia paid over US$3 million in debts owed by the Solomon Islands to the ADB and the World Bank, to allow the re-engagement of both organisations in the country.

There is no admission that the current problems may have had their roots *not* in traditional ethnic conflicts (of which there are no historical records) but in: (a) the unequal economic development put in place by Britain, the former colonial power; (b) the economic policies imposed by the IFIs; (c) the corruption that arose when local parliamentarians and businessmen, lured by

greed, sought to attract overseas investors for the timber and fishing industries, in the name of economic growth for the nation.

The 'solution' provided for the Solomons in the National Economic Recovery and Development Plan (NERDP) is very much in line with the 'top-down' good governance paradigm dictated by the IFIs. Critics who know the Solomons say that no serious consideration is given to the possibility of adopting another economic model more suitable to the country. Moreover, as John Roughan (2003) writes:

> 'National recovery should foster increased communal engagement, strengthen civil society's formal and informal bodies and empower individuals, especially women, to participate in decision making and peace building efforts... Our enemy has never been a bad economy but poor leadership. Bad economic conditions didn't destroy the nation – people did. The cure centres on people understanding the root causes of their soul-sickness and not glibly jumping to the conclusion that if we get a good handle on the economy the roots of our social unrest will be cured as well.'

In other words, the 'top-down' paradigm of good governance (in which Western style political and economic models are dominant) has little chance of success unless, strong civil society organisations are recognised and empowered to provide good governance from the 'bottom-up'.

It is interesting to note that the paper on the Solomons, entitled *Our Failed Neighbour*, by Elsina Wainwright from the Australian Strategic Policy Institute (ASPI) became the blueprint for the recent

Fiji and the Pacific

Australian intervention in the Solomons. In that paper Wainwright suggested that the Solomons could be a testing ground for a policy turn towards military intervention and direct control of parts of the financial and government bureaucracy by Australian technocrats.

Papua New Guinea

At the 2003 Pacific Forum meeting, PNG's Prime Minister, Sir Michael Somare, refused to accept John Howard's criticism that PNG was coming close to being a 'failed state'.

Referring to Australia's aid to PNG, Somare noted that a large percentage of it is 'boomerang aid' because, out of the A$330 million given in aid:

- 31% is used to employ Australian consultants;
- 38% is for procurement by Australian contractors with hardly any PNG sub-contractors awarded jobs.
- Somare pointed out that PNG has never had any military coups and that, despite 'public challenges' to the government of the day, 'respect for the democratically elected government has always prevailed'. Both Somare and Qarase (Fiji's Prime Minister) were sceptical about the suggestion by an Australian parliamentary committee, that consideration should be given to the South Pacific moving towards an economic and political bloc similar to the European Union, with the use of a common currency based on the Australian dollar.
- PNG does, however, undoubtedly face many severe problems. There are issues of corruption and cronyism, serious levels of uncontrolled urban drift, unemployment and social strife, ineffective government institutions, serious law and order problems, a worsening HIV/AIDS

epidemic and increasing poverty and inequality. PNG relies heavily on overseas aid along with massive loans from the World Bank, the International Monetary Fund and the Asian Development Bank. Also, due to the number of political parties, there is always the danger of political instability.

- In an article in PNG's *Post Courier* (15th August, 2003), the former commander of the PNG Defence Force, Major General Jerry Singirok, thinks that all the characteristics of a 'failed state' already exist in PNG. He warns that:

'PNG must now brace itself as it may be the next country to be 'restored' by a Pacific intervention force led by Australia. We cannot escape the inevitable onslaught as precedence (sic) has now been set in the Solomon Islands.'

He goes on to paint a possible scenario for Australian intervention and the justification under which it could take place.

Conclusion

It seems that, following the much talked about 'war on terrorism', a number of PICs are currently seen by Australia not only as unstable or struggling but as 'failed states' and a 'clear and present danger' to Australia's national security. The prescribed cure is imposing 'good governance' as understood by the IFIs and major bilateral donors. This 'top-down' paradigm of good governance is to be achieved by a powerful mix of direct military and bureaucratic control (under the cover of local figureheads) and an intensified forced march towards free-market capitalist globalisation.

Rather than listening to the people of PICs and assisting them to find models that would suit their own needs, the IFIs and

Fiji and the Pacific

bilateral donors such as Australia seek to impose their own structures and policies for development. It is in effect arrogant domination.

The 'top-down' paradigm of good governance (building a strong government) is bound to fail unless it is worked in tandem with the 'bottom-up' paradigm, in which a strong civil society is empowered to speak up and be heard.

References

Asian Development Bank:

Priorities of the Poor in Papua New Guinea. ADB. Manila. 2002.

Priorities of the People — Hardship in Samoa. ADB. Manila 2002.

Millennium Goals in the Pacific. ADB. Manila.2003

Priorities of the People — Hardship in Vanuatu. ADB. Manila.2003.

Priorities of the People — Hardship in the Marshall Islands. ADB. Manila. 2003.

Chinkin, Christine. 'The United Nations Decade for the Elimination of Poverty: What Role for International Law?' in *Current Legal Problems* vol.54. Oxford University Press.2001

Commonwealth Human Rights Initiative *Human Rights and Poverty Alleviation — a Talisman for the Commonwealth*. New Delhi. 2001.

Commonwealth Foundation. *Citizens and Governance: Civil Society in the New Millennium*. The Commonwealth Foundation. London.1999.

Human Rights and Poverty Education. The Commonwealth Foundation. London. 2001

Commonwealth Heads of Government. *The Durban Communiqué November 1999*. Commonwealth Secretariat. London. 1999.

Duncan, Ron and Steve Pollard 'A Framework for Establishing Priorities in a Country Poverty Reduction Strategy' in *Asian Development Review Vol.19 no.1.2001*

Foster, John W. 'Crisis Time: Repossessing Democratic Space — Governance and the Promotion of Rights in International Cooperation and Aid', A discussion Paper for the Reality of Aid. North-South Institute. Canada. 2003

Government of Fiji. *Strategic Development Plan 2002-2004 — Rebuilding Confidence, Stability and Growth*. Ministry of National Planning. Suva. 2001

Hughes, Helen. *Aid Has Failed the Pacific*. The Centre for Independent Studies. Issue Analysis No. 33. Sydney. 2003

Khan, Chantelle and Kevin J. Barr. *Christianity, Poverty and Wealth at the Start of the 21st Century*. ECREA. Suva. 2003

Kim, Iggy 'Australia: The Pacific's Free — Trade Bully' Asia-Pacific Action Group paper, August 2003.

Knight, Barry, Hope Chigudu and Rajesh Tandon. *Reviving Democracy: Citizens at the Heart of Governance*. Earthscan. London. 2002

Meltzer, Alan H (Chairman). *Report of the International Financial Institutions Advisory Commission*. United States Government: Washington D.C. 2000.

O'Gorman, Frances *Charity and Change — from Bandaid to Beacon*. World Vision. Melbourne. 1992

Ratuva, Steven. *Baseline study on civic education needs and attitudes towards democratic governance*. UNDP/ Fiji Parliament Survey Report (Draft). ANU. Canberra. 2003

Roughan, John. 'National Recovery Plan ... Misses the Point' (Unpublished Paper)

Singh, Kavaljit. 'Aid and Good Governance' — A Discussion Paper for the Reality of Aid. Public Interest Group. India. 2003.

Stiglitz, Joseph. *Globalisation and its Discontents: How to Fix What's Not Working* Lecture, University of Manchester, 4th April 2001.

Subramani, Professor (Chairman). *Poverty in Indo-Fijian and Minority Communities of Fiji*. Ministry of Multi-Ethnic Affairs, Government of Fiji. Suva 2003.

Tucker, Geoff. 'More than a Military Solution', *The Fiji Times* 7thJuly 2003.

Fiji and the Pacific

UNDP and Government of Fiji. *Fiji Poverty* Report. Suva. 1997.

UNDP. *Human Development Report*, Oxford University Press. New York. 2000.

Van Genugten, Willem and Camilo, Perez-Bustillo (eds) *The Poverty of Rights*, Zed Books, London. 2002.

Wainwright, Elsina. *Our Failed Neighbour* Australian Strategic Policy Institute. Canberra. 2003.

Notes

[1] In the Pacific, 'look North' is understood as PICs looking for assistance to Malaysia, China, Indonesia, etc — sometimes to spite Australia, the E.U. and other regular donors.

Governance within the Consultative Group On Indonesia: partnership or domination?

Sugeng Bahagijo, International NGO Forum on Indonesia (INFID)

The prospect of Indonesia[1] growing its economy and social spending to pre-crisis levels and meeting the Millennium Development Goals is bleak. Progress will require radical but necessary reform of creditor policies, as well as the ability of the Indonesian government to regrow its economy and finance development projects. At country level, reform could start with the Consultative Group on Indonesia (CGI).

This paper looks at the development of the CGI forum. As an aid coordination forum for Indonesia, the CGI met annually and provided loans and grants. This paper considers the governance aspect of the CGI process.

The term 'governance' is broad and has many meanings. Here it is used in the sense of how much decision making within the CGI is really in the hands of the recipient country. Indicators of governance include the nature of economic analysis being used within the CGI, how the agenda is prepared and how final decisions are being reached.

The World Bank, as the lead agency or chair of the CGI, basically controls the process and the decision making. The Bank can choose which analysis is supported and which issues are deemed important. At the same time, the Bank is not a neutral party in the process, since it is both a lender as well as coordinator of the donors' forum.

Brief history of the CGI[2]
The Indonesian donor forum, the IGGI (inter-Governmental Group on Indonesia) first met in February 1967 in Amsterdam. The delegates from Indonesia were led by senior minister Sri Sultan Hamengkubowono.[3] The IGGI continued until 1992, when the Indonesian government dissolved it.[4]

In March 1992, Indonesian Minister JB Sumarlin sent a letter to the World Bank, asking it to set up the Consultative Group on Indonesia (CGI). The Bank agreed in a letter dated April 1992. The first meeting of CGI was held in Paris in July 1992.[5] Since 1997, the issues discussed in CGI meetings have been getting broader. Not just macroeconomic policies and aid related issues, but also social and political issues, such as corruption, legal reform, governance and forestry.

Since 2000, there have been several significant changes in the CGI organisational set up: (i) for the first time, a CGI meeting has been held in Jakarta, Indonesia; (ii) for the first time, CGI meetings officially invite a number of NGO representatives as observers[6]; (iii) working groups have been established.[7]

Indonesia

Governance in CGI: the role of the World Bank

CGI is not a Paris Club or London Club meeting, where decisions on debt relief are being made. The forum is a country level aid coordination meeting designed primarily for giving new loans and grants to Indonesia. Based on a request by Indonesia and the amount of finance being requested, CGI member countries pledge or commit their new or extended loans and grants.

This is true in a formal and procedural way. But experience shows that unofficial outcomes also involve radical changes in macroeconomic policies and the budget and priorities of the developing country. In short, this can perpetuate the problem rather than solve it. Besides being a kind of donor coordination, the CGI forum is also a forum on what type of economic analysis and economic policy is being supported and opposed.

Governance in the CGI forum matters, because it involves the power to decide on the agenda and what decisions should be made. The core of the issue is who decides and who will be affected by such decisions.

Why the World Bank? Because the Bank in Indonesia, by design and by historical development, has been playing a very important role in leading the CGI process. At the very least, it has three crucial roles (a) As chair of the CGI forum, aid coordination is held under its leadership; (b) The Bank is the one of the largest providers of loans to Indonesia, together with Japan and the ADB; (c) It has more leverage and influence relative to the smaller bilateral donors and the UN agencies operating in Indonesia, such as UNDP, Unicef, or the ILO.

Two elements are important in assessing the role of the World Bank in the CGI. The first is the Bank's analysis. What kind of policies is it advocating and is it opposing?

Secondly, what agenda is being discussed and what is it choosing not to be discussed.

To start with the analysis of the Bank, in addition to its Country Assistance Strategy as the basis for its lending and non-lending operations, the Bank produces the CGI Brief/Report for the CGI meeting. The 2003 document is entitled *Beyond Macroeconomic Stability.* It is 63 pages long, plus a large number of statistical annexes, ranging from economic indicators to poverty indicators, from debt statistics to government finances.[8]

The heart of the CGI Brief 2003 is macroeconomic analysis and financial sector analysis, based on the government White Paper.[9] In addition, it has sections on legal reform, decentralisation and poverty reduction, where the Bank gives its views and opinions on progress and the problems experienced.

The main thrust of the document is to support and praise the White Paper, while continuing to push for more results and implementation in other areas that the Bank deems important, such as the investment climate, privatisation, governance (anti corruption, legal reform and so on) and decentralisation.

The key reason for the Bank supporting the White Paper is that it is a continuation of, rather than an alternative to, the previous macroeconomic programme under the IMF.

The key positions of the CGI brief are expressed in the following quotes[10]:

The white paper comprises the measures needed to achieve a healthy fiscal position, lower inflation and sufficient international reserves.
The white paper lays out a host of measures to continue financial sector reform and restructuring. Recognising the dire shape that

Indonesia

Indonesia's investment climate is in, the white paper aims to improve it. The measures proposed on trade are less promising and hardly support the goal of accelerating export growth.
Better governance is key for reducing policy and legal uncertainty and therefore improving the investment climate. Poverty reduction is not the main focus of the white paper, but the macroeconomic stability and higher growth the paper aims for is one of its pillars.

The brief also praises a number of actions taken by the Indonesian government in continuing the previous programme of privatisation. For instance, on the macroeconomic position, it says '... in addition, and quite remarkably for an election year, the government also remains committed to continued privatisation – 10 enterprises in total will be on the block to raise more domestic financing to cover deficits'.

In the investment area, the brief said, 'the white paper is a good start to tackle some of the difficult issues.'

In other areas, such as trade, the document sharply opposed government measures that the Bank viewed as against the principle of full trade liberalisation. Again, to quote directly from the document:

'...already protectionist measures, such as import registration and licensing, have cropped up in recent years...the announcement of an expansion of counter trade seems counterproductive.'

Yet the document is silent on a number of urgent issues that have hindered Indonesia's economic growth, such as the possibility of launching an expansionary fiscal and monetary programme, and resolution of the debt problem.

While the problem is the unsustainabilty of Indonesia debt, the document only mentions the technical issues and the management side of the problem. It does not discuss other policy options or alternatives on how to reduce the debt burden. The document admits that 'although the debt ratio to GDP was declining, the debt level remains high'. It supports government measures to: (a) limit borrowing by regional government and (b) to have a stronger debt management office with the aim of more transparency and better reporting (moving the debt management office to the treasury office). In addition, the document adds two measures to be taken by the Indonesia government: (a) better capacity in handling market risk (interest rate, liquidity, exchange rate), and (b) developing a secondary market for debt.

Consistent with its position as a creditor, it does not matter that Indonesia's recovery is hindered by a high debt burden, as long as Indonesia honours its commitment to pay the debt. It does matter that the Indonesian budget is not empowered to lead investment: '...the increase in external debt service pressures in the coming years means less financial resources for investment,' says the Bank. What to do then? The Bank's best bet is for Indonesia to rely more on international investment as an engine for investment. The Bank concludes 'it is critical that Indonesia attracts new foreign savings to satisfy its investment needs by improving its investment climate'.

More of the budget is to refinance the debt
In the budget for 2004, it is projected that Indonesia will need fresh money from CGI

Indonesia

donors of about US$2.4 – 3billion. What is interesting is that, while gross financing is estimated at about US$10 billion, a huge chunk of financing, estimated at US$7.6 billion, is for debt repayment (principal debt repayment or amortisation) both for external debt (US$5.2 billion) and domestic debt (US$2.4 billion). Only about US$2.9 billion is for development projects and programme expenditure in 2004.

In short, the document offers nothing new in policy and measures that could help the Indonesian economy and the debt problem. The document is rich with figures and information but short on ways to strengthen the current fragile recovery.

Why does the Bank decide to comment extensively on the government White Paper and not produce its own analysis and projections? It is the first time the Bank has analysed the government programme at such great length, producing an almost a point-by-point commentary in several areas. Usually, the Bank will only describe the main policies of a government, and then go on with its own projections and analysis on topics that it sees as important.

There are several possible explanations. First, the Bank would like to project the image that it is supporting a home-grown economic programme drafted by the Indonesian government, rather than one imposed from outside like the previous IMF programme. The Bank will thus avoid any criticism both inside and outside Indonesia. In particular, for bilateral donors, it may be that the Bank is making a very clear statement that it supports a programme by Indonesia for Indonesia.

Secondly, as the Bank sees the content of the economic programme as essentially a continuation of the previous IMF programme, it has little reason not to support it – since it is in line with

Bank's own analysis. For instance, on privatisation and on contractionary fiscal and monetary policy, both the Bank and the White Paper are genuine allies, basically sharing the belief that there is no alternative to the neoliberal way.[11]

Thirdly, given the sharp differences in the Indonesian cabinet, especially between minister Kwik Kian Gie, Chairman of Bappenas, and Minister Budiono-Dorojatun (Minister of Finance and Coordinating Minister for the Economy) the Bank would like to make it clear to Indonesian policy makers which side it is on (the former is critical of IMF and World Bank policies, while the latter advocates fiscal constraint and austerity measures.)[12]

How the agenda is being formed

The agenda of the CGI meeting covers a wide range of topics, including not just financing needs or gaps within next year's budget, but also legal and security reform. So, for example, the December 2003 CGI meeting covered fiscal sustainability as well as discussing the progress, or lack of progress, on issues of legal reform, security reform, forestry, decentralisation and poverty reduction.

The typical CGI meeting takes 2 days. The first day is called a pre-CGI meeting and is devoted to gathering inputs and reports, both from government and donors, including from working groups. The second day is the official CGI meeting, where the vice president of the Bank is chair and the co-chair is the coordinating minister for the economy. This meeting discusses the official statement and official reply, and comments from Indonesian government delegates. It agrees the amount pledged by donors, based on requests by government of Indonesia.

Two of the inputs being discussed at the December 2003 forum were highly significant in terms of their contribution to the

Indonesia

Table 2. Agenda of CGI meeting, 2003, December

Pre CGI meeting/day one	13th meeting of the CGI
Introduction Session I: infrastructure (government present its programme on infrastructure Session II: Policy Dialogue (simultaneous meetings) forestry decentralisation ODA Effectiveness Session III: Supreme Court Reform Presentation and Policy Dialogue (simultaneous meetings) Supreme court reform agenda Poverty reduction Health Session IV: The role of Security in Development: a Dialogue	Opening statements Welcome by Bank Indonesia Governor Statement by Doroddjatun Kuntjoro-Jakti, Coordinating Minister for the Economy Statement by Chairman, Mr. Jemal-ud-din Kasum, Vice President, East Asia and Pacific Region, World Bank Session I: Macroeconomy issues, investment climate and financial reform Session II: Poverty Reduction and Governance reform Session III: Financing Requirements for 2004 and beyond Statement by the World Bank Tour de Table: CGI members Closing Business Approval of Press Conference Chairman's Closing Remarks Closing Remarks by the Head of the GOI Delegation Arrangement for next meeting

Indonesia

Table 3. Overview of CGI meeting agenda

Year	Agenda	CGI Brief
2001, CGI meeting	Fiscal sustainability, legal and justice reform, forestry, small and medium economy, decentralisation, poverty reduction and effectiveness of aid	The imperative for reform
2002, CGI meeting	Fiscal sustainability, legal and justice reform, small and medium enterprise, decentralisation	None
2003, CGI meeting	Pro-poor growth and investment, governance, issue of Bom Bali and Aceh, poverty reduction, effectiveness of aid	Indonesia: maintaining stability, deepening reforms
2004, CGI meeting	Macroeconomy, decentralisation, poverty reduction, investment, forestry, etc.	Beyond macroeconomic stability.

governance process of the CGI forum — and as alternative policy proposals from Indonesia.

One came from the Bappenas/National Development Planning Body, headed by the state minister. The study[13], after drawing attention to the donor-driven process — both in regard to the topics being discussed in the CGI and in the working groups — recommended, among other things, that the CGI should be led by Indonesia, as opposed to the World Bank. This is a remarkable document in the light of Indonesia's 'good boy' style of diplomacy with donors and creditors[14] over many years. This was the first time, since the dissolution of IGGI in 1992, that the Indonesian government had addressed the role and existence of the CGI forum. It advocated that after two years' preparation, when Indonesia would be ready to assume the leadership/chair, the World Bank should agree with the proposal.

The second input was the analysis and recommendation of Kwik Kian Gie on the debt problem, both domestic and external. With regard to aid effectiveness, Minister Kwik argued that aid flowing into Indonesia, no matter whether efficient or less efficient, would not be effective in helping the Indonesian economy and budget, if it were just going into debt repayment, rather than

Indonesia

into development projects, or for strengthening existing or new government agencies, such as the anti-corruption commission. Minister Kwik challenged the CGI forum to find better solutions on debt repayment, so that the government could have sufficient resources to meet the dire need for development projects and job creation.[15]

Minister Kwik has attended the CGI meeting for each of the last three years and presented a similar analysis. But he has received the same response – basically no response – from both multilateral and bilateral donors. The best response has come from a bilateral government statement that said it shared some of Kwik's analysis. This, however, is a diplomatic way of saying no rather than a positive response[16] from donors who are concerned with the debt burden and its deadly effect on the Indonesian budget.[17]

The German government has so far made the most positive response to the debt problem, by granting Indonesia a bilateral debt swap for education. Though the value of this debt is not significant compared to those held by Japan, ADB, and the World Bank, it is nevertheless a recognition of the problem and the possibility of it being addressed.

Ways forward

Is there an alternative to CGI governance? Is there another perspective on Indonesia's economic needs and interests that is more pro-poor?

It is imperative that the voice and influence of both the Indonesian government and people be expanded within CGI process, both on the choice of economic policy and the processes through which the policy is being made.

On CGI governance, one modest organisational reform option is to take up the proposal from Bappenas. This proposal involves the CGI process being led by Indonesia, with the full support of bilateral donors. Both the process and the agenda of the CGI meetings, including chairing of working groups, could be led by the Indonesian side. The obvious benefits are that it will increase the ownership of the programme and will strengthen the donor-recipient relationship.[18]

The other option is to dissolve the CGI and let Indonesia deal with its creditors and donors one by one. The benefits are that Indonesia would have more freedom and flexibility. Many countries, including Malaysia, Thailand and Brazil, are dealing with donors and creditors without a CG-type forum and Indonesia could do the same.[19]

As far as analysis is concerned, it is imperative to produce more alternative and independent studies on the macroeconomic aspects of Indonesia's programme, so as to avoid a monopoly of policy and knowledge by the World Bank and IMF. Like a patient and doctor, the patient needs to ask a second opinion from other doctors, if the first doctor is only making suffering worse.

In this regard, it is worth mentioning three reports: a) the report and analysis by a team of Indonesian economists and activists, called 'Indonesia Bangkit' [Indonesia Rise up][20]; b) the study by UNDP (2003)[21] and c) the report by the Independent Evaluation Office (IEO) of the IMF.[22]

The 'Indonesia Bangkit' team was led by Dr, Rizal Ramli, who was Finance and Coordinating Minister of Economy under President Wahid. Advocating a more expansionary economy and fiscal policies to create more jobs, the Bangkit is very much opposed to IMF austerity measures.

The IEO report is investigating IMF interventions in countries suffering from capital account crises. The countries being studied are Indonesia, Korea and Brazil. The report acknowledges mistaken IMF policies in

Indonesia

handling the Indonesian crisis in 1997, even though it denies that the IMF is entirely to blame.

The UNDP study, led by Terry McKinley, shows that the current contractionary macroeconomic approach is significantly responsible for the slow pace of recovery. The report argues that it is possible to have a more expansionary fiscal and monetary policy, which is necessary for pro-poor growth and job creation. It also shows that more effort is needed to address colossal Indonesian debt.

The three reports contain a number of useful policy proposals that are very relevant for a CGI forum seeking solutions to Indonesia's development difficulties. The test for the CGI forum, as long as it is led by the World Bank, is whether these independent studies will be considered important enough to be incorporated into official and non-official discussions within the CGI.

While gross financing is estimated at about US$10 billion, a huge chunk of financing, estimated at US$7.6 billion, is for debt repayment (principal debt repayment or amortisation) both for external debt (US$5.2 billion) and domestic debt (US$2.4 billion). Only about US$2.9 billion is for development projects and programme expenditure in 2004.

Notes

1. Among the five crisis-ridden countries, even after 6 years under IMF tutelage, Indonesia is the slowest economy. Indonesia post crisis, is severely indebted. Its Human Development Index remains below its neighbouring countries. About half of population is living in poverty, earning less than 2 dollars a day. In terms of state capacity to provide peace and security, Indonesia also belongs to the fragile states, one level above being considered a failed state.

2. The figures and data in this section draw heavily on the Bappenas Report (2003) 'Peran dan Keberadaan CGI' [The Role and Existence of CGI], Jakarta: Bappenas

3. From the donors' side, the delegates are from the US, British, IBRD, IMF, OECD, UNDP, OECD, and ADB. From 1967 to 1974, the IGGI met twice annually. But since 1975, because of better economic development, the IGGI met once a year.

4. Indonesia could not accept the Netherlands government, which Jakarta saw as using development assistance to intervene in the internal affairs of Indonesia. Jakarta was upset with Dutch pressure and criticism of human rights violations in East Timor.

5. 19 countries attended the meeting, including the US, Australia, Japan, Canada. Also participating in the meeting were 13 institutions such as from IMF, The ADB, Unicef and UNDP.

6. INFID was one of those invited to CGI meetings. Other NGOs included groups working on environment, forestry, women and anti-corruption.

7. The pledges and commitments from CGI meetings between 1992 and 2003 total is about $58 million. Not all pledges wherefrom government, since part of the fund is disbursed directly to non government organisations. Data from Bappenas covering 2000 shows that out of $5.44 billion, about $88.6 million is for NGOs.

8. See CGI Brief 'Beyond Macroeconomic Stability', The World Bank, December 2003.

9. For the complete document and progress on implementation, see Coordinating Minister of Economy, at www.ekon.go.id

10. CGI Brief, ibid., page. i-iii

11. See, Mohan Rao, 'Lessons and Policy Alternatives Facing Indonesia,' Paper for INFID Conference, 2002. see www.infid.org.

12. It will send messages as well to the Indonesian parliament on which policies the Bank supports, as the Bank knows very well that its position is taken seriously by Indonesian parliamentarians as well as by those within government. By doing so, the Bank makes clear to Minister Kwik and its supporters, that the Bank rejects his analysis and policy proposal.

Indonesia

[13] The study is prompted by several factors, among others, raising awareness of the perils of the debt trap suffered by Indonesia, both inside and outside the Indonesian government. It is illustrated by increasing public pressure, as well as by the MPR (Indonesian people assembly) decree that government should find a strategy to reduce Indonesian dependency to external loans and renegotiate its debt.

[14] In Indonesia, it is well known that Indonesia's approach to its donors/lenders is called 'Good Boy' which means that Indonesia is never late in fulfilling obligations resulting from loans to creditors.

[15] Under the current macroeconomic programme, with 3-4% growth, maximum job creations is only half the level necessary to cope with new entrants into the job market. It is estimated that each year, there are about 1.5 million Indonesians searching for jobs. Current estimates on unemployment or underemployment suggest it affects about 25 million people. It is equal to the size of Malaysia's population.

[16] It was at the pre-CGI meeting on the topic of ODA effectiveness, that Minister Kwik Kian Gie as the Chair of Bappenas, delivered his paper.

[17] Kwik Kian Gie, 'CGI dan Utang Pemerintah', [CGI and Government Debt] Kompas, 10 December, page 36.

[18] The World Bank and other donors may oppose this proposal, which could weaken Bank's control of the CGI. But it could also support the idea, producing more ownership from the Indonesian side and better prospects for implementation. It could play a role by increasing its production of policy options or alternatives, working together with local academics and independent experts.

[19] Some observers and NGOs are convinced that CGI is more a cartel of creditors than a partner for development. They believe that an alternative is to negotiate bilaterally with each donor/lender.

[20] See Tim Indonesia Bangkit, 2003. Jakarta;

[21] On the UNDP study, see Terry McKinley et all, *The Macroeconomy of Poverty Reduction in Indonesia*, 2004, forthcoming.

[22] On the IMF report, see IEO report at IMF websites

Security and development as an emerging issue

Koshida Kiyokazu, Pacific Asia Resource Center

In the past, Japan's ODA has been described as a trinity of ODA, Investment and Trade. But a new trinity of ODA, NGO and the Military is emerging, as Japan becomes much more involved in peacekeeping and emergency operations linked to the wider security agenda.[1]

This shift towards a security agenda is not affecting Japan alone. Other reports — for example from Australia — suggest that the Australian government has already included defence expenditure and Australian Federal Police activities in East Timor and the Pacific Rim within total Australian assistance to developing countries. (See *The Reality of Aid 2002*, page 159). And ideas about a new definition of ODA have been discussed at the OECD's Development Assistance Committee (DAC). These discussions raise concerns about the inclusion of security measures, such as counter-terrorism activities, within the definition of ODA. Reflecting the critical awareness of new notions of ODA, NGOs from the Reality of Aid network have been examining the emerging security agenda and its potential impact on development. Key issues of concern regarding the post-September 11 situation and its impact on development are:

1 the adoption of a broader definition of terrorism in many countries and the introduction of major anti-terrorism legislation;
2 the redefinition of aid and ODA, within the framework of geopolitical interest;
3 the danger of ODA becoming more based on selectivity and conditionality, reflecting donor interests.

The Japanese government recently pledged new ODA to Mindanao entitled 'Support Package for Peace and Security in Mindanao'. This includes support for peace building and the fight against terrorism. But this project may bring a new threat to grassroots people and communities, by supporting police and para-military groups.

After 11 September, many nations re-emphasised security as their most crucial issue. Since the United States launched the global war against terrorism and urged most of the world to join this war, global militarism has been expanded under the name of the global security. It is in this context that many countries are amending their national policies, including ODA policy, in line with the global security agenda.

Case study: Japan's ODA

Japan's 1992 ODA Charter laid out the basic themes of Japanese ODA. The charter had four major principles:

Asia/Pacific

1 Environmental conservation and development;
2 Any use of ODA for military purposes or for aggravation of international conflicts should be avoided;
3 Full attention to trends in recipient countries' military expenditures, their development and production of weapons of mass destruction and missiles, their export and import of arms, in order to maintain and strengthen international peace and stability;
4 Full attention to efforts towards democratisation and introduction of market-oriented economy.

Murai Yoshinori, an ODA researcher in Japan, analysed this charter as follows:
1 Political and strategic will that military power should not be established in the Third World came to the front line of aid policy;
2 Democratisation, human rights and enlargement of freedom were linked to aid;
3 The development of market-oriented economies was linked to aid.

Thus, in line with the establishment of global economic governance, under the US/IMF, World Bank and WTO, and the establishment of global military governance by US and UN, the principles underlying Japan's ODA have changed.

Prior to the institution of the 1992 Charter, there was heated discussion in Japan about the country's international contribution. When the Gulf War broke out, the government decided (in line with Japan's Peace Constitution) not to dispatch Japan's Self Defence Forces, but to provide huge amounts of aid. Japan provided US$1.1 billion in aid to multilateral forces and US$0.2 billion worth of aid to surrounding countries (Egypt, Turkey and Jordan). Leading

conservative politicians claimed that an international security regime, based on the UN's Peace Keeping Operation, should be established. They argued that Japan should join this regime. As Murai pointed out, behind this lay the US interest in utilising the UN to pursue its own agenda.

But ten years later, in 2003, a shift in Japan's ODA was accomplished, bringing it more directly in line with the US-led approach to global security policy. The new ODA Charter adds Japan's own security and prosperity to its purpose, and 'the prevention of terrorism' is also included in the principles of ODA implementation. This shows that Japan's national interest (on security and prosperity) is to support the US led counter-terrorism war. In the past, Japanese ODA policy has been to tacitly support US interests. But this attitude has changed and become an explicit policy.

A group of politicians and élite bureaucrats called *kantei* (Prime Minister's office) leads this policy change. A bureaucrat in this group clearly stated that the ultimate raison d'être of the nation state is security and, since Japan faces multiple global threats, diplomacy should respond to this. This bureaucrat also mentioned that utilising ODA is one of the important tools for such diplomacy, so Japan's ODA should be shifted more to peace consolidation or peace building. This implies that Japan's prohibition on ODA being used for military purpose should be withdrawn.

After these views had been put forward, the government reviewed the ODA Charter in August 2003. The new ODA Charter has several significant points in relation to security:
1 It makes clear that ODA implementation should consider the national interest;
2 It introduces a new concept of human security and peace building in order to make linkages between counter terrorism, war, and ODA;

Asia/Pacific

2 The terms 'terrorism' and 'conflict' are included to open the way for Japanese ODA to be used for military purposes;
3 The strategic use of ODA is strengthened.

Many NGOs and community based organisations, international institutions, and the majority of governments have publicly stated that ODA's main purpose is to alleviate global poverty. But security concerns and poverty alleviation are difficult to reconcile. It is a time to re-consider what ODA is really for.

DAC's move to counter terrorism

The trend towards promoting security as a priority for aid is not only happening in Japan. In April 2003, the Development Assistance Committee (DAC) of the OECD endorsed its policy statement, 'A Development Cooperation Lens on Terrorism Prevention: Key Entry Points for Action'. This paper initially emphasises the importance of donor commitment to poverty reduction and human rights, quoting the internationally agreed UN Millennium Development Goals (MDGs). If this were all the statement did, NGOs would see it as in line with the proper objectives of official aid.

NGOs are concerned, however, that several sections of the statement may be interpreted as opening the door for the redirection of aid from poverty reduction towards a counter-terrorism and security agenda. Throughout the statement, there is the suggestion that donors may need to recalibrate current aid approaches and allocations to take account of terrorism prevention. This clearly opens up the possibility, not only of making terrorism prevention a goal of development cooperation, but of giving it precedence over the existing and internationally agreed goals of development. The statement emphasises that strengthening governance is crucial, as is

support for democratisation and modernisation, finance and security.

But what the statement does not sufficiently take into account is the fact that counter-terrorism operations are mainly implemented by the police and military, in particular foreign military forces. And the statement makes no reference to the United States' National Security Strategy, which declares that combating terrorism is an obligation for all countries. The US has increased military assistance to developing countries for combating terrorism since 11 September.

Aid to Iraqi rehabilitation

Prior to the donors' meeting for Iraq, the World Bank and Coalition Provisional Authority appealed for assistance towards the costs of rehabilitating Iraq over the period 2004 to 2007. The World Bank estimated US$35.6 billion was needed for priorities, such as electricity, water and education. The CPA estimated US$19.4 billion for rehabilitating oil-related equipment and security. The total amount of US$55 billion was quite big money, compared to costs for rehabilitating Afghanistan (US$4.5 billion) and East Timor (US$0.52 billion).

For this huge Iraqi rehabilitation budget, the US, Japan, the UK, Spain, South Korea and the EU pledged to contribute large amounts (see Table 4)

Adding to this new aid money, Iraq holds a huge amount of foreign debt. The total amount is still unidentified. Official loan debt (Paris Club debt) alone is estimated at US$21 billion. Aside from official debts, Iraq has unpaid war reparations to Kuwait and unpaid military related debts. The Washington-based private think tank, Center for Strategic and International Studies (CSIS), estimates the total outstanding amount at US$380 billion. Based on this amount, each person in Iraq shoulders a US$16,000 debt burden. But the

Asia/Pacific

Table 4. Donor pledges for rehabilitation of Iraq

Country	Pledged amount (US$ billions)	Troops dispatched
US	20.3	130,000
Japan	5	
World Bank	3 to 5	750
MF	2.5 to 4.25	
Kuwait	1.5	11,000
Saudi Arabia	1	
UK	0.91	850
Australia	0.83	
EU	0.236	1 300
Spain	0.3	
Iran	0.3	3 000
Italy	0.236	
Germany	0.23	470
Korea	0.26	
UAE	0.215	150
Turkey	0.05	
China	0.024	

huge amount of money flowing into Iraq during Saddam Hussein's regime can be described as odious debt.

The US urges donor countries to cancel the debt. Countries such as Japan are reluctant, but might succumb to this pressure. If a government like Japan decides to cancel Iraqi debt, it might acknowledge that the money spent supporting Saddam Hussein's regime was odious. This would imply not only the responsibility of the regime itself, but also the responsibility of donor countries that helped to fund it. Debt cancellation for the heavily indebted poor countries still encounters many obstacles from international society. But Iraqi debt might be very quickly dealt with by donors. This double standard on debt issues emerged after September 11, in preparation for the war in Afghanistan. Many donors, including the World Bank and IMF, cancelled or re-scheduled debt owed by Pakistan in order to make the Pakistani regime more pro-US.

Under the slogan of global security, many donor countries have put security issues at the heart of their policies. This move can be described as a state-led human security approach. This idea, however, presupposes that all the insecurity comes from poor and undemocratic countries in the South. Along with this logic, is the idea that to eliminate the root of this insecurity, a US-led alliance for combating global terrorism is needed, with 'good governance' criteria strictly applied when aid is being allocated.

Global NGO and CBO networks should speak out on the clear purpose for ODA — to end poverty. NGOs must insist that donors commit more actively to achieving the MDGs. Shifting ODA to counter-terrorism simply perpetuates the vicious cycle of war and poverty.

If a government like Japan decides to cancel Iraqi debt, it might acknowledge that the money spent supporting Saddam Hussein's regime was odious. This would imply not only the responsibility of the regime itself, but also the responsibility of donor countries that helped to fund it.

Notes

As a loyal ally of the USA, Japan is contributing huge amounts of aid for 'peace building' operations — and the Japanese government uses the term 'All Japan' to illustrate that Japanese involvement includes enterprises, NGOs and Self Defence Forces.

How donors reject governance and human rights: two case studies of hydropower and water supply projects in Nepal

Gopal Siwakoti 'Chintan', Nepal Policy Institute[1]

Nepal is arguably the most beautiful country in the world. Its peoples are among the richest in cultural diversity and the best in resource management through community ownership and the local, ethnic and indigenous practices. If the national resources were properly used, the 23 million people of this country could have all they want. They have Mount Everest and many of the other highest mountains in the world to attract tourism, a huge amount of freshwater resources, flora and fauna, the most fertile valleys and plains for agriculture and animal husbandry, wildlife and natural ecosystems. But the country is now regarded as the poorest in the world — very hard to believe. Nepal was made poor and is now being made the poorest!

The era of economic dependence and poverty began with Nepal's defeat in a war with the British East India Company followed by an 'illegal' Soogauli Treaty in 1816. As a result, Nepal lost its vast fertile land and the rivers from Darjeeling in the East to Kumau-Gadhawal in the West. The British began to recruit large numbers of Nepali youth into

their army — brave mountain fighters, known as the *Gurkhas*.[2] Hundreds of thousands of *Gurkhas* either gave their lives or suffered injuries in the two World Wars and other regional conflicts, from the Far East to the Falklands, but today they are still treated as virtual mercenaries. The 'export' of these youth from the rural areas of Nepal and their migration to towns is linked to widespread poverty and the socio-cultural disintegration of their various ethnic communities. Nepal is now known for its continuing export of the youth, either as security guards and British soldiers, or migrant workers in many countries, where they are treated as slaves or severely exploited. The hills and paddy fields are now turning into deserts and all the productive forces have flown either to cities or abroad. Nepalis never got a chance to develop themselves but rely on the sympathy of the donors even for a small hospital or drinking water supply.

As a result, Nepal at present is on the verge of collapse due both to chronic poverty and a Maoist civil war, which began in 1996 with demands for rapid democratisation and drastic land reforms.[3] Even the World Bank

Nepal

has recognised this fact recently by describing the Maoist insurgency as 'clearly a political movement with a firm political philosophy' and has further blamed the '[h]orizontal inequality and social exclusion' as well as the '[f]ailure of governance'.[4] What it does not mention is its own responsibility, and that of other donors, for the creation of such situations by the imposition of severe aid conditionalities in favour of economic liberalisation and privatisation in a feudal-agrarian society such as Nepal. Now more aid is coming in the form of military assistance and arms' supply than help in addressing the root causes of the Maoist conflict and other problems.[5]

In the five decades of international aid in Nepal, development never meant something local managed by the Nepalis and for the Nepalis; it was a complete dependency syndrome. It always meant a project run by foreigners with no transparency and accountability regarding outcomes. It was also considered as the most sacred area, to be untouched by public scrutiny or criticism. Various studies clearly show that foreign aid only benefited the local feudal-lords and other member of the élite, e.g. the Royal family and their relatives, and the army, which became more rich and also corrupt and powerful. Nepal's acceptance of globalisation and its joining of the World Trade Organisation has made the country just a dumping ground for foreign goods, with the sell-out of its vast national resources — both human and natural. These days, Nepal receives foreign loans and assistance not to build its economy but to destroy it, including the dismantling of public institutions and community systems.

One of the main reasons for the failure of the past 14 years of parliamentary rule in Nepal is the complete domination by international aid agencies and bilateral donors through their conditional loans and aid. The 'sovereign' Parliament and the elected governments remained largely as the agents of the foreign interest lobby. Thus we are never allowed to express our own needs and priorities. There are even cases of the government refusing to release secret dealings and agreements with the International Financial Institutions to Parliament and even the Supreme Court. The spirit of democratic governance[6] was taken over by donor-driven corporate governance, and human rights and the rule of law were subject to corporate rules. As a result, Nepal's adoption of a democratic constitution and laws, as well as the ratification of dozens of major international human rights and environmental instruments, remained totally ineffective as the governments have always been compelled to comply with the donors' pre-conditions and corporate obligations.

Recent experiences show that it is the donors who are mainly responsible for leading Nepal into the current economic mess and political collapse. The Maoist armed uprising is widely regarded as the result of the mockery of elections, a 'sovereign' Parliament that failed to address chronic poverty, and the failure of political commitment, due to destructive lending conditionalities and the militarisation of the state, including the Palace. What we really needed, after the democratic change of 1990, was real democratisation and the decentralisation of political power, as well as economic resources. The rhetoric of 'good governance' was in fact defined by the donors and went against the very fundamental principles of human rights-based democratic governance.

In this context, the following two cases provide the most interesting examples of the donors' inability to respect their own policies and procedures in promoting good

Nepal

governance and human rights. They also provide some details of how the people and the communities, who are supposed to be the targets of development, are denied access to their own resources and benefits. The first case of Kali Gandaki 'A' is a story of why the donors do not want to learn lessons from their mistakes; the second case of Melamchi River diversion is about how the local resources are transferred, against the will of the local people who own them and how cheaper and better available alternatives to water supply in another basin — the Kathmandu Valley — are being bypassed.

Kali Gandaki 'A' Hydroelectric Project

The Kali Gandaki 'A' (KGA) is Nepal's largest hydroelectric project, 144 MW, built in the western region of Nepal with conditional loans from the Asian Development Bank (ADB) and the Japanese Overseas Economic Cooperation Fund (OECF), now Japan Bank for International Cooperation (JBIC). Begun in 1997 and completed in 2002, this project is considered as a costly one compared to the original forecast. The reasons were the delays, and corruption. The notorious Italian Impregilo SPA company was the main contractor.

The implementation of the KGA was the result of the cancellation of the Arun III Hydroelectric Project by the World Bank in August 1995.[7] Activists and experts had presented the KGA as a better, and cheaper, alternative to Arun III. But it did not happen. The cost escalated from US$250 to US$360 millions by the time of its completion. The civil construction cost was increased by 67%. The ADB, instead of supporting cost reduction measures, was mainly concerned with compliance to its conditionalities and increasing electricity tariffs.[8] At present, Nepal has one of the highest tariffs in the world.

Struggle for access to information

The Arun III campaign represented a major shift in the development debate in Nepal. It was the first big campaign that questioned transparency and accountability in a foreign-funded project. In Arun III, the struggle for access to project documents and information was won both at the level of the Supreme Court and the World Bank's Inspection Panel, in October 1994, in the first case ever filed — in which the author was one of the main claimants.[9] The Court, in its landmark decision, set clear guidelines and procedures for seeking and receiving information on any issues of public interest, including development projects, as provided for article 16 of the 1990 Constitution of Nepal.[10]

Despite these achievements, the fight for the right to information in the KGA was not so different from Arun III, except for the accessibility of the loan agreement and Environmental Impact Assessment (EIA) reports. Even then these documents were no use to the local people, as they were all written in English, apart from some small information booklets. Most interestingly, none of these documents was available during the decision making time. The feasibility studies, cost-benefit analyses, and EIA reports, as well as the copies of the contracts, all of which were crucial for any critical debate and decision-making, have never been made available, even since the completion of the project.

Public consultation/participation

In any project, the holding of public consultation meetings is essential for ensuring effective and meaningful participation by the local/affected people. This is also the most important element when it comes to practising good governance.

Unlike in Arun III, some public meetings were held in the KGA project sites and in a Five Star hotel in Kathmandu. The local participants in these meetings were all selected at the instigation of the project officials. Activists were prevented from attending local meetings and presenting their views; those who tried to distribute printed information faced both verbal and physical abuse and harassment. The project also recruited some local politicians and leaders to systematically attack the critics and to blindly defend the project. The ADB officials present in these meetings remained silent and turned a blind eye to what was happening.

The issue of local benefits

When the project loan was being considered, the ADB and the OECF officials were accompanied by ministers and Members of Parliament to the project site and garlanded with flowers. The local people were given sweets and drinks for coming to listen to the 'donors', the ministers and the politicians promising them everything imaginable. It was out of the question to raise any critical voice in such a hostile situation. The project officials were even engaged in creating pseudo local groups and arranging fake letters of support to the ADB. Later on, some of these thugs were also used for spying on the local people and suppressing their voice.

The local people were brutally suppressed when they began to demand the promised jobs and effective implementation of the social and environmental improvement plans. There was an incident reported in the media in which an unemployed youth who had joined the protesting crowd was allegedly killed by the police, in the Impregilo office compound. No charges arose from this but about 32 local people demanding jobs were charged by the local authority, under the Public Offence Act. They were set free upon the deposit of their personal property for bail. The charges were

dropped only after the completion of the project. The formation of independent unions was virtually banned and the genuine union leaders were fired for their activities. The local traditional village women were exposed to vulgar aspects of western culture and life-style, and were offered only low-level and low-paid household work at the residence of Impregilo masters. No letters of appointment or contracts, which are required by the Nepal Labour Act, were given to workers and labourers. The terms and conditions of hiring and firing were in violation of all domestic and international labour laws and standards. The minimum basic pay and benefits provisions were also ignored. The Head of Impregilo once said to the author that it had no obligations to respect any domestic, international, or ADB rules and regulations on such matters.

The displaced people, however, had no choice but to accept whatever money was made available for compensation. There was, and still is, no provision for the true representation of the affected people in the land acquisition and compensation processes. The *Bote* indigenous peoples were provided with neither proper resettlement nor guaranteed jobs. Instead, they had to lose their traditional livelihoods permanently. Planned income generation programmes were not adequately implemented.

Several public meetings and protests were organised by the local people against the NEA, the Impregilo, and the ADB during the construction period. The people even complained that the ADB officials were hiding from them to avoid complaints, and that they were largely relying on inaccurate internal reports to judge the project performance. These reports were never made public for comment, despite requests. The activists and the media were also prevented from meeting the local people and visiting the project sites. In some cases, armed

Nepal

police were used to arrest and expel them from the area before reaching the place. The people believed that the local administrative and police officials were paid bribes, on a regular basis, to give 'protection' to the project. As a result, at a later stage, the KGA sites were virtually turned into security zones.

The ADB back in Manila knew of all these incidents but never bothered to make inquiries about them. The complaints made by the local Village Development Committee officials and other groups were either ignored or poorly addressed. It was only after a detailed complaint was made by the Water and Energy Users' Federation-Nepal (WAFED) to the ADB in June 2003 that a high-level mission was sent to study the problems. The Mission responded to WAFED in November, admitting that there had been serious violations of the ADB policies and promising that the mitigation plans would be complied with as soon as possible. The Mission had also agreed, in a meeting last January, to monitor continuously the post-project impacts and to develop mitigation plans as and when required. If this is done, it will be something exceptional in the case of such projects.

Melamchi Water Supply Project

The Melamchi Water Supply Project (MWSP) is the first inter-basin river diversion project planned for the supply of drinking water for about two million people living in Kathmandu Valley, the capital of Nepal. The MWSP has been on the political agenda and the donors' priority list for about 20 years but has never been followed through, due to conflicts of interest among the donors — mainly between the World Bank[11] and the ADB. The World Bank decided to pull out from the MWSP in 2002 for the very simple reason 'that important options have not been explored to utilize the water resources within the

valley'. The distribution system needs to be fixed first, but even then it will only benefit the richest 5% of the population, at the expense of other needs and priorities in the country.[12] Now the ADB is leading the project with the Japanese Bank for International Cooperation, Japan International Cooperation Agency (JICA), the Swedish International Development Cooperation (SIDA), the Norwegian Agency for Development (NORAD), the Nordic Development Fund (NDF), the OPEC-Fund, and the Norwegian NORPLAN as a consultant.

The main political issue related to the MWSP is whether it is the best option for supplying drinking water to the capital and, if so, how it will be done. So far, various studies, including those conducted by the ADB, clearly show that the MWSP is not necessarily the best option, since there are several other options within the Kathmandu Valley. These include the groundwater resources, rainwater harvesting and best management practice over the existing river and stream sources. Another option is the rehabilitation of existing old infrastructure that is regarded as the main reason for the loss of up to 70% of existing water supply due to leakages and inefficiency. However, all decisions have already been made to implement the MWSP at whatever cost and without any regard to the fundamental issues of how the new policies and institutions will be set up and at what price, and how, the water will be supplied to the Kathmandu population.

ADB taking a big chance

After the repeated failures of the World Bank — in the cancelled Arun III and the KGA and the MWSP from which it has pulled out — the ADB has been taking a big chance in monopolising Nepal's huge water and energy sector investment. Despite its gross failures

Nepal

in the implementation of its various policies, e.g. on information, public participation, environment, compensation and resettlement, indigenous peoples etc., the ADB is doing all it can to undermine the existing public institutions and associated welfare policies of the government, in water, energy and other social sectors. The ADB's main objective in the MWSP is guided by the desire to bring in foreign private management of the water supply system. If all goes well for the ADB and other donors in bringing the country into the international water mafia, Nepal will have to face the collapse of its public institutions, moral strength and skills — e.g. the Nepal Water Supply Corporation, which has a duty of providing safe and clean drinking water as a public service.

It is interesting to see how countries like Norway and Sweden, so well-known for their social welfare systems and democratic values, can be equally bad when it comes to their investment and operation for profit in other countries. One can feel ashamed for NORAD and SIDA in this regard. They have not shown any interest and have not even acknowledged the issues raised by the local groups in the Melamchi Valley, or by WAFED in Kathmandu. The same goes for the JBIC, unless it is specifically challenged under the newly developed complaint procedures. There seems to be a collective vested interest with the ADB to go for the dismantling of Nepal's public water authority, diluting development needs and priorities, and creating a good environment for foreign corporations. It is unfortunate that even the Nordic countries, instead of sharing their rich experiences of public service and social welfare, should unhesitatingly join the international financial and water mafia, for the benefit of their national companies and investment agencies.

Local concerns fall to international interests

As in the case of KGA, the people in the Melamchi Valley have been fighting for access to basic project documents for years, but without any significant success. The massive public campaigns and dialogue with the ADB and MWSP officials have produced little information in Nepali. In any case, these Nepali or English information documents, even if fully available, have no real use, since all decisions about the project have already been made. As regard public participation and consultation, as required for the EIA, the road survey, the land acquisition, compensation and resettlement, the development and implementation of the Social Upliftment Programme (SUP)[13] there was a complete lack of transparency and democratic processes. The inputs and suggestions provided by the local people during the meetings have never been properly considered or incorporated into the project documents and programmes, making these exercises mere formalities. The local people have totally rejected the SUP, as prepared by NORPLAN, endorsed by the ADB and implemented by the MWSP as inaccurate, inadequate and imposed by the consultants. The people in the Melamchi Valley want to see the SUP thoroughly discussed, designed, and implemented with their full consent, according to local needs and priorities — including social and economic programmes for the poor *Tamang* communities, who are known for the 'sale' of their daughters and/ or tolerance of trafficking, due to poverty and illiteracy. It is yet known whether or not there is any budget for comprehensive environmental mitigation plans.

The MWSP also has failed to satisfy the local people in terms of how much water will be required in the Melamchi Valley for their livelihoods and ecosystems and how much

Nepal

water will really be left for diversion. This is an important issue that the local people are confronting about maintaining a minimum, but adequate, flow of water as needed for sustaining the existing irrigation for the most fertile agricultural land, the *ghattas* (traditional water mills) and other activities, including the needs of future generations. The existing EIA is full of flaws and does not incorporate a vast range of indirect economic and social impacts. The reduction in the flow of existing water will lead to the closure of hundreds of *ghattas* and irrigation canals, including those funded by the ADB on loans. There will be a loss of electricity in some villages, and many will be unemployed due to the collapse of their cottage industries. There is also no adequate study of, and income generation programme for, over 50 *Majhi* families — a fish-dependent ethnic group. There is going to be a major conflict in the future over water rights, if these issues are not settled properly, and now. The people in the Melamchi Valley are also demanding a major share of the profit from their freely supplied water from the people of Kathmandu Valley, through a levy to fund local development and mitigate any future impacts. The proposed provision of a minimum of 0.4 cubic metres (400 litres)/ second of water flow may not be adequate at all, bringing into question the credibility of the whole scheme.[14]

The other issues of local concerns include the need for effective and guaranteed provisions for skill development training and employment for the locals, and either no or less use of technicians and labourers from outside. This issue has already generated conflict between the local people and the contractors. In principle, there is a provision for a minimum 30% of local jobs during construction. There is also a fear that Royal Nepal Army may be used to suppress

the local voice, since a new army barracks has been set up in the area at project cost. However, the MWSP and the ADB are denying it, and let's hope this will not be the case; although there have, reportedly, already been some incidents.

Denial of alternatives to water supply in Kathmandu

The most important question that the MWSP, and for that matter the ADB and other donors, have not dared to discuss publicly is the existence of much better, cheaper and easier solutions for water supply in Kathmandu. In the first place, no rivers can meet the demand for water supply in the capital if the population continues to grow at in the current rate, which is due to the centralisation of most of the country's scarce resources, illegal migration from India, and the influx of hundreds of thousands of people from Maoist conflict areas. Secondly, there are already huge amounts of groundwater that are yet to be explored and regulated. Furthermore, there is a large potential for rainwater harvesting, including the best management of existing surface water from ponds and streams around the Bagmati River basin. And, thirdly, enough water could be saved by the rehabilitation of old water supply infrastructure and addressing other technical/institutional leakages. So the problem is not the lack of alternatives, but the denial of these alternatives due to the big project mind-set and the role of the water mafias.

Even if the Melamchi is to be considered the only suitable option for water supply in Kathmandu, the MWSP, together with the ADB and JBIC, has a duty to discuss these issues in public and with experts in the country. Unfortunately, there have not even been proper public consultations with the Kathmandu population — the direct beneficiaries or potential victims of such an ambitious and costly project. It is still not too late to do this, since the major project construction work is yet to begin. The recent studies of the donors cannot simply be ignored, even if the opinions of the Nepali experts and activists are to be ignored.   For example, the February 2003 study of JBIC clearly says that the 'improvement of the [existing] distribution network, even if it is implemented alone, can deliver a better service to customers by distributing the existing water resources through the improved distribution system. Further, by reducing water losses it should be possible to offer more hours of service to customers in areas where the distribution system has not been improved.'

Privatisation first!

There is another highly sensitive issue of equity and social justice in the proposed water supply system in Kathmandu. The price of water is going to be very high. The bringing in of a foreign private operator, or private management, will add extra, unnecessary costs because of the high profit-making approach of the project. There is no provision yet for making water available to more than 30% of the population who are poor and live in slums or have no income. The connection charge is also going to be high 'to suppress demand and subsidise consumption tariffs'. The study shows that many will not be able to pay the connection charge. unless it is paid on an instalment basis or included in the tariffs.[15]

The problem with the ADB and other donors is that they are not really interested in supporting and building the local capacity for water supply at an affordable price. This could range from collaboration among the five municipalities in the Kathmandu Valley, the involvement of the local private sector, and the communities. There could also be local cooperatives. But this is simply

not the objective of the donors. They want to force Nepal towards the ultimate privatisation of its water supply system and the gradual dismantling of the Nepal Water Supply Corporation in favour of foreign companies. Due to strong opposition, from within and outside the government, the ADB is becoming flexible regarding absolute privatisation. It is now proposing a public-private partnership through international management contracts, as in the case with Nepali banks. The ultimate results and impacts, however, will be the same – the sale of water for 'profit' in place of 'service' and the virtual collapse of public utilities and their duties. What Nepal really needs is the reform of the existing Nepal Water Supply Corporation, with full autonomy from donors and the government, as well as the involvement of local municipalities, the private sector, and community cooperatives. What is also important is the philosophy and approach to water as a 'social good' and a 'human right', and not as an 'economic commodity' for corporate profit.[16] One also needs to take into account the very strong social, cultural and religious value of water in Nepali society as a free gift of nature, not something that can be privatised and commercialised for profit and at unreasonable cost.

Comparative findings

These two case studies are Nepal's most widely debated donor-driven development projects – one is completed, the other is in process. Based on the above details of these projects, the following conclusion may be drawn regarding how international aid agencies operate in Nepal in violation of the very basic principles and practices of good governance and human rights:

1. *Right to information*

The right to information is a human right,

Nepal

recognised by the International Covenant on Civil and Political Rights and many other international instruments. This is also a fundamental right under the Constitution of Nepal and has been widely expanded in various public interest cases. The Final Report of the World Commission on Dams[17] is another international document that has emphasised the need for free and prior informed consent of local people and indigenous communities, for example, in all water and energy development projects. These must be respected and implemented by all those involved in financing such projects.

2. Right to meaningful public participation

Free and prior informed consent must be obtained as evidence of effective and meaningful public participation

3. Environmental Impact Assessment and mitigation measures

The conduct of EIA is the most important element in deciding whether a project is good or bad. The main proble m with the EIA and the mitigation measures in the above studies has been the complete lack of access to information and public participation. There was also a lack of recognition of local ownership with regard to the implementation of the mitigation measures.

The affected people and the local communities should have adequate control and ownership over the EIA process and the development and implementation of mitigation plans. All the related costs should form part of the projects, including the mitigation of post-project impacts.

4. Compensation and resettlement

The compensation and resettlement measures in both of these projects have been both arbitrary and inadequate. Most of the compensation has been paid in cash with no offer of land for land for compensation or resettlement. Melamchi is the first project in Nepal with a resettlement component, due to the ADB policy. However, no consideration has been given to guaranteeing at least the same, if not better, living standards, for people displaced by the projects. The affected people must be given the choice of cash or land, and there must be adequate representations in the decision-making bodies that decide the amount and methods of compensation and/or resettlement plans.

5. Sharing benefits

One of the negative aspects of the foreign funded projects is the denial of benefits to the local people and communities upon which the success and future of such projects depend. The authorities should first distribute the project benefits to the affected people and communities. In addition, they also need to guarantee a certain amount of profit for long term local development and environmental mitigation, in addition to overall district or village-level development.

6. Freedom from destructive conditionalities

None of the above projects have come to Nepal without the overall vested interests of donors being reflected in severe lending conditionalities. They range from compulsory global procurement provision to tariff increases and privatisation. Conditionalities imposed on such infrastructure projects largely ignore the use of local resources and capacities, as well as local needs and priorities. As a result, the projects become unnecessarily costly and are also dependent on foreign donors and consultants throughout the project cycle.

Nepal

Conclusion and recommendations

The KGA and the MWSP cases demonstrate that no project goes to any country unless it meets the donors' criteria, which are largely guided by economic globalisation and corporate rule. Donors pay no attention to any internationally agreed framework of human rights and democratic governance for sustainable development. They do not care about domestic laws and regulations, let alone the needs and priorities of the people. When the IFIs, because of public pressure, do adopt such policies and mechanisms, it is simply a cosmetic exercise. What all these aid agencies need to honestly recognise is that no 'governance' can be 'good' without being 'democratic'. 'Good' and 'democratic' governance cannot be achieved without the full recognition and implementation of basic human rights — civil, political, economic, social, environmental, and cultural. The violations of these human rights and democratic principles by aid agencies, as in the case of Nepal, will certainly bring more poverty, more debt burden, and the collapse of national institutions that are the foundations of that society, as against the stated goals of national or local development... There are alternatives for local development and national prosperity,

based on locally owned democratic development, rather than the present unfair and undemocratic rules of the game. The people and the communities are the best alternatives to globalisation and corporatisation. The lack of a human rights approach to development and aid management will contribute to more violent conflicts, civil war and global population movement. What we urgently need is a more principle-based governance in the international aid system, which is neither above international human rights law nor immune from responsibility for their wrong polices and development crimes.

Nepalis can continue to be poor as domestic servants in India, security guards in Hong Kong, Brunei and on foreign ships and brave, but badly exploited, fighters in the British army. The rest of Nepalis will be forced to live in more and more poverty and related conflicts. But this should never be the destiny of a prosperous and dignified country in the 21st century. International development aid should primarily be for the recipient countries and their people, not the local elites and international business.

Nepalis never got a chance to develop themselves but rely on the sympathy of the donors even for a small hospital or drinking water supply.

Nepal

Notes

[1] Nepal Policy Institute (NPI) is a research, training and advocacy organization involved in providing critical inputs for policy reform in Nepal's public sector policies, membership to the WTO and other regional free trade agreements, and its relations in bi-lateral and multilateral 'donors' and lenders, including the United Nations agencies. It also promotes the incorporation of human rights and environmental principles into national and international policy-making, e.g. Nepal Development Forum (NDF) for the real achievement of Millennium Development Goals. NPI also participates in national and international campaigns to prevent the adverse effects of the existing national and global economic and trade policies and programmes, the international financial and trade institutions, and transnational corporations.

[2] The 'Gurkhas' or 'Gorkhalis' are named after the old Gurkha Kingdom in the western region of Nepal. It is now one of Nepal's 75 districts.

[3] Upreti, BR (Dr.), 'Forty point demands of the Maoists', The Price Of Neglect: From Resource Conflict To Maoist Insurgency In The Himalayan Kingdom, Bhrikuti Academic Publications (2004), Kathmandu, p. 368.

[4] The World Bank, Nepal: Country Assistance Strategy, 2004-2007, Report No. 26509-NEP, Washington, DC (2004), p. 9.

[5] The US, UK, Belgium and India are the main countries providing military assistance and exporting arms to Nepal. These are being grossly misused by the autocratic King and the Royal Nepal Army over the past two years to cross all the democratic and revolutionary forces.

[6] See for details, O S Saasa, G C Gurdian, Z Tadesse & G Siwakoti 'Chintan', 'Democratic Governance', Improving The Effectiveness of Finnish Development Cooperation: Perspectives From The South, Ministry of Foreign Affairs of Finland, Helsinki (2003), pp. 137-167 & 178-180.

[7] See, 'The Shelving of Arun III in Eastern Nepal', Encyclopedia of Sustainability: Successful Campaigning against Large Dams, Both ENDS, Amsterdam at www.bothends.org, and also, 'Nepal: Arun III Proposed Hydroelectric Project & Restructuring of IDA Credit-2029', Inspection Panel Investigation Report, The Inspection Panel, Washington, DC, 1995.

[8] To know more about the ADB, see, The Asian Development Bank: In Its Own Words, an analysis of

project audit reports for Indonesia Pakistan, and Sri Lanka, SG Fried, S Lawrence & R Gregory, Environmental Defense, Washington, DC (2003); and Focus on the Global South, An Overview of the ADB's Decision Making Processes and Policies: Good Governance or Bad Management, Bangkok (2002) at www.focusweb.org

[9] The author was the main claimant.

[10] See, also for various WAFED activities, www.wafed-nepal.org

[11] To know more about the World Bank's equally disturbing policies, see, 'Water Resources Sector Strategy: Strategic Directions for World Bank Manageent ', The World Bank, Washington, DC (2003) and 'Gambling with People's Lives: What the World Bank's New 'High-Risk/High-Reward' Strategy Means for the Poor and the Environment', a report by Environmental Defense, Friends of the Earth & International Rivers Network (2003).

[12] 'The answer is no', an interview with the World Bank President Ken Ohashi, The Nepali Times, July 19, 2002, Lalitpur, p. 1.

[13] SUP-identified five key areas of activities are: local income generation, health, education, electrification and buffer-zone management with the budget of about US $6 million. It is a separate component from the EIP mitigation plans. It was prepared and is being supervised by NORPLAN.

[14] See for details, M. Bhattarai, D. Pant & D. Molden, Socio-Economics and Hydrological Impacts of Inter-sectoral and Interbasin Water Transfer Decision: Melamchi Water Transfer Project in Nepal, selected paper presented at 'Asian Irrigation in Transition-Responding to the Challenges Ahead', April 22-23, 2002 at Asian Institute of Technology, Bangkok, Thailand.

[15] A Etherington, J Wicken & D Bajracharya, 'Preparing for Private Sector Management of Kathmandu Urban Water Supply' (Discussion Paper, Draft), September 2002, p. 15.

[16] See, also, R Stavenhagen, Needs, Rights and Social Development, Overarching Concerns, Paper Number 2, United Nations Research Institute for Social Development, Geneva (2003).

[17] The World Commission on Dams, Dams and Development: A New Framework for Decision-Making, Earthscan Publications Ltd., London and Sterling, VA (2000), also at www.wcd.org

USAID's *AGILE*: toying with governance to globalise the Philippines?

Jennifer del Rosario-Malonzo, IBON Foundation, Inc.

Although poverty reduction remains the goal of development aid, a donor's use of 'governance' may hold back human development. This happens when governance is used not only to set the selection criteria for recipients, but also to veil the agenda of restructuring government policies and programmes, according to neoliberal prescriptions.

Aid conditionality, which invariably entails policies pushing for integration into the global economy, contradicts the principles of good governance, which should be based on a collective decision-making process that promotes participation, access and empowerment of the disenfranchised and vulnerable populace. Conditionality takes away the essence of collective decision-making and action, as it imposes decisions from outside, regardless of national circumstances and the will of the people.

There is an even greater aberration in governance — the use of aid intended for poverty reduction to ensure the implementation of globalisation policies. This is revealed through an examination of a United States Agency for International Development (USAID) project in the Philippines, called *Accelerating Growth,* *Investment and Liberalization with Equity* or AGILE.

The AGILE programme came under fire when Philippines senators, working on revisions to the Anti-Money Laundering Act, questioned its influence and the work of its 'technical consultants' on a wide array of Philippine policy areas. One senator noted that AGILE's website was deleted in the heat of the debate on its existence and influence.[1] At present, the same set of objectives, actions, plans and achievements listed under AGILE comes under the name *Economic Governance Technical Assistance* (EGTA) programme.[2]

AGILE (and now EGTA) implements most of USAID's economic development and governance activities in the Philippines.[3]

Neoliberal economic reform and governance

According to USAID, its Office of Economic Development and Governance 'assists Philippine Partners in job creation and poverty reduction, by reducing the constraints on investment caused by corruption and poor governance, including the barriers to competition that inhibit domestic and international investment.'[4]

Philippines

USAID points to two goals in corruption mitigation: 1) To make institutions, policies and practices transparent and accountable; and 2) The removal of competitive barriers to development of infrastructure and trade. The second goal 'levels the playing field' and is seen to 'allow for expanded and efficient private and public investment, full participation in the multilateral trade system, and expanded job creation.'[5] (See List 1 for examples of activities).

List 1. Ongoing and planned activities under USAID Economic Development and Governance programme.[6]

Making institutions, policies, and practices transparent and accountable

- strengthening management at the Bureau of Internal Revenue;
- modernising import valuation and other operations at the Bureau of Customs, consistent with the WTO agreement;
- strengthening of the Philippine Securities and Exchange Commission to prevent stock market manipulation;
- improving transparency and efficiency of government procurement;
- strengthening and enforcement of commercial law through the Department of Justice and the courts; and
- improving transparency and accountability of banking institutions and addressing money laundering issues.

Removing competitive barriers to development of infrastructure and trade

- providing assistance to improve the competition and regulatory framework for ports, shipping, aviation, power, roads, information and communication technology, and grain marketing;
- helping to implement activities under the WTO framework for grain sector reform, biotechnology, customs valuation, intellectual property rights, plant variety protection, and sanitary and phytosanitary measures.

USAID's Economic Development and Governance programme reflects the wish list of US transnational corporations that seek to remove every single trade and investment measure put in place to protect the domestic economy. Although the Philippines has long embraced globalisation, there are still constitutional and other legal barriers that hamper foreign economic operations.

List 2 shows some of the economic barriers that the US wants removed. Clearly, those measures that cannot be achieved immediately through trade and investment negotiations are pursued through programmes that masquerade as development aid.

Philippines

USAID also conveniently lumps together corruption and economic barriers as undesirable impediments to development. But protective measures and other regulations have been instituted precisely because national development can only be achieved without undue foreign competition.

List 2. Some Philippine foreign trade barriers that the US wants removed.[7]

Import policies

- Tariff-rate quotas (TRQs) — several US agricultural exports, such as corn, poultry meat, and pork are affected by TRQs, where imports outside the quota are subjected to higher tariff.
- Quantitative restriction on rice — the US wants the Philippines to consider imposing a tariff on rice, in advance of the WTO Agreement on Agriculture, to encourage imports.
- Customs barriers — the Bureau of Customs' current regime must be reformed to minimise what some US exporters describe as 'import harassment'.

Standards, testing, labelling and certification

- Industrial goods — the Generic Act of 1988 requires pharmaceutical firms to put the generic name of products on the packaging of their brands.
- On agricultural goods, action is being suggested on: the Department of Agriculture's 'inappropriate' use of Veterinary Quarantine Certificates; the government's policy of zero tolerance for methanol in wine products; restriction on fresh fruits from Texas due to phytosanitary concerns.

Government procurement

- The Philippines is not a signatory to the WTO Government Procurement Agreement. Preferential treatment of local supplies is practised in government purchases of pharmaceuticals, rice, corn, and iron/steel materials for use in government projects. Another perceived problem is the requirement of 60% Filipino ownership for contractors in infrastructure projects in water and power distribution, telecommunications, and transport systems.

Services barriers

- Constitutional restriction on 40% foreign ownership of telecommunications firms. No market access or national treatment for satellite services and no commitment on resale of leased circuits/closed user groups.
- The Philippines only agrees, in the WTO, to allow 51% foreign equity participation in the insurance sector. Current policy means 70% of total banking assets must be controlled by Filipino banks at all times. There is a total restriction on foreign ownership in the rural banking system.

Philippines

- Foreign equity in securities underwriting companies is limited to 60%. Most Favoured Nation (MFN) exemption on foreign equity participation in security firms is perceived as a problem.
- Prohibition on foreign-flagged vessels engaging in domestic carriage services, as well as prohibition on foreigners becoming crew members or officers on Philippine-flagged vessels.
- Restriction on 100% foreign ownership of air express carriers and airfreight forwarding firms.

Investment barriers

- Foreign investments are hampered, due to constitutional or other legal constraints on foreign ownership, in the retail trade, mass media, advertising agencies, natural resource extraction, educational institutions, public utilities, commercial deep-sea fishing, government procurement contracts, rice and corn processing, and private lands.
- Foreign investments are also restricted for reasons of national security, defence, public safety, and morals.

'Globalising' the Philippines through AGILE

It was in February 2003 that AGILE's activities were made public, when Senators working on the Anti-Money Laundering Act revealed the existence of a group that allegedly influences Philippine economic policy-making through satellite offices in several vital government agencies. The programme claims its aims are to 'accelerate economic policy reforms, generate growth, create jobs, and reduce poverty.'[8]

Surprisingly, AGILE had already been working for more than four years before it was 'uncovered'. What is not surprising though, is that it was conceived during the administration of President Fidel V. Ramos, who embraced and aggressively promoted liberalisation, deregulation and privatisation.

With the Philippines firmly committed to the liberalisation of its economy, USAID saw technical assistance as a way to accelerate implementation. It collaborated with the Department of Finance (DoF), the National Economic and Development Authority (NEDA) and the Coordinating Council of the Philippine Assistance Program (CCPAP) to create a programme that would 'support economic policy liberalization and enhance competition in the Philippines.'[9]

Funded under the Philippine Assistance Program Support (PAPS)[10], AGILE's project costs were then estimated at US$28.4 million, of which USAID would provide US$21 million, while the balance, plus VAT expenditures of US$7.4 million, would be provided 'in cash and in kind' by the DoF and other government agencies, as well as private sector groups who would receive AGILE assistance for their advocacy.

The Philippine government supervises AGILE through a Steering Committee composed of representatives from the DoF (which acts as Chairperson), NEDA, USAID and two members of the private sector.[11]

AGILE found a ready niche in the Philippine bureaucracy. Its influence extends over practically every major government

Philippines

agency, as seen in List 3, which enumerates agencies that have availed themselves of AGILE consultants' services. From finance to agriculture, and even to the judicial system, AGILE was able to supply its services.

AGILE and USAID conditionalities

AGILE works in accordance with the USAID-Philippines' Strategic Objective No. 2, 'Improved National Systems for Trade and Investment,' with the following prescribed results: 1) Fiscal Resource Mobilisation and Allocation Improved; 2) Trade and Investment Policies Liberalised; and 3) Financial Markets Improved. AGILE includes all the areas of the said results packages.[13]

This project is claimed to be a step in the evolving USAID-Philippines cooperation for economic growth. AGILE concentrates on policy reform activities, acting as the 'main policy design and implementation vehicle for policy reform work under the Strategic Objective No. 2'. Although the initial policy areas covered by AGILE were competition, and trade and investment, the programme is also tasked with having a hand in any economic policy issue that has an impact at the national level.[14]

Thus, the policy areas in which AGILE is involved are wide-ranging: competition and competitive structure; agriculture; tariff and non-tariff barriers; WTO issues; financial markets, including securities markets; inter-island and overland transportation; industrial relations; intellectual property rights; fiscal policy; telecommunications; development planning and economic statistics; privatisation of public infrastructure; tax administration and microfinance policies.[15]

AGILE's policy work supposedly uses 'a mix of diagnosis, technical assistance and advocacy.'[16] But a look at AGILE's activities

---

List 3: Government agencies that have used AGILE's services[12]

Bangko Sentral ng Pilipinas (BSP)

Department of Finance (DoF)

Department of Budget and Management (DBM)

Securities and Exchange Commission (SEC)

Department of Justice (DoJ)

Department of Agriculture (DA)

Department of Transportation and Communications (DoTC)

Bureau of Customs (BoC)

Bureau of Internal Revenue (BIR)

National Telecommunications Commission (NTC)

Philippines

reveals an alarming picture: *they ensure the implementation of globalisation policies that ultimately benefit corporate interests, by subverting national sovereignty.*

AGILE's Achievements: subverting national sovereignty?
In June 1998, AGILE began operations, with the project's implementation being awarded to a consortium led by Development Alternatives, Inc. (DAI) as prime contractor, and Harvard Institute for International Development, Cesar Virata and Associates and Price Waterhouse Coopers as subcontractors.[17]

DAI is an American corporation registered in Bethesda, Maryland. It describes itself as 'a professional services firm' whose role is 'to provide information that facilitates good decision making and to help translate decisions into action.' It runs many technical assistance projects across the globe, with 13 long-term projects in Asia.[18]

It was DAI's website featuring AGILE that came to the attention of Senator Sergio Osmeña, who delivered a privileged speech questioning AGILE's role in Philippine policy-making.[19]

AGILE boasts a number of significant achievements. But a look at what are described as its major successes, in its first three years of operation, demonstrates how it was gradually restructuring the Philippine economy, to make it more accessible and attractive to US transnational corporations and American investments. (See List 4).

List 4. AGILE's 'major accomplishments', 1998-2001

- Assisted in the enactment of the Electronic Commerce Law, which legally enables electronic transactions in the country;
- Assisted in the enactment of the Countervailing Measures Act, the Anti-Dumping Act and the Safeguard Measures Act, intended to neutralise the adverse effects of unfair trade practices and import surges;
- Assisted in the enactment of the Retail Trade Liberalization Act, allowing foreign firms to engage in retail trade in the Philippines;
- Assisted in the issuing of a circular mandating the use of a uniform system of accounts to enable fair and reasonable rates and tariffs in the telecommunications industry;
- Assisted in the enactment of the Customs Valuation Law and the Establishment of the Super Green Lane to ensure an efficient customs system;
- Assisted the Securities and Exchange Commission in the Rules of Procedure on Corporate Recovery;
- Assisted in the issuing of EO 262, reforming the government procurement system; Provided the DoF with a framework for evaluating and monitoring government's contingent liabilities;
- Assisted in the drafting and enactment of Road User Charges Law;
- Assisted the Department of Interior and Local Governments and DoF to streamline the procedures for the issuing of municipal bonds;
- Assisted in the enactment of the General Banking Act of 2000, which paves the way for ensuring better capitalisation and supervision of the banking industry;
- Assisted in designing the Securities Regulation Code, which promotes the development of capital markets.

Philippines

A number of these claimed accomplishments address complaints of American firms about obstacles to doing business in the Philippines, such as the reform of the government procurement system, reform of the customs system and the passage of the E-Commerce bill. An important achievement, in terms of market access for US corporations, is the liberalisation of retail trade, which allows the entry of transnational corporations (TNCs) into a sector traditionally reserved for Filipino-owned firms. (See case study 1).

Case study 1. AGILE and retail trade liberalisation

The Philippines agreed to liberalise retail trade under the 1994-1997 'exit' programme from the International Monetary Fund (IMF). However, passing legislation liberalising the sector was difficult, because of strong opposition from the retail industry.

The liberalisation of the retail trade was part of AGILE's agenda from its conception. One of the original agenda items, under its Policy Agenda No. 5: Liberalise and Facilitate Investments, was to enact amendments to the 1954 Retail Trade Nationalization Act. The law had been enacted to prevent non-Filipino citizens from gaining a monopoly in an important sector of the economy.

Because of legal challenges in the Supreme Court to such liberalisation laws as the Downstream Oil Industry Deregulation Act (which had been overthrown by the Court in 1996, before a later version of the law was enacted in 1998) and the Mining Act, AGILE provided legal assistance in the drafting of retail trade liberalisation legislation.

According to 'A Revised AGILE Life of Contract Work Plan', dated October 1998, the project would hire three legal specialists as consultants, to undertake a legal analysis of two Bills, then pending in Congress, which focused on competition policy, power sector reform and amendments to the Retail Trade Act. Their expected output was a compilation of draft Bills, legal analysis of, and legal memoranda on the proposed Bills.

Since AGILE was aware of the strong opposition to the liberalisation of the sector, it also arranged for extensive public relations activities to make it more acceptable to the general public.

A DAI 'Statement of Work', dated August 2000, but seemingly concerning activities dating from before that, acknowledged strong resistance to liberalisation from domestic industry. In response to this, DAI decided to 'focus not only on analyzing the efficiency gains from the proposed liberalization of retail trade...(but) would also promote constituency building for the passage of a retail trade liberalization law by March 2000.'

Specific activities undertaken by DAI included: building broad public support, mobilising small and medium-scale enterprises, and informing consumers of the benefits of liberalisation. Consumer advocacy groups such as the Foundation for Economic Freedom would undertake these activities, thus effectively concealing the exact role of US aid in the process.

AGILE's activities finally bore fruit on 7 March 2000, as ousted President Joseph Estrada signed the Retail Trade Liberalization Act of 2000 into law.

Philippines

AGILE also claims to have had a hand in making the Arroyo government accept biotechnology and in paving the way for the commercialisation of genetically modified crops in the country. Case study 2 details the role that AGILE played.

Case study 2: AGILE and the Commercialisation of Biotechnology

Previous administrations, starting with Corazon Aquino, all expressed support for the exploitation of biotechnology in the Philippines. But President Gloria Macapagal-Arroyo seemed to have reversed that position in the early days of her assumption of power.

Arroyo said, during a Malacañang press conference in early February 2001, that her government would no longer allow research on genetically modified (GM) crops. She cited a groundswell of opposition to the introduction of GM crops and foods as the reason for her position.

However, by July 16, she had overturned her pronouncement by approving a policy statement on biotechnology that promotes its 'safe and responsible use'.

On 3 April 2002, the Department of Agriculture issued Administrative Order No.8 — Rules and Regulations for the Importation and Release into the Environment of Plants/ Plants Products Derived from the Use of Modern Biotechnology.

What made the current government change its position on GM crops? Apparently, the visit of the US-Philippines Business Committee of the US-ASEAN Business Council from 22-25 April 2001 affected the president's stand. Commercialisation of GM products was one of the important issues raised by the US business mission during their visit, which also produced a Business Framework Agreement between the US mission and its Philippine counterpart.

AGILE claimed the issuing of the policy statement and the DA guidelines as among its 'achievements' towards commercialising biotechnology products in the country.

According to the DAI 'Statement of Work', dated August 2000, AGILE's assistance in the commercialisation of biotechnology involved the following:

- Reviewing, revising and streamlining guidelines governing the importation and laboratory testing, as well as field trials, of biotechnology products;
- Preparing the guidelines for the commercialisation and marketing of transgenic plants by August 2000, and their subsequent publication by October 2000;
- Supporting the efforts of the US Department of Agriculture in mounting a public information campaign on the benefits of biotechnology products and in assuaging fears about their use and application.

As expected, the first beneficiary of government's new policy on biotechnology was the US agrochemical giant Monsanto, which was granted a permit by the DA's Bureau of Plant Industry for the commercial planting of its Yieldgard Bt corn in the country on 4 December 2002.

Philippines

Technical assistance or manipulation?

Reacting to the claims of AGILE, Senator Sergio Osmeña said, 'We have essentially here a group funded by the United States government, or their funding agency called USAID. It practically brags that they are directing, subverting, influencing, manipulating our very own economic policy.'[20]

AGILE personnel, however, reiterated that it is merely a technical assistance project designed to promote investments and accelerate economic growth in the Philippines.'[21]

In the Senate hearings on the group's activities, some disturbing revelations surfaced, making it clear that AGILE is actively involved in lobbying for policy changes and even in the drafting of laws.

During the 19 February hearing, for instance, Senator Manuel Villar said AGILE was involved in all phases of legislative work. Senator Villar cited the enactment of the Corporate Recovery Act, wherein he observed that AGILE personnel were present at every hearing, 'shepherding' the Bill, involving themselves in the Technical Working Group and drafting the final details of the Act.[22]

He added that AGILE's participation even extended to the bicameral meetings and the formulation of the Act's implementing rules and regulations.

The senator also pointed out that AGILE-sponsored Bills were given priority over those on education, health, local government and other areas. He underscored the fact that the participation of AGILE in the legislative process has been grossly underestimated.[23]

Aid for lobby groups to push liberalisation

AGILE officers admitted they had provided aid to lobby groups that were aggressively working for policy changes that would liberalise the airline and shipping industries.

Dr David Tardif-Douglin, Managing Partner of AGILE, disclosed to the Senate that DAI had funded public relations firm Policy Research Information Strategy and Media Services, Inc. (PRISM) to do an advocacy campaign for air transport liberalisation and ports modernisation for two advocacy coalitions.[24]

Dr Tardif-Douglin said this funding was within the scope of AGILE's work statement, which includes providing assistance for air transport liberalisation and ports modernisation to increase competition.

AGILE's work plan said that PRISM designed, managed and implemented all media efforts for the Freedom to Fly Coalition and the Coalition for Shipping and Ports Modernization from 15 March to 31 July 2001.[25]

The plan pointed out successes, such as the resumption of air flights to Taiwan and increased capacity to key markets like Malaysia and Singapore. It also boasted about halting the implementation of EO 59 (issued by ex-President Joseph Estrada in 1998) and the establishment of direct competition to government's port monopoly.

EO 59 mandated the unification of all facility operators and service providers in every government port into one corporation. Estrada revoked the order in 2000.

Senator John Osmeña III, charging AGILE with having an ulterior motive beyond providing technical assistance for the Philippines, stressed that AGILE worked against a presidential order when it funded a campaign against EO 59. He also noted that, though he filed the open skies Bill given to him by the Freedom to Fly Coalition, he was unaware that AGILE had drafted it.[26]

Where is Poverty Reduction?

While AGILE pursues the globalisation of the Philippines, it leaves out one main goal of development aid — the eradication of poverty.

Philippines

In fact, as the economy continues to be restructured according to the designs of the US, more and more Filipinos become mired in poverty, marginalised and deprived of basic social and democratic rights.

As of 2000, the government estimated that 32 million Filipinos were poor. The latest Annual Poverty Indicator Survey reports that, of the families belonging to the lowest 40% of the income bracket, only 56% has access to electricity, 67% has access to secondary education, and 70% has access to safe drinking water. Unemployment is rising, with some 3.6 million Filipinos jobless as of October 2003.[27]

The AGILE experience illustrates how aid money can distort governance and further limit the rights of people to empowerment and genuine development.

The USAID funding of projects like AGILE runs counter to development cooperation; it is undeniably a form of foreign interference in national affairs. It undermines democratic governance and hinders the Filipino people from choosing and pursuing their own course to economic and social progress.

USAID's Economic Development and Governance programme reflects the wish list of US transnational corporations that seek to remove every single trade and investment measure put in place to protect the domestic economy.

Philippines

Notes

1 Senator John Osmena III claimed that the AGILE web page, which was still posted three days prior to the Senate hearing, was deleted from the website of DAI. Committee of the Whole Journal of Meeting, p. 10. Senate of the Philippines, Twelfth Congress, Second Regular Session, 28 February 2003.

2 DAI website (www.dai.com) now features EGTA in its Back to Asia Projects.

3 USAID website (www.usaid-ph.gov)

4 ibid.

5 ibid.

6 ibid.

7 US Trade Representative website (www.ustr.gov)

8 USAID website (www.usaid-ph.gov)

9 Philippine Assistance Program Support Project (PAPS - Project No. 492-0452) AGILE Joint Project Implementation Letter No. 55, signed by Kenneth G. Schofield of USAID and concurred by Roberto F. de Ocampo as Chairman of CCPAP on 21November 1997.

10 Project No. 492-0452.

11 AGILE Joint Project Implementation Letter No. 55 states that the DOF shall act as the lead agency of the government of the Philippines in implementing AGILE. It will also chair the Steering Committee, which shall hold semi-annual meetings.

12 DAI website (www.dai.com)

13 AGILE Joint Project Implementation Letter No. 55.

14 ibid.

15 ibid.

16 ibid.

17 Dr David Tardif-Douglin, a directly salaried staff member of DAI, explained that DAI along with the other firms was hired by USAID to implement AGILE. Committee of the Whole Journal of Meeting, p. 10. Senate of the Philippines, Twelfth Congress, Second Regular Session, 28 February 2003.

18 DAI website (www.dai.com)

19 Minutes of session. Senate of the Philippines, Twelfth Congress, Second Regular Session, 18 February 2003.

20 ibid.

21 Statement of Dr. Ramon Clarete, AGILE Chief of Party, to the Senate. Committee of the Whole Journal of Meeting, p. 2. Senate of the Philippines, Twelfth Congress, Second Regular Session, 28 February 2003.

22 Committee of the Whole Journal of Meeting, p. 2. Senate of the Philippines, Twelfth Congress, Second Regular Session, 19 February 2003.

23 ibid.

24 Dr. Clarete denied funding such activity but Dr Tardif-Douglin admitted he knew about the contract with PRISM, which was worth P3.721 million.

25 Senator John Osmena III read portions of the contract to the body. Committee of the Whole Journal of Meeting, p. 14. Senate of the Philippines, Twelfth Congress, Second Regular Session, 28 February 2003.

26 Committee of the Whole Journal of Meeting, pp. 14-15. Senate of the Philippines, Twelfth Congress, Second Regular Session, 28 February 2003.

27 Data from the National Statistics Office.

The problematics of 'governance' in the Arab experience

Chafic Cheaib, Arab NGOs Network on Development (ANND)

The globalisation process has given rise to a number of new development approaches and concepts, the most significant of which is the concept of 'governance'. The use of this concept was, and still is, controversial in development literature and among researchers interested in the Arabic region. Attempts to arabise the concept led to three different proposed translations. This suggested that the meaning of the concept was not clear and needed to be redefined through discussion, whereas it had been adopted in development literature *before* it was explained or understood.

The concept of 'governance' has replaced that of 'empowerment' in development literature. Empowerment was elaborated through a series of evaluations at the political, economic and social levels. It also focused on assessing liberalism and criticising the adoption of market liberalisation and economic legislation without taking into account the social impact. It criticised the unjust and unequal relations between the North and the South. Democracy, transparency and participation were considered as necessary political and economic conditions and essential components in any development process.

Such clear and specific standards have been replaced by new, highly ambiguous expressions. If we examine the new theories on 'governance', we can easily detect this changing trend. This change has happened at a time when it became clear that the promises made during the Rio Summit, in 1992, had not been kept. On the contrary, today more than ever the world is suffering from poverty and environmental degradation, while in certain parts of the world wealth is increasing.

The concept of 'good governance' is presented as a means of regulating the performance of both parties in the relationship, in a framework governed by globalisation. 'Good governance' is used as a tool by the dominating power in the relationship to verify whether the countries of the South are respecting the standards and basis of 'good governance', as defined by WTO, World Bank and IMF – economic liberalisation, structural adjustment, privatisation, reducing the state's role, fighting corruption and, more recently, fighting terrorism.

On this basis, rich countries decide whether to give poor countries development assistance, or reschedule their debts, or grant them economic and commercial facilities, or allow them to join international and regional institutions. In the framework of these adopted policies, the attention shifts from the main element, which is the

Middle East

relationship between the two parties (in its political, economic, social, and intellectual dimensions). This relationship is the foundation that allows us to understand and analyse the historic dimension and the results of the current situation, with the increase in underdevelopment, poverty, and the degradation of living conditions.

The social model of 'governance'

When speaking of building human capabilities in order to reduce poverty, it is worth noting that this is a first attempt to define a problem present all over the Arab world, albeit with some distinctions between regions. Despite the lack of necessary data, Arab countries are considered among the poorest in the world (except for the Gulf countries) according to the World Bank statistics for 2001/ 2002. Although it has been widely recognised that the problem in the Arab world is very serious, and is likely to worsen, the social model of governance tried, simply, to define the problem and examined its main characteristics. It also tried to propose a package of general policies aimed at eradicating poverty. The package focused on procedures and completely ignored political, economic and social policies.

Some analysts argue that in the war against poverty the centre of attention has shifted from modifying economic policies and integrating them in radical social policies to a focus on governance. Therefore, universal (and national) policies are no longer responsible for causing poverty. The responsibility lies now with poor countries and their governments. These governments lack the necessary knowledge that allows them to govern society and help people in poverty. Poor countries, on this analysis, are poor simply because they don't know how to become rich, and how to seize and benefit from the opportunities of globalisation. This

is due to bad 'governance' and lack of knowledge. [On] this pretext, bad governance became the primary cause of poverty in the world, and good governance the only solution for it. The great distortions in international and national economies, which are the main cause of poverty, were completely ignored.

The roles and responsibilities of political and economic forces (internal and external) are usually completely absent from any discussion regarding the issue of poverty in the Arab region.

Political perspectives

All Arabic approaches to 'governance' consider that the exercise of political power at all levels (based on the principles of participation, transparency and accountability), in addition to economic and social practices, helps to define and to evaluate the impact of this new concept. These approaches focus on political priorities and on examining public and popular state institutions.

The lack of a scientific political basis in discussing issues related to 'good governance' increases ambiguity. The 'evangelical-ethical' trend we find in development literature is thus subject to various interpretations. In the end, what really counts is the balance of power and interests, while ambiguous promises, present in every declaration, in every memorandum and every conference, remain unfulfilled.

The powers dominating the current international relations network have a different understanding of 'good governance' from that of those concerned with the interests of social forces and the basic mission of sustainable human development. They are trying today to protect their regimes, through an adjustment policy that ignores calls for change and the objectives of change.

Middle East

The true meaning of these issues can only be tested in practice, at the political, economic and historic levels. This understanding should enable 'the powers' to express clear and precise positions in a particular region. They should be able to define whether the international system is capable of accomplishing international missions aimed at strengthening and protecting the human rights charter, in all its aspects, starting with the right to live in dignity, democracy and development.

When, however, they are faced with the realities of the Arab region, as was the case with the 'Arab Human Development Report', they abandon generalities and positions of principle (that characterise all international reports) and express specific positions and orientations. The report has made great contributions on several levels, especially in its approach to development issues in the Arab world. However, it did not discuss the specific and essential problems of Arab countries, especially issues related to 'good governance'. Not only did the report not deal with these problems, it also focused on some partial aspects of democratic openness and considered them encouraging.

The approach doesn't even examine the crisis affecting the regimes, or the challenges that have entered a critical phase since the second Gulf war and the invasion of Kuwait. This critical phase continued when Israeli forces reoccupied Palestinian Authority territories, a few days after the presentation of the Arab peace initiative (during the Beirut summit in 2002). This approach is very tolerant towards Arab official regimes. Thus it avoids discussing the plans being prepared for this region, and stated during the 1990s in what is called 'The Middle Eastern Project'.

International forces and their regional allies, especially within the Arab official regimes, are responsible for underdevelopment in the Arab region and for obstructing the development process at all levels. External powers are protecting the dominant powers of the official Arab regimes ignoring all the requirements of 'good governance', such as democracy, accountability, transparency and human rights.

The same economic, political and social forces, whose interest lies in achieving the democratic aspects of 'good governance', are striving for the success of the democratic development project. They must be challenged forcefully. At stake, is the biggest social coalition that emanated from the slogans and missions of the Rio Summit. We need to protect it from the wild military globalisation that is dominating today's world.

Poor countries, on this analysis, are poor simply because they don't know how to become rich, and how to seize and benefit from the opportunities of globalisation. This is due to bad 'governance' and lack of knowledge.

Part IV
Latin America

Decentralisation processes in Latin America: achievements and challenges for international cooperation[1]

Felipe Caballero & Mariano Valderrama[2]

In this essay, we assess the interventions of international cooperation in the area of decentralisation and local development in Latin America. Based on the results, we offer a number of reflections on the form in which international cooperation could more adequately adapt to local situations in the region, promoting socio-economic development, citizenship, and democratic institutionality.

The importance that issues of government and local development have acquired, in the work of international cooperation and development organisations during the last decade, is obvious. It is thought that local governments provide the opportunity for greater participation by the population in decision making and that they represent an important factor in the democratisation of society. The collection edited by Charles Reilly[3] reports on this new tendency, which is undoubtedly related to the decentralisation and reform of the State in Latin America, and which is being put into practice by a number of countries in the region. It is also found to be associated with the process of 'redemocratisation' — such as a return to the electoral system for local authorities — after authoritarian periods or as a product of peace accords.

The support of countries like Germany, Canada, United States, Italy and Switzerland for the decentralisation process, is related to the history of the decentralised political and economic configuration in these nations.

This tendency not only influences the actions of official cooperation, it also affects private aid. A study undertaken by the Latin American Association for Popular Organisations (ALOP) highlights the new importance that Latin American NGOs have been assigning to the strengthening of civil society at the level of local development. In Uruguay, the priority that the vast majority of NGOs have accorded to local concerns is notable. There are agreements in such areas as nursery management, youth centres, health programmes, regulations for precarious settlements and so on. In Colombia, NGOs are allocating a new level of priority to the issues of management, development and consensus building at local level. This coincides with the fact that municipal government resources increased considerably, after the passing of the 1993

Latin America

Law 60. Something similar occurred in Chile, where local governments' own income sources increased by 36% between 1985 and 1991. NGOs have joined planning committees and are frequently responsible for carrying out the proposed projects. This changes their approach to dialogue with the people and with governments. Brazil has had noteworthy experience in participation and budget allocation at the municipal level, with popular administrators, and in numerous councils (federal and state as well as municipal) linked to particular public policies and/or defence of the rights of certain sectors of the population (children and adolescents). This is the result of the process of institutionalisation of popular participation embodied in the 1988 Constitution.

In Bolivia, the Popular Participation Law passed in 1994, decentralised the budgetary process in the Republic and instituted mechanisms for the participation of social organisations in local management.[4] In Peru, a survey of a sample of 89 NGOs highlighted the fact that the majority of these organisations work with local governments. In recent years, coordinating bodies have been set up by the Metropolitan Municipality of Lima and NGOs, with programmes in health, food and lodging or urban development.

We will focus our attention on local development support programmes in Bolivia, a country in which international cooperation has played a very important role, representing about 50% of investments. Decentralisation in Bolivia is of particular interest, not only because of a significant transfer of public resources (the Popular Participation Law granted the municipalities one fifth of the Republic's budget) and the leading role assigned to the municipalities, but also because of the way in which the population has been integrated into local development planning.

International cooperation in Bolivia

The decentralisation policy is reflected well in the area of international cooperation where various organisations have begun to develop programmes directed at local development. A rapid overview of implemented programmes follows:[5]

European Commission: food security support programme (PASA)

This was a five-year programme, which began in 1997. It had US$60 million in financing and had as its principal objective the funding of programmes and projects aimed at reducing food insecurity in the poorest municipalities. Its main efforts were directed at: promoting economic activities to develop agricultural production, guiding investment for projects that were complementary to other development actions, and strengthening popular participation methods and administrative decentralisation, through the financing of projects that form part of municipal, departmental and national development strategies.

Its intervention strategy was based on two complementary components. The territorial component covered 78 municipalities, where local and regional projects were supported. The sectoral component involved support for programmes of national or sub-national interest.

There have been numerous criticisms of the implementation of PASA. It is felt that national government and public departmental bodies have used their influence to ensure the allocation of jobs and resources to further party interests and clientelism. For this reason, international donors and public opinion suggest that the public management of departments and social programmes needs to be reformed. In the case of PASA, it would be convenient for the European Commission to push for greater social monitoring, setting up civil society

Latin America

Table 5. Characteristics of PASA-funded projects

TYPOLOGY	NUMBER	US$ MILLIONS	%
Processing facilities	2	0.02	0.04
Warehouse facilities	2	0.03	0.05
Support for the tourist sector	2	0.17	0.29
Commercialisation services	5	0.18	0.31
Emergency actions	1	0.69	1.20
Institutional strengthening	5	0.92	1.59
Preinvestment	34	1.68	2.91
Support for farming production	24	7.54	13.06
Risk precautions	71	10.45	18.10
Training, technical assistance services	45	13.64	23.62
Roads infrastructure	115	22.42	38.83
	306	57.74	100.00

Source: PASA Minutes 1997-2002.

monitoring mechanisms for this type of programme.

Germany: support programme for decentralised public management and the fight against poverty (PADEP)

This programme is meant to increase efficiency and transparency in decentralised public management. It considers three areas of intervention:

a. Regulatory and institutional frameworks for decentralisation policies,
b. Sectoral, territorial and institutional development strategies,
c. Independent income, transfers, credit market and capital for municipalities and prefectures.

In the municipalities of Chaco and Norte de Potosí, and corresponding associations of municipalities, as well as in intermediary municipalities for departmental capitals, PADEP supports the strengthening of management capacity, which includes the quality of access to public services, local strategies against poverty, financial management, and conflict management. Cooperation with departmental prefectures is aimed at strengthening strategic planning.

Denmark: sectoral programme of support for decentralisation and popular participation

Between 1997 and 2002, the Sectoral Programme of Support for Decentralisation and Popular Participation were implemented

Latin America

through the Danish International Cooperation Agency (DANIDA), and covered 27 municipalities in the most economically depressed areas in the departments of Chuquisaca and Potosí. Its method of operation was the transfer of resources to municipalities that had prioritised productive infrastructure (roads, bridges, irrigation systems) in local development plans. The total expenditure amounted to US$15 million.

Denmark has decided to concentrate its future cooperation with Bolivia on the National Indigenous Development Programme, including sanitation and native community land title processes in the highlands and lowlands of Bolivia; it will no longer, therefore, allocate resources for municipalities.

Netherlands: programme to implement popular participation and administrative decentralisation

A donation of US$14.6 million from the Dutch government made the implementation of this programme possible between 1994 and 2002. It was aimed at strengthening the institutional capacity of the 314 municipalities and the nine prefectures in Bolivia, to enable them to carry out their executive responsibilities in effectively. It included: the contracting of technical personnel for the National Secretariat for Popular Participation, currently the Vice-Ministry of Popular Participation, support in obtaining legal status for local social organisations, training on the Popular Participation Law in approximately 150 municipalities; and financial support for the setting up of local development organisation.

Aid for decentralisation and popular participation was channelled through the Ministry of Sustainable Development and the vice-ministries of Popular Participation and Government Coordination.

The programme allowed greater popular participation in planning, execution, and the monitoring and control of municipal and prefectural development plans.

The Netherlands also supports the recently established Federation of Municipal Associations (FAM) in carrying out its functions. These consist of defending municipal interests vis-à-vis the national government and providing technical services to its members.

The Dutch government is also developing a programme of cooperation in Productive Rural Development (DPR) in Bolivia. This has the aim of fighting poverty through the promotion of sustainable economic growth, improvement of income levels and the creation of employment in rural areas.

Switzerland: Rural Development Programme (PADER) and Municipal Democracy Support Programme (PADEM)

The Rural Economic Development Promotion Programme has been underway since 1998, as part of an agreement between the Bolivian government and the Swiss Agency for Development and Cooperation (COSUDE). With an allocation of US$1.9 million, it is directed at generating a new vision of rural economic development, based on economic stimulation at the municipal, departmental and national levels. The target of PADER's efforts is the private investor (small, medium-sized producer, processor and marketer).

The programme has been criticised for concentrating its support on current, successful experiences in high profit areas, instead of developing new initiatives.

Swiss cooperation also finances PADEM, which aims to contribute to the equitable and sustainable development of rural municipalities, through the active participation of communities, as part of the implementation of the Popular Participation Law.

Among the activities being developed in the programme are workshops with indigenous peasant organisations in selected municipalities, municipal workshops and the preparation of proposals by various local actors, training for local promoters in the municipalities, regional courses, and mass dissemination of information from the municipalities.

PADEM operates directly in 18 selected municipalities in the departments of La Paz, Chuquisaca, Oruro, Potosí, Beni, Santa Cruz and Cochabamba. From these, its influence spreads to almost a hundred neighbouring municipalities. The first phase of the project went from April 1996 to March 1999. A second phase was implemented from April 1999 to March 2002. A third phase was begun in April 2002.

World Bank: Rural Community Development Project

From 1994 to 1997, the Rural Communities Development Project (PDCR I) was carried out through the National Secretariat for Popular Participation, now the Vice-Ministry of Popular Participation. It included a provision for institutional strengthening at the municipal level, with a budget line of US$4 million, for: the formation of a consultative team within the National Secretariat for Popular Participation; the accreditation of NGOs, consulting firms and independent professionals in participatory municipal planning methodology; technical follow-up and evaluation of processes and products stemming from the participatory formulation of 90 municipal development plans; and, finally, the monitoring and evaluation of 1600 projects involving investment in productive infrastructure, which were at that time submitted to the Peasant Development Fund.

From 1998 to 2002, the Participatory Rural Investment Project (PDCR II) used a loan of US$5 million for the strengthening of institutions at the municipal level. This was aimed at: consolidating the consultative team of the Vice-Ministry of Popular Participation; undertaking technical monitoring and evaluation of the processes and products of participatory formulation of 100 municipal and 13 indigenous district, development plans; as well as the training of 35 supervisory committees as social auditors, as defined by the Popular Participation Law.

Private aid: Network of Promotions and Education Networks Programme (AIPE): 'Productive Peasant Municipalities' (2000 to 2002)

The Productive Municipalities programme, implemented by AIPE with financial support from the Dutch NGO NOVIB, contributed to the development of productive municipalities in order to strengthen the peasant economy, stimulate local economic development in an equitable manner and reduce levels of rural poverty. It was developed during the three-year period 2000 to 2002 with a budget of US$387,272, with the intention of continuing during the 2003 to 2005 period. The network has 29 members, of whom 15 participate in the Productive Municipalities programme, albeit with different levels of commitment.

AIPE prepared the conceptual and operational proposal for the programme, based on concrete experiences of its members, in coordination with other institutions such as PADER/COSUDE, GTZ (German Technical Cooperation) and the Vice-Ministry of Strategic Planning and Popular Participation. The coordinated effort facilitated the preparation of a Guide for the Formulation of Municipal Economic Development Strategies (EDEM)[6].

Latin America

The municipal economic development strategy was put forward as a medium to long-term process as part of the concept and methodology of participatory municipal planning. It describes the State/Civil Society relationship on development matters in municipalities and with associations of municipalities. It is directed at creating a shared vision of municipal economic development and enhancing consensus among actors, applying the principles of complementarity, concurrence and subsidisation among public and private investors.

The AIPE Productive Municipalities project has been guided by the following objectives:

- Modification of 55 municipal development plans, introducing the concept of Productive Municipalities;
- Preparation of analytical summaries of experiences related to the productive development model;
- Training of member NGO promoters.

Bolivia Assessment

The relevance of the new municipal leadership role in local development and the democratic life of the country is unquestionable. The role of promoter and consensus builder, in political and development spheres, breaks away from the centralist and charity-oriented vision of public policies. The popular participation method has democratised management of local government. It has given the peasant population more influence, counteracting the former practice of giving the urban population a disproportionate weight in decision making, even in predominantly rural municipalities. There is agreement that municipalities use resources more efficiently, and more in line with people's needs than departmental prefectures and national Government do.

Despite the advances that have been made, there are still some significant obstacles to local economic and social development. Democratisation has not been extensive in departmental governments, where the authorities (Prefects) are designated directly by the central government, using partisan criteria. Prefects control a large portion of public expenditures (45% of the Republic's budget), which results in a high level of managerial inefficiency and corruption. For their part, departmental councils have not managed to convert themselves into instruments for participatory and transparent resource management. There is also a lack of synergy and complementarity among municipal and departmental roleplayers. This situation presents a serious problem for aid operations.

There is also great frustration with the inoperability of national development and compensation funds. As we have pointed out, the resources from the Productive and Social Investment Fund should be at the disposal of municipal investment projects. However, of more than 3,600 projects presented by municipal governments to this Fund, to date only 12 have reached the tender stage. International cooperation has encouraged the formulation of municipal development plans, which include investment projects presented to the Productive and Social Investment Fund and the Peasant Development Fund, whose procedures are completely bureaucratic.

Another important obstacle, preventing local development programmes from having greater impact, is the lack of clear rural development policies and the limitations that global economic policies impose on marginal areas. International cooperation has been promoting local productive development, without being completely clear under what conditions, and in which sectors, it can be achieved. The evidence shows that under the

Latin America

current neoliberal economic system, the Productive Municipalities model does not have the same viability, nor the same methods of operation in different areas. There are various examples of projects implemented in municipalities (such as schools and medical centres) that have subsequently been abandoned, when the population migrates for lack of economic alternatives.

Perspectives on decentralised aid operations

In the light of the above assessment, we present several recommendations regarding the way in which donors could better adapt to local situations in the region to promote socio-economic development, citizenship and democratic institutionality:

1 The work of international cooperation should be continued and strengthened at the local level. The assessment reveals the importance that local development strategies have acquired in the democratisation of political life and the economic development of Latin America. New opportunities have been opened up for the exercise of citizenship, especially for vast sectors of the rural population. It has been proven that possibilities for participation and the fiscal review of socio-economic development programmes are greater at the local than the departmental and national level. It would be advisable to give priority in Bolivia to local, rather than departmental aid, and to consider reforming departmental management (with regard to democratisation and transparency) as an urgent matter.

2 The case of Bolivia highlights the importance of decentralised aid through private development organisations. At a time when, for example, the European

Union is considering reducing funds for this type of work, it is worthwhile underlining its importance. NGOs in the Andean and Latin America regions have been providing valuable examples of building a common approach to local development with municipalities, local public bodies, social organisations and other actors. They have also played a role in monitoring and social oversight of public policies and programmes.

3 The participation of civil society in foreign aid programmes should be reinforced. Up to now, the design of country strategies has not involved the participation of national counterparts, or the opinion of civil society. However, this contradicts the pronouncements on 'ownership' by the South in international cooperation. It also contrasts with the progress made by other aid agencies. In the same way, it would be important to reinforce social monitoring of foreign aid programmes by civil society.

4 Transparency in the management of international aid should be increased. Information available through the internet is generic and incomplete. It does not allow users to be informed about details, the progress of expenditures, advances in project implementation, or the results of evaluations.

5 Greater coherence and complementarity must be sought between aid programmes on decentralisation and local development, and macro programmes and policies.

We have already referred to problems that have been encountered in working to democratise the management of social and investment programmes (which include support from external donors) to make them more transparent and to avoid their use for

Latin America

political clientelism. As we have seen, many of the programmes directed by international cooperation, in agreement with national governments, have not been characterised by an efficient and transparent administration of resources. In Bolivia, we need to rethink the functioning of the Social Investment Fund and the operations of departmental prefectures. The democratisation of departmental governments constitutes a central task. This will have an impact at the local level.

We also need to rethink macroeconomic policies and market systems, as they affect the viability of local development, within the context of the national and international

economic scene. Indicators show there is a growing deterioration of living standards in the interior. There are few zones that have the comparative advantages that would allow them to compete successfully in the international market, or even in their own national market.

Decentralisation in Bolivia is of particular interest, not only because of a significant transfer of public resources... and the leading role assigned to the municipalities, but also because of the way in which the population has been integrated into local development planning.

Bibliograpy

AROCENA, José: El desarrollo local, un desafío contemporáneo (Local Development, a Contemporary Challenge), Caracas-Montevideo, CLAEH & Nueva Sociedad, 1995

Association of Municipalities of Peru and others Municipios rurales y gestión local, (Rural Municipalities and Local Management), Lima. 1998.

Barrenechea Lercari, Carlos and Julio Díaz Palacios (editors). : Desarrollo local. Visiones y propuestas en el marco de la globalización y descentralización (Local Development. Visions and Proposals in the Context of Globalisation and Decentralisation), Lima, ESAN-USAID, Local Governments Development Project. 1999.

Castillo, Marlene (editor). Planificación, participación y concertación en ámbitos rurales de la sierra peruana 1994-98, (Planning, participation and consensus building at the rural level in the Peruvian sierra 1994-98) Lima, PACT-USAID. 1998.

Coanqui, Calixto. El modelo PREDES: Crónica de una esperanza frustrada (The PREDES model: Chronicle of frustrated hopes), in: Ruralter magazine, N° 16-17, 1997-98, La Paz. 1998.

Graduate School of Business Administration. Gobiernos locales y desarrollo en América Latina: Los casos de Perú, Bolivia, Colombia y Chile, (Local governments and development in Latin America: The cases of Peru, Bolivia, Colombia and Chile) Lima, ESAN-USAID, Local Governments Development Project. 1998.

García de Chu, Inés and María del Carmen Piazza (editors). Sociedad y gobierno local: Espacios de concertación y democracia, (Society and local government: Opportunities for consensus and democracy) Lima, Desco. 1998.

Grompone, Romeo. La descentralización y el desprecio de la razón política (Decentralisation and contempt for political reason), in: Bruno Revesz (editor) Descentralización y gobernabilidad en tiempos de globalización, (Decentralisation and governability in times of globalisation) Lima, CIPCA, IEP. 1998.

Haour, Bernardo. Globalización y descentralización vista desde una ONG de provincia (Globalisation and decentralisation as seen by a provincial NGO), in: Bruno Revesz (editor): Descentralización y gobernabilidad en tiempos de globalización, (Decentralisation and governability in times of globalisation) Lima, CIPCA, IEP. 1998.

Negrón, Federico and Valderrama, Mariano (editors). Concertación Regional y Cooperación Internacional (Regional Consensus and International Cooperation), Lima, ALOP-CEPES-IFCB, 2001.

PACT Planificación participativa y concertación en ámbitos rurales de la sierra peruana (Planning, participation and consensus building at the rural level in the Peruvian sierra), Lima. 1998.

Programa de Desarrollo Local XLAEH: Desarrollo local en la globalización (XLAEH: Local Development Programme, Local Development in the context of globalisation), Montevideo, CLAEH, 1999

Latin America

Quedena Enrique. Descentralización y gestión estratégica del desarrollo local, Bolivia, Ecuador y Perú (Decentralisation and strategic management of local development, Bolivia, Ecuador and Peru), Lima, School for Development and RURALTER. 2002.

Reilly, Charles A. New urban policies, NGOs and the Latin American decentralisation. Arlington, Virginia (U.S.): Interamerican Foundation. 1994.

Romero, Ana María, Julio Díaz Palacios, Maria Rosa Boggio and Giovanni Bonfiglio. «Fortaleciendo los gobiernos locales. La experiencia del PDGL-ESAN» (Strengthening local governments, the Experience of PDGL-ESAN), Lima, ESAN-USAID. 1998.

Salazar, Carlos (editor). *Espacios de concertación para el desarrollo rural* (Opportunities for consensus-building in rural development), Lima, Desco. 1998.

SER-ITDG 'Las municipalidades y su papel en la democratización y el desarrollo del país» (Municipalities and their role in the country's democratisation and development), II Mayors' Seminar, Lima, May. 1998.

Training workshop for peasant mayors: 'Tejiendo nuestra democracia' (Weaving our democracy), Lima, CCP, CEPES, CEAS, CICDA, SER, GPC and RIAD. 1999.

URIOSTE, Miguel: Desarrollo Rural con Participación Popular (Rural Development with Popular Participation), La Paz, Tierra Foundation, 2002

URIOSTE, Miguel. Bolivia: descentralización municipal y participación popular (Bolivia: municipal decentralisation and popular participation), Lima, III Session of the Decentralisation Forum. 2002.

Notes

1 This chapter has been edited by the Reality of Aid Management Committee and has been translated from the original Spanish by Susan Murdock. The edited English version has been reviewed by the author.

2 Felipe Caballero is a Bolivian economist and independent consultant. Mariano Valderrama is coordinator of the working group on international cooperation of the Latin American Association of Development Organizations (ALOP) and is a researcher with the 'Citizen Proposal' Group, a Peruvian NGO platform that promotes the decentralisation process.

3 Charles Reilly (editor): New urban policies, NGOs and municipal governments in Latin American democratisation). Arlington, Virginia (U.S.): Interamerican Foundation, 1994.

4 For more on the topic of the NGO/local governments relationship, see the Urban Poverty and Development Magazine, No. 5 (FICONG) on municipal NGOs, their relation to local development programmes. FICONG has also edited a book on the same theme in Ecuador.

5 Much of the information on international cooperation projects in Bolivia was provided by the economist Felipe Caballero.

6 'Methodological Guide for Further Developing the Municipal Planning Process related to Economic Development' (EDEM). This was incorporated into the 'Guide for the Elaboration and Modification of Municipal Development Plans' (PDM's), by the Ministry of Sustainable Development and Planning (2000).

Empowerment of people in poverty and civil society participation in international cooperation[1]

Mariano Valderrama, Peruvian Citizen Proposal Group[2]

Recently, the theme of the struggle against poverty and the focus on rights-based development strategies have won a new prominence within the international donor community. The proclamation of the Millennium Development Goals in United Nations forums, agreements reached at Summits and as part of the Monterrey Consensus, and the weight now placed on the struggle against poverty by the international donor community, giving greater voice and leadership to people in poverty, attest to this new outlook.

In this essay, we will try to assess the progress that has been made, paying special attention to multilateral organisations (IDB, World Bank and the European Union) and taking a close look at the area of social programmes and decentralisation that offer special opportunities for development with a rights focus.

We will assess international donor approaches, policies and programmes, with respect to the rights of people in poverty and the participation of the population in aid programmes, including the following aspects:

a) A mapping of the various opportunities and mechanisms for public participation in the programmes of the multilateral banks in Peru and an analysis of their impact.

b) A review of concrete policies applied by the World Bank and the IDB in Peru, to analyse the coherence between discourse and practice and to identify critical points for advocacy work. Through a succinct mapping of financial assistance provided by the World Bank and IDB, we will examine two other programmes: the National Compensation and Social Development Fund (FONCODES) and the National Programme for Management of Watershed and Soil Conservation (PRONAMACHCS).

c) An examination of the new scenario regarding the incorporation of the rights of the poor and their participation in aid programmes. We will focus our attention on processes of decentralisation and of the reorganisation and transference of social programmes to the local govern-ments, examining the role of international donors, and the possibility of advocating greater participation by the poorest sectors of the population in these processes.

Latin America

Dialogue between multilateral institutions and civil society on stategies for the struggle against poverty and for empowerment and citizen participation in Peru

World Bank
We will briefly review the various calls made by the World Bank, for the formulation of proposals such as 'Country Strategies' and 'Strategies for the Fight against Poverty', with civil society participation.

In 1993, the World Bank and the executive of the Ministers Council in Peru, convened the first forum on poverty, bringing together public functionaries, donors, NGOs, academics and business representatives. In 1999, a second forum was held, in which five priority areas were identified – nutrition, health, education, water and sanitation. Regional meetings were held in Cusco, Tarapoto and Piura. A diagnostic analysis was carried out and strategies defined for each area. The third forum, developed between 2000 and 2001, focused on the issue of poverty and employment, while the fourth focused on decentralisation.[3]

The Bank has also worked with the National Social Development Conference (CNADES) and the Roundtable on the Struggle against Poverty, and has held consultations and developed projects, with indigenous populations and groups of Afro-Peruvians.

Among the most interesting World Bank initiatives to promote citizen participation and the rights of people in poverty, are the following:

- At the end of 2001, the World Bank, together with DFID, promoted the study 'The Voices of the Poor in Peru' to analyse the extent of popular participation. Guidelines developed in a 1999 global study were applied to our country.[4]

- Civil society leaders have been consulted on the new World Bank assistance strategy.
- The website 'Window on Civil Society', sponsored by the World Bank, is offered as a space to facilitate citizens exercising their right to monitor the institutions charged with administering the State's resources.
- With the 'Cuanto Institute', Citizen Rating Cards have been developed, enabling people to voice opinions on the quality of social programme services.
- Consultants have been hired to provide independent analyses of the budget.
- Training modules on strategic planning and participatory budgeting have been promoted.
- At Development Fairs, contests have been held to encourage civil society projects.
- One of the interesting experiences in promoting citizen participation was the Social Monitoring System (SIVISO) for the empowerment of the poor. This was led by the Public Defender's Office, with support from the Ministry of Economy and Finance and the Interministerial Committee on Social Affairs, with assistance from the World Bank Technical Assistance department.

The follow-up on the various projects was problematic, owing to the limited human and financial resources available.

Finally, we should draw attention to the emphasis placed by the World Bank on the issues of empowerment, citizen participation and transparency in negotiations of social reform programme loans. Capacity building is to be undertaken in rural communities and local civil society for participatory planning, social monitoring and the transparency of public programmes for poverty reduction. Nevertheless, as we will see, the

Latin America

participation of the people in the design, management, and evaluation of the projects is very secondary and limited.

Interamerican Development Bank
Dialogue between the Interamerican Development Bank and civil society in Peru is a recent development. Under the authoritarian government, the IDB representative in Peru shared the *Fujimorisimo* hostile attitude toward civil society organisations. There has been a self-critical evaluation of the process and the IDB has convened civil society representatives to discuss its country strategy for Peru.

The IDB's dialogue with civil society began in 2000, with a series of preliminary meetings to gather opinions and suggestions on the Bank's policies and activities in our country. Following this, various organisations were invited to enter into dialogue with the IDB on a number of substantive issues: the Poverty Reduction Strategy and promotion of equity, modernisation of the state and regional integration. The first participatory discussion on the Country Strategy Document for Peru for the five-year period 2001-2006 was also held. Further, support was given to various activities of the Roundtable on the Fight against Poverty (including participatory budgeting) and the Annual Conference on Social Development (CONADES).

The Civil Society Advisory Council was set up in 2001, formed by some 70 organisations, including: member-based social and labour organisations, human rights organisations, the Roundtable on the Fight against Poverty and NGOs. Participating on behalf of the Peruvian state, were representatives from the Ministry of the Economy and Finance and the Peruvian International Cooperation Agency.

The Advisory Council has reviewed the first annual report on Bank activities and has divided into working groups to monitor 4 programmes being implemented by the Bank:

- Camisea Gas Project
- FONCODES
- Housing project
- Land Titling Project

IDB's representative in Peru, has indicated the Bank's commitment to civil society participation in the discussion phase of new projects and during the implementation, evaluation, and review of programmes. IDB also organised a Regional Conference for Dialogue with Civil Society, in Lima.

Nevertheless, the participation of civil society is concentrated more on expressing points of view on policies than on the management of programmes and projects.

Assessment of empowerment and civil society participation processes
Undermining local ownership, citizen participation, and empowerment in multilateral cooperation are the 'conditionalities' that prescribe neoliberal recipes and constitute a dogma that is not open to debate.

A second element, recognised by the World Bank itself, is the fact that dialogues are not binding on the Bank. Often, meetings with civil society organisations, are seen as exercises used by the Bank to validate its proposals, without making any commitment to incorporate participants' input, and without defining mechanisms for civil society to participate in, and monitor, their implementation.

Civil society participation in the activities of multilateral financial organisations has taken place in two separate spheres. On the one hand, there has been policy dialogue at the highest national and international levels, with the visible presence of civil society. Here there has been overrepresentation by large metropolitan NGOs. On the other hand, there has been miniscule participation by project beneficiaries.

Latin America

Beneficiary participation has been understood as a practical methodology or technique to incorporate the population in programme implementation, to improve management, and to increase the impact. Participation by the population has been centred on small, local infrastructure initiatives, without opportunities being created for the population in a given zone or region, to share its collective vision or evaluation of the programmes.

Evaluation of social programmes supported by international cooperation: progress in the areas of participation and empowerment

In this section, we first evaluate progress and limitations regarding participation and empowerment of the poor in social programmes supported by international donors during the period of *Fujimorista* authoritarianism. We will then examine the new scenario that opens with the process of democratic transition, decentralisation and transference of social programmes to local governments.

In analysing social programmes, we focus on the FONCODES and PRONAMACHCS case studies, because these without a doubt constitute the most important programmes in the fight against poverty. They also receive most resources from international financing bodies.

Currently, the most important financing available to FONCODES is the US$150 million credit allocated by the IDB. Two other programmes are also underway, supported by the Japan International Cooperation Bank (JBIC) for US$161.5 million. In the past, FONCODES has also relied on significant support from the World Bank, which has just approved a new programme loan of US$150 million for the social sector (Programmatic Social Reform III). This programme includes the areas of health, education and

community support. The Bank is also discussing a new loan for decentralised social programmes, to be transferred to regional and municipal governments.

PRONAMACHCS has a US$51 million credit from the World Bank, for the Relief from Rural Poverty Programme, and three loans from the JBIC for $149.4 million (for the period 1997 to 2004).

FONCODES is an independent body, established by the central government in 1991 as a temporary agency, directly dependent on the Executive. It was set up as a political instrument to counterbalance the negative effects of structural adjustment programmes on the most vulnerable sectors of the population. It aims to improve living conditions for the poorest, generate employment, respond to basic needs in health, nutrition, sanitation and education and promote the participation of poor people in the administration of their own development.

In these programmes, the participation of the population was to take place through the formation of Main Executing Groups (*Núcleos ejecutores*) to represent the community under FONCODES. Under PRONAMACHCS, planning was to be done through consensus building at the community level. These mechanisms allowed only limited participation by the population and did not prevent the programmes from being used for political ends, specifically, the regime's objective of perpetuating its power and re-electing Fujimori. In this context, it became clear that multilateral institutions, who knew about the situation, did not use the means available to them to correct the situation.

PRONAMACHCS and FONCODES have different mechanisms for participation by the population:

The PRONAMACHCS methodology is based on participatory planning and

Latin America

community management, within a rural development strategy based on the sustainable use of natural resources. It endeavours to have the community identify with the project and fulfil the planned agreements. Members of PRONAMACHCS meet with authorities from the peasant organisation to outline the project in general terms (objectives, components and activities) and to bring together all the information relevant to the commitments, the work methodology, and schedule. Once the peasant community has agreed to participate in the project, a work plan is prepared with PRONAMACHCS technicians, as part of the participatory planning process. A participatory diagnostic survey is then carried out, with emphasis on the current state and use of natural resources, using special techniques to help the peasants remember the physical characteristics of the community 20 or 30 years ago and to analyse the significance of recorded changes (such as deforested hillsides and erosion).

Community leaders are encouraged to propose an ideal situation for the community, with regard to natural resources (basically water and soil). The work and activities required to achieve this objective are set out. The community should also establish the order of priority for the work, based on their own needs and the logic dictated by the proposed plan, from which first year activities are derived. PRONAMACHCS technicians give shape to the plan with regard to the activities, timetable and financial requirements. Once they know the work and activities to be carried out , the timetable and costs, the same PRONAMACHCS technicians process the formal approval with the Departmental Office and then deposit the necessary funds in a bank account in the name of the community leader and the PRONAMCHS technician; they are jointly responsible for the project.

The contribution of FONCODES, in the context of the fight against rural poverty and other social funds in Latin America, is the provision of funds to the community, so that the community can take responsibility, through the Main Executing Group, for project implementation. The term Main Executing Group is used for institutions or organisations that receive FONCODES financing for project execution. Organisations have to register with F ONCODES to become eligible to present and implement projects, either for their own benefit, or for a social group they have been formed to support.

Main Executing Groups have the advantage of legal status. They are able to sign contracts, intervene in administrative and judicial procedures, and carry out all the functions required to execute funded projects. The Main Executing Groups are responsible for: (i) maintenance of separate and specific accounts for managing programme resources; (ii) maintenance of proper records; (iii) accountability to FONCODES regarding the use of programme resources; and (iv) the preparation and submission of financial information required by FONCODES.

The Main Executing Groups have a functional nature:
- They organise the demands made by the population;
- They allow for private administration of funds without the entangled bureaucratic procedures used for public expenditure. This gives them greater flexibility and makes it possible to lower costs (for example, they pay for shift work without including salary benefits that are standard in public works).

Some additional differences in the operating systems of the two organisations are the following:

- FONCODES places all the responsibility for project execution on the community, which appoints people to the Main Executing Groups and divides up the supervision. PRONAMACHCS is jointly responsible for execution, which it directly supervises and monitors.
- PRONAMACHCS undertakes a process of participatory planning; FONCODES only requires that the community request the project.
- PRONAMACHCS has multi-year projects and maintains an ongoing presence in the community around a single integral plan; FONCODES manages each sub-project in an isolated manner.
- FONCODES does not include institutional strengthening components for the community organisation, nor a focus on regions or micro-regions that encompass various communities.
- The participation of communities in PRONAMACHCS' programmes, takes place within a range of activities that is more limited than in the case of FONCODES, which also finances social infrastructure, electrification, roads, and productive projects.
- However, the fact that the work of PRONAMACHCS, in contrast to that of FONCODES, is more ongoing and is framed within these plans, and that a larger role is given to the community organisation, means that the effect on the community's institutional capacity is more significant and sustainable.
- Despite the progress it has made, FONCODES has demonstrated great difficulty in introducing new elements into its project cycle such as participatory planning, environmental impact and training and follow-up for project sustainability.

There are weaknesses in both FONCODES and PRONAMACHCS on the strengthening of local governments in poor rural areas.

While FONCODES does delegate project execution to representatives of organised groups of the population, in most cases this is done without making linkages with local governments. Problems in coordination and complementarity thus continue to exist between FONCODES and the municipalities. These are significant, most of all during the phase of conservation and project maintenance, a stage in which FONCODES does not participate directly.

A pilot project, the PREDES project, was developed from 1994 to 1996, with Dutch and German financing. The project created District Development Committees in which municipalities, communities, NGOs and other public institutions participated in the design of a district development plan and the setting of priorities for projects, which were then presented to FONCODES. However, although it was a positive experiment, it was not continued.

The new democratic context and international cooperation, decentralisation and social programme policies

With the return to democracy, there is awareness of the need to reorient the administration of social programmes so as to banish the practice of political clientelism that was rife during *Fujimorismo*. The government of President Valentín Paniagua promoted a more transparent and participatory administration. The Roundtable on the Fight against Poverty was constituted as a coordinating body for the State and civil society. It promotes departmental development plans and participatory budgeting as a means for gathering proposals from the population.

Latin America

At the beginning of President Toledo's administration, a broad agreement was proposed, between the Peruvian government and international cooperation bodies, for coordinated action in the fight against poverty and the strengthening of democratic institutionalisation, with strong civil society participation. This consensus was clearly expressed by the Roundtable on Cooperation, held in Madrid in October 2001.

During the Roundtable, the government announced the launch of its emergency programme 'To Work'. This aimed to fight poverty through the immediate creation of jobs. It was also announced that the government would make advances in the rational and institutional administration of social programmes. In order to guarantee efficient and transparent use of resources, it would create a modern Peruvian Agency for International Cooperation. The reform of social programme management was to be complemented by a process of modernisation and decentralisation of the State.

Following the agreements made in Madrid, both the government and international cooperation institutions saw the need to prepare, together with participants from civil society, a Strategy for Fighting Poverty. The aim was to design a policy for integrating and rationalising various existing programmes and establishing a plan of action with results' indicators. The State Policies in the National Agreement on Social Equity and Social Justice, were to be incorporated, as they provided a solid base for social development work in Peru.[5]

The dialogue that took place during the transition government was integrated into Peru's new social policy. This in turn became the basis for the Social Charter, prepared by the Roundtable on the Fight against Poverty. The Charter was submitted for consideration by the new government, which took office in July 2001. The government of President

Alejandro Toledo ratified the principles and commitments of the Social Charter and, in order to formalise them, formulated and published the 'Social Charter Policy'.

The desire to reach consensus with civil society was made evident by the importance that FONCODES – the principal management entity for social programmes – attached to it. There was even a proposal to establish, within FONCODES, a third managerial unit (together with that of social infrastructure and productive development), which would be responsible for the strengthening of local public and private institutional capacity..

FONCODES also suggested that projects be chosen and designed, using the framework of previously agreed-upon development plans and involving the participation of local governments and community representatives. Furthermore, it went so far as to suggest that European Commission and German donors should support projects aimed at strengthening local capacities.

Support was received from DFID in the UK for the promotion of a new social programmes management strategy, to be carried out in conjunction with municipalities and civil society organisations. The programme agreement between FONCODES and DFID proposed to:

a) Define intervention strategies and apply and validate mechanisms that introduce more participatory, and clearer, State strategies (via FONCODES) for working with civil society in the planning, selection, execution, monitoring and evaluation of development projects.

b) Contribute to the definition of national policies and standards to enhance links between civil society and the State in the fight against poverty, and to the generation of employment and promotion of economic and social development, contributing to the democratic decentralisation process.

Latin America

c) Stimulate the leadership role of the municipalities and the former Transitory Councils for Regional Administration (CTAR) and their capacity for building consensus with regard to local development planning, with participation by government authorities and civil society.

d) Mobilise local capacity, so that social actors can efficiently undertake project management in the fight against poverty and create new and better conditions for planning their own local development.

These new directions, however, did not always receive support from aid agencies. The IDB did not consider a new Management for Strengthening Local Institutionality necessary; nor did it approve of the active participation of municipalities in FONCODES projects. According to the IDB, there was full participation of the population through the Main Executing Groups, as it organised citizens who form these groups and name their four office bearers – president, secretary, treasurer and financial officer. The president and the treasurer have signing authority on the bank account, which FONCODES opens and supervises. The issue of local government participation in the management of the Fund's social projects did not interest the IDB; it finally agreed with the government, after a long and arduous discussion, that the financial officer of the Main Executing Group would be a representative proposed by the municipal district.

With the departure of former FONCONDES director, Pedro Francke, and his replacement by a leader of the ruling party, much less emphasis was given to the proposal to create a Management for Strengthening Local Institutionality and to link projects to agreed-upon development plans and the municipalities.

DFID, which had promoted the new unit for strengthening local institutionality, had to negotiate the continuation of its experimental initiatives through a Unit for Consensus, in which it endeavoured to link the work of the Fund to the Roundtables for Consensus or their equivalent, through tools such as integrated plans generated by strategic and participatory planning processes. 'Zone Facilitators' were created in some areas to act as promoters in support of putting the above mentioned focus into practice.

The strength of the dialogue with aid agencies on a strategy to fight poverty was lost when Pedro Francke, who had led the process, left the position of Technical Secretary of the Interministerial Committee on Social Affairs. There was a period of many months during which his replacement was not determined. It was obvious that integration of social programmes was beginning to meet resistance from some influential leaders in Fujimori's ruling party, which managed programmes such as PRONAMACHCS and the Office for Popular Cooperation.

At the beginning of 2003, the Ministers' Council approved the document 'Bases for the Strategy for Overcoming Poverty and Economic Opportunities for the Poor'.[6] This raised the need to restructure the ministerial organisation and the administration of social investment and to design for this purpose 'institutional and management tools that ensure the completion of government objectives'.

Together with the formation of a new ministry as the governing body for policy on capacity building for poor and marginalised people, and the promotion of social capital – that is, Social Development – it was necessary for the State to have three Funds, which would function as second level institutions in close relation, complementarity, and/or agreement with local and

Latin America

regional governments and civil society. These Funds would take on three specific and specialised tasks for overcoming poverty:

- An initial Local Social Development Fund (FONDEL) for investment in social infrastructure, productive projects for income generation and local capacity building for local social development in the districts and among populations with high levels of poverty.
- A second Food Security and Assistance Fund (FONASOL) that would make social investment resources available, for strategies and programmes aimed at both food security in districts with high levels of poverty, and food assistance for children as a first priority, (since children are the future foundation for human resources);
- A third Family Assistance Fund (FONAFAM) which would make social investment resources available to provide support for groups and people at high physical or moral risk, for neglected or marginalised social sectors and for assistance to families and individuals that face catastrophic situations.

In practice, this new strategy has remained at the level of a proposal. There is a problem of superimposition of bodies (PCM, CND, MIMDES) that are involved in the issue of social programme administration, and their transference to local governments. MIMDES has suggested, as an alternative, the creation of a single fund. This idea is supported by the Ministry of Economy and Finance, on the basis of budgetary criteria, as it would mean sharing the administration of various programmes among fewer management bodies.

There is also considerable resistance by various bodies to becoming integrated. PRONAMACHCS was under the autonomous control of the Ministry of Agriculture.

Subsequently, it was decided, by decree DS 036 in 2002, that this organisation should be integrated with FONCODES. In April of 2003, this decision was reiterated but Ivanhoe Vega, the Director of PRONAMACHCS and influential leader of the governing party, opposed it. It would appear that the proposal to integrate of this body has been discarded.

Conclusion

We conclude with a number of general observations.

It would appear that the progress made by multilateral and bilateral external aid institutions and by national governments themselves, in the areas of empowering people in poverty and civil society participation in development programmes, is greater at the conceptual level than in practice.

Mechanisms set up for direct participation by beneficiaries do not allow them real control over programmes, nor do they manage to prevent the practice of clientelism by governments with partisan intentions.

Also, the broad discussion in Latin American regional and national forums is divorced from the isolated, limited and predominantly local way in which participation by beneficiary populations has been carried out. Participation takes place community by community in each project, without opportunities for exchanges between beneficiaries from different regions, not even within the same department, to facilitate the integration of experiences and grassroot points of view into a national perspective.

The current government of President Toledo has not been able to implement its proposal to rationalise the use of social programme resources (funded in part by international aid agencies) and to make their allocation more transparent. Successive changes to the Cabinet and movement back

Latin America

and forth on policies, have led to a lack of continuity regarding these proposals. Pressure by party officials to control these programmes has had a negative impact on the realisation of such proposals.

Participation by the population has been centred on small, local infrastructure initiatives, without opportunities being created for the population in a given zone or region, to share its collective vision or evaluation of the programmes.

English definitions of acronyms

CND	National Decentralisation Council
DFID	Department For International Development (of Britain)
FONCODES	National Compensation and Social Development Fund
IDB	Interamerican Development Bank
MIMDES	Ministry of Women and Social Development
PMC	Presidency of Ministers' Council
PREDES	Centre for Disaster Prevention and Research
PRONAMACHCS	National Programme for Management of Watershed and Soil Conservation.

Notes

1   This chapter has been edited by the Reality of Aid Management Committee and translated from the original Spanish by Susan Murdock. The edited English version has been reviewed by the author.

2   Mariano Valderrama is coordinator of the Working Group on International Cooperation of the Latin American Association of Development Organisations (ALOP) and is researcher from the 'Citizen Proposal' Group (Grupo Propuesta Ciudadana), a Peruvian NGO platform that promotes the decentralisation process. This contribution is a summary of a larger report sponsored by this platform.

3   It is necessary to examine the type of institutions convened for these dialogues. We have the impression that civil society participation has referred mainly to what could be called mesocratic sectors, with little representation from popular sector organisations and has referred more to the discussion of policies than to the design and monitoring of specific projects.

4   For an assessment of World Bank consultation processes with civil society, see the document by D. Hellinger at http://www.iadb.org. See also the document by Manuel Chiriboga: 'Las ONG y el Banco Mundial: Lecciones y desafíos'. en. La Realidad de la Ayuda Externa, América Latina al 2000, Lima ALOP.

5   The policies are: a) Poverty reduction and promotion of equal opportunity; b) Universal access to adequate, free quality public education and promotion of culture and sports; c) Universal access to health services and social security; d) Access to full-time, dignified productive employment; e) Promotion of food security and nutrition; f) Strengthening of the family, protection and promotion of children and youth.

6   Supreme Decree N° 002-2003-PCM.

Part V
OECD

Millennium Development Goals

The Millennium Development Goals

Goal 1: Eradicate extreme poverty and hunger

- Halve, between 1990 and 2015, the proportion of people whose income is less than US$1 a day;
- Halve, between 1990 and 2015, the proportion of people who suffer from hunger.

Goal 2: Achieve universal primary education

- Ensure that, by 2015, children everywhere, boys and girls alike, will be able to complete a full course of primary schooling.

Goal 3: Promote gender equality and empower women

- Eliminate gender disparity in primary and secondary education preferably by 2005 and in all levels of education no later than 2015.

Goal 4: Reduce child mortality

- Reduce by two-thirds, between 1990 and 2015, the under-five mortality rate.

Goal 5: Improve maternal health

- Reduce by three-quarters, between 1990 and 2015, the maternal mortality ratio.

Goal 6: Combat HIV/AIDS, malaria, and other diseases

- Have halted by 2015 and begun to reverse the spread of HIV/AIDS;

- Have halted by 2015 and begun to reverse the incidence of malaria and other major diseases.

Goal 7: Ensure environmental sustainability

- Integrate the principles of sustainable development into country policies and program and reverse the loss of environmental resources;
- Halve, by 2015, the proportion of people without sustainable access to safe drinking water;
- Halve, by 2015, the proportion of people without access to adequate sanitation [WSSD 2002];
- Have achieved, by 2020, a significant improvement in the lives of at least 100 million slum dwellers.

Millennium Development Goals

Goal 8: Develop a global partnership for development

- Develop further an open, rule-based, predictable, non-discriminatory trading and financial system;
- Address the special needs of the Least Developed Countries;
- Address the special needs of landlocked countries and small island developing states;
- Deal comprehensively with the debt problems of developing countries through national and international measures in order to make debt sustainable in the long term;
- In cooperation with developing countries, develop and implement strategies for decent and productive work for youth;
- In cooperation with pharmaceutical companies, provide access to affordable, essential drugs in developing countries;
- In cooperation with the private sector, make available the benefits of new technologies, especially information and communications.

Governance and poverty: can the goals get donors back on track?

Shennia Spillane, Australian Council for International Development

Governance was introduced into aid programmes ostensibly as an attempt to enhance poverty reduction. Donors justify the inclusion (and increasing prevalence) of so-called 'good governance' activities in their aid programmes by claiming that they are essential for sustainable development to end poverty.

Today the 'governance' sector covers an ever-wider field of activities ranging from economic policy, to human rights, to counter-terrorism. The governance bandwagon has picked up speed recently, particularly with the increasing influence of the anti-terrorism agenda. Now, more than ever, there are serious questions to be asked about the implicit and explicit political objectives of the donors' agenda and the effect of the increasing funds poured into governance. The contribution of governance aid to poverty reduction is still asserted, but seldom tested or proven. Instead, the ill-defined 'governance' sector provides a space for pursuing a range of donor interests with aid money.

The Millennium Development Goals (MDGs) require, among other things, a commitment from donors to focus their aid squarely on poverty reduction through the fulfilment of basic rights. Achievement of the MDGs alone will not eradicate poverty, but the effort required even to achieve them leaves no room for competing priorities. The MDGs, while imperfect, may offer an opportunity to assess the governance aid agenda against specific poverty reduction outcomes, and to reopen the debate on donor approaches to development. But the MDGs will only help if donors are prepared to accept the challenge of some good governance of their own, through accountability for their contribution to achievement of the Goals.

Donors and Governance — not an easy answer

Aid donors began to focus on 'good governance' because they argued, with some justification, that corruption, weak financial management and low planning and implementation capacity within developing country governments, was preventing aid and domestic financing from reaching the people for whom it was intended. In short, 'poor governance' was undermining poverty reduction. Few could argue with the principle that if weak and/or corrupt governance kept essential resources from the poor, addressing these problems was a necessary activity.

Whether the complex, and very political, issues of governance in sovereign states

Millennium Development Goals

could, or should, be resolved by outsiders, would always be a more difficult and contentious question.

Nevertheless, good governance has increasingly become a major focus in the aid programmes of many donor governments, including the United Kingdom, Sweden, the United States and Australia, not to mention multilateral donors and international financial institutions. In the Australian case, for example, governance is now the single biggest sector in the aid programme; in 2003-04, governance activities will absorb 21% of all Australian aid.

Donor approaches to good governance do not often examine, but rather take as given, the links between aid programmes for 'good governance' in developing countries and the outcome of less poverty. Donor activity rests on the simplistic assertion that donors understand what policy settings and institutional structures will lead to the best outcomes in economic growth and, thus, poverty reduction. Critics note that when the so-called 'Washington Consensus' economic model failed (repeatedly) in the developing world, donors blamed recipients' poor implementation of it and rushed to strengthen that, rather than addressing the logical question about the appropriateness of the model in the first place.

In the early years of the 21st century — in the wake of the Latin American and Asian economic crises of the 1990s, in the light of the ongoing global debt crisis, and facing as big challenges as ever to eradicating poverty and realising global equity — there is no choice but to reject donor confidence that the neo-liberal model of good governance is a recipe for poverty reduction.

... then along came terrorism

Perhaps the most troubling trend of all in the field of governance aid, which has intensified over the past two years, is the increasing use

of 'governance', as a broad and ill-defined descriptor to signify a handy catch-all sector under which to place a widening array of projects and programmes, in pursuit of donor objectives that have little to do with direct poverty reduction.

The starkest example of this is the increasing use of governance aid to further donors' national security interests. In particular, increased aid for various counter-terrorism activities has been slotted under the 'good governance' heading, using governance rhetoric to justify spending aid money on national security objectives.

Recent collaborative work by international NGOs, has demonstrated the breadth of the trend towards pursuing national security through aid. NGOs have observed counter-terrorism being established or increased as a development priority in the aid programmes of Australia, Japan, the USA, UK, European Union, and Denmark. In the programmes of these donors, and no doubt others, the nature and direction of aid have shifted to accommodate the national security and anti-terrorism agendas of the donor governments.[1]

Most donors have made some attempt to justify such aid spending by linking counter-terrorism to development. In February 2002, US Secretary of State Colin Powell made the connection between development assistance and counter-terrorism, saying 'we have to show people who might move in the direction of terrorism that there is a better way'.[2] The Australian Government has justified an increasing focus on counter-terrorism in its aid programme by claiming that 'stability and security... [are] critical preconditions in tackling poverty'.[3]

Other donors have perhaps been more honest, construing the connection the other way around. Japan's ODA Charter, revised in 2003, says 'Japan will proactively contribute to the stability and development of

Millennium Development Goals

developing countries through its ODA. This correlates closely with assuring Japan's security and prosperity and promoting the welfare of its people.'[4] In 2003, the Danish Government commissioned a think-tank to explore how Danish development cooperation could be used 'as an instrument in the prevention of terrorism'.[5]

Donor countries in the OECD DAC have turned their collective minds to the role of development cooperation in counter-terrorism. The result in April 2003 was the policy paper *A Development Cooperation Lens on Terrorism Prevention: Key Entry Points for Action.*[6] While general statements in the paper note the importance of donors' commitment to poverty reduction and human rights, the paper is infused with the suggestion that donors may need to 'calibrate' current aid allocations and approaches to take account of terrorism prevention. NGOs have expressed serious concern that this OECD paper, and the trend in donor thinking it reflects, opens the door for terrorism prevention increasingly becoming a goal of development cooperation in its own right.[7]

There is little doubt that conditions of poverty, combined with perceptions of global injustice and alienation, contribute in some circumstances to the creation of environments that can breed instability and conflict and, in extreme cases, acts of terror. At the same time, NGO research has suggested that 'linking acts of terrorism and their prevention with the goals of development cooperation... is highly problematic.'[8]

Poverty reduction arguments are evidently not the driving motivator, nor the guiding principle, for donors' new governance and security agendas. Recognition of the importance of stability and security for effective aid implies the need for a greater commitment to *poverty-focused* assistance,

to address the causes of conflict and provide greater economic and social equity to affected peoples. Simplistically combating symptoms through law enforcement, financial regulation and the like, is not an adequate response. As one NGO commentator has noted, if alleviating poverty reduces terrorism, there is no need to create a new counter-terrorism goal in aid programmes. All that such a link implies is the need to step up poverty-focused aid in order *to eradicate poverty.*[9]

There may be merit in the proposition that many types of aid directed at counter-terrorism may ultimately contribute to poverty reduction. More stable and better-governed states, for example, can benefit from international trade and growth more easily and, under the right circumstances, the resulting growth can lift the living standards of those in poverty. But where spending scarce aid funds is at stake, doing things that may possibly, eventually, make some contribution to reducing poverty is not good enough — regardless of the foreign policy or national security benefits for the donor. Donors must ensure that their programmes are the *best*, most effective way to use their limited resources to eradicate poverty. Much of the present aid for counter-terrorism activities would fail this test.

In fact, a glance at the types of anti-terror activities now being funded by large amounts of aid, reveals that the security threats being countered are almost always those directed towards rich countries and peoples, rather than threats to people in the countries of the terrorists' origin, or those they work through. Australia provides aid to small, poverty-trapped countries in the Pacific Islands to prevent international terror groups from laundering money, *through* them, towards Australia and other western countries. Even aid targeted at restoring stability to conflict-ridden states is now

Millennium Development Goals

described as preventing fragile states from becoming 'havens' or 'breeding grounds' for terrorists.[10] Much aid is being provided to assist Indonesia to counter international terrorist threats, while the world largely chooses to ignore the human suffering caused by conflicts within Indonesia's own territory, such as in Aceh.

While it is understandable that rich countries want to protect their citizens and their defence and security interests, by combating international terrorism, it is questionable whether diverting scarce aid money to this end is the appropriate way to fund these policy pursuits. That is to say, strengthening money-laundering regulations and customs police in East Timor or Nauru, may be in both governments' national interests, but is it an activity truly and primarily directed at reducing the burden of poverty for the citizens of such countries?

Regardless of any links that happen to exist, the language of donors' statements on counter-terrorism and aid leaves little doubt that the ultimate goal of such aid is security, not development. Like other donor-driven political priorities before it, counter-terrorism activity has too easily found a home under the catch-all category of aid for 'good governance'.[11] When it comes to their governance aid programmes, in particular, many donors need a reality check.

Can the Millennium Development Goals help?

The MDGs are fast becoming the international 'main game' in global development discourse. Eight simple goals, backed up by 14 hard targets and 49 measurable indicators, with a definite deadline of 2015, were endorsed by some 148 world leaders through the Millennium Declaration. Since that time, the MDGs have been vigorously promoted, developed and refined, chiefly by the UN but also, increasingly, by developed and developing country governments and other international institutions.

Anecdotal evidence suggests that civil society's reaction to the MDGs has been mixed. Some critics point out that several of the targets are restatements of UN Goals that the world failed to achieve, as promised, by 2000. Others, importantly, wonder whether the Goals represent the same old donor-driven agenda in a new guise. Critics also berate the lack of civil society and recipient community participation in both the development of the Goals themselves and in the mechanisms being used for their implementation (such as MDG Country Reports and Poverty Reduction Strategy Papers).

It is certainly true that the MDGs are neither exhaustive nor perfect. Among other things, they lack an explicit grounding in human rights, neglect to take account of the specific needs of marginalised groups such as people with disabilities and ethnic minorities, and lack a clear interaction with goals and standards established in other forums.

Nevertheless, there is a compelling argument that the MDGs represent the best opportunity in recent history to transform development debates and to achieve real results in poverty reduction. The Goals already have the UN, the World Bank and many donor governments talking about increased commitment to development, new approaches and accountability for real results in poverty reduction. At the very least, the MDGs represent a potentially powerful advocacy tool that NGOs and local communities can draw on, to hold developed and developing country governments to account for their own commitment to combat poverty.

For the first time there is a coherent set of priorities and a definite deadline. The Goals are easily understood, measurable and patently achievable. While they are not the

Millennium Development Goals

complete recipe for poverty eradication, their achievement would represent a major step. Most importantly, they have *already been agreed* by the vast majority of the world community. The Goals represent specific commitments to which donors can (must!) be held accountable.

The relevance of the MDGs to the governance debate is that they provide an internationally agreed framework to focus the aid and development agenda where it belongs — on action to *eliminate poverty*. Further, if taken seriously, the MDGs absolutely require aid to be used to that end, because all current aid resources and more will need to be directed to the Goals if they are to be achieved. The World Bank and others estimated that, in 2002, global aid added up to no more than half of the annual aid needed between now and 2015 to achieve the Goals.[12]

Governance provides an ideal example of the potential of the MDGs to sharpen aid priorities and to refocus on the basics. There is, quite appropriately, no specific MDG on Governance. That is because governance is not, and should not be, a development goal in itself. Governance activities for their own sake, or for the pursuit of objectives other than — or only distantly related to — poverty reduction, will not achieve the MDGs.

Instead, governance assistance is a means that should be employed, only where it can *most effectively* augment the ability of people in poverty to realise their basic right to a life free from poverty. If governance activities are not optimally contributing to the achievement of this, donors 9should simply not be spending aid money on them. Donors' own commitment to achieving the MDGs, demands that governance assistance be rigorously assessed against tough targets, embodying the real priorities that should be at the centre of aid efforts — poverty reduction through meeting basic needs.

The catch in this equation, though, is equal accountability for achievement of the MDGs. With the support of international donors and the UN, developing countries are doing an enormous amount to account for their progress towards achieving Millennium Goals 1 to 7. Meanwhile, Millennium Development Goal 8 — *develop a global partnership for development* — touches on the reforms needed to donors' approaches and the rules that govern the global economy, if the Goals are to be achieved. But Goal 8 is not as specific as the other Goals and lacks an adequate mechanism for holding developed countries accountable. The latter is a major unresolved problem with the MDGs as a whole. If the MDGs are an opportunity to reopen the discussion about policy and practice on governance with donors, they also make it necessary for NGOs and others to demand better accountability from them.

There has been some discussion about Goal 8 accountability in the international system. Various proposals have been made, including incorporation of MDG targets into OECD DAC peer review assessments, use of the IMF Chapter IV mechanism, and more directed use of the 'Commitment to Development' Index pioneered by the Centre for Global Development and *Foreign Policy* magazine in 2003.[13] These are some of the options. NGOs and others are publicly beginning to push hard for more work to be done on this crucial issue, in the lead-up to the UN Secretary-General's 2005 progress report on the MDGs.

But to date, donors have conspicuously failed to come to the party. Very few donors have indicated that they are even considering reporting against MDG Goal 8 in any structured way. Indeed, unless there is a much stronger demonstration of political will on the part of donors to account for their contribution to the Goals, their good faith in

Millennium Development Goals

claiming to support the MDGs must be exposed as a sham. NGOs in OECD countries have a role to play in ensuring their governments are accountable for the integrity and effectiveness of their aid. MDG Goal 8 can, and should, provide a strong basis for a global effort towards better donor accountability between now and 2015.

Getting Donors Back on Track

Governance, rights and poverty reduction are natural allies. But seeing them in this way and adopting approaches that maximise all three, requires a donor re-think about why good governance should be pursued with aid, what sort of activities can truly improve governance, and a genuine donor re-commitment to the ultimate goal of poverty reduction. Now more than ever, donors are imposing 'good governance' which fits their own agendas, rather than genuinely prioritising a better standard of life for those in poverty around the world. Donors' own commitment to achieving the MDGs by 2015, presents perhaps the best opportunity for NGOs to advocate for bringing governance back to the basics – to poverty reduction – and for the international cooperation that will make it a reality. What is needed is a display of good governance from the same donors who so vigorously promote it. A start would be a transparent accountability mechanism for donor performance against MDG 8.

If alleviating poverty reduces terrorism, there is no need to create a new counter-terrorism goal in aid programmes

Millennium Development Goals

Notes

1. Information collected and distributed by the NGO Global Security and Development Network during 2003; see http://www.bond.org.uk/advocacy/globalsecurity.htm

2. Speech at the World Economic Forum, February 2002.

3. Counter-terrorism and Australian Aid, Australian Agency for International Development, Canberra, August 2003.

4. Revision of Japan's Official Development Assistance Charter, unofficial translation, Ministry of Foreign Affairs of Japan, August 2003: http://www.mofa.go.jp/policy/oda/reform/revision0308.pdf

5. Development Cooperation as an instrument in the prevention of terrorism, Ministry of Foreign Affairs Research Report, Edited by Timo Kivimaki, NIAS Copenhagen, July 2003.

6. OECD DAC, 22-23 April 2003, available at www.oecd.org.

7. Joint statement by members of the Global Security and Development Network on the Development Assistance Committee policy statement and reference document 'A Development Cooperation Lens on Terrorism Prevention: Key Entry Points for Action', London, 30 October 2003.

8. Tornlinson, Brian, A CCIC Commentary on 'A Development Lens on Terrorism Prevention: Key Entry points for Action', Canadian Council for International Cooperation, Ottawa, October 2003.

9. Gaughran, Audrey, Shifting Goalposts: Aid and Terrorism, British Overseas Network on Development (BOND), available at www.bond.org.uk.

10. See for example comments made by Australian Foreign Minister Alexander Downer MP in relation to Australian intervention in the Pacific: Security in an Unstable World, National Press Club, Canberra, 26 June 2003: http://www.foreignminister.gov.au/speeches/2003/030626_unstableworld.html

11. In some cases, this goes so far as to be directly contradictory — assistance provided to developing countries to draft and implement restrictive and draconian anti-terrorism laws and regulations, has in some cases undermined core good governance principles relating to fundamental civil rights, transparent justice systems, and a free media.

12. The Costs of Attaining the Millennium Development Goals, World Bank, Monterrey, Mexico, March 2002.

13. On discussion of accountability proposals, see for example http://www.undp.org/oslocentre/docsoslo/events/Achieving%20the%20MDGs%20Strengthening%20Mutual%20Accountability/bergen-final-summary.pdf On the Commitment to Development Index specifically, see http://www.cgdev.org/rankingtherich

Civil society participation in EC Aid: a cornerstone of good governance?

Mikaela Gavas, BOND

'Whatever the development question you ask, the answer is Good Governance.'

Rt Hon Clare Short, Former UK Secretary of State for International Development, Valladolid, 7 March 2002

All aid actors, whether donors, recipients or implementers, now underline the importance of civil society participation in the development process. But, has there really been a paradigm shift? What does the European Commission mean when it talks about 'participation' and 'stakeholders'? What institutional and attitudinal changes are necessary, to enable poor people to truly participate in decision-making?

In its White Paper on European Governance, the European Commission refers to people's increasing distrust in institutions, a widespread image of the Union as 'remote and at the same time too intrusive' and the need to 'connect Europe with its citizens'.[1]

Upon his nomination in 1999, European Commission President Romano Prodi made 'good governance' -- an expression that, for the European Union (EU), encompasses bottom-up participation through public partnerships with civil society — one of the main priorities of his mandate. The Commission emphasised the need for a stronger interaction with civil society and a 'reinforced culture of consultation and dialogue'[2]. Participatory democracy entails 'opening up the policy-making process to get more people and organizations involved in shaping and delivering EU policy'[3]. The Union had to become less top-down and complement its policy tools 'more effectively with non-legislative instruments'[4]. The EU, therefore strongly commits, in unequivocal terms, to promoting a more participatory democracy as a global principle of good governance.

The biggest challenge, however, is how to translate laudable principles into operational dialogue structures and practical programming orientations, bearing in mind that the concept of 'participatory development' implies a cultural revolution for most EC developing country partners.

This paper looks at the rhetoric on promoting good governance as communicated at various EU institutional levels. It examines the extent to which the principle of participatory democracy, as a fundamental element of good governance, is being implemented in developing countries.

European Commission

Defining 'good governance'

The concept of 'good governance' is difficult to define with precision, but it has been influenced by the international debate on the relationship between human rights, governance and economic development, incorporating elements of each.

For the United Nations Development Programme (UNDP), it is '... among other things participatory, transparent and accountable. It is also effective and equitable. And it promotes the rule of law. Good governance ensures that political, social and economic priorities are based on broad consensus in society and that the voices of the poorest and the most vulnerable are heard in decision-making over the allocation of development resources.'[5]

For the World Bank, it is '... epitomized by predictable, open and enlightened policy making; a bureaucracy imbued with a professional ethos; an executive arm of government accountable for its actions; and a strong civil society participating in public affairs; and all behaving under the rule of law.'[6]

Numerous European Commission communications on development cooperation, both of a general nature and region-specific, have incorporated discussion of the importance of good governance. According to the European Commission Communication on Governance and Development, 'governance is a meaningful and practical concept relating to the very basic aspects of the functioning of any society and political and social systems. It can be described as a basic measure of stability and performance of a society.'[7]

The Commission lists a number of concepts that, when developed within a society and political system, provide for a transition from governance to good governance. These concepts are human rights, democratisation and democracy, the rule of law, civil society, decentralised power sharing and sound public administration. The Communication is a step forward in defining governance within EC development cooperation. But there is little emphasis on enabling civil society participation and little attention to how civil society can be supported in building capacity to respond to, and influence, governments.

Civil society participation: a fundamental element of good governance in EC policy

Since the Joint Declaration of November 2000 on the European Community (EC) Development Policy by the Council of Ministers and the European Commission[8], the promotion of human rights, democracy, the rule of law and good governance have become integral elements of EC development cooperation. Strengthening democratic systems in developing countries therefore lies at the heart of Community efforts to encourage 'the most wide-ranging participation of all segments of society',[9] thereby creating conditions for greater equity and greater participation by the poorest in the development process.

The key conditions for effective dialogue and cooperation between partner countries and the EU, encompass institutional capacity building in partner countries and good governance, 'with a view to ensuring transparent and responsible management of all the resources devoted to development'. These parameters will guide the distribution of Community development aid 'in order to allocate it to where it has the greatest chance of reducing poverty efficiently and sustainably'.[10] Institutional capacity building represents one of the European Commission's six priorities for action, to maximise the impact of Community development policy.

Furthermore, the Compendium on Cooperation Strategies in the Cotonou

European Commission

Partnership Agreement between the EU and African, Caribbean and Pacific (ACP) countries, identifies, among other things, capacity building of 'non-state actors' (NSAs) and the strengthening of structures and mechanisms of information, dialogue and of consultation between NSAs and the national authorities as an area of support provided by the Community.[11].

Articles 9 and 10 of the Cotonou Agreement state that development centred on the human person, entails 'respect for and promotion of all human rights'. The Articles state that 'democracy based on the rule of law and transparent and accountable governance are an integral part of sustainable development', and that 'greater involvement of an active and organised civil society' is essential to maintaining and consolidating a stable and democratic political environment.

Underpinning these articles is the recognition that at the heart of governance and development are two linked concepts, the one a result of the other. Firstly, that a working concept of good governance must be based on a recognition of the promotion of economic, social, political and cultural rights. This rights-based approach to development is not country specific. Secondly, that governance and good governance is therefore predicated on the strengthening of transparency and accountability, with active citizens' organisations engaging on a regular, open and systematic basis with elected representatives in their countries. In other words, participatory democracy is a direct result of the rights-based approach to development.

Civil society participation in EC development programmes

The key features of civil society organisations include: autonomy from the state and the market and development through a fundamentally endogenous process; CSOs are established voluntarily by citizens who have common values, concerns, needs or interests; and they are organised around the promotion of an issue or the interests of a particular section of society. CSOs are seen as increasingly crucial agents, because of their knowledge, experience, low-cost, flexibility, and ability to bridge the critical gap between strategic goals and their practical realisation.

Commission Communication on NSA participation

In November 2002, the Commission published a Communication on the 'Participation of Non-State Actors in EC Development Policy', followed by 'Guidelines on Principles of Good Practices for the Participation of Non-State Actors in the Development Dialogues and Consultation'[12]. Both seek to align EC aid firmly with the principle of 'local ownership' by recipient countries. Yet, in sharp contrast with the Commission's adamant will to enhance participatory democracy, the key terms of this approach, such as 'non-state actor' (NSA) and 'participation' and their place in the context of wider EC aid reforms lack clear definition. This questions the very legitimacy of the system.

While the paper uses the broad term 'non-state actor', to include non-governmental organisations (NGOs), social partners, business associations and the media, its substantive content deals exclusively with NGOs. It seems ironic that the very document that aims to ensure 'an adequate level of consultation and participation in all partners' countries' is itself developed with very little official consultation or input from civil society organisations in Europe and without any consultation with the developing world.

European Commission

Criticism of 'ad hoc-ness'

The EU's relationship with associations of development NGOs undertaking policy dialogue in Brussels itself has been strewn with problems. The organisations themselves complain that any consultation they enjoy is entirely ad hoc; they often also accuse the Commission of consulting when it wants to legitimise its own perspective, rather than genuinely to listen and respond to alternative viewpoints. This ad-hoc consultation practice may be a result of limited staff numbers, as Commission staff have genuinely struggled to cope with the myriad of demands from literally thousands of organisations — local, national and international. But even if the Commission did consult with NGOs on a consistent basis, there would still be a problem: the Commission assumes that NGOs are representative of civil society as a whole and this leads it to the misconception that policy has been made in a participatory manner.

Criticism of inconsistency

The participatory approach to development, which aims to increase the ownership of development strategies by the countries and populations concerned, is an innovation in ACP-EU Cooperation. The Cotonou Agreement, signed in 2000 between the EU and the ACP, makes the participatory approach at all levels of cooperation a legally binding, well-structured obligation, which aims to encourage dialogue between the national authorities and the NSAs in the country. Participation is not limited to project implementation, but extends to political dialogue, policy formulation and monitoring and evaluation of progress.

Although the EU's main policy document is the Communication, it is only the Cotonou Agreement that places a legal requirement on EC Delegations for NSA participation. In the regulation for Latin America, the

Commission simply states that current regional, sub-regional and country strategy papers have a strong civil society component and that growing support to civil society can be perceived in the new generation of agreements. Yet, the agreements in force between the Commission and Asian and Latin American countries do not contain a legal obligation to consult civil society. There is a serious inconsistency for delegations, regarding the simultaneous implementation of the regulation for Asia and Latin America (ALA), which essentially ignores civil society actors,[13] and the Communication on NSAs that does indeed apply to all developing countries.

Linking EC Delegations and NSAs

According to recent EC literature, the role of the EC Delegation is that of observer and facilitator. It is to facilitate the engagement of NSAs in policymaking and implementation of cooperation policies and, in particular, to provide technical assistance in programming. According to the EC, the Head of Delegation (HoD) will play an increasingly important role in the selection process of co-financing projects, presented as NSAs' own initiatives. In this context, the HoD is expected to ensure that there is an acceptable degree of consistency between these initiatives and the whole cooperation strategy.

In the framework of the Cotonou Agreement, most ACP Governments, in agreement with the EC, have undertaken to provide support to NSAs by reserving a European Development Fund (EDF) for this purpose in their respective Country Strategy Papers. In the implementation process of these innovative provisions, the ACP national authorities, the EC Delegations and the NSA representatives are expected jointly to identify the range of actors and activities to be supported. As far as the management of the funds and the funding decisions of NSA

European Commission

activities are concerned, the HoD will be the main person responsible.

The decentralisation of resources and responsibilities to EC Delegations, which began in 2001, and is expected to extend to all Delegations before the end of 2003, is intended to improve the quality of the participatory approach in EC development policy. The ongoing rationalisation of development aid instruments, which aims to facilitate sound management and coherence of development programmes, also provides an opportunity to clarify the EC's approach to working with NSAs. Good co-ordination between the EC Delegations and Headquarters is crucial.

According to the EC, the participatory approach must be implemented while respecting both the particular situation in each partner country and the central role of the Government, complemented by the local authorities, the business sector and other NSAs. The EC identifies lack of political will to involve NSAs on the part of the national governments, and the poor structuring and capacity of NSAs, as two important issues that Heads of Delegation often face. Interestingly, this is not necessarily just in the poorest countries. A useful tool for overcoming these issues may be Country Strategy Paper consultations that, from the outset define policy towards NSAs. They give NSAs the opportunity to emerge, to present their ideas, to promote debate in society and to add to the rooting of democratic systems.

Box 7. Participation in Senegal

A BOND research project on the participation of southern civil society representatives in the decision making processes and implementation of EU development programmes, was conducted in Senegal during August 2003.[14]

The choice of NSAs invited to participate in the EU programming process was essentially based on a national assessment of available information. Yet, the multitude of civil society organisations made it difficult to involve them all in consultation. A 'pragmatic' approach was therefore adopted, with co-opted representatives of some of the most visible organisations and those known for their expertise.

In February 2001, an open consultation process was launched with NSAs in order to draw up Senegal's Country Strategy Paper with a 'central group', comprised of six Dakar-based NSAs playing a coordinating role. Subsequently, five issue-based 'technical working groups', comprising 66 co-opted NSA representatives were established focused on: macro-economic adjustment and budgetary support; social sectors the poverty reduction, transport and trade, good governance and non-state actors.

Seven more working groups, comprised of the same participants, were then set up to identify projects in accordance with the agreed areas of cooperation between the Government of Senegal and the EU: good governance, transportation, hygiene, budgetary support, trade, culture, Non-State actors. These groups met four or five times, concluding with a three-day workshop to develop strategies for the particular areas. NSAs were invited to participate in all groups; however, substantial participation only took place in the group on good governance.

European Commission

In general, NSAs were pleasantly surprised at the invitation from the EC Delegation and the Government of Senegal to participate in the identification of areas of cooperation between Senegal and the EU. Prior to this, there was a lack of knowledge on the EU's activities in the country. However, some critical NSA voices have suggested that participants mostly represented an urban Dakar-based 'NGO elite' and little effort was made to reach out to smaller, grass roots or regional organisations. As a result, a lack of consideration was given to a number of serious concerns in the Country Strategy Paper. Agriculture, in particular, was not considered a focal sector despite studies showing that agrarian people constitute approximately 60% of the population most affected by poverty in Senegal.

All of the meetings of the different technical groups were held at the offices of the EC Delegation in Dakar, but all the costs of engaging in the consultation were borne by the NSAs themselves. Furthermore, the process suffered in its entirety from a lack of clear terms of reference and a precise work plan, which would have framed objectives and mandates within a clear timetable. Most participants also deplored the way in which NSAs were brought into the process on the basis of co-option without any prior preparation, no mandate and therefore no legitimacy from their constituencies. Finally, there was a noticeable ill-preparedness, lack of knowledge and expertise among NSAs, on the policies outlined in the Cotonou Agreement, and how these should be implemented.

Participation: actual or nominal?

Effective consultation with NSAs presupposes that they are properly organised and have access to adequate information. NSAs need the financial and technical ability to respond adequately to consultation. They need to be able to articulate issues on their areas of concerns, in a manner that is taken seriously and acted upon.

But an official of the Kenyan Ministry of Planning and Development was candid enough to admit that NSA participation in the elaboration of the Kenyan Poverty Reduction Strategy Paper (PRSP), on which the Kenyan Country Strategy Paper was based, was purely cosmetic, in that the process was government driven. Most, NSAs received documentation late and as a result, even though they were sitting at the table, NSAs could not effectively participate, so civil servants ended up dominating the process, as

well as writing the reports. Although on the surface, NSAs can be said to have been consulted, since they were allowed to sit at the table, their participation was hampered by lack of information. The lack of consultation with civil society in drawing up the Kenyan Country Strategy Paper, seemed largely to be based on lack of understanding about the supposed benefits of involving civil society groups in discussions about policy.[15]

Conclusion

Most academics and development practitioners agree that ownership of development strategies, by those they are intended to benefit, provides the best guarantee that strategies will succeed. Many of today's buzzwords around public-private partnerships, good governance and sustainability, are equally dependent on participation by a healthy and functioning

European Commission

civil society in developing countries. Consultation is not an exact science measurable in numbers alone. The quality of involvement, particularly from the poorest and most marginalised, is important when the Commission's activities are assessed. It is a cornerstone of good governance that consultations and their results are not an 'add on', but integrated into the mainstream processes for the delivery of EC aid. This should include all relevant policy instruments. The first test of whether such a commitment is serious, will be the forthcoming 'Mid-term Review' of existing agreed Country Strategy Papers.

To date, limited attention and resources have been made available to governments for strengthening democracy, respect for human rights and civil society engagement in democratic and participatory processes. Implementation of the principle of NSA participation in the development process will evolve over time and will require identification of best practices, flexibility and institutional innovation. Yet, it is the principle of participatory development — not simply the operation of consultation processes — that must be the ultimate arbiter as to whether the good intentions of the Commission really do make a difference.

Notes

[1] *European Governance, A White Paper*, COM(2001)428 final, Brussels, 25.07.2001, p 3.

[2] Ibid, p 16.

[3] Ibid, p 3.

[4] Ibid, p 4.

[5] *Governance for Sustainable Human Development*, A UNDP policy paper UNDP 1997, p 2-3.

[6] *Governance: The World Bank's Experience*, World Bank 1994.

[7] Communication from the Commission to the Council, the European Parliament and the European Economic and Social Committee: *Governance and Development*, COM(2003) 615 final, Brussels, 20.10.2003, p 3.

[8] The European Community's Development Policy — Statement by the Council and the Commission: http://europa.eu.int/comm/development/body/legislation/docs/council20001110_en.pdf#zoom=100

[9] Ibid, p 3.

[10] Ibid.

[11] Partnership Agreement between the Members of the Group of African, Caribbean and Pacific States and the European Community and its Member States —

Compendium on co-operation strategies: http://europa.eu.int/comm/development/body/cotonou/compendium/comp12c_en.htm

[12] Communication from the Commission to the Council, the European Parliament and the Economic and Social Committee: *Participation of non-state actors in EC development policy*, COM(2002) 598 final, Brussels, 07.11.2002.

[13] The European Parliament has introduced recommendations to the Regulation proposed by the Commission supporting civil society participation.

[14] Researched by Moussa Ba, a consultant with *Sahel Ingenieurs Conseils* based in Dakar and coordinated by INTRAC, an international training and research NGO. The BOND research project, 'Ensuring Civil Society Participation in European Commission Development Assistance Programmes' seeks to measure the effectiveness and impact of the EC's development assistance programme by evaluating the nature and quality of civil society participation in the development of EC Country Strategy Papers in four developing countries. The research will be published in March 2004.

[15] BOND EC-PREP Research, 'Ensuring Civil Society Participation in EC Development Assistance Programmes', Kenyan Study by Halima Noor, p. 47.

Part VI
World Aid and Donor Reports

Global pledges sacrificed to national interests

Tony German and Judith Randel, Development Initiatives

The first *Reality of Aid* report was published in 1993, the year after the Earth Summit (UNCED) held in Rio. At the Earth Summit, donors pledged modest increases in aid — US$2.5 billion, or an extra 4%. But, as graph 1, ODA from all DAC donors, shows, donors collectively failed to fulfil their commitments. In fact aid fell by 24% in real terms between 1992 and 1997.

So in 2002, when donors gathered for the Financing for Development Summit in Monterrey, Mexico, aid was less than it had been in the year when they gathered in Rio. It is against this background that pledges to produce more resources for the fight against poverty must be seen.

The real terms decline in aid during the 1990s followed many years of gradual growth in global aid. See graph 2: the long-term trend in ODA.

But though aid grew by 117% over more than four decades, this does not mean that donor countries have become more generous, because over the same period donor countries have become very much richer.

Graph 3, the growing gap, shows how the growth in aid per person from donor countries compares with how much more wealthy people in donor countries have become. The

Graph 1.

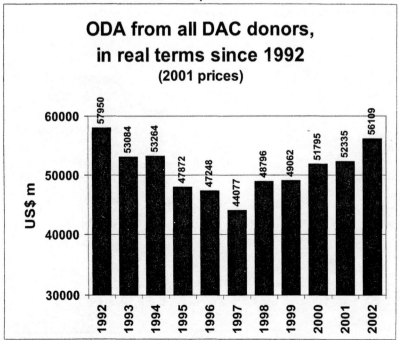

ODA from all DAC donors, in real terms since 1992 (2001 prices). US$ m. 1992: 57950; 1993: 53084; 1994: 53264; 1995: 47872; 1996: 47248; 1997: 44077; 1998: 48796; 1999: 49062; 2000: 51795; 2001: 52335; 2002: 56109.

World Aid Trends

Graph 2.

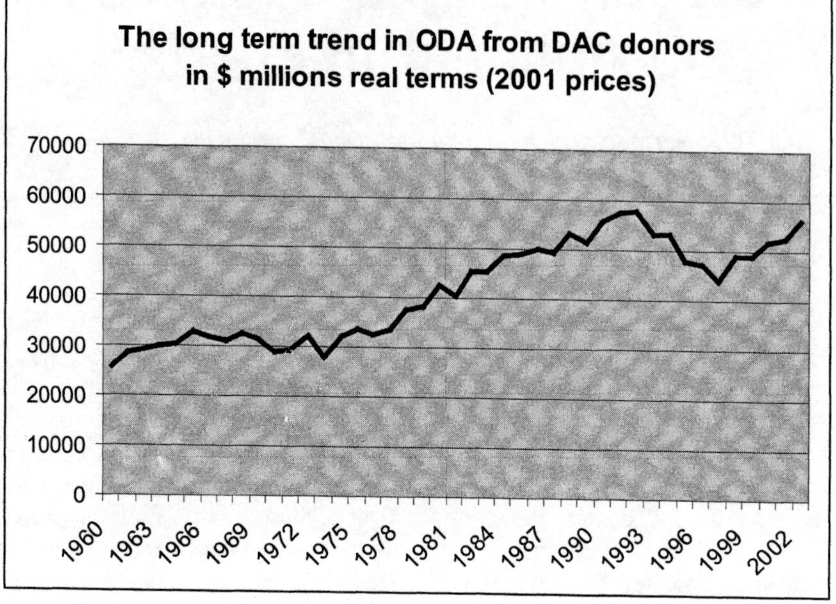

The long term trend in ODA from DAC donors in $ millions real terms (2001 prices)
70000
60000
50000
40000
30000
20000
10000
0
1960
1963
1966
1969
1972
1975
1978
1981
1984
1987
1990
1993
1996
1999
2002

Graph 3.

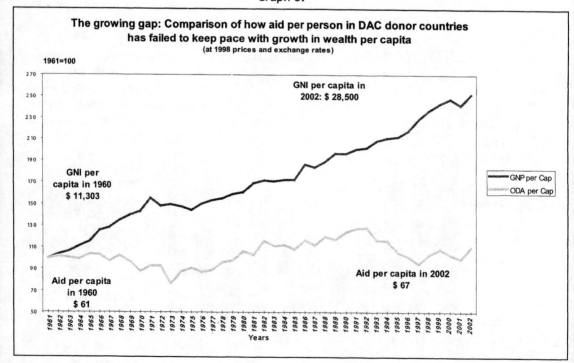

The growing gap: Comparison of how aid per person in DAC donor countries has failed to keep pace with growth in wealth per capita
(at 1998 prices and exchange rates)
1961=100
GNI per capita in 2002: $ 28,500
GNI per capita in 1960 $ 11,303
Aid per capita in 1960 $ 61
Aid per capita in 2002 $ 67
GNP per Cap
ODA per Cap
Years

World Aid Trends

picture is clear. Wealth in donor countries has gone up by 152% from US$11,303 per person to US$28,500. By contrast aid per person has risen by less than 10% from US$61 to US$67.

Looking at the detail of who gives what in ODA, graph 4 shows aid volume from each donor in 2002, which totalled US$58,274 millions.

G8 donors — the USA, Japan, France, Germany, the UK, Italy and Canada (in descending order of volume) — together provided almost three quarters of DAC aid in 2002.

But it is also the G8 donors who have been mostly responsible for the decline in aid over the 1990s.

Graph 4.

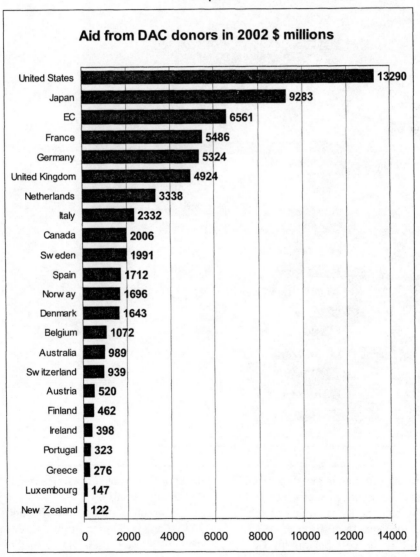

Aid from DAC donors in 2002 $ millions

Donor	$ millions
United States	13290
Japan	9283
EC	6561
France	5486
Germany	5324
United Kingdom	4924
Netherlands	3338
Italy	2332
Canada	2006
Sweden	1991
Spain	1712
Norway	1696
Denmark	1643
Belgium	1072
Australia	989
Switzerland	939
Austria	520
Finland	462
Ireland	398
Portugal	323
Greece	276
Luxembourg	147
New Zealand	122

World Aid Trends

Graph 5.

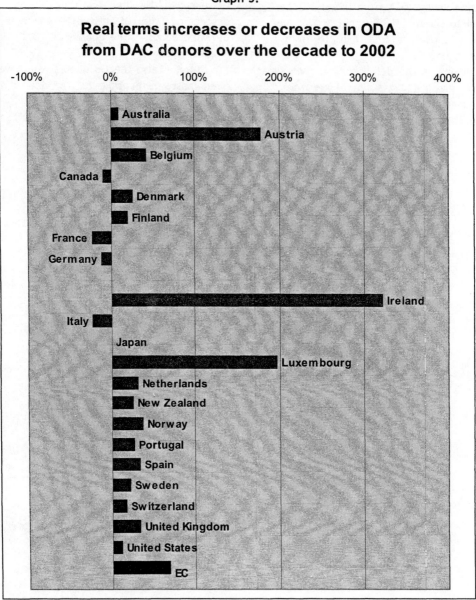

Real terms increases or decreases in ODA from DAC donors over the decade to 2002

The only non-G8 donor giving over US$3 billion a year (substantially more than Italy and Canada) is Netherlands, which at 0.81% GNI in 2002 manages to perform more than twice as well as the best performing G8 donor in terms of aid as a percentage of GNI (France 0.38%).

As graph 5 shows over the decade to 2002, Canada, France, Italy and Germany have all allowed their aid to decline

World Aid Trends

significantly in real terms — the only DAC donors to have allowed a decline.

Of course aid from individual donor countries can fluctuate from year to year for many reasons. But when looked at over a decade, countries cannot excuse a decline on the basis of short-term factors. A fall over ten years can only be seen as evidence that political priority is being given to domestic considerations, rather than to global poverty reduction.

The question of how much political priority is being given to poverty reduction within aid spending can be viewed in several ways. One basic measure is whether aid is flowing to very poor countries or to those who are somewhat better off.

As figure 1 shows, in 2002, 34% of global aid went to the Least Developed Countries (LLDCs). The 49 LLDCs all have:

- a low income,
- weak human assets (poor nutrition, high child mortality, low school enrolment and adult literacy rates),
- high level of economic vulnerability (for

example instability in agricultural production and exports).

Other Low Income Countries (including India, China, Ghana, Indonesia, Pakistan, Nigeria and Zimbabwe) received 29% of global aid.

Lower Middle Income Countries received 33% of aid. This group of countries includes Bolivia, Bosnia and Herzegovina, Egypt, Fiji, Iraq, Morocco, Palestine, Papua New Guinea, Peru, the Philippines and Yugoslavia.

Just 4% of aid went to Upper Middle Income Countries in 2002, and whereas in 1994, 3% of aid went to High Income Countries, no aid now goes to such countries. See figure 2. Share of aid to poorer countries.

In terms of whether aid has shifted to different regions over the decade to 2002, the major changes are a 5% fall in aid to Far East Asia and a 5% rise in aid to South and Central Asia.

The share of aid to Sub-Saharan Africa has risen from 33% to 36% and Europe's

Figure 2.

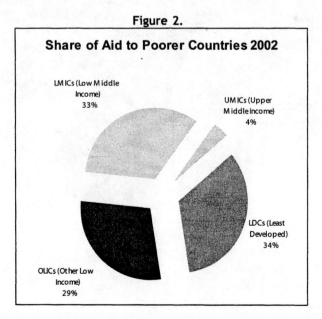

Share of Aid to Poorer Countries 2002

LMICs (Low Middle Income) 33%

UMICs (Upper Middle Income) 4%

LDCs (Least Developed) 34%

OLICs (Other Low Income) 29%

World Aid Trends

share of aid receipts has more than doubled from 5% to 11%. See figure 3.

. In 2002, it was still the case that just five donors — Denmark, Netherlands, Sweden, Norway and Luxembourg were meeting their commitments to achieve the UN 0.7% target for aid as a share of national income, established in 1970.[1] See Graph 6.

Graph 7 shows the long-term trend in aid as a percentage of GNI over the 20 years to 2002. The period shows a marked decline, with aid now hovering around 0.23% GNI, compared to around 0.33% at the end of the cold war and into the early 1990s.

Graph 7 presents two different ways of measuring average GNI performance by donors. One method is to take a simple or unweighted average. The other is to take

the total aid spending as a share of the total GNI of donor countries. The latter method produces a weighted average — skewing the figure towards bigger countries, such as Japan and the USA, who are among the worst performers on aid as a percentage of GNI. The effect is to produce a lower average. *Reality of Aid* thinks a fairer measure of the relative generosity of donor countries is the unweighted average, which the DAC calls 'average country effort'. In 2002 this stood at 0.41% GNI compared with the 2002 weighted average of 0.23% GNI.

Reality of Aid has always acknowledged that aid can have the effect of reducing poverty when it is spent on promoting broad — based growth — every dollar does not have to be spent directly on basic

Figure 3.

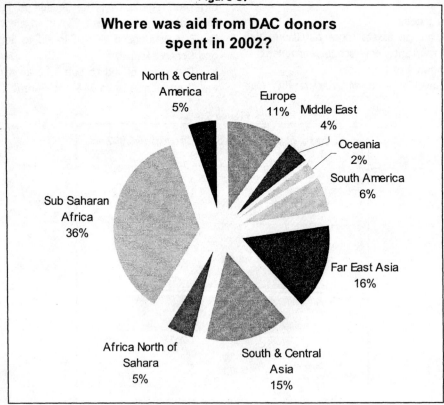

Where was aid from DAC donors spent in 2002?

World Aid Trends

Graph 6.

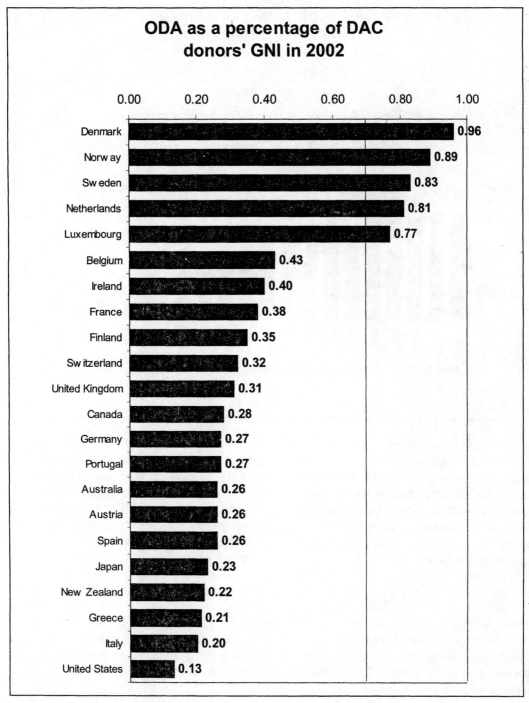

ODA as a percentage of DAC donors' GNI in 2002

Denmark	0.96
Norway	0.89
Sweden	0.83
Netherlands	0.81
Luxembourg	0.77
Belgium	0.43
Ireland	0.40
France	0.38
Finland	0.35
Switzerland	0.32
United Kingdom	0.31
Canada	0.28
Germany	0.27
Portugal	0.27
Australia	0.26
Austria	0.26
Spain	0.26
Japan	0.23
New Zealand	0.22
Greece	0.21
Italy	0.20
United States	0.13

World Aid Trends

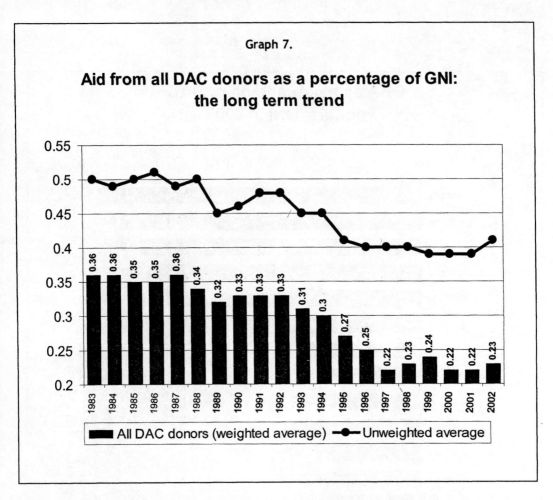

Graph 7.

**Aid from all DAC donors as a percentage of GNI:
the long term trend**

All DAC donors (weighted average) — Unweighted average

needs. However, successive reports have also highlighted the ways that aid is all too easily diverted to projects that have much to do with export promotion and winning geopolitical influence (and latterly security). The case has repeatedly been made that for aid to sustain both public and political support in the North, and to be seen as genuine partnership in the South, the chain of causation between every dollar spent and ultimate benefit to people in poverty should be credible and proximate.

The dangers of aid being spent on projects where the benefits to northern and southern élites are obvious but the benefits to poor people are at best speculative, are shown all too well in this *Reality of Aid* report. Therefore it is essential to have rigorous assessment of who will benefit from aid before money is allocated, and evaluations that examine which groups are benefiting and have benefited, both during and after programmes.

But it is also possible to look at current spending, to see how much is going on projects that have a reasonable chance of bringing some direct benefits to poorer income groups – and especially to see how much is being allocated to the basic rights and needs of the most vulnerable. See figure 5.

World Aid Trends

Figure 4.

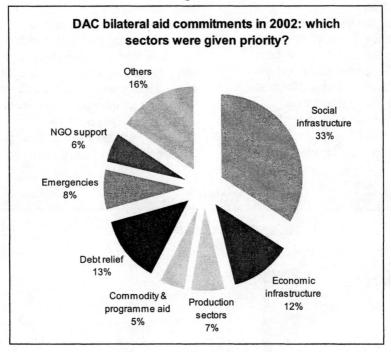

DAC bilateral aid commitments in 2002: which sectors were given priority?

Others 16%
Social infrastructure 33%
NGO support 6%
Emergencies 8%
Debt relief 13%
Commodity & programme aid 5%
Production sectors 7%
Economic infrastructure 12%

Figure 5.

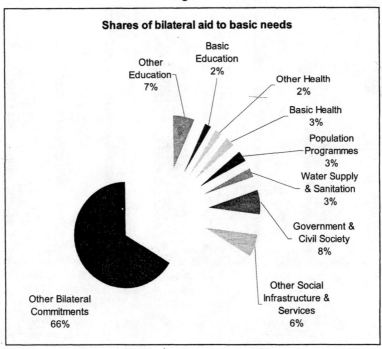

Shares of bilateral aid to basic needs

Other Education 7%
Basic Education 2%
Other Health 2%
Basic Health 3%
Population Programmes 3%
Water Supply & Sanitation 3%
Government & Civil Society 8%
Other Social Infrastructure & Services 6%
Other Bilateral Commitments 66%

World Aid Trends

Prospects for aid and the Millennium Development Goals

When the Financing for Development Summit took place in Monterrey, Mexico, DAC aid figures for 2001 had just been released showing global aid at just over US$52 billion. In 2002, global ODA rose significantly to over US$58 billion.

Estimates prepared for the FfD meeting in the Zedillo report[2] suggested that to achieve the Millennium Development Goals, an additional US$50 billion per year in aid would be needed.

At Monterrey, donors collectively pledged an additional US$16 billion. If donors deliver on these pledges, global aid will rise from 0.23% in 2002 to 0.29% GNI in 2006. But this amount will be far short of what is required from donors to help achieve the MDGs by 2015.

Graph 8 presents a picture of current aid spending and how donors could

Graph 8.

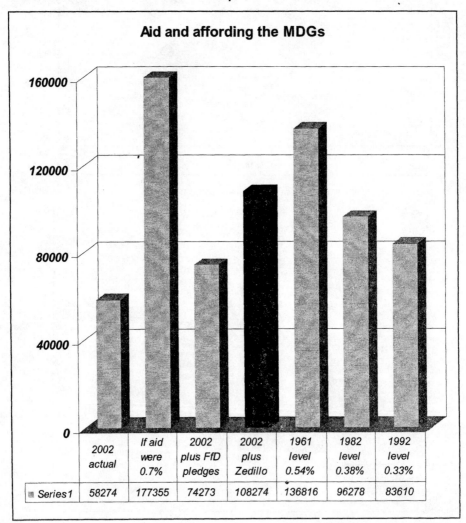

Aid and affording the MDGs

	2002 actual	If aid were 0.7%	2002 plus FfD pledges	2002 plus Zedillo	1961 level 0.54%	1982 level 0.38%	1992 level 0.33%
Series1	58274	177355	74273	108274	136816	96278	83610

World Aid Trends

increase aid to the necessary levels.
- Column 1 shows the actual level of aid achieved in 2002 — US$58 billion or 0.23% GNI.
- Column 2 shows what aid would have been if donors in 2002 were giving 0.7%. On that basis, aid would have totalled US$177 billions, which is three times the 2002 level.
  In 2002, the USA alone spent almost twice this amount (US$349 billion) on arms. The UK, France, Germany and Japan collectively spent another US$149 billions in 2002.[3]
- Column 3 shows aid at its 2002 level plus US$16 billion increases pledged at FfD — not enough to fund the MDGs.
- Column 4, coloured black, shows the

2002 level of aid plus the US$50 billion estimated as necessary to achieve the MDGs. (It is obvious, comparing column 4 and column 2, that if aid was at 0.7%, the MDGs would be very easily funded).
- Column 5 shows what aid would have been in 2002 if donors were giving the same percentage of GNI in aid as they did in 1961 when at 0.54% of GNI, aid was at its highest level ever. This would more than fund the MDGs.
- Column 6 shows 2002 aid if GNI percentage had been at its 1982 level. Not far off what is needed.
- Column 7 on the right shows what aid would have been in 2002 if the GNI percentage achieved in 1992 had been sustained.

No room for complacency as aid rises modestly in 2003.

In April 2004, just after final copy for this Reality of Aid report was sent for publication, the OECD DAC released provisional figures for aid in 2003. This brief note aims to update the discussion in Part V of Reality of Aid 2004 on aid volume and aid as a percentage of GNI.

As shown in graph 9, total aid from DAC donors rose from $58.3 billion in 2002 to $68.5 billion in 2003. Substantial increases in aid from some of the largest (G8) donors — the United States (16.9%), the UK (11.9%) and France (9.9%), outweighed big falls in aid from Japan (-8.9%) and Italy (-16.7%).

In real terms, the figures for 2003 represent a rise of 3.9% to $60.540 millions at 2002 prices. This follows a 7.2% real terms increase between 2001 and 2002.

As graph 10 shows, recent increases in aid have now restored the cuts that occurred after 1992. But as a DAC statement accompanying the new aid figures

noted, there is no room for complacency. Aid levels remain far short of what is needed to achieve the MDGs. Only 5 DAC donors met the UN aid target of 0.7% GNI in 2003 (see graph 9).

As discussed on page 185, any increases in aid volume need to be seen very much against the background of growing wealth in donor countries — the gap is still widening between rich and poor. Single digit real terms increases in aggregate aid volume may be welcome, but they fall far short of what is required to meet the challenge of eliminating absolute poverty.

World Aid Trends

Graph 9.

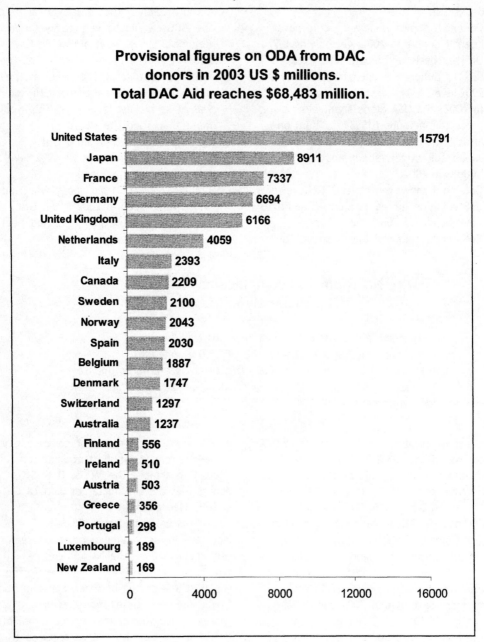

Provisional figures on ODA from DAC donors in 2003 US $ millions. Total DAC Aid reaches $68,483 million.

United States	15791
Japan	8911
France	7337
Germany	6694
United Kingdom	6166
Netherlands	4059
Italy	2393
Canada	2209
Sweden	2100
Norway	2043
Spain	2030
Belgium	1887
Denmark	1747
Switzerland	1297
Australia	1237
Finland	556
Ireland	510
Austria	503
Greece	356
Portugal	298
Luxembourg	189
New Zealand	169

World Aid Trends

Graph 10.

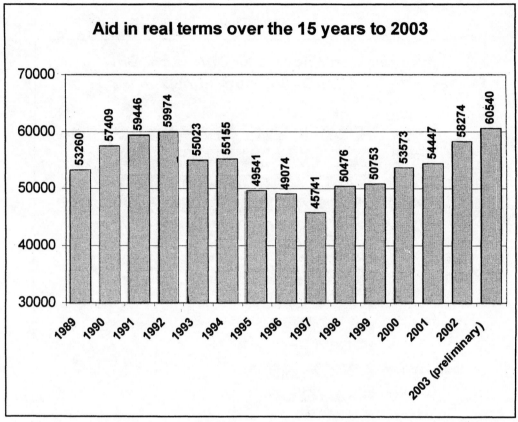

Aid in real terms over the 15 years to 2003

The message from the graph is that, in the past, donors have managed aid levels as a percentage of GNI that would exceed the Zedillo requirements. What was pledged at FFD will not even restore aid to the levels of just over a decade ago, let alone provide donors' share of what is needed to achieve the MDGs.

Less than one quarter of what the USA, UK, France, Germany and Japan spend on arms each year, would provide enough funding to ensure that aid played its part in the goal of halving poverty by 2015.

Less than one quarter of what the USA, UK, France, Germany and Japan spend on arms each year, would provide enough funding to ensure that aid played its part in the goal of halving poverty by 2015.

Notes

1. The Pearson Commission Report recommended the 0.7% GNP target in 1969, and the target was adopted by the UN in 1970.

2. http://www.un.org/reports/financing/

3. http://www.cdi.org/news/mrp/global-graph.pdf

World Aid Trends

Graph 11.

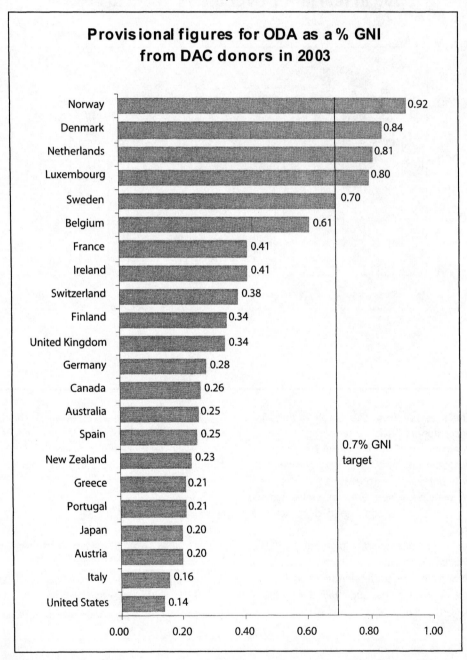

Provisional figures for ODA as a % GNI from DAC donors in 2003

Country	% GNI
Norway	0.92
Denmark	0.84
Netherlands	0.81
Luxembourg	0.80
Sweden	0.70
Belgium	0.61
France	0.41
Ireland	0.41
Switzerland	0.38
Finland	0.34
United Kingdom	0.34
Germany	0.28
Canada	0.26
Australia	0.25
Spain	0.25
New Zealand	0.23
Greece	0.21
Portugal	0.21
Japan	0.20
Austria	0.20
Italy	0.16
United States	0.14

0.7% GNI target

Australia

Box 8. AUSTRALIA at a glance

How much aid does AUSTRALIA give?

In 2002, AUSTRALIA gave

US$989m or 1,821m Australian Dollars

This means that, in 2002, each person
in AUSTRALIA gave

US$51 or 93 Australian Dollars

In 2002, aid from AUSTRALIA rose by

US$116m in cash terms. Because of inflation
and exchange rate changes, the value of aid
rose by 4.9% in real terms

How generous is AUSTRALIA?

AUSTRALIA gave 0.26% of its national wealth in 2002. This compares with the average
country effort of 0.41% and AUSTRALIA's previous own highpoint of 0.65% in 1975.

AUSTRALIA was less generous than 14 other donors, but more generous than in 2001 when
aid was 0.25% of GNI.

How much of AUSTRALIA's aid goes to the poorest countries and people?

41.9% of total bilateral aid (US$324) went to Least Developed and Low Income Countries
where 3.5 billion people (60% of the global population) live and where average incomes
are less than two dollars a day.

How much of AUSTRALIA's aid was spent on basic health, basic education, water supply and sanitation?

AUSTRALIA spent

1.29% of its bilateral aid (US$8.42m) on basic education
3.19% of its bilateral aid (US$20.75m) on basic health
0.65% of its bilateral aid (US$4.23m) on water and sanitation

Security issues dominate over direct poverty reduction

Shennia Spillane, Australian Council for International Development (ACFID)[1]

Developments in 2002-03 have given Australian civil society increasing cause for concern about the quantity and quality of Australian ODA. The scarce aid funds that remain in Australia's budget are in danger of increasing diversion to 'whole of government' priorities, particularly with regard to national security.

The Australian Government still claims to support the UN aid target of 0.7% of Gross National Income (GNI),[2] yet Australian practice indicates otherwise. Despite enjoying 'one of the strongest economies of the developed world'[3], with one of the highest growth rates in the OECD, Australian aid in 2002 rose, just a little, to 0.26% of GNI, from the historically low 2001 figure of 0.25% GNI. An ever-increasing proportion of this ODA is in fact spending by non-aid government agencies, particularly to fund Australia's controversial immigration policies. At the international level, Australia has chosen to remain largely disengaged from initiatives such as the Financing for Development process and the Millennium Development Goals, and has made no commitment to increase aid.

There has been an overt shift in the focus of Australian aid, with the inclusion of several new initiatives for counter-terrorism capacity building. These include bilateral counter-terrorism programmes with Indonesia and the Philippines, a 'Peace and Security Fund' for the Pacific Island Countries, and a contribution to an Asia-Pacific Economic Cooperation (APEC) fund for counter-terrorism capacity building.

This agenda conflates the combating of terrorism with combating poverty. While it is necessary and legitimate for governments to support an effective programme to combat terrorism, Australian NGOs have argued that the resources for these activities should come from national security budgets, not from the overstretched aid and development budget.

At the same time, there is a more subtle and fundamental shift toward prioritising security in aid programme strategies, especially in Australia's immediate region. Some of this is understandable and can be seen as necessary to help establish the conditions required for sustainable development; such as investing in effective police and judicial systems in the Solomon Islands, where any development had become virtually impossible due to the serious breakdown of law and order. But it appears that addressing security is increasingly taking precedence over other priorities for dealing with the causes of suffering and conflict, such as addressing urgent human needs for food, clean water,

Australia

basic health and education services.

In a November 2003 statement to Parliament on the Australian aid programme, the Minister for Foreign Affairs focused heavily on aid as an instrument to promote regional security and to combat terrorism. Minister Downer's central theme was that 'our aid is contributing in no small part to Australia's national interest by helping create those conditions essential for enhanced regional stability and security, and poverty reduction.'[4]

This statement represents a notable variation on previous expressions of the central objective of Australian aid. For the first time, poverty reduction is placed second to security in the aid rationale. While there is some acknowledgment of the relevance of meeting basic needs — particularly basic education — in countering terrorism, the strong emphasis is on activities to boost policing and law enforcement and to strengthen financial systems — activities that contribute to the national security of Australia and, in some cases, the partner country, but whose links with poverty reduction remain largely unproven.

Australian interventions even in the Pacific Island Countries, a long-term focus of the Australian aid programme, are now often characterised as actions to guard against 'failed states' in the region. In 2003, Australia initiated and led a 'Regional Assistance Mission to the Solomon Islands'. This consisted of a military and police intervention supported by at least A$87m in ODA, particularly focused on the provision of Australian governance assistance through technical advisers in a range of government ministries. The intervention was described by Australia's Foreign Minister as an Australian-led 'coalition of the willing', intended to counter the security threat posed by a 'failed state' in Australia's neighbourhood.[5]

This was followed in December 2003 by the announcement of a major bilateral initiative in Papua New Guinea, which will cost some A$800m over five years. The initiative, designed 'to help PNG address its key challenges... in the areas of policing, law and justice and economic and public sector management', will involve the placement of 230 Australian police personnel and some 65 Australian bureaucrats in PNG Government agencies.[6] The implications of this significant new programme for the overall profile of the aid budget are not yet clear.

Other key developments in the Australian aid programme during 2003 included:

- A commitment of some A$120m to the reconstruction of Iraq over two to three years, following Australia's military participation in the US-led war.[7] Unlike the A$650m in new money given to the military to fund the war, only around A$38m in new funding has been provided for aid to Iraq — the remainder will be sourced by reallocating existing aid funds.

- An increase in total Australian aid to Indonesia by A$30m or 22.2%, focusing on governance, counter-terrorism cooperation, secular basic education, and health and reconstruction in Bali.

- The release in March 2003 of a new policy on aid for water and sanitation, *Making Every Drop Count*. Although many NGOs welcomed the policy's support for a strong focus on water and sanitation in the aid programme, it was regrettable that no new funding accompanied the policy statement. There have been welcome increases in Australian aid for water and sanitation over the past two years, but such increases only occur through redistribution of funds within a stagnant aid budget.

Australia

- Increases in trade-related technical assistance, food security initiatives, and humanitarian and emergency funding (though, at least initially, spending in Iraq will account for much of the latter increase). Australia also opened its market to tariff- and quota-free access for all goods produced in the 49 Least Developed Countries, and East Timor, from July 2003.
- A decline in the proportion of Australian aid allocated for projects and programmes through NGOs, to represent less than 5% of aid spending.[8] This decline is partly due to changes underway in the mechanisms for government-NGO funding. Nevertheless, government support for the work of civil society in developing countries (both directly and through Australian NGOs) will warrant close monitoring over coming years.

Governance, human rights and Australian Aid

Governance has been an element of Australian aid programmes for many years, but has received particular emphasis over the past five years, doubling as a proportion of aid spending. By 2003-04, 'governance' represented the largest single sector in the Australian aid programme, accounting for A$370 million or 21% of aid spending. Aid funding allocated for basic rights in 2003 included 12% for health, 5% for basic education and 3% for water and sanitation.[9]

Australian governance aid is primarily directed towards strengthening institutions for economic and financial management and public sector reform, which accounts for 55% of governance spending.[10] Some 60-70% of good governance activities focus on personnel at senior levels in government or industry.[11] Australian NGOs have been critical of the extent to which Australian governance

assistance involves the placement of Australian 'experts' as technical advisers within the governments of developing countries in the Pacific and South East Asia. These projects are known as 'boomerang aid', because the money mainly ends up in the pockets of Australian consultants and companies. Moreover, while recognising the importance of sound economic governance, Australian and regional NGOs question the use of governance aid to impose Australian systems and approaches that may not be appropriate to the social, cultural and technological context.

While Australian policy notes the importance of support for human rights and civil society as part of improving governance in developing countries, these areas attract only 20% of governance spending. Australia claims a strong tradition of support for human rights in the Asia-Pacific region, including through aid, but in recent years such support has been reduced to only one small element of a broader 'governance' agenda. Like much aid for governance, there is a strong emphasis in Australian projects on the 'supply side' of good governance, with less attention being paid to strengthening the ability of affected communities to exercise their human rights and demand transparency and accountability from their governments.

In addition, Australian policies and actions on illegal immigration continue to undermine the country's international credibility on human rights. Official rhetoric focuses on border protection and criminalising people smugglers, at the expense of protecting the human rights of asylum seekers and refugees. Meanwhile, draconian measures continue to be employed to prevent asylum seekers gaining access to Australia and to detain indefinitely those who do enter. The substantial costs incurred in pursuit of these policies are counted as Australian ODA.

Australia

Australian support for good governance has also shown its limits when it comes to issues of global governance. In 2003, the Australian government continued to express strong cynicism about the UN and other multilateral forums; it explicitly supported bilateralism and 'coalitions of the willing' in preference to the multilateral rules-based system.[12] Australia has remained largely disinterested in issues related to the quality and justice of global financial governance, such as reform of the IMF, and the failure of international debt mechanisms. Even in trade, where Australia has been an active player in the WTO and sometimes acted in concert with developing countries, the government has simultaneously pursued bilateral trade agreements with the United States and with key Asian trading partners. It seems that while Australia is keen to 'provide' its own version of good governance to developing countries, the pursuit of good governance does not extend to the international system and Australia's own role within it.

Notes

[1] The author would like to acknowledge useful input and comments for this chapter provided by Graham Tupper, Kathy Richards and Garth Luke.

[2] The Hon Alexander Downer MP, Minister for Foreign Affairs, *Australian Aid: Investing in Growth, Stability and Prosperity*, Eleventh Statement to Parliament on Australia's Development Cooperation Program, September 2002, Canberra, p22.

[3] Statement by the Hon. Peter Costello, Treasurer of Australia and Governor of the IMF and the World Bank for Australia, at the joint annual discussion [of

the IMF and World Bank], 23 September 2003, Dubai; available at http://www.treasurer.gov.au/tsr/content/speeches/2003/016.asp; quoting the IMF unsourced).

[4] The Hon Alexander Downer MP, Minister for Foreign Affairs, *Twelfth Annual Statement to Parliament on Australia's Development Cooperation Program*, Canberra, November 2003; available at http://www.ausaid.gov.au/publications/pubout.cfm?Id=1317_3443_8330_1968_7137

[5] See speech of The Hon Alexander Downer MP, Minister for Foreign Affairs, *Security in an Unstable World*, at the National Press Club, Canberra, 26 June 2003, available at http://ww.foreignminister.gov.au/speeches/2003/030626_unstableworld.html

[6] *New Era of Cooperation with PNG*, Media Release FA158 by the Minister for Foreign Affairs Alexander Downer MP, 11 December 2003: http://www.foreignminister.gov.au/releases/2003/fa158_03.html

[7] Downer, above n.iv, at p6.

[8] Aid Budget 2003-04, *Overview and Analysis*, Australian Council for Overseas Aid, May 13 2003, Canberra, http://www.acfid.asn.au/campaigns/aid/budget_analysis2003-04.pdf.

[9] *Ibid. Actual figures for Australia's spending on basic social services in 2002, are given in the Australia at a glance box.*

[10] *Australia's Overseas Aid Program 2003-04*, Federal Budget Statement by the Hon Alexander Downer MP, Minister for Foreign Affairs, Canberra, 13 May 2003, p5.

[11] Drawn from OECD DAC reporting 2001, quoted in an ACFOA Good Governance paper by Kathy Richards, to be published late 2003 at www.acfid.asn.au.

[12] See for example, speech by The Hon Alexander Downer MP, above n.v..

Austria

Box 9. AUSTRIA at a glance

How much aid does AUSTRIA give?

In 2002, AUSTRIA gave   US$520m or 552m Euros

This means that, in 2002, each person
in AUSTRIA gave   US$65 or 69 Euros

In 2002, aid from AUSTRIA fell by US$13m in cash terms. Because of inflation and exchange rate changes, the value of aid fell by 8.4% in real terms.

How generous is AUSTRIA?

AUSTRIA gave 0.26% of its national wealth in 2002. This compares with the average country effort of 0.41% and AUSTRIA's previous own highpoint of 0.38% in 1985.

AUSTRIA was less generous than 15 other donors and less generous than in 2001 when aid was 0.29% of GNI.

How much of AUSTRIA's aid goes to the poorest countries and people?

42.5% of total bilateral aid (US$154.7m) went to Least Developed and Low Income Countries where 3.5 billion people (60% of the global population) live and where average incomes are less than two dollars a day.

How much of AUSTRIA's aid was spent on basic health, basic education, water supply and sanitation?

AUSTRIA spent

0.27 % of its bilateral aid (US$1.22m) on basic education
1.41% of its bilateral aid (US$6.48m) on basic health
2.89% of its bilateral aid (US$13.26m) on water and sanitation.

Belgium

Box 10. BELGIUM at a glance

How much aid does BELGIUM give?

In 2002 BELGIUM gave   US$1072m or 1137m Euros

This means that, in 2002, each person
in BELGIUM gave   US$104 or 110 Euros

In 2002, aid from BELGIUM rose by   US$204m in cash terms. Because of inflation
and exchange rate changes, the value of aid
increased by 14.8% in real terms.

How generous is BELGIUM?

BELGIUM gave 0.43% of its national wealth in 2002. This compares with the average
country effort of 0.41% and BELGIUM's previous own highpoint of 0.60% in 1975.

BELGIUM was less generous than 5 other donors and more generous than in 2001 when
aid was 0.37% of GNI.

How much of BELGIUM's aid goes to the poorest countries and people?

48.8% of total bilateral aid (US$346.9m) went to Least Developed and Low Income
Countries where 3.5 billion people (60% of the global population) live and where average
incomes are less than two dollars a day.

How much of BELGIUM's aid was spent on basic health, basic education, water supply and sanitation?

BELGIUM spent

1.01% of its bilateral aid (US$7.48m) on basic education
4.45% of its bilateral aid (US$32.98m) on basic health
1.75% of its bilateral aid (US$12.99m) on water and sanitation.

Concern as Foreign Affairs swallows the aid budget

Han Verleyen, 11.11.11, Coalition of the Flemish North South Movement

Elections

In 2003, Belgium held federal elections, which resulted in a huge defeat for the Green Party and a confirmation of the Socialist-Liberal coalition.

In the former government, the Green Party's Eddy Boutmans held the post of State Secretary for Development Cooperation. The tensions between the departments of Foreign Affairs and Development Cooperation were almost legendary. Foreign Affairs made several attempts to get a stronger hold on the competences and budget for development cooperation.

After the elections, the Belgian government appointed a Minister for Development Cooperation and no longer a State Secretary under the Minister of Foreign Affairs. This did not, however, result in a greater autonomy for the Department of Development Cooperation. The budget for development cooperation was fully integrated in the budget of Foreign Affairs. There are no immediate consequences for the competence of the Minister but the tendency to downgrade development cooperation to an instrument of Foreign Policy is very obvious. Moreover, budgets for conflict prevention and humanitarian assistance had already been lifted out of the section on development cooperation

are fully transferred to the competence of the Minister of Foreign Affairs.

Budget

An important achievement of the former State Secretary was the adoption of a law that obliges Belgium to reach the 0.7% target by 2010. In the meantime, government has to explain annually the efforts it makes to increase the budget. For 2004, the government has promised to raise the Development Cooperation budget to €847 million and to achieve an overall ODA-budget of €1.3 billion.

In the current negotiations on the 2004 budget, this commitment has been repeated, but the rise in the budget is a fake! The Development Cooperation budget has been artificially increased by introducing ODA-accountable budget lines from other departments into the development cooperation budget. Normally these expenses are added to the Dev-Co budget, to calculate the overall ODA-budget. The so-called rise in the budget can also be partially attributed to the detailed scrutiny applied to the budgets of other departments, to find ODA-accountable expenses.

Focus on Central Africa

The new government renewed its commitment to Central Africa as a focal

Belgium

point for Belgian Development Cooperation. Belgium supported elections in Rwanda, and is engaging actively to support the Peace Conference to be held in Congo in June 2004. The focus of Belgian aid in Congo is on strengthening the public services, health and support to small enterprises. The Minister announced that aid to Congo will be doubled next year. It is unclear, however, how this increase will be financed, given the general decrease in the budget for bilateral cooperation.

Partner countries dropped

The government has decided to reduce the number of partner countries from 25 to 18. Bangladesh, Ethiopia, Ivory Coast, Burkina Faso, Cambodja, Laos and SADC have been removed from the list. The criteria for the selection were, among other things, the focus on Central Africa, the impact and visibility of Belgian Cooperation, the share in the total amount of ODA to the partner countries, the quality of ongoing programmes and projects and the quality of policy dialogue with the governments involved. Poverty focus has also been mentioned as a criterion, but this is not reflected in the list of countries excluded: apart from SADC, all countries affected by the decision are LDCs.

The 11.11.11, Coalition of the North-South Movement is in favour of more concentration, but stresses the need for continuity. With each new government, the list of partner countries changes, and the criteria used are not very clear.

Another dangerous evolution in Belgian development cooperation is the shifting focus to 'Migrant countries'. The government agreement and the Development Cooperation policy note both refer to the need to focus aid on the countries of origin of asylum seekers in Belgium. Both policy documents also carefully introduce the idea of a partial reorientation of ODA to Balkan

states. This is so far not reflected in the selection of partner countries but the near future will prove whether or not this shift can be noticed in practice.

11.11.11 strongly opposes migration pressure as a new criterion for aid. In the long run, the aim of ODA is of course to improve living conditions. A possible side effect can be a reduction in the number of asylum seekers or immigrants. This cannot, however, be the basis and goal of a long-term cooperation relation with partner countries. Making aid dependent on its effects on migration will lead to a rapidly shifting, unsustainable, and poor quality cooperation.

Governance and human rights in the Belgian Aid programme

The Belgian Law for development cooperation mentions the strengthening of democracy, governance and human rights as a central aim of Belgian Development Cooperation. Since 1994, Belgian Development Cooperation has been obliged by law to draft annual reports on the human rights situation in partner countries, and to assess development cooperation policies accordingly. But the significance of both the law and the few annual reports that have been drafted is limited.

The budget for Foreign Affairs has a specific budget line for conflict prevention, peace-building and human rights. This budget line has been lifted from the general budget for development cooperation and transferred to the Foreign Affairs budget. 11.11.11 deplores the transfer. The link between development cooperation and highly political and sensitive issues such as conflict prevention, governance and human rights should be strengthened, not weakened.

Human rights and good governance do not figure as such among the core issues for development cooperation, as defined in the

Belgium

policy note from the new Minister for development cooperation. He wants to focus on health (HIV, malaria and poverty-related diseases), childrens rights, gender and water. These priorities for Belgian Development Cooperation are defined in terms of rights, for example the right to health, food or education. Human rights, good governance and democracy are stressed as important issues in different policy declarations. In interviews, the Minister refers to human rights as an important benchmark, against which to assess the quality of democracy and democratic institutions.

The Belgian government does not maintain a strict political conditionality policy in the promotion of governance and human rights. Likewise, performance in the field of human rights and good governance do not figure among the criteria for the selection of partner countries.

Rather than making aid directly dependent on progress, Belgian development policy aims to contribute to improvement in the field of governance and human rights. The policy note on conflict prevention and peace building stresses the need for an 'encouraging and supportive policy to underline the necessity of good governance, the state of law and respect for human rights as the basis for structural stability'. It further clarifies that aid has to be oriented towards capacity building for good governance in the framework of a long-term commitment. 11.11.11 supports this approach: political conditionality to contribute to human rights and good governance has rarely proved to be effective. Attaching strings to aid can only be useful when based on a strong demand from civil society.

Governance and human rights in the context of PRSPs
When discussing the importance of Poverty Reduction Strategy Papers (PRSPs) for Belgian development cooperation in his policy note, the Minister does not refer to human rights or governance issues. The Millennium Development Goals are much more prominent, in the policy note as a whole, and in the chapter on PRSPs.

However, the Minister puts great faith in PRSPs, as a national policy framework for poverty reduction and a vehicle for participation of civil society in the planning process and the development debate. Though recognising the importance and weight of PRSPs in the current development thinking and policies, 11.11.11 calls for a much more critical analysis of PRSPs and a critical assessment of the value of participation and the ownership aspects in their drafting.

Security, Migration and combating terrorism
The autonomy of Belgian development cooperation is threatened by the increasing influence of issues such as security and migration. Development cooperation funds (€3 million in 2003) have been used for the rebuilding of Iraq (Foreign Affairs competence), and for Asylum policy or Migration issues (€70 million in 2003; Internal Affairs competence). Both the governmental agreement (July 2003) and the policy note of the Minister of Development Cooperation (October 2003) carefully introduce the need to redirect development funds to Migrant countries (see above).

Global governance
Belgium is not a prominent actor in discussions on the reform of international institutions. It pleaded for a more significant role for the UN in the context of the US-Iraq conflict but this was not linked to concrete proposals for reform. At the WTO summit in Cancun, however, Foreign Affairs Minister Louis Michel did plead for an Economic and

Belgium

Social Security Council, to provide a social and economic framework for world trade. This idea was introduced by the Socialist Party in the governmental agreement. 11.11.11 is supportive of each step to integrate world trade in a social, economic and ecological framework, and to make trade subordinate to human rights and ecological norms.

Making aid dependent on its effects on migration will lead to a rapidly shifting, unsustainable, and poor quality cooperation.

Canada

Box 11. CANADA at a glance

How much aid does CANADA give?

In 2002, CANADA gave   US$2,006m or 3,150m Canadian Dollars

This means that, in 2002, each person
in CANADA gave   US$64 or100 Canadian Dollars

In 2002, aid from CANADA rose by   US$474m in cash terms. Because of inflation
                                             and exchange rate changes, the value of aid
                                             rose by 31.2% in real terms

How generous is CANADA?

CANADA gave 0.28% its national wealth in 2002[1]. This compares with the average country effort of 0.41% and CANADA's previous own highpoint 0.54% in 1975.

CANADA was less generous than 11 other donors but more generous than in 2001 when aid was 0.22% of GNI.

How much of CANADA's aid goes to the poorest countries and people?

35.5% of bilateral aid (US$533.9m) went to Least Developed and Low Income Countries where 3.5 billion people (60% of the global population) live and where average incomes are less than two dollars a day.

How much of CANADA's aid was spent on basic health, basic education, water supply and sanitation?

CANADA spent

3.99% of its bilateral aid (US$68.77m) on basic education
3.08% of its bilateral aid (US$52.98m) on basic health
1.67% of its bilateral aid (US$28.73m) on water and sanitation.

DAC aid performance statistics for Canada for 2001 and 2002 are different than CIDA's and CCIC's calculation of Canada's performance for those years because the DAC figures are based on a calendar year and not CIDA's fiscal year. In 2001 CIDA multilateral contributions were minimal in the DAC statistics because two payments were made in 2002, but in two different fiscal years for CIDA. CIDA reports its fiscal year performance for 2001/02 at 0.27% of GNI (compared to 022% in the DAC report) and CCIC has estimated 2002/03 at 0.27% (compared to the DAC's 0.28%).

Doubling the budget is just one of the challenges

Brian Tomlinson, Canadian Council for International Cooperation (CCIC)

On the night of November 2003 when Canada's new Prime Minister, Paul Martin, was elected leader of the Liberal Party, his guest, Bono, challenged him to assume aggressive leadership for global justice — on cancelling debt, promoting fair trade, eradicating poverty and HIV/AIDS in Africa. As Prime Minister, Martin set out the new vision for Canadian foreign policy, through which he intends to assume greater international leadership 'in developing new thinking about how the international community governs itself'.[1]

Whether the Prime Minister lives up to the challenges posed by Bono remains to be seen. In his early initiatives, Martin sought to 'improve' Canada's relations with the United States (participation in continental missile defence), but also to create a forum for North/South dialogue, to bridge and change relationships with developing countries. While the directions for Canadian international cooperation policy are not yet clear (February 2004), it seems likely that they will be distinguished by both significant change as well as continuity with the previous Chrétien government. These directions are to be elaborated in an International Policy Review during the later half of 2004.

Chretien's 2003 Federal Budget fulfilled his aid commitment made at the 2002 UN FfD

Conference. This Budget increased Canadian aid by 8% for 2002/03 and for each of the next two years up to 2004/05. The Budget renewed the pledge to double assistance by 2010, with a focus on nine priority countries and half of the increase going to Sub-Saharan Africa.[2]

As expected, the new Prime Minister honoured the commitment of 8% increases in his March 2004 budget. Canada's aid performance is expected to be 0.28% of GNI in this year.

Table 6. Canadian Aid Performance (including 8% annual increases)

2000/01	0.25% of GNI
2001/02	0.27% of GNI
2002/03	0.27% of GNI
2003/04	0.26% of GNI
2004/05	0.28% of GNI
2005/06	0.28% of GNI
2009/10	0.32% of GNI

Note: CCIC Estimates 2002/03 to 2009/10.

If the government were to achieve a doubling of aid by 2009/10, Canadian aid might reach 0.32% of GNI in that year. CCIC is challenging the new government to adopt

Canada

a plan to reach the UN goal of 0.7% by 2015, and at the same time to contribute Canada's fair share of new aid resources needed globally to achieve the UN Millennium Development Goals.[3]

During the International Policy Review, Canadian civil society organisations (CSOs) will continue to press the government to match its international ambitions for leadership in North/South relations with the resources that developing countries expect Canada to commit to meet its stated obligations to the MDGs and to poverty eradication.

During the past three years, there have been significant changes in Canadian international cooperation policy. These will continue to inform changes to both the delivery and content of Canadian ODA under the new government.[4]

- In September 2002, CIDA adopted a new overarching policy, 'Canada making a difference in the world: Strengthening aid effectiveness', which outlines new approaches to aid. These include 1) increased participation in donor coordinated engagement with government through sector-wide approaches (SWAps) and Budget Support for PRSPs, 2) increased sector and country focus for Canadian aid, 3) programmatic approaches and a move away from a project orientation, and 4) reduction in the tying of Canadian aid. Canadian CSOs welcomed the policy's principles of local ownership, a focus on poverty and greater coherence in Canadian aid efforts. They have, however, been frustrated by the absence of any strategic reflection on roles for civil society in these new approaches.[5]
- CCIC has noted a sharp decline in the involvement of CSOs in implementing CIDA programming between 1999/00 and 2002/03 (from 28.7% of ODA to 16.6%), even prior to the new aid directions. For CIDA's nine priority countries, the role of the Canadian and beneficiary governments in the direct implementation of bilateral programmeshas increased over this period from 39% to 52%, while CSO and private sector implementation decreased accordingly.[6] Given the emphasis in the September 2002 policy on SWAps and Budget Support, the marginalisation of partnerships with CSOs will probably only be attenuated in the coming years. CCIC continues to seek a CIDA overarching policy framework that clarifies the important role for CSOs in the development process.[7]
- In his first international policy pronouncements, Prime Minister Martin has underlined the importance of the 'Montreal Consensus', adopted by G-20 finance ministers in 2001, whereby conditions favourable to sustainable growth in developing countries must 'ensure that the appropriate social policies are in place — so that the benefits of that growth will reach all citizens in an equitable way'. Martin adds, 'we must do all these things in an inclusive way so that these policies respond to the needs citizens themselves express'.[8] CIDA has expanded its support for social development priorities — basic education, primary health, child protection and HIV/AIDS — since 2000. Issues of governance will also play a significant role in future Canadian aid and foreign policy relationships with developing countries.

Overall support for improved governance in developing countries has increased, rising from 10.5% of total CIDA programming in 1995 to 16.4% in 2002/03.[9] Governance

Canada

initiatives include both strengthening the public sector as well as civil society/human rights. CIDA's governance programme funding in 2002/03 was split almost equally between civil society/human rights and strengthening the government sector. The latter will rise substantially as disbursements for SWAps and Budget Support increase. In the past, CSOs have been major partners in CIDA's governance programme, implementing fully 38.8% in 2002/03.[10]

- In 2003, CIDA adopted a policy framework on private sector development (PSD) in Canadian development cooperation. Positively, it promotes a broad definition of the private sector, including the informal economy, and subjects all PSD initiatives to three analytical lenses - a pro-poor lens (livelihood strategies for the poor), a business lens and a governance lens.[11] In 2003, Prime Minister Martin was co-chair for the UNDP Commission on the Private Sector and Development. He has intimated that its recommendations (expected in early 2004) will inform future programming priorities for CIDA. At DAVOS in 2004, PM Martin indicated that building a strong indigenous private sector in the developing world is essential for reducing poverty and that this 'will become a focus of [Canadian] foreign policy'. It is hoped that such a focus will retain CIDA's poverty lens for determining appropriate Canadian initiatives.
- In 2003/04, the government's commitment to poverty reduction in Africa and to nine priority countries may have been undermined by very large CIDA aid commitments in Afghanistan and post-war Iraq. Between 2002 and 2004, C$350 million was committed for humanitarian and reconstruction programmes in

Afghanistan, the largest single country pledge ever made by Canada.[12] A 2000-strong military force and leadership of NATO's International Security Assistance Force add to this commitment. Afghanistan policy is being closely coordinated between Defence, Foreign Affairs and CIDA. Canadian CSOs are concerned that Canada may be contemplating support for joint military/aid Provincial Reconstruction Teams (PRTs). According to CSOs, PRTs will increase insecurity for the population, CSOs and government personnel, in part because the lines between military and humanitarian mandates are blurred. For Iraq, in October 2003, Canada announced commitments of C$300 million in reconstruction aid. Most of this is being disbursed through UN and multilateral facilities.[13] In January 2004, Canada agreed to cancel C$750 million in Iraq debt as part of a multilateral agreement. CCIC will be closely monitoring CIDA's 2003/04 aid statistics, to ensure that these reconstruction funds do not compromise the government's 2003 Budget commitments for additional aid to Sub-Saharan Africa and for long-term development.[14]

- New Canadian international initiatives will be accompanied by increased inter-departmental coordination, or the whole-of-government approach, which is being piloted for Canadian management of its Afghan policy. Such an approach may affect the ways in which Canada delivers its ODA, including the possibility of greater integration of CIDA resources within the Department of Foreign Affairs. CCIC and its members are deeply concerned that such restructuring may affect the content of Canadian aid efforts, greatly diminishing resources devoted to long-term poverty reduction

Canada

in the poorest countries, in favour of other more immediate Canadian foreign policy interests. An important indicator of these tensions is Canadian interest in a broader definition of ODA at the OECD DAC, to include resources devoted to security and the 'war on terrorism', further undermining the poverty focus of international assistance.[15]

Notes

[1] Honourable Paul Martin, 'Reply to the Speech from the Throne', House of Commons, 3 February 2004.

[2] In December 2002, the government announced that future increases in Canadian aid would be concentrated in nine countries — Bangladesh, Honduras, Bolivia, Ethiopia, Tanzania, Mozambique, Senegal, Mali, Ghana. CIDA is implementing its strategies for improved aid effectiveness in these nine countries with these enhanced resources. At least half of the aid increases is to be devoted to Africa's development needs.

[3] An elaboration of CCIC's budget plan to achieve the 0.7% target for aid and other proposals for revitalising Canada's leadership in relations with developing countries, see 'Recommitting to the Millennium Development Goals' (http://www.ccic.ca/ e/docs/002_aid_2003-10-21_call_on_government_to _meet_its_un_commitments.pdf and 'Towards a Canadian Foreign Policy for Global Justice and Equity' (http://www.ccic.ca/e/docs/002_policy_2003- 12-9_global_justice_policy_brief.pdf) on CCIC's web site, www.ccic.ca.

[4] Many of these changes will not be known in their specifics until after a federal election expected for April/May 2004. See the CCIC web site, www.ccic.ca for further developments in Canadian aid policy in the post-election period.

[5] For CCIC's critique of the new aid directions for CIDA see 'CIDA's Canada making a difference in the world: A policy statement on strengthening aid effectiveness: CCIC's summary highlights and implications' athttp://www.ccic.ca/e/002/ aid_cidas_canada_making_a_difference_inthe_world.shtml and 'Report on the CCIC/CIDA Dialogue: Local Ownership: Roles for Southern and Canadian Civil Society Organizations, March 20/21 2003' at http://

www.ccic.ca/e/docs/002_aid_2002_ccic- cida_dialogue.pdf.

[6] These statistics have been calculated by CCIC based on a review of the implementing agent for all bilateral projects and Canadian Partnership Branch projects in these two years, based on project statistics provided by CIDA. Included are those agencies implementing humanitarian assistance projects in Multilateral Branch. The information available for other programmes in Multilateral Branch or Policy Branch was not complete.

[7] As noted below, such a policy framework for the private sector has been developed and published in 2003 on the initiative of the past Minister for International Cooperation.

[8] Prime Minister Paul Martin, 'Prime Minister Paul Martin speaks to the inauguration ceremony of the Special Summit of the Americas, Statement by the Prime Minister', January 12, 2004, Monterrey, Mexico.

[9] Treasury Board, 'Canadian International Development Agency: Performance Report', various years.

[10] CCIC calculations based on CIDA project statistics for 2002/03 for the Geographic Branches and Canadian Partnership Branch. The coding of Government and Civil Society includes the following sub-codes- strengthening civil society, human rights, landmines clearance, demobilisation, post-conflict peace-building (UN), free flow of information, elections, government administration, legal and judicial development, public sector financial management, and economic development policy/planning. These statistics include the first two as civil society strengthening and the last four as strengthening government and the public sector. Support for 'elections' amounted to 1.2% of total governance disbursements in 2002/03.

[11] The CIDA strategy for the private sector is found at http://www.acdi-cida.gc.ca/cida_ind.nsf/AllDocIds/ C21E4EA87075A4CE05256CC2006FE2F3?OpenDocument.

[12] So far, CIDA current bilateral commitments to Afghanistan are C$73.8 through the World Bank, C$45.4 through UN organisations, and C$15.1 through Canadian partners.

[13] These commitments for Iraq include C$100 for pre- war humanitarian assistance in early 2003 (of which C$55 million went to UN organisations), and C$200

Canada

million for post war reconstruction, of which C$40 million was directed to UNICEF, C$100 million for the Fund Facility for Iraq, C$5 million to CARE and C$10 million to help train Iraq police officers. The cancellation of Iraq debt will not affect budgetary allocations, but will be included in Canadian ODA in the year that the debt is cancelled.

14 The 8% increase to Canadian aid for 2003/04 was approximately C$230 million, with an additional

C$423 million added in supplementary budget estimates during the fiscal year.

15 See 'A CCIC Commentary on A Development Cooperation Lens on Terrorism Prevention: Key Entry Points of Action', A Policy Statement by the Development Assistance Committee, OECD, April 2003, produced by CCIC in November 2003, located at http://www.ccic.ca/e/docs/002_aid_2003-11_ccic_commentary_dac_terror_prevention.pdf.

Denmark

Box 12. DENMARK at a glance

How much aid does DENMARK give?

In 2002, DENMARK gave   US$1,643m or 12,956m Krone

That means that, in 2002, each
person in DENMARK gave   US$305 or 2,408 Krone

In 2002, aid from DENMARK rose by   US$9m in cash terms. Because of inflation and
                                         exchange rate changes, the value of aid fell by
                                         5.8% in real terms

How generous is DENMARK?

DENMARK gave 0.96% of its national wealth in 2002. This compares with the average
country effort of 0.41% and Denmark's own previous highpoint of 1.06% reached in 2000.

DENMARK was the most generous of all 22 DAC donors, but less generous than in 2001 when
aid was 1.03% GNI.

How much of DENMARK's aid goes to the poorest countries and people?

54.0 % of total bilateral aid (US$560.4m) went to Least Developed and Low Income
Countries where 3.5 billion people (60% of the global population) live and where average
incomes are less than two dollars a day.

How much of DENMARK's aid was spent on basic health, basic education, water supply and sanitation?

DENMARK spent

2.68% of its bilateral aid (US$22.59m) on basic education

0.49% of its bilateral aid (US$4.17m) on basic health

3.57% of its bilateral aid (US$30.13m) on water and sanitation.

A world of difference – indeed

Jesper Heldgaard, freelance journalist, and Lars Anderskouv,
Mellemfolkeligt Samvirke[1]

'A World of Difference'. That is the title of the Danish Liberal-Conservative government's 'Vision for New Priorities in Danish Development Assistance 2004-08', which was launched in June 2003. And the government, which took over from the Social Democrat-Social Liberal government in November 2001, has certainly not wasted time in making changes to Danish development policy that means a world of difference from the policy of the recent past.

As recently as October 2000, the Liberals and Conservatives in the Danish Parliament voted in favour of a new strategy 'Partnership 2000', which confirmed years of broad consensus in Denmark on development policy. But following the November 2001 elections, the new government – with a narrow majority in Parliament and supported only by the nationalist Danish People's Party – has made sweeping changes in Danish aid.

This should come as no surprise. The government was voted in on promises to finance better Danish health care out of the aid budget. The long-held perception that a broad majority of Danes were in favour of the high spending on aid has been challenged. Aid has – for good or ill – moved to centre stage and has suddenly become part of the on-going battle for public spending resources in Denmark.

Highlights of the reality of aid under a new Danish government are:

- The goal of maintaining Danish ODA at 1% of GNI has been dropped.
- In 2002, the new government cut DKK1.5 billion (about US $168.5 million) from the total 2002 aid budget. Danish ODA is likely to decrease to 0.83% of GNI in 2004.[3]
- The special Environment, Peace and Stability Facility (EPSF), which was to reach 0.5% of GNI – on top of the 1% of GNI for aid – by 2005, has been abolished.
- While poverty reduction remains the overriding aim of Danish aid, development policy is increasingly integrated into foreign policy and perceived as a tool to overcome threats to national security. Thus, the fight against terrorism has been introduced as a new priority of Danish aid. Direct support to fight terrorism is increased and aid to programme countries is made dependent on their active involvement in the fight. Also, a new, special initiative to promote democracy in the Arab world will be allocated a yearly DKK100 million from the aid budget.

Denmark

- Development no longer has its own Minister, but falls under the Minister of Foreign Affairs. This confirms the perception that development policy is not seen as an area in its own right by the present government.
- Dramatic cutbacks in aid are announced and new strategies launched and implemented, without consulting partners in Denmark or in the South, or other stakeholders, such as opposition parties. Not even the Board or the Council for International Development Co-operation are consulted before major decisions are made.
- The aid budget is increasingly used to promote what a DAC peer review of Danish aid in 2003 called 'domestically inspired priorities'. The government[4] has threatened to cut aid to countries that refuse to take back nationals who have been refused asylum in Denmark; support for refugees in adjacent areas has been increased, in order to reduce the influx of refugees to Europe; support has been introduced for projects in developing countries that will contribute towards meeting Danish obligations under the Kyoto Protocol to reduce carbon dioxide emissions.
- Three of the 18 programme countries for Danish aid — Eritrea, Malawi and Zimbabwe — were dropped in 2002. This happened at the same time as the DKK1.5 billion cut in the aid budget but the government claimed that aid to the three countries was stopped because of their poor human rights and democratisation record.[5]
- Aid to another two programme countries, Egypt and Bhutan, will be phased out over a ten-years period, reducing the total number of programme countries to 13.
- Social sectors are given higher priority, not in absolute amounts compared to aid under the former government, but relative to the reduced aid budget. Five new sector programmes will be launched within education, two within health, and another two within water and sanitation.
- The private sector receives more attention and funds. The budget for the Private Sector Development Programme has been increased and the programme has been expanded to cover all programme countries despite a very critical evaluation of the programme in 2001.[6] Denmark has also embarked on comprehensive business sector support programmes in Tanzania and Ghana, and similar support will be launched in Vietnam.
- Danish development NGOs have suffered the 10% cut in government funding and future support will depend on their ability to demonstrate popular support in Denmark.
- Denmark has decided to untie bilateral aid and invite tenders from all EU countries.

The distribution of multilateral (some 45%) and bilateral (some 50%) aid will remain the same. Multilateral aid will increasingly be focused on health and population, while organisations like ILO, UNESCO and UNIDO face decreased Danish funding.

Denmark no longer the lead donor

The goal of maintaining Danish ODA at 1% of GNI has been dropped. A broad majority in the Danish Parliament agreed on this goal way back in 1985 and it was first reached in 1992. In 2000, Danish ODA peaked at 1.06% and was set to increase further due to the special Environment, Peace and Stability Facility (see below). In early 2002, however, the new government cut DKK1.5 billion

Denmark

(about US$168.5 million) from the aid budget. This cut has since been made permanent, and the future aid budget is to remain at the current level.

Aid funding has to be balanced against domestic priorities. In November 2003, the government resisted suggestions by the Danish People's Party to cut a further DKK2 billion annually from the aid budget. However, the aid organisation of the Danish trade unions was singled out and overnight lost its long-term state-funding, amounting to DKK44 million annually. This was seen as a politically motivated decision.

In 2002, the Danish ODA:GNI ratio fell to 0.96%. It is expected to decrease to 0.92% in 2003 and to 0.83% in 2004. A further, although less dramatic, decline can be expected in the years to come, as growth in the Danish economy no longer automatically translates into growth in ODA.

The government has been very reluctant to use the ODA:GNI ratio as an indicator of Danish commitment to fighting world poverty, claiming that the quality and efficiency of aid are as important factors as the quantity. In a report on Denmark's efforts to fulfil its commitments in relation to the eighth Millennium Development Goal, the government stated that 'over the next five years the Government will maintain development assistance at a level that means that Denmark will continue to be in the leading group and which at the same time will ensure a stable political and economic framework for long-term and sustainable development efforts.'

Taken together, these decisions mean that the gap between what total Danish aid would have amounted to, if the policy under the previous government had been maintained, and total aid under this government, widens year by year. In 2005, Danish aid is projected to reach only 71% of what was projected under the former government.[8]

Special window for environment, peace and stability closed

Denmark has abolished its special Environment, Peace and Stability Facility (EPSF). Until 2001, it was on track to reach the target of 0.5% of GNI – on top of the 1% of GNI for aid – by 2005. Both parties in the coalition government had supported the EPSF since its in 1992, but in 2003 the government unilaterally announced the end of EPSF.

Danish Cooperation for Environment and Development (DANCED) in the Ministry of Environment, which was responsible for environmental support to middle-income countries and East and Central Europe, has been closed down. Remaining activities that used to be financed under EPSF have been integrated into the aid budget and are now administered by Danida.

The government insists that environment is still a priority area, but in absolute terms, environment receives less funding. And the automatic increase built in under EPSF no longer exists.

More assistance for the (less) money

'More for the money' is a slogan of the Danish government, even when it comes to aid. The government has continually claimed that the world's poor have not suffered from the cutbacks in the Danish aid budget. What has been lost in quantity has been gained in quality and efficiency. The issues of tied aid and cutbacks in Danida staff provide interesting examples of this thinking.

In 2003, the Danish government gave in to growing EU pressure to untie aid. From 1 January 2004, Denmark started to apply EU rules when purchasing goods and services and tendering building and construction works as part of Danish

Denmark

bilateral aid and support for Eastern Europe. By doing this, Denmark averted a legal case on the issue — one that the Danes stood no chance of winning.

While the DAC peer review of Danish aid welcomes this move, it requires Denmark to go further and open up procurement for aid to the least developed countries, to firms from countries that are not members of the European Union. Denmark is one of only five DAC members that have not yet fully implemented this DAC recommendation.

While Danish governments have in the past claimed that aid tying did not lead to overpricing, the government now boasts that the untying will make available up to DKK300 million over the next five years to fight poverty.

More efficiency is expected of the staff of the Ministry of Foreign Affairs. In September 2003, the Ministry started implementing both a modernisation plan and a long-prepared decentralisation plan to deploy staff from Copenhagen to Danish embassies in developing countries.

These plans, however, coincided with dramatic cuts in the budget for administration of aid — from DKK650 million in 2003 to DKK595 in 2007. This has caused concern as to whether there are sufficient resources to implement the ambitious plan to move administration and decision making closer to beneficiaries.

Danish NGOs wake up to harsh realities

Danish development NGOs have for years enjoyed substantial government support. As pointed out by the 2003 DAC review, 'Danish NGOs receive most of their financing from the government, with little coming from traditional fund-raising activities.' The new government wants to change this situation.

In 2002, NGOs had their government support cut by 10%. From 2004, support for large NGOs has been cut by another 5%. The money saved will go to small NGOs that are seen to have more popular backing and to projects involving alliances of Danish NGOs. Further, the large NGOs were warned that further cuts will follow unless they are able to demonstrate popular support.

One of the first moves of the government, when it came to power, was to close down a number of advisory boards and committees. The NGO Liaison Committee was one of these, leaving NGOs with no regular and formal dialogue with the Minister and parliamentarians. This has done little to build an atmosphere of confidence between NGOs and government.

The sudden decision in November 2003 to stop long-term funding to the aid organisation of the Danish trade unions, the LO/FTF Council, also provoked protests from the NGO community. Only six months earlier the Minister for Foreign Affairs, Per Stig Møller, had confirmed his support to the council.[10] Yet, the decision was made without any warning or dialogue. The NGOs protested that such decisions make all long-term planning impossible.

Responsible partners

Time and again, the responsibility of developing partners is stressed in the papers and strategies of the Danish government. 'To eradicate poverty in the developing countries, the countries themselves must first and foremost pursue a sensible policy', it says in 'A World of Difference' under the subheading 'Human Rights, democratisation and good governance'.

The government promises unwavering support to countries that actively promote human rights, democracy and good governance, fight corruption and take part in the fight against terrorism.

On the other hand, the government

Denmark

will not tolerate lack of respect for human rights, democracy or good governance. This was precisely the reason given for the abrupt closure of the Danish aid programmes in Eritrea, Malawi and Zimbabwe in 2002.

Critics have, however, claimed that this was just an excuse to cut the aid budget, a view reinforced by the fact that the government tolerates lack of multi-party democracy in countries such as Uganda and Vietnam. More importantly, as noted in the DAC review, the 'unilateral and abrupt withdrawal from Eritrea, Malawi and Zimbabwe raised the question of Denmark's commitment to the longer-term partnership concept'.

Danish bid for a seat in the UN Security Council

'We no longer want Denmark to sail under a flag of convenience,' Prime Minister Anders Fogh Rasmussen has stated several times as the main reason for joining the American-led coalition that toppled Saddam Hussein and occupied Iraq. Denmark does want to play a more prominent role in the international fight against terrorism — and development aid is increasingly seen as one

of several tools that can reduce threats to peace and world stability arising from: poverty, lack of democracy and human rights, radicalisation, extremism and religious intolerance.

Support for the American-led invasion of Iraq does not mean, however, that Denmark has given up on the United Nations. On the contrary, it is actively seeking support to become a member of the UN Security Council in 2005-06. Here, Denmark will advocate firm deadlines for countries targeted by Security Council resolutions and concrete sanctions if the UN does not adhere to resolutions to make itself more efficient.

There is less talk of using the position as an international platform to advocate an increased fight against world poverty and injustice. The international image of Denmark has certainly changed. Denmark may not sail under the flag of convenience any more when it comes to a military effort to fight a perceived threat of terrorism and weapons of mass destruction, but its high international profile in the fight against poverty has been tarnished.

Notes

1 This chapter covers the period January 2002 – December 2003.

2 Royal Danish Ministry of Foreign Affairs: A World of difference. The Government's Vision for New Priorities in Danish Development Assistance 2004-2008. June 2003. http://www.um.dk/publikationer/danida/dansk_udviklingssamarbejde/en_verden_til_forskel/en_verden_til_forskel.pdf[3] Development Today, Vol XIII - No 12. August 2003.

3 Development Today, Vol XIII - No 12. August 2003.

4 OECD, DAC: Development Co-operation Review. Denmark. Volume 4, No. 3. 2003.

5 Royal Danish Ministry of Foreign Affairs: Redegørelse for Regeringens Gennemgang af Danmarks Udviklings- og Miljøsamarbejde med

Udviklingslandene. January 2002.

6 Royal Danish Ministry of Foreign Affairs: Evaluation, Private Sector Development Programme. 2001. http://www.um.dk/danida/evalueringer/eval2001/2001-1/

7 Royal Danish Ministry of Foreign Affairs: 2015 Målene, Mål 8: Skabelsen af et globalt partnerskab. Hvor står Danmark? September 2003

8 Besparelserne på u-landsbistanden – en analyse. May, 2003. http://www.u-land.dk/presse/nalysebistand.rtf

9 Royal Danish Ministry of Finance: Forslag til Finanslov for finansåret 2004. August 2004. http://www.fm.dk/visNiveau1.asp?artikelID=4770

10 Jyllands-Posten. May 27, 2003.

European Union

Box 13. EUROPEAN UNION AND EUROPEAN COMMISSION at a glance

In this section, EU refers to EU member states together, whereas when EC is used, this refers to the European Commission's development programme, funded by member states.

How much aid is spent through the EUROPEAN COMMISSION?

In 2002, the amount of aid from EC
member states spent through the
European Commission was   US$6,561m or 6,962m Euros

This means that, in 2002, every person in the European Union gave US$17 or 18 Euros for aid spending through the European Commission.

In 2002, aid spent through the EC rose by   US$204m in cash terms. Because of inflation and exchange rate changes, the value of aid rose by 2.1% in real terms.

How generous are EU member states?

The EU member states gave 0.35% of their collective wealth in 2002. This compares with the average country effort of 0.41% and the EC's own previous highpoint of 0.46% in 1989.

EU member states collectively were more generous than in 2001, when aid was 0.33% of collective GNI.

How much of the EC's aid goes to the poorest countries and people?

37% of total EC aid (US$2,317.1m) went to Least Developed and Low Income Countries where 3.5 billion people (60% of the global population) live and where average incomes are less than two dollars a day.

How much of the EC's aid was spent on basic health, basic education, water supply and sanitation?

The EC spent

0.32% of its bilateral aid (US$20.55m) on basic education
1.45% of its bilateral aid (US$93.93m) on basic health
1.47% of its bilateral aid (US$95.1m) on water and sanitation

Soft power ambitions compromising EU development aid?

Howard Mollett, BOND

The European Union is often described as 'an economic giant, but a political dwarf'. This chapter looks at how EU foreign policy reforms have set the agenda for European Community (EC) official development assistance and policy relating to democracy, human rights and governance in developing countries in 2002-03. These reforms reflect the alliances and conflicts between institutional actors in Brussels and the European capitals as much as the needs of people living in poverty.

Competing priorities undermine poverty focus

The European Community is the world's third largest aid donor, with an ODA spend of more than US$6,5 billion in 2002.[1] More than half of EC aid is allocated to middle income countries, many of them along the Union's borders, that are important in terms of trade or migration policy.[2]

Provisional figures for 2002 do suggest an improvement, with 52% of total aid going to low-income developing countries (donor best practice is approximately 70%). Those EU member states with a weak commitment to development, and policy constituencies preoccupied with EU foreign policy and enlargement, consistently argue for directing resources to the strategically important 'near-abroad'. As Eastern Europe and Central Asia have become foreign policy priorities, annual aid to these regions increased to US$7 per capita in 2002. Annual gross national wealth per capita in these countries averages US$1,739. In contrast, South Asia — home to two thirds of the world's poorest people, with annual gross wealth per capita of just US$514 — only received US$0, 27 per capita in annual EC aid.

Development in the policy mix: coherence or co-option?

In an attempt to patch up divisions over the war in Iraq, 'coherence' became this year's buzzword for EU foreign policy. But coherence at what cost? EU policy makers increasingly refer to aid as an 'instrument', with the boundary between coherence and co-option being unclear. The war on terror has dominated the foreign policy agenda. The EC, along with European bilateral donors, endorsed an OECD DAC statement calling for aid to be 're-calibrated' in line with counter-terrorist objectives. Mid-2003 saw the UK and Spanish governments proposing that aid should become conditional on developing countries accepting 'immigrant repatriation' clauses in their cooperation agreements. The EU Security Doctrine suggests: 'The challenge is to bring together the different instruments and capabilities: [...] European assistance

European Union

programmes, military and civilian capabilities from member states and other instruments such as the European Development Fund. [...] Diplomatic efforts, trade and environmental policies, should follow the same agenda. [...] In a crisis, there is no substitute for unity of command.'[3] The trend is for policy to reflect the needs of European integration rather than development cooperation. Pro-development policy coherence in trade or agriculture, for which EU-level coordination has much potential, remains more rhetorical than real.

Early days for participation policy
Sectoral allocation for each aid recipient country is determined by its EC Country Strategy Paper process. This is ostensibly 'locally owned' and based on participatory consultation. Sadly, to date, evidence of this is mixed. As a direct consequence, there is little evidence that EC sectoral spending is meeting the basic needs of people living in poverty. Figures for aid under the Cotonou Agreement with African, Caribbean and Pacific (ACP) countries indicate that while the transport sector represents 31% and macroeconomic and budgetary support 21.4% of total allocation, education and health represent only 6.3% and 4.3% respectively.[4] European parliamentarians have lobbied for a minimum allocation of 35% for social sectors in the 2004 budget.

In 2003, the EU published new policy and guidelines for EU in-country delegations on the participation of 'non-state actors' in EC aid programming. Civil society groups welcome these proposals, but criticise the absence of any legally binding commitment. The stated aim is to make EC aid democratically accountable; first results will be seen in 2004, with the publication of 'Mid Term Reviews' of the Country Strategy Papers. (See EU chapter by Mikaela Gavas)

2003 to 2004: re-writing the EU rulebook
The EU policy framework is undergoing a major review. A draft EU Constitutional Treaty seeks to establish a new legal basis for development cooperation and humanitarian aid. But it explicitly subordinates them, in the institutional hierarchy, to a newly consolidated foreign policy agenda and a proposed EU Foreign Affairs Minister. Talks have also begun with the aim of overhauling the entire EU budget for 2007 to 2013. The European Commission's calls for 'increased flexibility' in the budget risk further compromising the focus on poverty reduction. The Commission has also proposed bringing Cotonou (ACP) aid resources, currently managed in a separate fund, into the general European Community budget. This could improve coherence and introduce European parliamentary scrutiny, but the risk is that funds would be siphoned off to other regions. By Autumn 2004, a new European Commission and a new European Parliament will be inaugurated; both may be substantially restructured with manifold implications for the political space for development.

Governance and rights
The 1990s were marked by recurrent crises in the 'failed states', authoritarian regimes and dysfunctional democracies of former European colonies in the developing world. 'Good governance' became both an objective of, and a condition for, EU aid. The inspiration for this approach is twofold: firstly, the success of political conditionality in relations with the EU accession countries of the former Soviet Union and Eastern Europe; secondly, a shift, among European social democratic governments, away from the crude 'anti-state' ideology of the early 'Washington Consensus' and a parallel increase in aid channelled through recipient governments' budgets. The Cotonou

European Union

Partnership Agreement, for example, thus marked the end of 'aid entitlements' for the ACP, according to which countries received fixed amounts regardless of performance.

Policy and operational framework

The EU Development Policy Statement of 2001, signed by the Commission and all member states, lists good governance, the rule of law, civil society participation, democracy and human rights as key priorities. While the EU institutions have horizontal structures to coordinate implementation of human rights policy, there is no focal point for governance. Coherent action on either is undermined by a lack of permanent expert staff and a split in the European Commission, along geographical lines, between DG Development (responsible for the ACP and development policy-focused) and DG External Relations (responsible for other third countries and foreign policy-focused).

The European Initiative for Democracy and Human Rights (EIDHR) is the main funding instrument for human rights programmes by DG External Relations, and is now focused on priority themes and regions. During the 1990s, EIDHR funding shifted towards support to civil society organisations, although it maintains a strong profile in electoral support. Regional and country strategy papers for those countries under the DG External Relations remit reflect the lack of a developmental policy framework. For example, relations with Asian countries are dominated by trade policy, with commitments on human rights and democratic governance in the draft Asia-Latin America Regulation and regional strategy papers being mostly preambular.[5]

The Cotonou Agreement with the ACP states that 'respect for human rights, democratic principles and the rule of law are essential elements of the partnership', with these commitments subject to performance reviews and continuing political dialogue. In problem cases, a consultation procedure is backed by the threat of a suspension of co-operation or other intermediary sanctions.[6] Good governance is defined as a 'fundamental element', which only leads to suspension in the case of serious corruption. Since 1995, all new cooperation agreements with third countries include 'democracy clauses' that allow for the suspension of relations if either party fails to respect the 'essential elements'.

The Cotonou Agreement includes a range of mechanisms for mutual accountability on issues such as democratic governance: for example joint parliamentary assemblies. In contrast to governance of the IFIs, Cotonou thus opens up a formal political space for Southern governments and activists in its own institutional structures. Arguably, this moves the donor-recipient relationship towards an innovative model of rights and obligation, rather than beneficence and paternalism. Developing countries under the DG External Relations remit do not benefit from this framework. As negotiations on trade under Cotonou demonstrate, the EU-ACP partnership is a flawed and imbalanced one; yet, incremental improvements, as exemplified by the 'Everything But Arms' agreement, have been achieved.[7]

Officials estimate that just under €2 billion (of a total €10 billion) is spent on initiatives with broadly defined governance implications, ranging from human rights projects to transport sector reform. How much of this currently contributes to pro-poor, rights-based development is not clear.

Until recently, governance has been something of a 'will-o'-the-wisp' concept in EC development cooperation. In the past year, however, there has been considerable improvement in the EU policy framework,

European Union

with the publication of a much-awaited EU communication on 'Governance and Development' in late 2003.[8] The communication's definition of governance includes both 'classical' issues relating to administrative reform and some attention to democratisation and global governance issues, albeit without any commitments on the latter. The emphasis is firmly on the responsibilities of recipient country governments. Governance is defined as 'the state's ability to serve the citizens'. Governance reforms are conceptualised as national/context specific processes that result in progress from 'governance' to 'good governance'. A thematic European Commission working group is drafting a handbook to guide in-country EU delegations and beneficiaries on best practice. EC aid officials hope that these documents will be effectively 'administratively-binding' through their inclusion in the project cycle. The handbook will include step-by-step suggestions and a logbook to record problems, thereby engendering a minimal level of evaluation and accountability. Civil society groups call for legally binding commitments and a more concerted political leadership to make the rhetoric on democratic governance a reality.

Limits to promoting democratic governance

Institutional capacity building: Yes. Ad hoc, project-based human rights initiatives and training: Yes. Diplomatic response, when politically expedient, to dysfunctional democracies in the former colonies (eg. Zimbabwe): Yes. Yet, outside of election monitoring, there are few EU instruments for, and little funding given to, political society in terms of the democratic accountability of legislative-executive relations, decentralised government or the functioning of pluralistic democratic systems.[9] EU policy remains

heavily predicated on the assumption that market-based economic reforms will spill over into broader political reform. Egypt, Tunisia, Vietnam, Uganda and Peru, during the Fujimori administration, are all examples of countries with bad and even deteriorating records on democracy that have been awarded generous EU aid to assist economic reform.[10]

The European Commission and EU member states have promoted a 'coherence, coordination and complementarity' agenda between bilateral and multilateral aid programmes, EU policy and the Bretton Woods institutions. New BOND research from Bolivia, India, Kenya and Senegal suggests that EC Country Strategy Papers have replicated and enhanced the World Bank and IMF country analysis and remit for development assistance.[11] This has resulted in World Bank macroeconomic policy prescriptions, imposed without proper consultation, being reinforced by EC aid.

Governance and foreign policy

According to Joseph Nye, in contrast to the 'hard power' global presence of the United States, the EU is endowed with 'soft power' — a hybrid of economic, social and political influence. Several recent analyses have concluded that democratic governance and human rights in developing countries come far below trade, regional stability and security on the list of EU policy priorities.[12] In 2003, the Commission announced a new €250 million programme — more than two and half times the total European Initiative on Democracy and Human Rights (EIDHR) budget[13] — to fund anti-migration measures in third countries that agree to sign readmission agreements. EU external policy projects its 'civil power' role by prioritising regional stability and democracy promotion in countries and regions of strategic importance: themes

European Union

that also help articulate a distinctly 'European identity' at home and abroad. Conflict resolution and crisis management – the so-called 'Petersberg Tasks' – are now the favoured channels for promoting Europe as a global player. Sub-Saharan Africa has been identified as an important region, precisely because 'it could contribute to the global affirmation of the European Security and Defence identity.'[14] Some analysts fear that, in this context, EU governance intervention will increasingly emphasise foreign policy-led initiatives focused on high profile conflicts, rather than long term development cooperation.[15] Others welcome this development as a means of securing increased and more effective political engagement with the problem of corrupt or oppressive regimes.[16]

Conclusions

The EU has much improved its policy framework, but its practice is undermined by the confusion over foreign and development policy remits. Assessing and supporting democratisation processes are inevitably challenging tasks, but the EU can still improve on the incoherence and gaps between micro project funding and the macro 'high politics' of diplomatic intervention. Making rights-based, democratic development a priority requires more than a handbook. It requires political will and resource allocation from the top levels of the EU and member state decision makers, and an opening of governance to those at the 'bottom', people living in poverty and political marginalisation.

Notes

1 European Community aid resources are those funds pooled by EU Member States and managed by committees and agencies of the European Community.

2 In 1990, 70% of EC development aid went to the poorest countries. By 2001, aid to low-income developing countries (LICs) had fallen to just 38% of total allocations. The rise to LICs in 2002/3 is largely accounted for by increased aid to Iraq and Afghanistan.

3 'A Secure Europe in a Better World', 12 December 2003 (EU Security Doctrine), pg 14.

4 The Cotonou Agreement. (http://europa. eu. int/ comm/development/cotonou/agreement). Figures from most recent 9th European Development Fund (Source, Aprodev).

5 See BOND analysis in 'Tackling poverty in Asia: EU aid, trade and political relations with Asia'.

6 Articles 96 and 97, Cotonou 2000, *ACP-EU Partnership Agreement signed in Cotonou on 23 June 2000*, (The ACP-EU Courier, Special issue Cotonou greement) (http://europa. eu. int/comm/ development/cotonou/agreement)

7 For analysis of Cotonou trade negotiations: www. bond. org. uk/pubs/eu/cotwto. pdf

8 Communication from the Commission to the Council, the European Parliament and the European Economic and Social Committee 'Governance and Development'. COM (2003) 615 final.

9 Dr Richard Youngs, 'Democracy Promotion: The Case of European Union Strategy', Centre for European Policy Studies Working Document nb. 167, 2001 p 8.

10 Ibid and see also Carlos Santiso 'Improving the governance of European foreign aid: Development co-operation as an element of foreign policy', Centre for European Policy Studies Working Document No 189, October 2002.

11 BOND research paper 'Implementors or Actors? Assessing civil society participation in European Community Country Strategy Paper processes', to be published in March 2004.

12 Gorm Rye Olson, Institute for International Studies, 'Promotion of democracy as a foreign policy instrument of Europe: Limits to international idealism', *Democratization*, Vol. 7, No 2, p 142-167.

13 Dr Richard Youngs, 'Liberalism and Security', forthcoming paper for the Foreign Policy Institute, 2004.

14 G. Lenzi, 'WEU's Role in Sub-Saharan Africa,' p 46-65 in W. Khüne, G. Lenzi and A. Vasconcelos, WEU's *Role in Crisis Management and Conflict Resolution*

European Union

in Sub-Saharan Africa (Paris: Institute for Security Studies of WEU, 1995), p. 48.

[15] Dr Chris Alden and Dr Karen E. Smith, 'Strengthening Democratic Structures and Processes in Africa: A Commentary on the Role of the EU', presentation at IEEI conference 'The Challenges of Europe-Africa Relations: An Agenda of Priorities', Lisbon, 2003 (www. ieei. pt).

[16] See Mark Leonard and Richard Gowan, 'Global Europe: Implementing the European Security Strategy' forthcoming from the Foreign Policy Centre, www. fpc. org. uk.

Finland

Box 14. FINLAND at a glance

How much aid does FINLAND give?

In 2002, FINLAND gave

US$462m or 490m Euros

That means that, in 2002, each
person in FINLAND gave

US$89 or 94 Euros

In 2002, aid from FINLAND rose by

US$73m in cash terms. Because of inflation
and exchange rate changes, the value of aid
increased by 11.5% in real terms

How generous is FINLAND?

FINLAND gave 0.35% of its national wealth in 2002 according to figures from the DAC.
This compares with the average country effort of 0.41% and FINLAND's own previous
highpoint of 0.76% in 1991.

FINLAND was less generous than 8 other donors, but more generous than in 2001 when
aid was 0.32% of GNI.

How much of FINLAND's aid goes to the poorest countries and people?

43.6% of total bilateral aid (US$109.6m) went to Least Developed and Low Income
Countries where 3.5 billion people (60% of the global population) live and where average
incomes are less than two dollars a day.

How much of FINLAND's aid was spent on basic health, basic education, water supply and sanitation?

FINLAND spent

2.2% of its bilateral aid (US$6.85m) on basic education

5.49% of its bilateral aid (US$17.1m) on basic health

6.77% of its bilateral aid (US$21.09m) on water and sanitation

Rights-based approach stresses participation – implementation is the challenge

Maria Suoheimo, KEPA

Finnish development aid has recently gone through significant changes both in terms of its quantity and the policy it is based on. Early 2003 saw a new government and, in response to NGOs who had been demanding 'more and better development aid', the new government committed itself to increasing Finnish development aid progressively to 0.7% of GNI by 2010, though 'taking into account general economic trends'. However, during the term of office of the current government, which ends in 2007, Finland's development aid will only increase from 0.34% to 0.44%. Nevertheless, in comparison with the previous government's expenditure on development aid, the amount will increase by one third, totalling US$136 million.

The government also took some concrete measures to respond to the NGOs' demands regarding the quality of Finnish aid. The Development Aid and Foreign Trade portfolios were merged into one and a new Development Policy Programme was drawn up, under the direction of the new minister. The new policy programme contained further promises regarding the distribution of the increasing grants: the government committed itself to raising the share of aid to the Least Developed Countries to 0.15% of the total amount of aid and is working towards raising the share of aid to NGOs to 14% by 2007.

By approving the policy programme, Finland made an even more explicit commitment to the international poverty reduction consensus, including the Millennium Development Goals, the Poverty Reduction Strategies and the harmonisation of donor aid practices. In addition to this, the policy specifies other fields of priority that reflect the Finnish political tradition and expertise, including gender equality, the combination of economic growth and fair income distribution, and environmental issues.

Good principles are not enough
More clearly than ever before, Finnish development policy now emphasises a rights-based approach, regarding extreme poverty as the biggest human rights problem of our times:

> 'Human rights and development
> are interdependent elements that
> support each other. The rights-
> based approach to development
> cooperation stresses the right of an
> individual to participate in society,

Finland

as opposed to becoming marginalised. Increasing the possibilities for individuals to participate in the improvement of their life is the key to poverty reduction.'

(Development Policy Programme 2004)

The policy thus defines respecting the right of developing countries and their citizens to make their own decisions, respecting human rights and democracy and promoting good governance, as key goals of Finland's development policy.

The policy similarly emphasises that developing countries are, to a large extent, responsible for their own development. The role of industrialised countries is to support the efforts of developing countries and to create favourable conditions for development. However, according to the policy programme, Finland cannot do this unless the cooperation and coherence of its different administrative branches is improved, by mainstreaming the development perspective into all decision making that affects development. The policy thoroughly analyses the challenges Finland has to tackle to achieve such coherence, particularly in the fields of defence policy, trade, agriculture and forestry, education, research and culture, as well as in health care, social politics, employment and immigration. The document also defines specific principles that each administrative sector should implement in order to achieve coherence. Moreover, Finland vows to promote actively the coherence of different sectors of policy in the EU.

It all depends on political will

The new policy is praiseworthy and ambitious, but the touchstone of its real significance will be its application. Without

efficient implementation, the document will remain a mere collection of good principles. It seems that the decisive factor in successful implementation is the ownership of different administrative branches, as the policy programme is largely an initiative of the Ministry for Foreign Affairs. If ownership is not achieved, the different ministries are hardly likely to commit to issues that thus far have not figured high on their political agenda.

Another crucial issue is solving the conflicts of interest between the different administrative branches. One of the most substantial weaknesses of the policy is that it does not propose concrete measures but merely declares general principles. Conflicts arising from the different interests of Finland and developing countries are not thoroughly discussed; the section on the agricultural sector, for instance, acknowledges that the most vulnerable developing countries have a special need to protect and support their agricultural producers, yet the same section also notes that coherence requires domestic agriculture, too, to be taken into account. Instead of suggesting concrete measures to improve the coherence of the agricultural policy of the EU through cuts in export subsidies, the document underlines that the EU and Finland have been consistently making unilateral concessions by adopting initiatives such as the Lomé and Cotonou Conventions, the General System of Preferences (GSPs) and the Everything But Arms initiative (EBA), to improve the market access of developing countries.

A concrete example highlighting potential conflicts of interest between Finnish agricultural producers and the farmers of developing countries is sugar production, which is strongly subsidised by the EU and provides a living for some 2800 Finnish farmers and sugar industry workers. A more global conflict of interests is reflected in the

Finland

dispute that is currently developing in Finland regarding the price that the paper and forest industry, the cornerstone of Finland's economic growth, will have to pay in order to meet the goals of the Kyoto Protocol. Finland is torn between its responsibility to ensure the growth of its economy and its commitment to developing international environmental management and preventing the adverse impacts of climate change, which would affect the poorest countries the most. Solving these kinds of conflict will require strong political will. However, unless the kind of coherence required by the new development policy programme is improved at the national level, the implementation of Finland's development cooperation will not be compatible with the principles of good governance with which the country requires developing countries to comply.

Finland, a leader in promoting partnership and transparency?

As stated above, the implementation of the planned changes requires a great deal of political will at the national level; the same applies to promoting the goals of the policy programme in the arena of international policy making. Finland should follow the example of its Nordic neighbours and become more active in international development policy making as an advocate of gender equality and solidarity, the values that have always characterised Nordic politics.

Fortunately, new winds now seem to be blowing in Finland. The signs of change are evidenced by the fact that the president of Finland, Tarja Halonen, and her Tanzanian counterpart Benjamin Mkapa, co-chair the ILO's World Commission on the Social Dimension of Globalisation. Furthermore, the Finnish and Tanzanian governments have initiated the Helsinki process on

Globalisation and Democracy. After the approval of the development policy programme, Finnish civil society has every right to expect the Finnish government to fervently promote within the international donor community principles such as partnership, transparency and the right of developing countries and their citizens to make their own decisions.

In order to reach this goal, Finland must have international credibility. Such credibility can be gained, for instance, by consistently increasing development cooperation funds. It seems, however, that the current government's commitment to increasing the funds is only an apparent one, as the goal of reaching 0.44% of the GNI by 2007 is so low that it seriously undermines the chances of the next government reaching the promised level of 0.7% by 2010. If the level of 0.7% is not reached within the timeframe, Finland's commitment to attaining the MDG goals by 2015 is going to appear quite superficial.

Another way for Finland to enhance its credibility would be to implement the principles declared in the country's development policy programme within its own aid regime. However, the transition of Finland's development cooperation towards increased sectoral and budget support, harmonisation of aid and promotion of partner country ownership calls for increased Finnish presence in the partner countries. Within Finland, the administration of development cooperation has been largely centralised in Helsinki; no large-scale decentralisation can be expected. At the domestic end of Finland's development cooperation administration, a good deal of attention has been paid to transparency and involvement of different interest groups and segments of civil society. However, this is not the case in many traditional partner countries, since few of Finland's missions have staff who are specialised in

Finland

development aid. The fine principles defined in Helsinki and the input obtained from Finnish interest groups go down the drain much too often, because of the lack of implementation capacity and development cooperation expertise of the Finnish missions.

Priority number one: hearing the voices of those in poverty

Finland pays budget and sectoral support instalments on the condition that partner countries make progress towards reaching the goals specified in the PRSPs (Poverty Reduction Strategy Papers). The indicators of progress, and how they should be monitored, are decided together between the governments and all the donors. These negotiations allow Finland's development cooperation administration to promote in partner countries the principles of transparency and involvement of diverse interest groups, which are well applied in Finland.

It is crucial that the emphasis of these PRSP negotiations should be on awareness of the needs of people living in poverty, outside the formal structures of society. The key condition for successful poverty reduction is ensuring that the poorest segments of the population have the opportunity to influence the PRSP and other national policies of their country. Donors are the ones who define the conditions and rules of sectoral and budget support. In its capacity as a donor, Finland must systematically promote the involvement of citizens of its partner countries in making decisions about issues that affect them. To achieve such access, it is important that the national and municipal budget policy of the partner countries be both transparent and participatory. The key challenge for the Finnish development aid administration in implementing the new development policy programme is taking these issues into account at the national level.

France

Box 15. *FRANCE at a glance*

How much aid does FRANCE give?

In 2002, FRANCE gave US$5,486m or 5,821m Euros

This means that, in 2002, each person
in FRANCE gave US$93 or 98 Euros

In 2002, aid from FRANCE rose by US$1,288m in cash terms. Because of
inflation

and exchange rate changes, the value of aid
increased by 22.1% in real terms

How generous is FRANCE?

FRANCE gave 0.38% of its national wealth in 2002. This compares with the average
country effort of 0.41% and FRANCE's own previous highpoint of 0.76% in 1965.

FRANCE was less generous than 7 other donors but more generous than in 2001 when aid
was 0.32% of GNI.

How much of FRANCE's aid goes to the poorest countries and people?

52.7% of total bilateral aid (US$1905.3m) went to Least Developed and Low Income
Countries where 3.5 billion people (60% of the global population) live and where average
incomes are less than two dollars a day.

**How much of FRANCE's aid was spent on basic health, basic education,
water supply and sanitation?**

FRANCE spent

3.4% of its bilateral aid ($161.07m) on basic education

1.31% of its bilateral aid ($62.34m) on basic health

3.98% of its bilateral aid ($188.78m) on water and sanitation

---

Increases promised in a 'freezing' climate

Amélie Canonne and Gregory Jacob, Observatoire français de la coopération internationale (OFCI), on behalf of the Centre de Recherche et d'Information pour le Developpement (CRID), with translation by David Sunderland

Since 2002, the French government has indicated that Official Development Assistance is a priority. In reality, its forecasts for 2003 were shown to be optimistically high. Whether there is the real political will to implement the full 2004 budget for ODA (€6.7 million, 0.43% of the national budget) remains to be seen.

After his re-election in May 2002, Jacques Chirac made a number of significant commitments, announcing a target for ODA of 0.7% GNI by 2010, as one of the four main priorities of his five-year tenure. In 2003, aid (not including that to French overseas territories) increased to €5.876 billion, or 0.38% of GNI.

French government budgets on aid are somewhat impenetrable and it is difficult to find a reliable breakdown of the figures. Nevertheless, two major factors explain the global increase of French Aid from 2002 to 2003:

- The increased French contribution to the European Development Fund (EDF), which grew by 127% according to the national Budget (Loi de France, LFI, 2002);
- Further steps to cancel bilateral debt under the Highly Indebted Poor Countries

(HIPC) Initiative, within the French framework for debt relief (Contrats-desendettement-développement, C2D). During 2003, the countries benefiting were Guinea, Madagascar, and Cameroon (Mozambique and Mauritania had begun to benefit in 2002).

Nevertheless, the official announcements have not been followed by concrete actions. For a start, the promised increases have been accompanied by substantial freezing of budget lines allocated to non-governmental and official development activities. In total, approximately €40 million earmarked for programmes and approximately €90 million of pledged funds, were frozen during 2003. This represented 10% of the total funds allocated to the Solidarity Priority Fund.[1]

French NGOs were particularly badly affected. On top of the freezing of the Solidarity Priority Fund, there were two other implications. Firstly, initial grants to NGOs allocated from the LFI budget stagnated. Secondly, a number of NGOs were immediately hit, as grants from the 'support to private and decentralised' budget (around €3 million) were frozen.

In total, the Cooperation Ministry had to freeze 18% of its programmed actions in

France

2003, according to its Minister, Pierre-André Wiltzer. This figure excludes the decline in direct support from other parts of the French political administration to development assistance, both in France and abroad.[2]

Before cutting off the funds allocated to 'typical' development assistance, the Government announced that nearly all of the increase in aid levels would go towards its debt relief commitments. This was despite the fact that, in November 2002, the Inter-Ministerial Council for International Cooperation and Development[3] had reaffirmed the principle of additionality (in that payments to bilateral debt relief should not adversely affect the aid budget).

The provisional 2004 Budget envisaged that there would be a natural progression from the aid budget for 2003. According to the Treasury, the commitment is €6.7 million, or 0.43% of the national budget. But, if the experience of 2003 is anything to go by, one can predict that increases in the aid budget will continue to be largely channelled to debt relief, and that there will be further cuts and freezes in 'typical' development assistance. Given the shrinkage to date, it is possible that in 2004 funds will simply go towards the frozen designated expenditure of 2003.

'Poor people are still waiting!' was the title of a press release in July 2003 from Coordination SUD, the principal French network of development NGOs. The release drew attention to the fact that the increase in aid, trumpeted by the French government, could be explained above all by sleight -of hand accounting that was made possible by the lack of transparency in the process used to put together the Budget.

When Bruno Delaye was Director of the General Directorate for International Cooperation and Development, DGCID[4] in 2003, he raised several alarming points in an internal memo to his supervising Minister,

Dominique de Villepin, concluding, 'It is time to end our illusions: we do not have the means to implement our policy'. The memo set this in the context of the earlier merger of the Development Ministry with the Ministry of Foreign Affairs, effectively criticising the fact that the government had differentially prioritised the work of each of the Ministries.

French 'democratic governance' outlined

Until recently, the French position on governance in southern countries had been characterised by its ambiguity. Even though France has been signing on to more and more international initiatives in the fight against poverty and progressively aligning its activities with those of the Bretton Woods institutions and the European Union, before 2003, France had not initiated any process to recognise 'governance' as a concept. French studies on governance had been very limited, although, in the field, French development cooperation had been engaged in similar sectors, particularly in sub-Saharan Africa (for example, financing 'democratic' election processes, administrative cooperation, and capacity building for civil society organisations).

The publication by DGCID, in 2003, of the general policy document 'For a democratic governance'[5], finally laid out French development policy in this area. Care was taken, however, not to link government aid administrators to the notion of governance. Instead the term 'humanism'[6] was stated as the key principle of French development cooperation, rooted in the 'system of universal values constituting a democracy' (of which the authors considered France to be an exemplary model). In effect, the DGCID promoted 'democratic governance' as its vision:

> 'French development cooperation
> sees the promotion of democratic

France

governance as a major objective. Building the rule of law, democratic values, and respect for human dignity all reinforce the capacity of partner countries to improve their public management.'

The interventions of French development cooperation in 'governance' are numerous and wide-ranging:

- *Democracy and public liberty*: support to organisations involved in democratic election processes, to local democracy and political processes involving decentralisation of power, support for the defence of human rights and fundamental liberties (in particular for women and minorities), encouragement for plural societies by promoting multi-party systems and capacity building for civil society organisations.
- *Security* support to police forces (for example establishing well-trained and well-equipped forces, recruited from all parts of society), support for the military (for instance helping develop security forces for democratic and civic purposes, increasing professionalism and transparency; improving financial management); support for the judiciary (such as reforming the judicial and penal systems) and support to conflict prevention and post-conflict management.
- *Public management*: support to participatory processes in public policy, fighting corruption (for example administrative reforms that are transparent; clear designation of responsibilities, consideration given to setting up international legal tools). A firmly integrated approach, like this, has cross-cutting effects on both programming and intervention. It

suggests that tools and methods will need to be reconsidered — not to mention changes in job specifications and competencies. It suggests the need to establish new terms of reference, and possibly completely different ways of measuring and evaluating work at both quantitative and qualitative levels. From this point of view, the structural reforms are at the moment embryonic. It seems that French development cooperation today will be confined in its operation (when aid is not being frozen) but under a new label — that of 'democratic governance'.

'Democratic governance' is, therefore, France's narrow approach. French development cooperation remains a tool for its diplomacy, which focuses little on democracy and human rights. France has a long history of supporting African dictators. It has often hidden behind multinational mechanisms, in order to indirectly impose sanctions against governments who are 'friends'. French acceptance of the term 'governance' rests largely on the security role of the state, tending to favour (directly or not) representation of France as a 'policeman'. In reality, the large majority of French development cooperation for governance is focused on national governments. Relations with, and support to, non-government actors are unclear, despite their expertise and competence in undertaking action and research related to institutional cooperation.

To conclude, France has affirmed that it is willing to consider the principle of governance and how it operates at local, national, and global levels. But the thinking of DGCID on the idea of global governance (on the institutions and standards that guide international public action, and the structure of a global government) is lacklustre, and weakly conceptualised in the form of 'democratic governance'.

France

Notes

[1] The Solidarity Priority Fund *(Fonds de solidarité prioritaire, FSP)* is the project Aid instrument of the Ministry for Foreign Affairs, originating from a recent reform of French development cooperation. Its remit is to support, through financial donations alone, countries in a solidarity priority zone (*Zone de solidarité prioritaire, ZSP)* by means of institutional, cultural, and social development, and research. It is a financial tool for partnerships with other countries, territories, and other donors, and also with NGOs that receive cofinancing for their projects.

Note that in December 2003 the Ministry of Foreign Affairs had a strike (including ambassadors) demonstrating against budgetary restrictions, for the first time in its history.

Conseil Interministérial à la Coopération Internationale et au Développement (CICID).

[4] *Direction générale de la coopération internationale et du développement*

[5] Ministère des Affaires étrangères, *Pour une gouvernance démocratique,* Document d'orientation de la politique de coopération française, Paris, 2003.

[6] Humanism: a belief or outlook emphasising common human needs and seeking solely rational ways of solving human problems.

Germany

Box 16. GERMANY at a glance

How much aid does GERMANY give?

In 2002, GERMANY gave   US$5,324m or 5,650m Euros

This means that, in 2002, each person
in GERMANY gave   US$65 or 69 Euros

In 2002, aid from GERMANY rose by   US$335m in cash terms. Because of inflation
                                                and exchange rate changes, the value of aid
                                                fell by 0.2% in real terms

How generous is GERMANY?

GERMANY gave 0.27% of its national wealth in 2002. This compares with the average country effort of 0.41% and GERMANY's own previous highpoint of 0.48% in 1983.

GERMANY was less generous than 12 other donors and it gave the same level of aid as in 2001.

How much of GERMANY's aid goes to the poorest countries and people?

45.3% of total bilateral aid (US$1,507.8m) went to Least Developed and Low Income Countries where 3.5 billion people (60% of the global population) live and where average incomes are less than two dollars a day.

How much of GERMANY's aid was spent on basic health, basic education, water supply and sanitation?

GERMANY spent
1.58% of its bilateral aid (US$72.78) on basic education

1.73% of its bilateral aid (US$79.64) on basic health

4.76% of its bilateral aid (US$218.75m) on water and sanitation.

Stabilisation at last, but at a low level

Peter Mucke, terre des hommes Deutschland e.V.[1]

The current federal government took office in late 2002, giving positive signals for development policy. The coalition agreement of 12 October 2002 (marking the second term for the SPD/Green government), reaffirmed the Monterrey Consensus of March 2002, whereby European governments had agreed on a binding timetable for achieving quantitative finance goals. The governing coalition parties jointly emphasised: 'In the EU context, Germany has committed itself to reaching a level of 0.33% by 2006, as an interim step towards reaching the goal of 0.7%.' The significant thing here is not just that, for the first time, a percentage figure was promised with a fixed deadline, but above all that the rise was expressly described as an 'interim step' towards the goal of 0.7%.

The coalition agreement, moreover, places development policy in the context of foreign and security policy: 'The federal government relies...on a concept of security that also takes account of economic, human rights and development policy aspects. In the context of a wider understanding of security (it) works for a balanced development of civilian and military capacities.'

The fact that this document relates the classical concept of development to national and international security interests has nourished the hope, among development policy makers, for a stronger position on development cooperation, particularly as the federal Chancellor stressed in his governmental declaration on 29 October 2002: 'Today security is less than ever to be achieved by military means, and certainly not by military means alone. Anyone who seeks to create and uphold security must ... also pacify the environment in which the use of force arises. (In) a world in which everyone has moved closer together we will not achieve security if we allow the fermenting of injustice, oppression and underdevelopment.'

During its first term, the coalition government stopped the downward trend in German ODA, which had prevailed since 1990. While ODA as a share of gross national income (GNI) was 0.41% in 1990, it hit rock-bottom in 1998 and 1999 at just 0.26%. From 2000 to 2002, it remained at 0.27%. German ODA has thus consolidated itself at a low level.

The federal ministry for economic cooperation and development (BMZ) stated in a press release on 22 April 2003: 'That makes it clear that initial steps are to be seen on the part of the German government to

Germany

achieve its goal of 0.33% of gross national income (GNI) for ODA by 2006.'

The BMZ budget is of particular interest in terms of Germany's future development contribution. In the last few years it has represented about two thirds of ODA. In addition, ODA grants come from other portfolios, including the Foreign Office (humanitarian aid), the Finance Ministry (World Bank group), the Ministry for Consumer Protection, Food and Agriculture (contributions to the FAO) and the Ministry for Education and Research (research promotion). German ODA also includes budgetary funds from the federal states (*Bundesländer*), the federal government having little influence on the amount and use of such funds.

In 2002, the BMZ spent about 3.8 billion Euro; its share of the federal budget amounted to about 1.6%. In relation to the target figures for 2003 and the draft budget for 2004, this share is continuing to fall.

In absolute figures, BMZ had an additional €9 million available to it in 2003, compared with 2002. The federal budget for 2004, adopted in November 2003, showed a decline to €3.74 billion. Even in the unlikely eventuality that the other portfolios and *Bundesländer* maintain their ODA grants at the present level, the modest percentage increases allocated by the BMZ will not be enough to increase ODA as a percentage of GNI.

If ODA as a share of GNI were to reach 0.33% in 2006 Germany would only have reverted to the levels achieved in 1977 and 1994. If this rate of increase was maintained, the fall in German ODA since 1983 could be made up for by 2020. Only then would a 'genuine' rise be feasible. If the same trend continued, the international goal of 0.7% would only be achieved in 2043.

Broad definition of poverty reduction

The overarching aim of German development cooperation is combating poverty. The substantive and regional orientation of bilateral cooperation must therefore be measured against this goal.

However, BMZ uses a very broad concept of poverty, including under 'combating poverty' the areas of education, health, water supply and waste water disposal, protection of human rights, peacekeeping and security, the protection of natural resources, good governance and global structural policy. With this broad definition, the share of resources available for the goal of poverty reduction would probably be raised from 56% (2001) to 60% (2002) and then to around 80% (2003). But this is mostly a matter of relabelling, which is not the same as effective action for achieving the MDGs.

The share of bilateral commitments to the least developed countries (LDCs) has remained almost unchanged in the last few years. A comparison of disbursements leads to a similar result. There have been no substantial changes, even between payments before and after 1998, which is when the change of German government occurred. The figures do not indicate any clear differences between the policies of the governments before and after 1998 in relation to their treatment of LDCs. Nor has an oft-heralded prioritisation materialised.

It is, however, pleasing to see the substantial rise in funds for development education, which has been continually called for by NGOs since the early 1980s. Until 1998, this budget item was always around 4 million Deutschmarks (2.045 million Euro). In 1998 it was the equivalent of €2.11 million. Development policy-makers within the present governing parties had, in 1998, promised to triple or even quadruple this sum, if elected. This promise has been fulfilled, absolutely and in relation to the overall amount (1998: 0.52%; 2003: 1.54% and 2004: 1.89%).

Germany

Assessment

For the third year in a row, Germany's ODA as a share of GNI remained static at just 0.27%. The downward trend can therefore be regarded as halted. But the promised turnabout has not happened. The chances of reaching the Millennium Goals on combating poverty have become remote — a finding that represents a low-point in development policy.

It is pleasing to witness the further rise in funding for development education and outreach, which enables NGOs, particularly small groups and initiatives, to contribute to the urgently needed support for development cooperation.

In the debate on the federal budget for 2004, representatives of the governing parties pointed to the significance of global forces that can either reinforce or undermine the effects of development cooperation. In fact, many inter-related interventions are needed at different levels in order to attain the millennium goals, above all, efforts to halve the number of poor and hungry people by the year 2015.

Governance and Human Rights in German Development Policy

Observing human rights and good governance are, according to the federal government, central concerns of German development policy. Back in 1991, the Federal Minister for Economic Cooperation and Development laid down the following five criteria for German development cooperation, which are applicable to this day[2]:

1. Respect for human rights
2. Participation of the population
3. The rule of law and guarantee of legal certainty
4. Creating a market-friendly and socially concerned economic order
5. Development orientation of government action.

In German development policy, good governance is understood as involving both strong and efficient public institutions and support for participation by civil society. This is reflected in the federal government's Programme of Action 2015, adopted in 2001.[3] Among the focal areas for action by the German government, it mentions, 'Realising Human Rights', 'Ensuring the Participation of the Poor — Strengthening Good Governance'.

These goals are both part of the country strategies and of the policy dialogue with recipient countries. Observing human rights is, however, by no means a fundamental condition for granting German ODA. The ten most important recipients in 2002 included China, Indonesia, Pakistan and Egypt — countries with a continuing record of human rights violations. Accordingly, in 2003, NGOs drew attention to massive human rights violations related to the building of the Three Gorges Dam in China. The dam was made possible, by, among other things, export loans from the German bank Kreditanstalt für Wiederaufbau (KfW) and Hermes-Buergschaften, Germany's export financing agency. That is an example of strategic and foreign trade interests, taking priority over the policy of the federal government on human rights and social policy objectives.

In the context of its bilateral development cooperation activity, Germany makes approximately €100 million available each year for projects promoting 'good governance'. Priority programmes exist in more than 30 countries. According to its own figures, German support focuses on democratisation and decentralisation processes, and legal, judicial and administrative reforms. Further, support is given to reforms in the area of budgetary and finance policy (including fiscal policy and administration) as well as anti-corruption measures.[4]

Germany

At the multilateral level, too, the federal government strives for greater consideration to be given to 'good governance'. The fact that the Monterrey Conference in 2002 explicitly named 'good governance' as a basic condition for development, is regarded by the federal government as one of the main successes of this conference. However, by strongly emphasising the responsibility of developing countries, and the internal conditions for development, it distracts attention from the external causes of poverty and the negative consequences of economic globalisation.

Another problematic element is that — under the heading of 'good governance' — the federal government calls on partner countries to guarantee a market-friendly economic order, and the creation of positive conditions for foreign direct investment. Such conditionalities prevent these countries from freedom of choice about an independent economic and industrial policy. They inhibit the search for alternative development models that go beyond a neo-liberal fixation on the (global) market. They therefore contradict the principle of 'ownership', which German development policy does support, for example under PRSP processes.

The promotion of PRSP processes constitutes a further important element in the focal area of good governance. In this context, the federal government particularly stresses the involvement of civil society. To quote the Programme of Action 2015:

'The German Government will support the elaboration of national poverty reduction policies, especially as part of the Poverty Reduction Strategy Papers (PRSPs). In particular, it will give support to civil society participation and broad-based consultation within society (including the participation of women's organisations and the compilation of gender-disaggregated data).'[5]

Germany has provided financial support to PRSP processes in countries such as Bolivia, Honduras and Nicaragua.

At the same time, the federal government is concerned that donor countries in the World Bank have the last word on the formulation of PRSPs. In a position paper prior to the Annual Meeting of IMF and World Bank 2003, Germany stated:

'The impression that has arisen in many countries that have fallen into the "PRSP cycle" is that ultimately the final approval of PRSPs is given in Washington. If meant seriously, ownership calls for serious reflection about PRSP self-restraint in the relevant board discussions.'[6]

German development policy expressly stresses the connection between 'good governance' and 'global governance'. According to BMZ, democratically legitimised states with efficient public structures are in a better position to articulate the interests of their population, in the framework of global governance and international instruments. At the same time, the ministry is also committed to democratisation and reforms in the global governance system. The German Minister for Development calls for a reform of the decision making and capital structures of the IMF and World Bank, for instance, through raising basic voting rights and introducing the principle of a double majority.[7]

Furthermore, since the Monterrey Conference, the Minister has advocated the creation of a new 'global council' under the umbrella of the United Nations, in which southern countries would be equally represented. Her demands are, however, not supported by the whole of the German government — in particular not by the Minister for Economics and Labour and the Minister of Finance. This, presumably, is why the positive words of the Minister of

Germany

Table 7. Financing German ODA (in million € and in percentages)

	1990	1997	1998	1999	2000	2001	2002	2003	2004
								Target	Budget
Federal budget: Single budget 23, (BMZ budget)	4,067	4,010	4,052	3,997	3,675	3,790	3,759	3,768	3,744
% of federal budget	1.8	1.8	1.73	1.62	1.50	1.56	1.57	1.46	1.51
ODA	5.222	5.193	5.020	5.177	5.458	5.571	5.650		
ODA share	0.41	0.28	0.26	0.26	0.27	0.27	0.27		

Development have so far not been followed up by the necessary action, specifically political reform initiatives by the whole of the federal government.

Notes

[1] Part I of this paper is based on the report 'Die Wirklichkeit der Entwicklungshilfe — Elfter Bericht 2002/2003', Deutsche Welthungerhilfe and terre des hommes, author Dr Ludger Reuke.

[2] See Klemens van de Sand: Menschenrechte als integraler Bestandteil der staatlichen Entwicklungszusammenarbeit. In: Klaus Dicke/ Michael Edinger/Oliver Lembcke: Menschenrechte und Entwicklung. Duncker & Humboldt, Berlin, 1997.

[3] Federal Ministry for Economic Cooperation and Development: Poverty Reduction — a Global Responsibility. Program of Action 2015. The German Government's Contribution Towards Halving

Extreme Poverty Worldwide. Bonn, 2001 (Program of Action 2015).

[4] BMZ: Kurzinformation zum Stand der Umsetzung der Internationalen Konferenz uber Entwicklungsfinanzierung (International Conference on Financing for Development, FfD), 18. — 22.3.2002, Monterrey/Mexiko. Bonn, 29 October 2003.

[5] Program of Action 2015, p. 28.

[6] BMZ: Deutsches Positionspapier. Fur eine qualitative Veranderung der Mitsprachemoglichkeiten in der Weltbank. Berlin, September 2003.

[7] Ibid.

Germany

Table 8. *Sectoral breakdown of bilateral ODA (promises*)*

Sector million €	2002	%
Social infrastructure services	1,634.195	33.5
Including:		
Education	734.612	15.1
including basic education	48.265	1.6
Health including basic health	161.134 84.506	3.3 1.7
Population policy including combating AIDS	55.423	1.1
Water supply, waste water/waste disposal	232.116	4.8
State and civil society	246.696	5.1
Other social services	204.213.	4.2
Economic infrastructure	540.743	1.1
Productive sectors	227.350	4.7
Multi-sectoral/cross-	527.474	10.8
commodity/programme aid	40.094	0.8
Debt relief	**1,304.086**	**26.7**
Emergency relief	233.400	4.8
Other	370.230	7.6
Total	4,877.573	100

*ODA net disbursements are not recorded on a sectoral basis by the BMZ.

Germany

Table 9. Bilateral ODA: Net disbursements to LDCs (in million €)

	Total *bilateral ODA*	*including:* to LDCs (percentage)
1996	*3,489.094*	23.9
1997	*3,226.008*	21.2
1998	*3,139.972*	24.6
1999	*3,076.282*	23.4
2000	*2,915.312*	24.1
2001	*3,186.130*	21.0
2002	3,531.194	24.6

Ireland

Box 17. IRELAND at a glance

How much aid does IRELAND give?

In 2002, IRELAND gave

US$398m or 422m Euros

This means that, in 2002, each person
in IRELAND gave

US$104 or 110 Euros

In 2002, aid from IRELAND rose by

US$111m in cash terms. Because of inflation and exchange rate changes, the value of aid rose by 25.7% in real terms

How generous is IRELAND?

IRELAND gave 0.40% of its national wealth in 2002. This compares with the average country effort of 0.41%. This is IRELAND's highest ever level of aid as a percentage of GNI.

IRELAND was less generous than 6 other donors but more generous than in 2001 when aid was 0.33% of GNI.

How much of IRELAND's aid goes to the poorest countries and people?

73.9% of total bilateral aid (US$197.5m) went to Least Developed and Low Income Countries where 3.5 billion people (60% of the global population) live and where average incomes are less than two dollars a day.

How much of IRELAND's aid was spent on basic health, basic education, water supply and sanitation?

IRELAND spent

5.07% of its bilateral aid (US$13.53m) on water and sanitation

IRELAND does not report its spending on basic education or health.

Aid target missed but the outlook is positive

Claire Martin and Howard Dalzell, Concern Worldwide

Ireland's long tradition of solidarity with the poor and dispossessed was born from its own experience of colonisation, poverty, famine and mass emigration. This tradition has been expressed in public support for East Timor, debt relief and the abolition of apartheid, which has been shared by many Parliamentarians and civil society institutions. This tradition has been encapsulated in the principles of solidarity, poverty focus, neutrality and partnership that underlie the aid programme.

Much new thinking was stimulated by the 2002 report of the Ireland Aid Review Committee, which identified key areas for programme development. The agenda for this Committee was influenced by the findings of the 1999 DAC Peer Review. Since then, a number of significant changes have taken place.

Multilateral

- Increased voluntary contributions to EU and to UN agencies that demonstrate a commitment to the reforms necessary to minimise overlaps and improve effectiveness.
- Ireland has decided to concentrate on four UN agencies that support its policy objectives. With these agencies, Ireland can become more actively involved, for example by seeking board membership. The agencies are the United Nations Development Programme (UNDP), the Office of the United Nations High Commissioner for Refugees (UNHCR), the United Nations Children Fund and the United Nations Family Planning Association (UNFPA).[end bullet list]

Bilateral

- Much energy has been put into building strong partnerships with host governments and into relating to host governments in harmonisation with other donors. To support this, there has been a move towards direct budget support related to Poverty Reduction Strategies. This has been a slow process and thus the Development Cooperation Ireland's (DCI)[1] programme retains a judicious mix of area-based projects, SWAps (sector investments) and budget support. This is based on a pragmatic approach to real obstacles to full and open support to each country, including accountability, capacity building, policy, human resources and governance issues.

Ireland

Human Resources
- The 1999 DAC Peer Review identified the need for substantial staff increases in DCI. Staff numbers have increased from 84 in 1998 to 147 in 2003;[2] while this is welcome, it will need to continue in line with the ever-growing budget. Employment conditions have also improved.
- There has been an increase from four to nine in Senior Management posts., three of which are filled by non-civil servants with development expertise. This management enhancement, coupled with clearer policies, has strengthened DCI's voice in discussions with partner governments and donors.
- To enhance programme development, DCI is committed to commissioning, or carrying out, research of the highest international standards.

Support in Ireland
- A 2002 survey revealed that there is huge support among the Irish population for helping developing countries, but that there is very little awareness of the impact that DCI has made. This finding has led to a new strategic approach to gain public ownership of the programme, in an effort to secure support for the achievement of the 0.7% goal. Initiatives include:
  - An improved website http://www.dci.gov.ie/ More interaction with parliamentarians;
  - Increased media exposure such as marking World AIDS Day with highly publicised events and launches of the UNDP's Annual Human Development Report and the UNHCR Consolidated Appeal. To assist developing countries to participate in the global economy, Ireland has decided to commit to building relations with the private sector by: Setting up an Information and Communications Technology Task Force; Initiating a Private Sector Task Force; Beginning an initiative to enable experienced professional people to volunteer assistance for short periods.

Focus
- DCI is committed to addressing the challenges presented by HIV/AIDS, which is now considered in policy formulation and in strategic and project planning, so that it informs all decisions. Funding has increased by €34 million annually to support this increased focus.
- A new policy focus on governance, democracy and human rights has been adopted and reflects the values that inform Ireland's foreign policy.

Promotion of Civil Society
- Three new co-financing schemes have been developed between DCI and its main NGO partners to put their relationship on a more strategic basis:
  - Multi-annual Programme Scheme – three year funding with impact and effectiveness judged through joint evaluations. HIV/AIDS Partnership Scheme – three year funding with close alignment between NGO and DCI policies. The Missionary Development Fund – a support framework for Irish missionaries to assist them with partner capacity building.

Ireland

Other Initiatives

- Establishment of an Advisory Board to provide strategic advice to the Minister of State.
- Establishing an independent Audit and Evaluation Committee, chaired by a member of the Advisory Board.
- Integration of APSO and the National Committee for Development Education into DCI to promote more strategic approaches and to work through a wider range of civil society partners.
- Expansion into East Timor and preliminary appraisal of countries in South-East Asia and Sub-Saharan Africa. Any further expansion would be limited to one or two countries, so as to maintain the advantages of focussing on a small number of countries.

Policy on Governance and Human Rights

Several statements have been made on Ireland's approach to governance and human rights of which the following are the most pertinent:

Statements by Minister of State Kitt

To the Joint Committee on European Affairs[3]

To announce grants to assist Human Rights and Democratisation projects[4]

To the Joint Department of Foreign Affairs/NGO Committee on Human Rights[5]

Address by the Minister for Foreign Affairs, Brian Cowen TD

To the Royal Irish Academy — 'New World Order?'[6]

These statements contain the following key points, confirming Ireland's commitment to good governance and respect for human rights.

Ireland is a board member of the UN Commission on Human Rights until 2005. It fully supports the Commission in its more dynamic and strategic approach and is participating in the Commission's programme to prepare guidelines and a handbook intended to improve the effectiveness and impact of its governance programmes.

During its EU Presidency in 2004, Ireland will coordinate EU activity across a wide range of human rights issues.

A grant of €826,610 for a Human Rights and Democratisation Scheme, which is intended to support small scale human rights and democratisation projects.

Ireland is the sixth largest individual contributor to the Office of the UN High Commissioner for Human Rights.

The appointment of a Minister of State with Special Responsibility for Development Assistance and Human Rights reflects the government's commitment to human rights as a central focus of Irish foreign policy.

Governance and Human Rights in Practice

The more focused approach to governance and human rights has not changed the overall pattern of aid distribution, but there have been some changes in modality.

For example, reports from the UN Group, and the Porter Commission, about Uganda's involvement in the DRC led to an outcry from an Irish NGO and much public debate. This resulted in the transfer of funds from Direct Budget Support to the more carefully targeted and controlled Poverty Action Fund. The governance/human rights approach has not directly affected country priorities, but preliminary investigation of potential priority countries will include detailed examination of the human rights and governance situation.

Ireland

Sectoral priorities have been little affected as, although it is staff intensive, human rights and governance work does not demand large amounts of money.

DCI is encouraging governments to include governance issues in Poverty Reduction Strategies. This includes setting targets for progress towards a small number of pre-agreed indicators that can be reviewed on a regular basis. Governments will thus be clear about donor expectations. This should lessen their apprehension about the need for rapid changes in governance standards. They will not be vulnerable to abrupt financial cuts, provided they implement their anti-poverty strategies.

Governance is a very broad area, as typified by the DCI programme in Uganda that includes the following initiatives:

Justice, Law and Order Programme – overcrowding in many prisons leads to contravention of basic human rights standards. Ireland is working with the Ugandan Justice Department to reform the justice system so as to minimise the number of prisoners, thereby improving prison conditions.

Support to the government-established Uganda Commission on Human Rights.

Support to the Democratisation Programme, including monitoring of elections and voter education.

Conflict Resolution – a project working through the Amnesty Commission in Northern Uganda.

DCI also supports decentralisation of government and civil society development, including the promotion of local initiatives.

Conflict resolution falls under DCI's remit and also under the Diplomatic Service of the Ministry of Foreign Affairs. Ireland intends to raise issues of conflict resolution during its Presidency of the European Union.

DCI has established a dedicated unit responsible for assessing policy coherence for development issues.

Global Governance

As a small neutral country, Ireland's foreign policy relies heavily on an effective United Nations for international peace and security. Ireland's funding of the UN and the Bretton Woods Institutions reflects both this and the need for institutional reforms.

To this end, recent Irish initiatives include:

Commissioning a study into systems for independent evaluation in UNHCR, UNDP and UNICEF;

A proposal that led to HIV/AIDS becoming a standing agenda item for all co-sponsors of UNAIDS; Tabling a resolution, approved by the UNICEF board, which required UNICEF to adopt results-based reporting and led to results-based management.

Outlook

The outlook is positive, as the programme will continue in the direction strongly endorsed in the 2003 DAC Peer Review. However, this review noted that Ireland had missed its 2002 0.45% target. The final expenditure for 2003 will fall below the level of 0.45% and the modest increases provided for 2004 mean that 0.45% will not be realised until at least 2005.

A decision has been made in principle to join the Asian Development Bank and the first steps for this were taken in October 2003. However, there remain doubts as to whether there will be enough funding to meet all planned expansion of the programme, including diversification into new priority countries. The biggest uncertainty is whether the 2007 target of 0.7% GNP will

Ireland

be realised, although this was recently reconfirmed in a statement by the Taoiseach, at the 58th General Assembly of the United Nations.[7]

Notes

1 In July 2003, Ireland Aid was renamed as Development Cooperation Ireland (DCI).

2 Review of the Development Cooperation Policies and Programmes of Ireland. DAC's Main Findings and Recommendations 2003. Page 8. Para 20.

3 12 November 2003 - http://www.irlgov.ie/iveagh/

4 17 August 2003 - http://www.irlgov.ie/iveagh/

5 24 September 2003 - http://www.irlgov.ie/iveagh/

6 14 November 2003 - http://www.irlgov.ie/iveagh/

7 Statement by the Taoiseach, Mr. Bertie Ahern T.D., to the General Debate at the 58th General Assembly of the United Nations. New York, 25 September 2003.

Italy

Box 18. ITALY at a glance

How much aid does ITALY give?

In 2002, ITALY gave US$2,332m or 2,475m Euros

This means that, in 2002, each person
in ITALY gave US$41 or 43 Euros

In 2002, aid from ITALY rose by US$705m in cash terms. Because of inflation and exchange rate changes, the value of aid fell by 32.6% in real terms

How generous is ITALY?

ITALY gave 0.2% of its national wealth in 2002. This compares with the average country effort of 0.41% and ITALY's own previous highpoint of 0.42% in 1989.

ITALY was less generous than 20 other donors but more generous than in 2001 when aid was 0.15% of GNI.

How much of ITALY's aid goes to the poorest countries and people?

78.2% of total bilateral aid (US$787m) went to Least Developed and Low Income Countries where 3.5 billion people (60% of the global population) live and where average incomes are less than two dollars a day.

How much of ITALY's aid was spent on basic health, basic education, water supply and sanitation?

ITALY spent

0.03% of its bilateral aid (US$0.32m) on basic education

0.21% of its bilateral aid (US$2.55m) on basic health

0.38% of its bilateral aid (US$4.58m) on water and sanitation

Debt reduction fails to reverse downard trend

Carlotta Aiello, José Luis Rhi-Sausi and Marco Zupi, CeSPI

The present phase of Italian development cooperation follows a decade, the 1990s, that was characterised by a crisis of Italian ODA. *Clean Hands*, the judicial process against generalised corruption, initiated in 1992, also involved Italian development cooperation, leaving it discredited in the eyes of the public.[1] Since then, Italian aid has gradually regained credibility, although it has not returned to the levels reached in the 1980s. In the mid-1990s, Italy embraced the development priorities stated at international level, principally poverty reduction, and has translated these into strategic guidelines (*Linee-guida della cooperazione italiana sulla riduzione della povertà*, October 1999) for its aid policy.

In 2000, the Jubilee campaign (Drop the debt) marked a turning-point in the Italian situation: public opinion espoused the cause of debt cancellation and showed renewed interest in development cooperation issues; government responded with a law on bilateral cancellation of poor countries' external debt, putting Italy in the forefront of the battle for debt reduction.

These are symptoms of an important cultural change; unfortunately its impact on ODA practice is not very great. Strong Italian commitment to debt cancellation (almost US$986 million in HIPC countries' foreign debt cancelled by Italy between October 2001 and October 2002) is good news; but since there is no real increase, this is no more than a goodwill initiative that pumps up the otherwise poor bilateral resources, without guaranteeing a reversal in the Italian trend towards ODA reduction. The trend towards a multilateralisation of aid has been confirmed in recent years. Italian ODA, except for debt relief, continues to flow mainly through the multilateral channel.

Another interesting new dimension of Italian ODA is the growing attention paid to neighbouring countries (the Balkans and Mediterranean). Led by national geo-political priorities, this trend is in line with the 'Wider Europe approach' of the EU. It is translated into a reciprocal strategy that opens up potential space for decentralised cooperation, as well as for Italian enterprises, in particular SMEs (in 2001 the Italian Parliament passed an *ad hoc* law aimed at promoting Italian investment in the region, and a specific Fund was set up).

The role of Italian enterpreneurship (which has followed the descending parabola of Italian ODA in the last decade and is now very weak) in future aid policy, depends on the outcome of the current debate on aid

Italy

reform and on the implementation of the EU sponsored neighbourhood policy.

Italian decentralised cooperation (i.e. international cooperation carried out by local authorities in coordination with other local actors) is the emerging factor in Italian development policy. It provides an interesting opportunity to implement the objectives of participation and involvement of different stakeholders from local communities, through international partnership. At the same time, NGOs are striving hard to play a more crucial role in Italian international cooperation, trying to overcome the many limitations imposed by the slow and complex bureaucratic aid management system.

Given these overall trends, a crucial point has been reached in respect of Italy's poor (and decreasing) ODA resources. Looking at the 2004 Italian budget, resources for 2004 are estimated at €571 million for ODA administered by the Directorate General for Development Cooperation of the MFA, a drop of almost €86 million compared to 2003; The amounts budgeted for 2005 and 2006 remain the same, without even allowing for the projected inflation rate. In 2004, the amount allocated to ODA activities (total ODA resources less administrative costs) falls to €528 million, a fall of 14.7% compared to 2003. Within this amount, the allocation for voluntary contributions to the EU, international organisations, banks and funds suffers most from the contraction, totalling $361 million, compared to almost $459 in 2003. Most of the other items are either unchanged or decreasing, the only exception being support to NGOs, which sees an increase from €39 to 50 million. But despite the increase, NGOs complain that these resources are too low and suffer from the very long, slow and confused bureaucratic procedures needed to transform commitment into disbursement. NGOs point to the amount

of credit they have been building up over the years.

Italian official statements (for example within the DAC forum) show a strong commitment to good governance and human righs. The priority role of human rights has recently been reaffirmed by the Minister of Foreign Affairs, in his December 2002 Human Rights Day declaration in Rome. Beyond the official declarations, it is not easy to identify what 'good governance' stands for in Italian development cooperation. The MFA view seems to focus on good governance in *public sector management*: a good example is given by the Italian initiative 'E-Government for Development', launched in Palermo in April 2002 in cooperation with UNDESA (United Nations Department for Economic and Social Affairs). The initiative is in its implementation phase in the first five beneficiary nations: Jordan, Albania, Nigeria, Mozambique and Tunisia. Another activity related to good governance and human rights is the *monitoring of elections*. Italy has a long experience in this field and has operated in many countries, although it does not have a well-defined strategy and election work does not represent a big portion of its ODA budget. A third dimension of good governance at the governmental level is access to *basic social services* (such as the strengthening of epidemiological systems). Last but not least, in the Italian case, good governance strongly interrelates with *debt relief*, in the sense that Italian Law 209 of 2000, which governs all actions related to debt, makes debt relief conditional on three considerations: protection of fundamental freedoms and human rights; rejection of war; commitment to poverty reduction and to social and human development.

It is not easy to quantify Italian official efforts in the field of governance and human rights. Looking at the top ten beneficiaries of Italian ODA in 2001 (Eritrea, Serbia &

Italy

Montenegro, Somalia, Afghanistan, Albania, Palestinian territories, Ethiopia, Mozambique, Honduras and Angola)[2], we can see how marginal the Italian efforts on good governance and human rights are in concrete terms. The main sectors to which Italian official resources have been committed are: economic and development policy/planning, elections and government administration. The two biggest commitments were for Somalia and Angola: a US$457,000 commitment for public sector financial management for the former, and a US$782,000 contribution to UNDESA for economic planning for the latter. Very small amounts (less than US$10,000) are committed to strengthening civil society and human rights. The country that benefited most from these commitments is Albania.

A widely-held opinion is that a major source of experience and lessons learned in the field of good governance is derived from Italian engagement in the Programmes of Human Development at Local Level (PDHL), which followed the Italian participation in the UNDP programme in Central America (PRODERE). This responded to the priorities stated at the Copenhagen Social Summit in 1995. Italian decentralised cooperation, if well-tuned, could be an important and effective actor in promoting good governance from a human rights perspective. Italy has given financial as well as operational support to UNDP/UNOPS programmes in many countries, among which Albania, Tunisia, Mozambique and Cuba are worth mentioning. These programmes, which have seen the active involvement of the Italian local administrations, were focused on the central idea that the strengthening of good relations between institutions and population is crucial to development.

The Italian experience with the PHDL programmes is largely over now, (the only surviving programme being the PASARP in Albania), being partly substituted by other programmes (APPI). But this vision of good governance is still crucial to Italian decentralised cooperation, which has been widely applied in contexts such as the Balkans and the Palestinian territories, and now uses its expertise in other programmes, such as City to City in the Federal Republic of Yugoslavia (UNOPS), the Italian Programme to fight desertification and poverty in the Sahel region (IAO and UNDP), and others. Another experience worth mentioning is Italian participation in the Network of the Local Democracy Agencies (LDAs), based in 11 municipalities in the territory of former Yugoslavia, and their Association (ALDA), comprising representatives of 14 countries. On the Italian side, 18 local authorities as well as seven NGOs are members of the Association.

Within this framework, Italian decentralised cooperation has had to engage with *institution building*, a sector that is new to the Italian experience. Another test was the recently concluded NEBAME project (Network for officials of central and local administrations in the Balkan and Mediterrean areas), and also by the biggest UNIVERSITAS programme (an Italian trust fund with ILO/UNDP).

Overall it can be said that the best contribution Italian decentralised cooperation has made to the promotion of good governance and human rights has less to do with technical issues and more with political activity in support of local communities and the strengthening of relationships between institutions and populations.

Finally, it is important to stress that decentralised cooperation is not fully reported in the ODA statistics, since the share taken from the local authorities' own budgets is not included in those statistics.

The same emphasis on capacity building and civil society can be found among Italian NGOs, who have grown more aware that

Italy

projects only work where there are good governance mechanisms. NGOs have translated this new awareness into action by turning away from 'technical' projects and committing themselves more strongly to projects focused on democratisation, civil society participation, human rights and partnership. The main difficulty NGOs face is Italian bureaucracy. In fact, they argue, it is impossible to sustain good governance processes within the limitations of a short-term perspective and restrictive and inflexible budget-oriented regulations.

On the national level, much effort is put into advocacy campaigning for better global governance, on the one hand, and into awareness programmes and training in human rights on the other. From the NGOs' perspective, this emphasis on global governance, rather than on democracy and human rights alone, represents a more comprehensive approach to governance issues, which more effectively reflects the idea of a rights-based approach, focussed on the need for a more coherent and strong

international institutional structure, capable of providing global public goods. From the NGO perspective, this approach also avoids the risk of a passive acceptance of the prevailing rhetoric on democracy, human rights and security, as the priorities of current international agenda, which reflect a new dimension of the westernisation of the world.

Notes

1. In order to ascertain possible criminal acts perpetrated within the Italian aid activities, in 1995 a Parlamentary Enquiry Commission was set up and a judicial process was started by the Penal Court of Rome. Although the judicial process did not find systematic corruption (only isolated cases of corruption were proved), a general disenchantment with Italian development co-operation still persists within public opinion.

2. OECD/DAC source. No data available for Afghanistan, Eritrea and Honduras.

Japan

Box 19. JAPAN at a glance

How much aid does JAPAN give?

In 2002, JAPAN gave | US$9,283m or 1,162b Yen

This means that, in 2002, each person
in JAPAN gave | US$73 or 9,120 Yen
In 2002, aid from JAPAN fell by | US$564m in cash terms. Because of inflation and exchange rate changes, the value of aid fell by 1.2% in real terms

How generous is JAPAN?

JAPAN gave 0.23% of its national wealth in 2002. This compares with the average country effort of 0.41% and JAPAN's own previous highpoint of 0.35% in 1999.
JAPAN was less generous than 17 other donors and its aid level remained the same as in 2001, when aid also stood at 0.23% of GNI.

How much of JAPAN's aid goes to the poorest countries and people?

61% of total bilateral aid (US$4,080m) went to Least Developed and Low Income Countries where 3.5 billion people (60% of the global population) live and where average incomes are less than two dollars a day.

How much of JAPAN's aid was spent on basic health, basic education, water supply and sanitation?

JAPAN spent

1.08% of its bilateral aid (US$101.27m) on basic education
0.85% of its bilateral aid (US$79.07m) on basic health
4.04% of its bilateral aid (US$378.0m) on water and sanitation

Muted celebrations for 50 years of Japanese aid

Tatsuya Watanabe, JANIC (board member)

The year 2004 marks the 50th anniversary of Japan's ODA. Though the war-worn country was still struggling hard to rise from the ashes, it started assisting less developed countries in 1954, by sending three development experts and receiving as many trainees. Following that small beginning, Japan progressed by leaps and bounds to become one of the largest donors.

However, this should hardly be a year of celebration. The decade-long economic hardship is taking its toll on Japan's ODA. The amount of aid has been decreasing for five years in a row.

Aid is also undergoing a qualitative change. The Government revised its ODA Charter for the first time in 2003. 'Strategising' was the buzzword and the distinct winner in the process was 'national interests'. This is a cause of concern for many NGOs and most probably for developing countries.

Japan's ODA peaked in 1999 at US$15.3 billion and then started going downhill. In 2002, it stood at US$9.28 billion — 40% less than the peak year and a mere 0.23% of GNI. There is no knowing when the downhill momentum will be arrested. The aid budget for FY2004 has been slashed by a further 4.8%.

The economic quagmire and a snowballing public debt — to the tune of six trillion dollars — have mercilessly cut into benevolence as well as budget. Recent national opinion polls show public support for ODA at an all-time low, with only 19% of those polled in favour of an increase.

The quality of aid is also suffering. The grant share of Japanese ODA in 2001-2002 lagged far behind other DAC countries, standing at 53.3% as against an average of 87.4%. The share of Japan's ODA provided to LDCs was 23.9% as against the DAC average of 34%. More revealing is the erosion of untied aid. In the face of rising criticism of the commercial nature of its aid, the Government made major efforts and accomplished 100% untying of its loan aid in FY1996. But erosion started the year after, as uncompetitive Japanese firms lost ground and started complaining vociferously. The decision was reversed and the untied portion of the loan aid kept slipping down — hitting the level of 60% in FY 2001.

ODA Charter revised

The ODA Charter, instituted in 1992, was revised by the reform-minded and nationalist Government of Premier Koizumi in 2003. Factors behind the revision were: 1) intensifying terrorism; 2) emerging

Japan

development issues; 3) the financial crunch; and 4) the desire to engage all concerned in development assistance. Far-reaching as the revision was, the Government allowed the public only two months to consider a revised draft. Public hearings and comment gathering via its homepage were little more than a ritual. The draft came through virtually untouched and was approved by the Cabinet.

The most significant change is in the objective of aid. Whereas the original Charter sought to help realise sound economic development in developing countries, the new one aims to 'contribute to the peace and development of the international community, and thereby to help ensure Japan's own security and prosperity'. Developing countries are sidelined and Japan's own security and prosperity — a euphemism for national interests — now take the front seat.

9/11 casts a long shadow over the new Charter. The four principles of the original Charter remain unchanged but the principle that cautions against military spending by recipient countries is now qualified by the proviso 'so as to maintain and strengthen international peace and stability, including the prevention of terrorism'. Poverty reduction is top of the four priority issues, which is an improvement over the original Charter. But the reason given is that poverty reduction is 'essential for eliminating terrorism'. Priority issues have a new entrant: peace-building that includes conflict prevention and post-conflict peace restoration. ODA is being transformed so as to serve Japan's national interest, which enshrines the strategic alliance with US above everything.

The new emphasis in policy is already evident on the ground. Despite deep public concern, the Government has bent over backward to support the US-UK occupation of Iraq. It has stretched constitutional constraints and sent military contingents to help reconstruction. It also pledged US$5 billion-worth of ODA, partly to ward off attacks on Japanese military by 'buying minds of Iraqi people'. Militarisation of aid is thus creeping in and resources for pure poverty reduction are being siphoned off.

Another major change is the clear departure from long-practised, request-based assistance. The new Charter tells ODA personnel to 'engage in policy consultation before requests are made'. Developing countries are likely to face more assertive, if not imposing, aid officials from Japan.

The new Charter has also not forgotten to promote commercial interests. It dictates 'appropriate use ... of the technologies and expertise of Japanese private companies, and ensuring appropriate protection of intellectual property rights'.

DAC's peer review of Japan's ODA was undertaken soon after the Charter revision in 2003. It aptly recommends the country to 'highlight that the primary objective of ODA is for the development of the recipient country' and 'ensure that narrower national interests do not over-ride this objective'. It also recommends that ODA should 'more fully mainstream poverty reduction', more clearly 'focus on poor countries or poor populations', and focus 'more investment in basic health and education services to reduce poverty'. It then asks the Japanese Government to 'make a policy statement on coherence for development' and to identify 'concrete measures to progressively untie the use of grant funds for primary contractors'.

On governance and Human Rights

Policy statements
The ODA Charters, both old and new, mention governance and human rights only in passing. The new one says, under the 'Basic

Japan

policies' heading, '[t]he most important philosophy of Japan's ODA is to support the self-help efforts of developing countries based on good governance .... Japan will give priority to assisting developing countries that make active efforts to pursue peace, democratisation, and the protection of human rights, as well as structural reform in the economic and social spheres'.

Then one of the four principles stipulates that '[f]ull attention should be paid for promoting democratisation and the introduction of a market-oriented economy, and the situation regarding the protection of basic human rights and freedoms in the recipient country'.

The second most important official document, 'Mid-term ODA Policy' (formulated in 1999 and soon to be revised), devotes just one section to support for democratisation and expects this support to lead to people's participation in governance and development, as well as to the promotion of human rights.

Guidelines

JBIC (Japan Bank for International Cooperation) — the implementing agency specialising in loan aid — developed, in collaboration with NGOs, the 'Guidelines for Confirmation of Environmental and Social Considerations' and put these into effect in October 2003. The JBIC Guidelines have been developed to ensure that potential environmental and social impacts are duly taken into consideration before a project gets approved by JBIC and during implementation by a borrower country. If a project is found to have undesirable impacts, JBIC may not approve it, or may stop lending. There is no direct reference to human rights, but such social aspects as involuntary resettlement, ethnic minorities, indigenous peoples, cultural heritage, gender, children's rights, HIV/AIDS are to be looked into.

JICA (Japan International Cooperation Agency) — the agency implementing technical cooperation — followed suit and is now formulating its own version. The draft JICA guidelines deal more directly with the issues. The policy section of the guidelines states that 'with respect for human rights and democratic governance system, JICA secures a wide range of stakeholder meaningful participation and transparency of decision-making, works for information disclosure and keeps efficiency for undertaking environmental and social considerations'. JICA also pledges to 'respect internationally established human rights standards, such as the International Convention on Human Rights, and gives special attention to human rights of vulnerable social groups ... in implementing cooperation projects'. The guidelines also stipulate that '[a]ppropriate consideration must be given to vulnerable social groups ... who may have little access to decision-making processes within society'.

Practice

In 1996, Japan introduced a programme called 'Partnership for Democratic Development (PDD)' with a view to promoting human rights and democratisation. It encompasses assistance to:

1) legal, administrative and law enforcement institution-building;
2) holding elections;
3) intellectual activities (research on human rights, training for opinion leaders, etc);
4) strengthening civil society (election education, media development, etc); and
5) enhancing women's status.

But the programme did not come with any financial commitment. The Government then opened a new window in 2001 called 'Governance Grant' for democratic

Japan

institution/capacity building. But budgetary allocation has been minimal — less than US$10 million (0.1% of total ODA) a year.

Japan's approach to human rights is characterised by 'carrot' instead of 'stick'. It seeks to constructively engage regimes that have poor human rights records and to change them by persuasion. Its application, however, has been selective: harsher to small countries and more lenient to large and resourceful countries such as China. Myanmar should be happy that it was categorised as one of the latter. A show of goodwill by the military regime was good enough for Japan to loosen the noose and restart ODA as early as 1995. But developments in the country to date show what constructive engagement has achieved in practice, making the rhetoric ring hollow.

Netherlands

Box 20. NETHERLANDS at a glance

How much aid does the NETHERLANDS give?

In 2002, NETHERLANDS gave   US$3,338 or 3,542m Euros

That means that, in 2002, each person
in the NETHERLANDS gave   US$209 or 222 Euros

In 2002, aid from NETHERLANDS rose by   US$166m in cash terms. Because of inflation
and exchange rate changes, the value of aid
fell by 3.3% in real terms

How generous is NETHERLANDS?

NETHERLANDS gave 0.81% of its national wealth in 2002. This compares with the average country effort of 0.41% and NETHERLANDS's own previous highpoint of 1.07% reached in 1982.

NETHERLANDS was the fourth most generous donor, but was less generous than in 2001 when aid was 0.82% of GNI

How much of NETHERLANDS's aid goes to the poorest countries and people?

55.2% of total bilateral aid (US$1,351.4m) went to Least Developed and Low Income Countries where 3.5 billion people (60% of the global population) live and where average incomes are less than two dollars a day.

How much of NETHERLANDS's aid was spent on basic health, basic education, water supply and sanitation?

NETHERLANDS spent

4.8 % of its bilateral aid (US$214.03m) on basic education

1.33% of its bilateral aid (US$59.37m) on basic health

2.78% of its bilateral aid (US$123.79) on water and sanitation

Mutual interests, mutual responsibilities

Nicole Metz, Novib/Oxfam Netherlands

In November 2003, the new Minister for Development Cooperation, Agnes van Ardenne (Christian Democrats), published a policy memorandum, entitled *Mutual interests, mutual responsibilities: Dutch development cooperation en route to 2015*, which outlines The Netherlands' new development policy. Some of its main features are:

- Sustainable poverty reduction remains the main objective of Dutch development cooperation and the Millennium Development Goals (MDGs) are the means of achieving it. To meet these goals, the Dutch government plans:

  to make everyone more involved in meeting the MDGs by 2015;

  to boost the quality and effectiveness of development cooperation;

  to make Dutch efforts and results more visible.[1]

- Bilateral assistance: Minister Van Ardenne has further reduced the number of countries that are eligible for Dutch bilateral assistance from 49 to 36. The selection is based on an analysis of national development trends and on

criteria such as IDA-eligibility, improvements in the quality of policy and governance, and the relative size and added value of Dutch development aid.

- 'Partnership' is a key concept. 'Development cooperation calls for commitment from everyone involved: The Netherlands, other donors, civil society organisations, the private sector, individual citizens and multilateral organisations, as well as the developing countries themselves. We have all committed ourselves to meeting the UN Millennium Development Goals by the target date of 2015.'[2] Several financial instruments have been put in place or maintained to implement the collaboration between the Ministry, private companies, and civil society organisations.

- The emphasis will be on an integrated, coherent and regional approach to foreign policy, on sustainable development, on the collaboration with the private sector, and on Africa.

- Aid will focus on four priority themes: education, reproductive health, HIV/AIDS, environment and water. An increasing part of the budget, up to 15% in-2007, is earmarked for education. As a result, The Netherlands came first in a comparison of donors by the Global Campaign for Education.

Dutch civil society organisations reacted to the proposed policies with mixed feelings. Novib/Oxfam Netherlands welcomed the clear commitment of the Dutch government to the MDGs, but was surprised that little attention had been given to the implications of geopolitical developments, such as the Iraq crisis or the failure of the WTO Cancun Ministerial Conference. With regard to the thematic focus, there is a risk that good governance and gender are being particularly neglected. The fact that the Dutch financial contribution to UNIFEM has been discontinued was strongly criticised. The Minister's choice for 'public-private partnerships' is a subject of lively debate among Dutch NGOs. They advise the Minister to set much clearer criteria for collaboration with the private-for-profit sector and to require that these 'partnerships' contribute effectively to the realisation of the MDGs.

Regarding the country focus, doubts were raised, both in and outside Parliament, about the justification for the proposed choices. On the one hand, relatively rich countries such as Brazil, China and India will no longer benefit from bilateral cooperation, though so-called 'pockets of poverty' exist in these countries. Bilateral relations could also be important because of the geopolitical role of these countries. On the other hand, a specific country list for private sector programmes, which includes some countries that are relatively rich, or have questionable human rights records, is being maintained, for strategic reasons — for example South Africa, Egypt, Pakistan, Indonesia.

Quality of aid

In early 2003, the implementation of Dutch development cooperation policy was criticised, when a group of 150 Dutch

'practitioners' working as experts, consultants and researchers in development cooperation programmes, published a critical 'open letter' to the government. This letter expressed grave concerns about the diminishing quality of Dutch aid, especially in relation to the introduction of the sector policy. They also openly questioned whether there had been sufficient common 'learning' in the Dutch development cooperation sector over the last few years. Specific issues mentioned in the letter, were the loss of control over, and diminishing quality of, the Ministry's staff, a lack of a clear and inspiring vision on development, and the absence of a clear implementation plan to 'mainstream' gender in all policies and operations.

The letter was discussed at a symposium with representatives from the Ministry of Foreign Affairs/NEDA.

'Contamination' risk

The Netherlands has generally shown serious commitment to the UN 0.7% of GNI target for development cooperation. In 2004, ODA will be maintained at 0.8% of GNI. Of this budget, 15% will be for education and 0.1% for environment and water. At least 50% of the bilateral aid has been reserved for Africa. At the same time, there is a shift in the allocation of funds within this budget, which increases the risk of its improper use ('budget contamination'). First, a large amount of the development aid budget has been reserved for the cancellation of debts related to export credit insurance, granted by the government to Dutch companies exporting to developing countries: €540 million (or 14% of the DC budget) in 2003. According to the Jubilee Netherlands Campaign, cancellation of debt due to export credits or guarantees cannot be counted as ODA, since this is rather an instrument of export promotion and the cancellation of the related debts does not incur real costs. This

Netherlands

position was supported by a European Union directive, which says that export insurance instruments should be cost neutral for the government. Also, the UN Financing for Development Conference in Monterrey (2002) decided that debt cancellation in general would be additional to existing ODA commitments. Second, the government proposes to extend the OECD/DAC standards for ODA, in order to include the implementation of a 'more integral international approach to (potential) crises' and the Clean Development Mechanism. Novib/Oxfam Netherlands has been objecting to these proposals from the start, because of the high risk of further diversion of ODA funds for non-ODA purposes.

Political support for ODA is slightly decreasing. Though parliament approved the proposed budget and policies for 2004, critical questions were asked referring to the effectiveness of aid, the need for coherence with international trade policies, as well as the critical international economic situation. This trend can be explained by the turbulent shifts in Dutch politics in the period 2001-2003, which included two consecutive changes of parliament and government. During this period, Dutch political debate seemed to be dominated by internal, rather than international, issues. The current government, a centre-right coalition of Christian democratic and liberal parties, came to power in early 2003.

Governance and human rights: high on the political agenda

As stated above, sustainable poverty reduction remains the main objective of Dutch development cooperation. In the vision of the Dutch government, 'poverty reduction and the promotion of human rights have to go hand in hand.'[3] According to the government, the responsibility for observing human rights lies primarily with national governments, though the international community can put pressure on a country to fulfil its human rights obligations.

'Good governance' is, in the government's vision, 'a political and institutional climate in which human rights, democratic principles and the rule of law are being protected, and in which human and natural resources, as well as economic and financial resources, are managed in a transparent and responsible way, in the interest of equitable and sustainable development.'[4]

Under the previous Minister, Eveline Herfkens, good governance was among the primary criteria for the selection of countries for bilateral aid relations. 'Ownership' was developed into the central philosophy. Countries that qualified as having 'good governance', were given sector-wide support on the basis of Poverty Reduction Strategy Papers. Instead of supporting concrete projects, Dutch funds were directly transferred to a sector ministry for its general policies and programmes — resulting in increased 'ownership' of recipient governments. A second group of countries were eligible for smaller funds from the so-called 'governance, human rights and peace-building' programme. These funds aimed to promote 'good governance', not necessarily through the bilateral channel. In spite of a recent budget reduction in the latter category, the new government's policy intends to include a more proactive approach to governance and human rights.

More than in the past, the efforts of the Development Cooperation and the diplomatic departments of the Ministry, as well as the embassies, will be integrated. The Netherlands intends to use its position more structurally than in the past, to try to influence recipient countries' policies. Embassies will prepare annual plans, addressing among other things, the steps

Netherlands

necessary for promoting human rights and good governance. There will be annual reporting on the results.

In addition, a specific budgetary provision has been made for a new category of 'economic governance' institutions — which means institutions that facilitate the functioning of markets, such as land registers, competition authorities and taxation systems.

Stability Fund focuses on global security

The Netherlands has played an active role in several areas affected by conflict, especially the Great Lakes Region in eastern Africa, the Horn of Africa and the Western Balkans. An integrated 'regional approach' is being developed, taking into account the often cross-boundary character of conflicts in these regions, and giving priority to these conflicts in Dutch diplomacy. The Defence, Foreign Affairs and Development Cooperation Ministers have collaborated in establishing a so-called Stability Fund, an initiative aimed at tackling global security problems, using an integrated approach. It is meant for projects related to conflict prevention and resolution, and post-conflict rehabilitation and demobilisation. For 2004, €64 million has been allocated to the Fund.[5]

Notwithstanding its traditional preference for multilateralism, The

Netherlands gave political (but not military) support to the invasion of Iraq by US and UK troops. After the war ended, Dutch troops joined the occupying forces in Iraq. Also, The Netherlands participates in peacekeeping forces in Afghanistan and Bosnia and has positioned a hospital ship off the coast of Liberia. Until 2001, Dutch troops were part of the UN peacekeeping forces in Ethiopia and Eritrea (UNMEE).

Novib/Oxfam Netherlands supports the government's intention to pay substantial attention to the impact of conflicts on human development, because Dutch (and European) foreign and development policy should be based on the principle of human security — instead of the narrow approach to (armed) security that is now central to international politics. In a reaction to the Minister, Novib welcomed the regional approach, but also warned of the risk of mixing (finances for) civil and military operations — which could lead to the above-mentioned 'budget contamination' as well as being an obstacle to humanitarian aid. The selection of regions and countries should be more carefully done. For example, West Africa should also be selected for a regional approach; there should also be financial support in conflict areas or regions, even if individual countries do not qualify for bilateral assistance.

Netherlands

Box 21. Arms Trade Treaty

In October 2003, Oxfam International, Amnesty International and the International Action Network on Small Arms (IANSA) started a joint campaign to 'Control Arms' by an international Arms Trade Treaty, as proposed by Nobel Laureates, among them former Costa Rican president Oscar Arias. Dutch Minister Van Ardenne was one of the first officials to express her support for this proposal. Novib/Oxfam Netherlands expects a lot from her in the second half of 2004, when The Netherlands, as chair of the European Union, will be in a good position to promote this initiative.

She can make a good start at home. The Netherlands is among the ten largest arms exporters in the world and is suspected of being a major transit country. There is hardly any control of transit, even though the port of Rotterdam is the largest in the world and Schiphol airport is the fourth largest airport in Europe. Available data shows, for example, large transhipments of military goods from the United States through the Netherlands, with Israel as the final destination. Novib/Oxfam, Pax Christi and Amnesty International propose to submit the transhipment of arms through The Netherlands to the same regulations as export, in order to ensure that arms are not flowing to countries in conflict, or to regimes that have a bad human rights record.

http://www.controlarms.org/

Notes

[1] Ministry of Foreign Affairs, Minister for Development Cooperation, 2003. Mutual interests, mutual responsibilities: Dutch development cooperation en route to 2015. http://www.minbuza.nl/default.asp?CMS_ITEM=MBZ257572

[2] Ibid.

[3] Foreign Affairs Minister De Hoop Scheffer and Development Cooperation Minister Van Ardenne, Beleidsreactie op het AIV advies getiteld 'Een mensenrechtenbenadering van Ontwikkelingssamenwerking', letter to the Adviesraad Internationale Vraagstukken (AIV), September 2003.

[4] Ref. to note 1.

[5] Budget for the Stability Fund: for 2005, €110 million; for 2006, €93 million; from 2007 onwards, €77 million per year.

New Zealand

Box 22. NEW ZEALAND at a glance

How much aid does NEW ZEALAND give?

In 2002, NEW ZEALAND gave — US$122m or 264m New Zealand Dollars

This means that, in 2002, each person
in NEW ZEALAND gave — US$31 or 67 NZ$

In 2002, aid from NEW ZEALAND rose by — US$10m in cash terms. Because of inflation and exchange rate changes, the value of aid fell by 1.1% in real terms

How generous is NEW ZEALAND?

NEW ZEALAND gave 0.22% of its national wealth in 2002. This compares with the average country effort of 0.41% and NEW ZEALAND's own previous highpoint of 0.52% in 1975.

NEW ZEALAND was less generous than 18 other donors and less generous than in 2001 when aid was 0.25% of GNI.

How much of NEW ZEALAND's aid goes to the poorest countries and people?

38.7% of total bilateral aid (US$35.5m) went to Least Developed and Low Income Countries where 3.5 billion people (60% of the global population) live and where average incomes are less than two dollars a day.

How much of NEW ZEALAND's aid was spent on basic health, basic education, water supply and sanitation?

NEW ZEALAND spent

2.69% of its bilateral aid (US$2.47m) on basic education

1.79% of its bilateral aid (US$1.64m) on basic health

1.29% of its bilateral aid (US$1.18m) on water and sanitation

New agency makes poverty elimination its mission

*Rae Julian, Council for International Development/
Kaunihera mo te Whakapakari Ao Whānui*

The most significant development in New Zealand's aid programme in the last couple of years has been the establishment of NZAID/*Nga Hoe Tuputupu-mai-tawhiti* in June 2002, as a semi-autonomous agency within the Ministry of Foreign Affairs and Trade (MFAT). This followed a major review of ODA, reported in *Reality of Aid 2002*. There are a number of key features of the new agency.

- **Permanent staff.** In contrast with the former division of MFAT, where most staff were rotated from the diplomatic corps, in order to widen their experience (development staff were not eligible for rotation), NZAID staff are selected for their skills and experience in development-related areas.
- **Semi-Autonomous from MFAT.** NZAID's increased autonomy has allowed it to take a development focus throughout all of its activities. This change is also demonstrated in the difference between the public statements of the Minister of Trade Negotiations, who espouses a neo-liberal trade agenda, and the Associate Minister of Foreign Affairs and Trade (with responsibility for ODA), who is more likely to reflect the position of developing countries, especially the Pacific.

- **An over-arching focus on poverty elimination.** This is the mission of the agency. Poverty is defined as: extreme poverty or the inability to meet basic needs; poverty of opportunity caused by lack of opportunities to participate in economic, social, civil and political life; and vulnerability to poverty through being likely to experience natural disasters or other circumstances affecting livelihoods or full participation in community and national life.
- **The Pacific Island Countries as the main developing country partners.** Currently just under half of the ODA goes to the Pacific. There are also significant programmes in South East Asia, targeted assistance for other developing countries, and funding for multilateral agencies.
- **A closer relationship with civil society.** A Strategic Policy Framework document, defining the extent of the partnership between NGOs and the then Development Cooperation Division of MFAT, was signed in 2000. The development of NZAID has enabled NGOs to participate in developing the strategic direction and core policies of the new agency. In addition to regular formal meetings, there have been numerous opportunities

New Zealand

to comment on country, regional and multilateral and strategy documents, share training, participate in joint working groups and generally provide advice. There has also been an increase in funding for NGOs.

- **A greater emphasis on working directly with civil society in developing countries.** This applies particularly to countries where governance is weak or where there is little government support for civil society. In some countries, for example, NGO funding mechanisms, which are administered mainly by local NGO representatives, have been established.

- **A change in education policy, towards basic education.** The previous education policy tended to place much of its emphasis on tertiary scholarships, mainly for students to come to New Zealand. This was seen as especially desirable from a diplomatic and political perspective, as many of the students went back to be leaders in their country, with closer links to New Zealand. Evidence showed, however, that the scholarships tended to be elitist, assisting a few privileged young people, while basic education in the country was often in a very poor state.

There are also some recommendations from the DAC Review in 1999 where less or little progress has been made:

- **Striving to maximise the use of developing countries' own services and goods in the implementation of projects.** Although NZAID does not have a policy of tied aid, there is still a tendency to use management service consultants from New Zealand rather than from the local community or from another developing country. This has

changed to some extent through the use of locally engaged aid administrators in some diplomatic posts and through the NGO funding schemes referred to above.

- **Setting a medium-term ODA/GNP (GNI) target.** As can be seen from the accompanying table, New Zealand features very low on the list of OECD countries that are committed to reaching the target of spending 0.7% of GNI on ODA. The 0.22% GNI figure for 2002 was less than the 0.25% GNI figures for 2000 and 2001. The Government, however, continues to express its commitment to meeting the goal:

'The government is absolutely committed to increasing the amount of aid we give, and giving it in the most effective way possible. We're only a third of the way to the internationally agreed target, but we're definitely heading in the right direction.'

Governance and human rights

- NZAID has developed a 'Good Governance' programme, which states as its objective: To promote, sustain and support human development by promoting good governance, including promotion and protection of human rights and strengthening participatory development, at regional, national and local levels.[2]

There is a Global Programme and a Pacific Programme (with a Budget of NZ$3.3m), reflecting NZAID's commitment to the Pacific as its primary area of focus. The programme will be delivered through key strategic partnerships — including those with developing country NGOs — seeding grants or pilot projects, conflict prevention and

New Zealand

peace building activities and a small grants scheme.

- *NZAID has not adopted a fully rights-based approach to development, although some preliminary discussions have taken place with the Human Rights Council of Australia, one of the chief proponents of the approach throughout the region. Instead, the NZAID policy is to mainstream human rights, recognising that: Human rights are at the core of all development policy and practice and will be reflected throughout the development programming cycle — from initial appraisal to evaluation and impact assessment.[3]*

- NZAID, however, does not operate in a vacuum. It must work closely with the Ministry of Foreign Affairs and Trade, as well as the international financial institutions, whose policies are more likely to focus on corruption and financial management than on the human rights aspects of good governance. A number of Pacific countries, such as the Cook Islands, Solomon Islands and Tonga, have been told that assistance depends on their reduction of the public sector. There is supporting rhetoric about retraining and the opportunities for development of a stronger competition-based private sector. Little heed is paid to issues such as population size, limited opportunities for business development, and the role of many public servants in supporting extended families or even as the principal source of cash income for a village in an outer island.

- NZAID has taken a leading role in ensuring that civil society organisations are also consulted as part of country strategy studies. This accords with the human rights principle of empowering people at all levels of society to participate in decision making that affects their lives. NZAID has also taken the step of working only with NGOs in countries where the governments were clearly in breach of basic human rights. For example, in Fiji after the coup of May 2000, all development assistance was suspended, apart from that channelled through NGOs and regional organisations.

- Issues such as security, migration and combating terrorism do not feature largely in NZAID's governance policies. New Zealand plays a role in peace-keeping throughout the world, but only the humanitarian aspects of these activities within the country of deployment are included within the calculation of ODA for the DAC report. Terrorism is a concern within Aotearoa/New Zealand, especially since the terrorist attacks in the United States and Bali. Special legislation has been introduced since that time. This has impinged on migration and refugee policy, for example, through the incarceration for ten months in solitary confinement of an elected Algerian parliamentarian, who had attempted to claim refugee status. This imprisonment was based on insubstantial reports from international security agencies.

- New Zealand is an advocate of the internal reforms at the World Bank and the International Monetary Fund, according to the Minister of Finance[4]. He has also expressed support for change in the governance and voting systems of the two institutions, stating that, 'A strong voice for developing countries is fundamental if the Bank is to function effectively'. The Minister for Trade Negotiations has stated his support for reform of the WTO:

'That the WTO needs reform to its democratic processes is self-

New Zealand

evident, given that it has just failed [at the Cancun Ministerial meeting] to significantly advance reforms that almost all of its members — especially its poorest and least developed — desperately need'.[5]

Conclusion

Governance issues are ranked highly on the ODA agenda of the New Zealand government, especially within the principal area of focus, the Pacific Islands region. Conditionality is not practised overtly and is not expressed in any NZAID policies but New Zealand's close links with international funding institutions associate it with their policies. Only time will tell whether NZAID will be able to resist pressures, both overseas and domestic, in order to pursue the policies it has

developed, which aim to benefit people in poverty and promote the rights of all those within its partner countries.

Issues such as security, migration and combating terrorism do not feature largely in NZAID's governance policies.

Notes

[1] *Marian's Environment:* Newsletter from the Associate Minister of Foreign Affairs and Trade, June 2003.

[2] *Guidelines for NZAID Good Governance Programme,* NZAID 2003.

[3] *Human rights policy statement,* NZAID 2003.

[4] Statement by Dr Michael Cullen, Minister of Finance, at Joint Annual Discussion of World Bank Group, September 2003.

[5] Letter to *Listener,* October 18, 2003.

Norway

Box 23. NORWAY at a glance

How much aid does NORWAY give?

In 2002, NORWAY gave   US$1,696m or 13,544m Krone

This means that, in 2002, each person
in NORWAY gave   US$373 or 2,977 Krone

In 2002, aid from NORWAY rose by   US$350m in cash terms. Because of inflation
                                        and exchange rate changes, the value of aid
                                        rose by 12.7% in real terms

How generous is NORWAY?

NORWAY gave 0.89% of its national wealth in 2002. This compares with the average
country effort of 0.41% and NORWAY's own previous highpoint of 1.17% in 1990.

NORWAY was the second most generous donor, more generous than in 2001 when aid was
0.8% of GNI.

How much of NORWAY's aid goes to the poorest countries and people?

47.5% of total bilateral aid (US$544.4m) went to Least Developed and Low Income
Countries where 3.5 billion people (60% of the global population) live and where average
incomes are less than two dollars a day.

**How much of NORWAY's aid was spent on basic health, basic education,
water supply and sanitation?**

NORWAY spent

5.52% of its bilateral aid (US$60.82m) on basic education

4.1% of its bilateral aid (US$45.18m) on basic health

2.34% of its bilateral aid (US$25.8m) on water and sanitation

Goals and focus remain but foreign policy influence grows

Gweneth Berge, Norwegian Church Aid

- Norway's Official Development Assistance (ODA) for 2003 was 14.39 billion Norwegian Krone, which represented a modest increase of NOK 856 million from the 2002 budget. The total constituted 0.93% of GNI, compared to 0.92% in 2002. The current government (Christian Democrat-Conservative coalition) has recommended a further increase in 2004 to NOK 15.29 billion, or 0.94% of GNI. This very modest increase does not bode well for Norway's goal of allocating 1.0% of GNI to ODA by 2005.
- Oil revenues continue to give Norway a budget surplus, which is invested in the National Petroleum Fund. In terms of GNI per capita, Norway is one of the richest countries in the world. There is no excuse for not meeting the goal of 1% GNI to ODA by 2005. Norwegian NGOs have challenged the government to meet this goal and to challenge other OECD donors to do the same.
- In her 2002 statement to the Norwegian Parliament, Minister of International Development Hilde Frafjord Johnson identified education as the government's main focus in development policy. A new education strategy has been developed and 15% of total development assistance

has been targeted for education initiatives.
- Norway continues to be the OECD country channelling the highest proportion of official development aid through civil society organisations (roughly 25% of ODA). There has been no indication of any dramatic decline in these proportions, but there have been indications that the trend to coordinate Norwegian NGO activities more closely with official aid priorities will continue.
- The international War on Terrorism and the militarisation of humanitarian aid have also become an issue in Norway. Norway has committed military personnel to the Coalition Forces in Iraq, where they are carrying out humanitarian work under British military command. This has raised domestic debate about how Norwegian military involvement in Iraq has confused the roles of military and humanitarian intervention and has thus increased the security risk for humanitarian aid workers in Iraq. Norwegian NGOs have also criticised the government for using the aid budget to finance military operations related to de-mining in Iraq.

Norway

- They have also criticised the government for including assistance to refugees in Norway in the aid budget. In 2003, NOK 648.5 million (4.5%) of the total ODA budget went to assist refugees in Norway. This is a slight decrease from 2002 but an increase compared to 2001.
- In 2002, the government launched Norway's 'Action Plan 2015 for Combating Poverty in the South'. The Action Plan is intended to be a broad-based guide to Norwegian development policy. Its overarching objective is to fight poverty and to contribute to achieving the Millennium Development Goals, within the framework of national strategies for poverty reduction. Main priorities in the Action Plan include:

Commitment to the need to increase ODA and affirmation of the goal of increasing development assistance to 1% of GNI by 2005.

The intention to channel 40% of total bilateral assistance to least Developed Countries and to intensify efforts to improve the international debt relief system.

A strong emphasis on human rights as integral to human development. The rights of the most vulnerable groups will be given special attention.

Giving priority to conflict resolution as a precondition for social and economic development.

Better policy coherence between aid policy and other relevant policy areas (At international level, for example, to promote better coherence with trade, investment and debt policy. At national level, to work for better coherence between aid policy and policies for trade, agriculture, energy and immigration).

Partner responsibility must be strengthened, governance improved, and corruption combated. The focus on recipient responsibility aims to give developing countries greater control over their own strategies for poverty reduction. Norway aims to scale down project assistance and to increase sector programme and budget support. Poverty Reduction Strategy Papers will be the foundation for this bilateral support.

Giving priority to donor coordination and alliance building with different civil society and private sector actors — both internationally and in the Norwegian context. There are increased demands on Norwegian NGOs to coordinate efforts among themselves. But many NGOs would give priority to coordinating efforts within their own international networks — including civil society partners in developing countries.

In general, Norwegian NGOs have supported the main policy directions in the plan, but have criticised the lack of clear priorities or benchmarks that are necessary to hold Government accountable for its stated good intentions. Some NGOs have criticised the plan for putting more emphasis on the responsibility of the recipients than on the rich and powerful development actors in the North — especially in relation to economic justice issues, such as debt and trade.

- A new White Paper for development cooperation is being prepared. It seems that the policy directions of the Action Plan will have a significant influence on the content of the White Paper. The

Norway

last White Paper on Development was written in 1995; the new one was due to go to the Parliament in April 2004.
- A major study (1998-2003) on democracy and power in Norway, concluded in 2003. One of the sub-studies, 'Development Aid, Foreign Policy and Power',[1] analysed the Norwegian model of close cooperation between aid and foreign policy actors: political leadership, civil servants, civil society, media and researchers. The analysis suggests that tight-knit relations between the various actors have led to the development of a 'National Regime of Goodness' *(nasjonal godhetsregime)* for development aid and peace work. Under this 'regime', the same individuals rotate in and out of top positions within public institutions, civil society organisations, and academia, which hinders any real critical debate on Norwegian aid policy. There are different views on the accuracy of this analysis and the debate is ongoing.
- As part of the Government's programme for modernising, decentralising and streamlining the public sector, a major evaluation of development aid administration was completed in 2003. The evaluation has led to a major reorganisation of NORAD and the Ministry of Foreign Affairs. As a result, a sizable portion of NORAD's staff and budget is being moved into the MFA. NORAD's regional desks and the policy unit are being integrated into MFA and there are plans to decentralise more decision making and more staff to embassies in Norway's partner countries. The goal is to achieve better coordination, less duplication of effort and more effective coordination of MFA, NORAD and the embassies. With the integration of NORAD's regional desks in MFA (and the Embassies), there is concern that specific

country competence will be weakened, due to MFA practice of rotating staff. Some NGOs are afraid that another consequence will be more politicisation of aid, with more funding flowing to the politically spectacular countries (e.g. Iraq) and programmes.

Norwegian support to good governance
Norway's *Action Plan for Combating Poverty in the South (2002)*, identifies 'good governance' as a critical factor in eradicating poverty and promoting development and lays out a comprehensive approach for supporting good governance.

In a 2002 speech, State Secretary for International Development Olav Kjørven, referring to the new Action Plan, said:

> *'There is a vital connection between open democratic and accountable systems of governance and respect for human rights on the one hand, and the ability to achieve economic and social development on the other. They are mutually reinforcing. We must recognise that the relationships[s] between the state, the private sector and civil society are key determinants of whether a nation is able to create and sustain equitable opportunities for its entire population. Governance can no longer be considered a closed system.'*

Norway's approach to governance will build on three main approaches:

1. *Efforts to evaluate and improve basic preconditions for good governance –* education, institutional development, anti-corruption work, democratic frameworks and observance of basic rights.

Norway

2. *Support to government reforms,* including: improved financial administration, public administration reforms (including decentralisation and capacity building for local government), developing the competence of government officials, reforms to secure a constitutional state that guarantees the rights of citizens and independence of the courts.
3. *Support for public watchdog functions,* including initiatives to improve supervision and control by government bodies, non-governmental institutions, governing and opposition parties, the media and civil society.

In the new Action Plan, the goal of good governance is to be pursued by, among other things, providing assistance for capacity-building. Countries that are willing and able to improve governance will, in general, be given priority in government-to-government allocations. In countries with poor governance, non-official channels of assistance (i.e. those defined as having public watchdog functions) will be given preference. In this case, criteria for support will be that initiatives reach people living in poverty and support forces of reform. In recent years, Norway has pursued a tougher policy on stopping development aid to countries with a deteriorating governance record. Governments that demonstrate bad leadership, practise corruption and allow serious rights abuses over long periods of time, will not be rewarded with Norwegian development aid.

Norway has, however, worked on good governance issues over a long period of time and prior to the Action Plan. Most notably, Norway has supported work on:

- human rights, especially through work to strengthen national human rights commissions;

- civil society, especially through support to strengthen civil society organisations and independent media;
- public financial administration and
- public administration reform, especially related to decentralisation and local government.

As such, the new Action Plan mainly articulates and consolidates existing practice in respect to good governance.

In 1999, Norway raised the issue of corruption as a serious constraint to development. The then Minister for International Development challenged NORAD to become an international frontline organisation in efforts to combat corruption. As a result, a special project was established within NORAD, and a two-year action plan was developed (*NORAD's Good Governance and Anti-corruption Action Plan 2000-2001*). The main goal of the plan was to prevent and curb corruption within a context of good governance.

An internal analysis in 2003 showed that NORAD spending on anti-corruption initiatives had more than tripled since 1999. Likewise, there have been good efforts to improve public financial administration in partner countries, mainly in Africa and countries where NORAD gives, or plans to give, aid via budget support. Internal NORAD assessments suggest that more needs to be done to strengthen support to the justice sector and to public administration reforms.

Using DAC sector code definitions for 'Government and civil society', estimates are that roughly 16% of total NORAD assistance (bilateral aid) went to good governance activities in 2003. Within this category, the largest proportion (29%) of funding went to strengthening civil society. This represented an increase from 16% of total 'Government and civil society' spending in 2002, and underscores the high priority the

Norway

Norwegian government has placed on civil society as a force for democratisation and nation-building, and on civil society organisations as a channel for assistance. A new mechanism to support independent media will be launched in early 2004. A free press is seen as an important tool for giving people in poverty a voice and documenting and exposing systematic and random abuses of power. The main goal will be support to strengthen the watchdog function of the media.

The other two areas where there has been an increase in the proportion of bilateral funding to good governance are economic and development policy planning, and public sector financial management. These trends correspond with NORAD's intention to increase funding to improve partner countries' financial administration systems and to support broad public administration reforms.

In her 2002 statement to the Norwegian Parliament on Development Cooperation, Minister of International Development Hilde Frafjord Johnson said that bilateral Norwegian cooperation was to be based on developing countries' own poverty reduction strategies: 'These PRSPs will form a basis for the mobilisation of the country's own resources and for the prioritisation of tasks between donors. But if these efforts are to succeed, this will require better governance.'

Good governance is seen as a prerequisite for the success of poverty reduction strategies. But are PRSPs a good strategy for promoting good governance?

Tensions between conditionality, which tends to be strengthened through donor coordination, and the ideal of national ownership become particularly evident in the context of PRSPs.

A recent study of the implementation of PRSPs in Malawi and Zambia[2] provides some insights:

'Civil society organisations played an active role in both Malawi and Zambia in formulating the PRSP, which gave these documents some measure of legitimacy. However, the national assemblies and political parties were marginalised in these policy-making exercises, which were driven by the respective executive branches of government, notably the Ministries of Finance. The donors found themselves in an ambivalent situation. On the one hand, in the interest of creating national ownership of the PRSP, they were expected to keep their hands off. On the other hand, they were apprehensive that the substantive nature of the final document would not satisfy the World Bank and IMF criteria for debt relief. As a result, the donors took an active part in the processes.'

The study maintains that because of good civil society participation, strong involvement of the national Ministries of Finance and a positive moderating role by donors, the formulation process has yielded PRSPs that are good policy documents. In both processes, the macroeconomic prescriptions are largely based on the donor consensus that poverty reduction requires growth and that growth is founded on a set of macroeconomic principles laid out in the World Bank/IMF structural adjustment programmes from the 1980s. Such structural reforms are still part of the economic conditions laid down by the external donors. However, in other areas (e.g. social sectors) there are indications that country ownership of PRSP in both countries is considerable.

The key question is how PRSPs will be implemented. National assemblies will be

Norway

critical for approving the national budgets into which PRSP initiatives should be integrated. But these assemblies have generally not been involved in formulating the PRSPs, do not enjoy the same sense of ownership, and may not be full participants in getting PRSPs implemented.

In Malawi, the modest involvement of parliament in the PRSP reflects the current subordinate position of the national assembly relative to the executive branch. A representative, accountable and functioning parliament is essential to the practice of good governance. One must ask if donor promotion of PRSP processes, which strengthen the role of the executive branch of government but marginalise the role of elected representatives, will strengthen or weaken a system of governance that is accountable to the people. If PRSPs are to be given such a central role in Norwegian development assistance, adequate attention must be given to initiatives that promote the involvement of civil society and elected representatives, as well as Ministries of Finance and Planning.

As with Norwegian development policy in general, policy on the issue of good governance is progressive, poverty-oriented and easy for Norwegian NGOs to support in principle. The question is how is this policy followed up in practice and how do these good governance initiatives actually have an impact on improving the lives of people living in poverty?

Notes

1. Terje Tvedt, Utviklingshjelp, utenrikspolitikk og makt – den norske modellen. Gyldendal Norsk Forlag AS, 2003.

2. E. Bwalya (University of Zambia), L. Rakner (Christian Michelsens Institute (CMI), L. Svåsand (University of Bergen), A. Tostensen (CMI), and M. Tsoka (Centre for Social Research, Malawi) 'Getting Rid of Politics? Comparing NGO-Donor Relations in the Implementation of Poverty Reduction Strategies in Malawi and Zambia' Conference paper, October 2003.

Portugal

Box 24. PORTUGAL at a glance

How much aid does PORTUGAL give?

In 2002, PORTUGAL gave · · · · · · · · · · · · · · US$323m or 342m Euros

This means that, in 2002, each person
in PORTUGAL gave · · · · · · · · · · · · · · · · US$31 or 33 Euros

In 2002, aid from PORTUGAL rose by · · · · · US$54m in cash terms. Because of
inflation and exchange rate changes, the
value of aid rose by 9.2% in real terms

How generous is PORTUGAL?

PORTUGAL gave 0.27% of its national wealth in 2002. This compares with the average
country effort of 0.41% and PORTUGAL's own previous highpoint of 0.36% in 1992.

PORTUGAL was less generous than 13 other donors and more generous than in 2001
when aid was 0.25% of GNI.

How much of PORTUGAL's aid goes to the poorest countries and people?

84.2% of total bilateral aid (US$156.6m) went to Least Developed and Low Income
Countries where 3.5 billion people (60% of the global population) live and where
average incomes are less than two dollars a day.

How much of PORTUGAL's aid was spent on basic health, basic education, water supply and sanitation?

PORTUGAL spent

2.49% of its bilateral aid (US$4.64m) on basic education

0.34% of its bilateral aid (US$0.64m) on basic health

0.17% of its bilateral aid (US$0.31m) on water and sanitation

Regression and expectation in Portuguese cooperation

Rita Veiga, Eline Feijão, Oikos

Since Prime Minister Durão Barroso's government came to power in March 2002, there have been some changes in Portugal's development cooperation policy. A new cooperation policy has been approved, based on the importance of Official Development Aid (ODA) for the development of recipient countries. But are there any crucial changes within this new policy?

- Portuguese bilateral and multilateral ODA totalled 342.295 million euros in 2002 (299.747 million euros in 2001).
- In 2002, the percentage of ODA in relation to the Gross National Income (GNI) was 0.27%, up by 0.02% on 2001.
- The commitment to reach the UN 0.7% target made at the Earth Summit in Rio during 1992 is definitely history. At the 2002 Financing for Development conference in Monterey, Portugal promised to aim at only 0.33%. However, the Cooperation Secretary of State, Manuela Franco, recently declared that even this percentage was unrealistic. So Portugal wants to invest in a better quality of aid in order to contribute to the Millennium Development Goals in accordance with the 'deep rootehaved traditions we have'.

- Despite comments in the DAC's 2001 Aid Review, on the need for aid to be allocated on the basis of a 'deliberate attempt to address poverty reduction', rather than as a result of historical ties, the largest part of the Portuguese bilateral aid still goes to the five Portuguese-speaking countries (PALOPs[1]) — Angola, Cape Verde, Guinea Bissau, Mozambique and São Tomé e Príncipe, plus East Timor. In 2001, 61% of bilateral ODA was transferred to PALOPs, 31.6% to East Timor and 7.5% to other countries. In 2002, those percentages were respectively 44.8%, 40.8% and 14.5%.
- Basically, the priority areas for Portuguese cooperation policy are still the same: education, poverty reduction, reinforcement of institutions and governance, and supporting business activities. But one of the priorities highlighted by the government, is the need to invest in education and training, especially to strengthen local elites.
- A new institute for development cooperation has been created. The IPAD[2] — Portuguese Institute of Development Aid — includes the former Institute for Portuguese Cooperation (ICP[3]) and the Portuguese Development

Portugal

Support Agency (APAD[4]). After a long period of internal restructuring of Portuguese Cooperation, in 2002, IPAD was officially created in January 2003. IPAD is supposed to supervise and coordinate development cooperation policy.

- The last Integrated Programme of Portuguese Cooperation and the last significant programmes being applied in each country are the ones prepared by the ICP in 2001-2002. The IPAD has not yet presented any new practical programme.

- After a promising 2001, when their relationship with the former ICP seemed to be maturing, NGOs could not find a governmental interlocutor during the following year. During the restructuring carried out in the public cooperation agency, there was no one available to deal with NGOs, until the IPAD was officially created in January 2003. Several inconsistencies and a general lack of direction soon became obvious and an open conflict eventually arose (see *IPAD vs NGOs*). Most Portuguese NGOs are rather small and a number of them are now struggling to survive.

The government's new cooperation policy highlights the importance of creating a more coherent approach characterised by 'coordination, control and evaluation of future development cooperation programmes'. These guidelines are in accordance with the restrictive economic policy that has been undertaken by the government in the last two years.

Despite the objectives outlined, it seems that between 2002 and 2003 most of the significant changes in cooperation policy were the result more of budget constraints than of improvements in development cooperation.

In general, it can be said that Portuguese

development cooperation policy has taken some backward steps, if not in objectives, at least in terms of practical initiatives undertaken by the government.

Good governance and human rights

With the second generation of structural adjustment programmes, good governance and respect for human rights became relevant areas of concern for development aid. In the cooperation policy of the European Union, aid depends on political conditionality. According to the European Economic and Social Committee's guidelines, good governance is an essential objective of development aid.

The Portuguese Programme for Development Cooperation (2002), responding to EU guidelines, considers the issues of democracy and good governance strategic area of intervention, with special emphasis on the strengthening of institutions. The Portuguese Programme for Development Cooperation in 2002 therefore includes commitments to:

- strengthen administrative capacity, using technical assistance and specialised training;
- support electoral processes and institutions working in this field;
- support the preparation of legislation appropriate to the needs and circumstances of each partner country;
- support the consolidation of the state-owned and the private media;
- strengthen civil society;
- use technical and military cooperation to consolidate the role of the armed forces as a guarantee of the democratic rule of law.

Despite the stated importance of good governance, Portuguese cooperation does not really depend on authentic political

Portugal

conditionality. Economic motivations still prevail over political ones, with too many agreements between Portugal and recipient countries being tied to commercial interests. The distribution of Portuguese aid is very much concerned with the commercial benefits obtained from the recipient nations, as a counterpart of development aid. In fact, the largest share of cooperation projects are for technical assistance to enterprises in the field. There are no relevant projects supporting institutional capacities or enhancing the political transparency of the state. They are not really concerned with improving the capacity of government and public administration.

Conclusion

In general terms, and as described by OECD Development Assistance Committee (DAC), Portuguese cooperation lacks both solid coordination and evaluation. The recommendations of the DAC have, however, been taken into account in the latest Programme for Development and Cooperation (2002), which underlines the importance of reducing poverty, reinforcement of the coordination of programmes and debt-relief procedures.

Despite the well-structured cooperation policy framework, goals such as support for education, poverty reduction and strengthening institutional capacities and good governance are far from being put into practice. Aid programmes still give insufficient attention to these areas.

Instead, Portuguese cooperation policy will give recipient countries what they want, provided that it is compatible with Portugal's own interests. Good prospects of business partnerships, which include commercial favours, are much more decisive than development goals.

The incoherence of cooperation policy explains the bad relationship between the IPAD and Portuguese NGOs. The Institute made up allegedly legal reasons for cancelling the allocation of financial resources to NGOs and unilaterally decided to impose new rules. It simply ignores the crucial role of NGOs, especially in designing and delivering development programmes and meeting the needs of the population.

Even considering the budgetary restrictions that the government has been enforcing, the whole thing seems pointless when you realise that the amount to be transferred from the IPAD to the NGOs is less than €1.4 million — for 25 projects that were selected (out of 57) in the first of two calls for proposals in 2003.

Portugal

Box 25. IPAD versus NGOs

According to João Gomes Cravinho, the former president of the Institute of Portuguese Cooperation, we are going through a period of regression, but also of expectation, in Portuguese international cooperation. There is regression because the laws that were approved by Parliament and government over the last four years for the implementation of real cooperation policies are not being put into practice.

In 1999, Parliament approved a law on the statutes of NGOs, and the Council of Ministers recognised the role of the NGOs in Portuguese Cooperation. Further, the Ministry of Foreign Affairs signed a protocol with the NGO Platform, in which it recognised the role that NGOs were to play alongside the government programme. For the first time in Portugal, the status of NGOs, as well as of their representative association, the Portuguese NGO Platform, was recognised. The principle of participation and public financing of the cooperation projects of NGOs was established, including the institution of an annual donation by the Ministry of Foreign Affairs.

However, during 2003, all these decisions were disregarded. Many difficulties arose when NGOs tried to get co-financing for projects they were to carry out; none could get any response from the state. Also, a law established to allow citizens to choose a social organisation to receive a small percentage of their tax contribution had little practical result. The NGO Platform appealed to the administrative court and saw its claims - both in relation to the co-financing of projects and to the tax concession that is still not happening — reinforced by experts' statements

João Gomes Cravinho nevertheless believes that some expectation is reasonable because, as he recalls, the Prime Minister, Durão Barroso, earned a good reputation as Secretary of State for Cooperation, at the end of the 1980s, both due to his valuable role in the mediation of the Angolan conflict and because he was the first to accept the opening up of dialogue with NGOs. It was Barroso who signed the first protocol for financing a cooperation project of a Portuguese NGO and, during his term as Secretary of State, the relationship between NGOs and the state improved significantly, as dialogue conditions were created to make mutual recognition and collaboration easier. NGOs now ask themselves if the people in charge in the Ministry of Foreign Affairs are going to resume the policy of dialogue and cooperation with NGOs that was started by the man who has become the head of the government.

Luís de França

Notes

[1] Países Africanos de Língua Oficial Portuguesa

[2] Instituto Português de Apoio ao Desenvolvimento

[3] Instituto Cooperação Portuguesa

[4] Associacão Portuguesa de Ajuda ao Desenvolvimento

Spain

Box 26. SPAIN at a glance

How much aid does SPAIN give?

In 2002, SPAIN gave   US$1,712m or €1,817m

That means that, in 2002, each person
in SPAIN gave   US$43 or 45 Euros

In 2002, aid from SPAIN fell by   US$84,23m in cash terms. Because of
                                             inflation and exchange rate changes, the
                                             value of aid fell by 10.3% in real terms.

How generous is SPAIN?

SPAIN gave 0.26% of its national wealth in 2002. This compares with the average country
effort of 0.41% and SPAIN's own previous highpoint of 0.3% in 2001.

SPAIN was less generous than 16 other donors and less generous than in 2001.

How much of SPAIN's aid goes to the poorest countries and people?

28,6% of total bilateral aid (€349 m Euros or US$328,5 m) went to Least Developed and
Low Income Countries where 3.5 billion people (60% of the global population) live and
where average incomes are less than two dollars a day.

How much of SPAIN's aid was spent on basic health, basic education, water supply and sanitation?[1]

SPAIN spent

2.9% of its bilateral aid (US$25.28m) on basic education

4.29% of its bilateral aid (US$37,4m) on basic health

1.58% of its bilateral aid (US$13,78m) on water and sanitation

Steps forward on quantity, backwards on quality

Marta Arias and Carmen González, Intermón Oxfam

After several years of decline and broken promises, the amount of Spanish Overseas Development Assistance (ODA)[1] rose to 0.30% of GNI in 2001 and then fell back to 0.26% GNI in 2002.

These figures, compared to previous years, and the new commitments signed up to at the International Conference on Finance for Development in Monterrey (0.33% GNI for 2006), could be seen as positive signs in the Spanish cooperation system. However, a closer look at the items that made up the past two years' growth, and the planned future resources, shows some worrying trends:

1) The extraordinary increase in 2001 was mainly due to a singular and controversial debt cancellation operation with Nicaragua.[2] Therefore, this **is not the result of a real change** in political will and commitment to developing countries.

2) The resources managed by the Foreign Affairs Ministry, recognised in the International Cooperation Law as the lead agency of the Spanish cooperation system, are stagnant. Meanwhile, the **Finance and Defence Ministries**, whose role and efficiency on poverty reduction have been frequently questioned by

different NGOs and academics, have **increasing resources** under their management.

3) Whereas Afghanistan, Iraq and Argentina have received significant amounts of funds from the Spanish cooperation system, declining resources are allocated to some of the Sub-Saharan African countries, even though they are priorities according to Spanish International Cooperation Law. These examples show how **geostrategic and political interests increasingly determine ODA allocation.**

The second term of the Partido Popular (Conservative Party) did not bring any progress on the urgently demanded reforms to the Spanish cooperation system:

- Commercial interests and the promotion of Spanish cultural and linguistic interests remain a strong influence on the decisions of ODA officials.

- The 10.4% figure for ODA to Basic Social Services as a share of total bilateral aid, and the 0.03% figure for ODA to Least Developing Countries in 2001, show that no real progress has been achieved on the fulfilment of commitments made on Basic Social Services (under the Copenhagen 20/20 Initiative) or on aid

283

Spain

Graph 12.

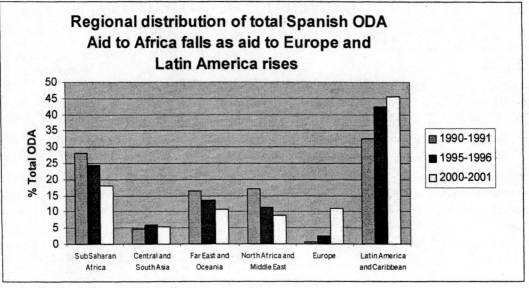

Source: OECD DAC Report 2002

to Least Developing Countries (target 0.15% GDP).

- Decreasing levels of ODA to Sub-Saharan African countries (from US$167 millions in 1997 to US$86 millions in 2001).
- The Spanish government is increasingly arguing in favour of allocating a major part of Spanish ODA towards Middle-income countries. But it is not taking the necessary measures to ensure that its assistance effectively targets poverty reduction.
- Humanitarian aid remains characterised by low quality and high costs. There is increasing Armed Forces participation and an unwillingness to increase participation within the United Nations.
- There is no improvement in dialogue with civil society.

On the positive side, some internal, national and international steps should be underlined: first of all, the improvement in Spanish cooperation planning and monitoring tools. Country and sector strategies are being elaborated and the monitoring report (*Plan Anual de Cooperación Internacional – PACI Seguimiento*) has significantly increased the data and analysis provided. Second, cooperation from regional and local governments is progressively improving both in quantity (14% of total Spanish ODA in 2002) and in coordination with central Cooperation Funds. Finally, under an EU agreement, debt relief provided to HIPC countries has been increased from 90% to 100% of commercial debt[3].

Governance and Human Rights promotion

Good governance is one of the top priorities in Spanish Aid (under article 7 of the International Cooperation Law). It is considered a specific requirement for sustainable development. Currently, Spain is

Spain

carrying out activities (mainly through technical cooperation) related to good governance and institutional development consisting of: judicial and legislative reform; administrative reform (including decentralisation); tax administration and financial sector reform; and training of police.

The 2001 DAC Review report on the Spanish cooperation system recommended that: 'Spain could ensure that the objectives and targets in each institutions building project are resulted-oriented and measured against improvement in the lives of citizens, particularly the poor'. It specifically encouraged Spain to 'engage in a sector approach in institution building, together with other donors. In fact Spain could take on a lead role in pursuing a sector approach in some Latin American countries'.[4]

Recently, Spanish authorities have been working on the development of a specific strategy on this area (pending approval). On the positive side, the strategy is likely to make a significant improvement in the planning and coordination of different actors (central, regional and local governments). However, it has received significant criticism on several questions. On the one hand, the lack of effective measures to follow up the DAC recommendations has been pointed out. On the other hand, there is also a lack of coherence between different Spanish cooperation policies. In its strategy documents, the Spanish government defends a very critical position towards some undemocratic or corrupt states. However, it maintains very favourable relations with, and makes no criticism of, the Chinese or Indonesian governments, where economic interests play a key role.

Notes

[1] The Spanish government signed up to reach 0.7%ODA/GNI during the 1996-2000 period. However, from 1995 to 2000 the average of Spanish ODA was 0.23% ODA/GNI. Aid fell from 0.28% GNI in 1994 to 0.22% in 2000.

[2] The origin of that debt (1980) was a concessional loan for the building up of a cellulose factory that never started functioning and which had previously been strongly criticised for its environmental costs.

[3] This is subject to the 'cut-off date', the date of the first meeting between a debtor country and its Paris Club creditors, after which no new credits are eligible for rescheduling.

[4] *DAC Journal* 2002, Volume 3, No. 2, OECD Paris, 2002.

Spain

Table 10. Spanish ODA Distribution by category

		1997	1998	1999	2000	2001	2002	2003 *
Bilateral	FAD credits	221.2	211.2	165.7	177.3	142.2	201.5	247.4
	Programmes and Projects AECl1	85.1	165.0	134.8	127.9	159.8	57.1	304
	Programmes and Projects other ministries	22.6	34.2	78.3	125.8	164.2		
	Cooperation from regional and local governments	139.1	185.8	196.1	13.9	208.2	261.4	308
	Aid to NGOs	75.3	76.6	97.0	90.2	88.0	99.2	-
	Food aid	2.8	12.0	7.4	5.0	5.7	8.6	-
	Emergency aid	17.7	26.2	68.3	42.2	25.5	19.8	-
	Microcredits	-	-	22.5	24.7	20.5	42.8	60.1
	Debt relief	92.0	134.3	60.9	18.7	434.9	125.3	124
	TOTAL Bilateral	755.8	845.3	831.0	825.7	1.249	1,059.2	1,282
Multilateral	UE	314.6	364.9	367.8	392.8	82.6	440.2	461
	IFIs	100.7	111.8	110.4	69.3	208.8	234.5	258.2
	Non IFIs	45.0	53.7	57.4	67.3	66.1	83.2	76.8
	TOTAL Multilateral	460.4	530.4	535.6	529.3	657.5	757.9	796
TOTAL		1,216.2	1,375.8	1,366.6	1,355.0	1,906.5	1,817.1	2,078

* Preliminary figures

Sweden

Box 27. SWEDEN at a glance

How much aid does SWEDEN give?

In 2002, SWEDEN gave   US$1,991m or 19,354m Krona

This means that, in 2002, each person
In SWEDEN gave   US$207 or 2,144 Krona

In 2002, aid from SWEDEN rose by   US$325m in cash terms. Because of inflation
and exchange rate changes, the value of aid rose by 10.9% in real terms. In Krona, aid from Sweden rose by 2.5 billion compared with 2001.

How generous is SWEDEN?

SWEDEN gave 0.83% of its national wealth in 2002. This compares with the average country effort of 0.41% and SWEDEN's own previous highpoint of 1.03% in 1992.

SWEDEN was the third most generous donor and more generous than in 2001 when aid was 0.77% of GNI

How much of SWEDEN's aid goes to the poorest countries and people?

38.4% of total bilateral aid (US$479.8m) went to Least Developed and Low Income Countries where 3.5 billion people (60% of the global population) live and where average incomes are less than two dollars a day.

How much of SWEDEN's aid was spent on basic health, basic education, water supply and sanitation?

SWEDEN spent

4.41 % of its bilateral aid (US$17.77m) on basic education

0.56% of its bilateral aid (US$7.02m) on basic health

1.97% of its bilateral aid (US$24.88m) on water and sanitation

Sweden aims for coherent approach

Magnus Walan and Ankin Ljungman, Diakonia

After a four-year process of formulating a new, coherent policy to cover both goals for development aid and Sweden's wider development cooperation, the Swedish Government presented the new development Bill to parliament in May 2003, and it was tabled with amendments in December.

The NGO development community generally welcomed the new policy. Some questions on the proposals were raised. NGOs were concerned that the Bill signalled Government unwillingness to reconsider existing trade polices and also a lack of willingness to change the rules and policies regarding arms exports. Parliament brought up some aspects of the NGO critique in their amendments to the Bill.

The Bill was entitled, 'Shared responsibility — Sweden's policy for global development'. According to the Government, Sweden is the first country to present a coherent policy for global development.

- The Bill proposes new goals for all aspects of Government operation, with the aim of contributing to fair and sustainable global development. Trade, agricultural, security, migration, environmental and economic policies should all promote global development.
- A poverty and human rights perspective should permeate the whole of Government policy.
- With this Bill, the Government has reformulated policy in order to contribute more forcefully to the fulfilment of the UN Millennium Goals. The overriding goal is to abolish world poverty, an intermediate goal is to halve world poverty by the year 2015.
- The Bill proposes that the Government should report each year to the elected representatives in the Riksdag, on the implementation of the policy. Each ministry will explain how its political decisions have contributed to fair and sustainable global development.
- Development assistance will be increased but must also be made more efficient.
- Instead of limiting the number of partner countries, the number will probably be increased. Sweden will work in all countries where its contribution is meaningful. But development assistance will be concentrated on fewer subject areas and sectors in each country.
- The goal of contributing 1% of Sweden's GDP in development aid remains unchanged.
- A new independent evaluation function will be introduced to monitor the fulfilment of objectives and the efficiency of development cooperation.
- Sweden will continue to address difficult and controversial issues.

Sweden

There are deep differences of opinion on issues relating to democracy and human rights, in particular in the matter of women's rights. Matters relating to sexual and reproductive rights are especially controversial, including the right to abortion, contraception and sex education, as well as the rights of homosexuals, bisexuals and transsexuals. The Swedish Government says it will continue to speak out on these issues.

The most outspoken development NGOs, such as Diakonia, Forum Syd and the Swedish Society for Nature Conservation, welcomed the general goals and principles of the new policies — but raised a number of concerns:

a) *Lack of clarity in instruments*
The Bill does not adequately indicate how the new policies will be implemented. It is not clear how this Bill will differ from other government statements regarding human rights in Swedish foreign policy and the rights of people living in poverty.

b) *Rights approach on trade policy?*
The Bill's own description of the present trade rules in the WTO indicates that there is no need to change the present rules and policies. This is a major weakness, because the Bill does not recognise the actual and potential conflicts between the trade institutions, regulations and policies and the conventions on human rights. This is particularly important in view of the overriding principle of formulating a rights approach in the new coherent development policy.

c) *Some steps for a new debt policy*
A similar critique came from the Swedish Jubilee Network regarding the macro economic policies of the World Bank

and the IMF, which often contradict a poverty oriented approach. The Government Bill did not deal properly with this contradiction. The Bill did, however, show willingness to discuss how a sustainable debt can be formulated, and some willingness to discuss the relationship between poverty eradication and debt reduction and the introduction of a debt arbitration mechanism.

d) *No willingness to include arms exports*
The Bill did not propose any amendment to arms polices and regulations. Sweden is supplying arms to conflicts such as the one between India and Pakistan. It is exporting arms to countries guilty of major human rights violations, despite legislation banning exports to such countries. Sweden is exporting arms to countries with major poverty problems, without any policies and regulations demanding impact assessment.

The Riksdag decided, on 17 December 2003, to adopt the Government Bill 'Shared responsibility: Sweden's policy for global development' (2002/03:122). The Bill means that the objectives of development policy for equitable and sustainable development now apply to government policies as a whole. As Carin Jämtin, Minister for International Development Cooperation, said at the time:

'Sweden will now be the first country in the world to have a development policy in which all policy areas share the same objectives. Development assistance is only one aspect of this policy. There should also be a development perspective in such areas as international trade, security and

Sweden

environment policy'.

The Bill also means that the policy will be based on two perspectives: the rights perspective and the perspectives of those in poverty.

'Individuals have the right to control their own lives. People are participants, with the will to develop, and our policy should focus on the reality of poor people and their needs,' says Carin Jamtin.

Amendments to the Bill by the Riksdag's foreign relation committee were welcomed by development NGOs. Some of the concrete issues were:

a) On instruments

Parliament did not specify how government should implement the new policies but requested strong co-ordination and asked for a proactive approach. Parliament also asked for departmental programmes to explain how the new policy should be implemented.

b) Further improvements needed on debt issues

The Riksdag requested a regular report from Government on Swedish policies in the World Bank and the IMF. The Riksdag will be able to present motions on this report. This will, according to NGOs, improve transparency and the debate around debt and development issues.

c) 'Arms exports must be included in the new government policy'

Parliament made clear a general will to include arms exports in the new government development policy. Parliament requested government to ensure that existing rules and policies on arms exports took into account the implications of the new policies on poverty, democratic governance and human rights.

It remains to be seen to what degree, and in what way, the Government will follow the Riksdag's amendments and comments on the Bill.

Reflections on the new approach

In January 2001, the DAC presented its review of Swedish development policy. The Government's Development Bill answers some, but not all, of the issues raised by DAC.

In line with DAC recommendations, poverty reduction has been confirmed as the overarching goal of Swedish aid, and greater attention has been given to the achievement of the Millennium Development Goals.

The Bill clearly responds to DAC recommendations on stronger mechanisms to support coherence.

Between 1975 and 1995, Sweden lived up to the ambition of the Riksdag that at least 1% of GNI should be set aside for development cooperation. But in 1993 this policy was abruptly changed by both right-wing and social-democratic led governments. The result was that between 1994 and 1999, Swedish aid plummeted from 0.96% to 0.7% GNI. After a strong advocacy campaign by civil society groups, the Social Democratic minority government, together with its partners the Green Party and the Left Party, made a promise that the goal of 1% of GNP should be fulfilled by 2006. The commitment to go back to 1% of GNI by 2006 represents a success for NGO lobbying — but there is a rather critical proviso — that achieving 1% depends on the availability of government resources.

Sweden's aid policy is meant to complement a country's own efforts, and Sweden therefore aims to develop partnership strategies, within which PRSP processes are regarded as central. Institution-building is seen as a cornerstone of the new aid policy. Cooperation and coordination between donors, the harmonisation of procedures and routines and untying of development assistance are also highlighted.

The Riksdag, in its amendment to the

Sweden

Bill, underlined the ambition that at least 25% of bilateral aid should go to the Least Developed Countries by 2010.

The DAC review in 2001 talked of Swedish aid going to more than 100 countries and the dangers of dispersion of resources and dilution of effort. The new strategy does suggest aid being focused on fewer sectors and subjects — but there is not much clarity on how this matches up to guidelines on phasing out and exit strategies that the government agency had wanted

Sweden is supplying arms to conflicts such as the one between India and Pakistan. It is exporting arms to countries guilty of major human rights violations, despite legislation banning exports to such countries. Sweden is exporting arms to countries with major poverty problems, without any policies and regulations demanding impact assessment.

Switzerland

Box 28. SWITZERLAND at a glance

How much aid does SWITZERLAND give?

In 2002, SWITZERLAND gave   US$939m or 1,462m Swiss Francs

That means that, in 2002, each person
in SWITZERLAND gave   US$128 or 200 Swiss Francs

In 2002, aid from SWITZERLAND rose by   US$31m in cash terms. Because of inflation
and exchange rate changes, the value of aid
fell by 5.0% in real terms

How generous is SWITZERLAND?

SWITZERLAND gave 0.32% of its national wealth in 2002. This compares with the
average country effort of 0.41% and SWITZERLAND's own previous highpoint of 0.45% in
1992.

SWITZERLAND was less generous than 9 other donors and less generous than in 2001
when aid was 0.34% of GNI.

How much of SWITZERLAND's aid goes to the poorest countries and people?

40.6% of total bilateral aid (US$310.6m) went to Least Developed and Low Income
Countries where 3.5 billion people (60% of the global population) live and where
average incomes are less than two dollars a day.

How much of SWITZERLAND's aid was spent on basic health, basic education, water supply and sanitation?

SWITZERLAND spent

1.59 % of its bilateral aid (US$12.24m) on basic education

2.87% of its bilateral aid (US$22.06m) on basic health

2.68% of its bilateral aid (US$20.61m) on water and sanitation

Joining the UN – but missing the UN target

Michèle Laubscher, Arbeitsgemeinschaft Swissaid/Fastenopfer/Brot für alle/Helvetas/Caritas/Heks

In 2002, the volume of Swiss ODA shrank by CHF 70 million to CHF 1.46 billion, dragging the GNP share down from 0.34% in the previous two years to 0.32%. This decline was mainly due to Switzerland's postponement of its contribution to the International Development Agency (IDA-13) from 2002 to 2003.

Despite having become a full member of the UN in 2002, the Swiss Government is unwilling to raise its ODA to the UN level of 0.7% GNP, sticking to its own target of 0.4% by 2010. But even this target is jeopardised by the large budget cuts the Government and a majority of the Parliament are planning for the next four years.

In September 2003, Foreign Minister Micheline Calmy-Rey explained that the overall government budget deficit had forced the Government to slow down the increase to a rate far below the annual 6.7% increase needed to reach the target by 2010. The Government required an ODA blanket credit line for 2004-07 totalling CHF 4.4 billion, which the Council of States (the Swiss Senate) cut by CHF 200 million[1].

This amounts to the biggest ODA credit line accorded to the Development Agency

(SDC) of the Ministry of Foreign Affairs and is destined solely for the South. A smaller credit line for Eastern European, Caucasian and Central Asian countries will be presented to the parliament in 2004.

Whether the CHF 4.2 billion credit will also get through the National Council (House of Representatives) remains to be seen. The swing to the right in the parliamentary elections of October 2003 puts it at risk. The Swiss People's Party (SPP), which won the biggest share of the vote, wants to cut it by almost a third. Being traditionally opposed to membership in multilateral institutions, it aims to clamp down on Swiss contributions to the UN, World Bank, International Monetary Fund and regional banks. The SPP has also announced its intention to push for deep cuts in the credit for the Eastern countries mentioned above.

The Government has come under growing pressure to link ODA to the willingness of partner countries to take back 'illegal' migrants and refugees who have been refused asylum. Up to now, it has refused such conditionality but there is no telling how long it may wish to hold out. Xenophobia, which the SPP has been stirring up for years, is increasing — although

Switzerland

expenditure on refugees within Switzerland has dropped sharply since 2000.

Swiss ODA is targeted at the poorest countries. Ten of the 17 priority countries in the South are in the Least Developed Country category, four are low-income countries and only three are lower or lower-middle income countries. But as the direct impacts on poverty were perceived to be unsatisfactory, the Swiss Agency for Development and Cooperation (SDC) started readjusting its focus in the aid programmes for Southern countries in 1999, through its Policy on Social Development, while poverty alleviation has only recently been incorporated into the programmes for Eastern European, Caucasian and Central Asian countries.

One result of the readjustment was the mainstreaming of gender equality, another being a stronger emphasis on empowerment of, and ownership by, the aid recipients. As to the allocation of bilateral aid in the Southern priority countries by sector, the biggest shares went to agriculture, education and culture, as well as water, infrastructure and transport. Although Switzerland doubled its spending on basic education between 1995 and 2002 to CHF 20 million, this sector still gets a mere 2% of total bilateral aid commitments.

The DAC Peer Review 2000 praised Switzerland for targeting its aid at the poorest countries, but also deplored its dispersal of aid across many recipients. Despite efforts to concentrate over the past years, in 2002 only 45% of the allocated bilateral aid was channelled into the 17 Southern priority countries. Besides these, the SDC has six special programmes in the South and in 11 key countries in Eastern Europe and Central Asia. Moreover, the State Secretariat for Economic Affairs (seco), which administers 16% of total ODA, has its own geographical priorities that are not always congruent with those of SDC. As a result,

humanitarian aid activities, such as peace promotion in Colombia and the aid channelled through Swiss NGOs, bilateral aid is spread over at least 70 countries.

SDC and, especially, seco are increasingly considering so-called public-private partnerships (PPP) in their aid programmes. They are following the World Bank line in arguing that the Millennium Development Goals can only be reached with the support of private capital. Bearing in mind the often disastrous experiences with PPPs in water and energy supply, and considering that in most cases the 'beneficiaries' and the donor community are heavily subsidising private companies, the Swiss Coalition of Development Organisations is opposing this new strategy.

Governance and Human Rights

In recent years, human security, human rights, peace promotion, and peace-keeping have become major issues in Swiss foreign policy. To provide a legal basis for the growing expenditure, the government in 2003 tabled a draft law for promoting human rights and peace and a line of credit of CHF 240 million for the next four years. The law and line credit were approved by the National Council (House of Representatives) without problems but the Council of States (Senate) cut the credit back to CHF 200 million in September. The credit is handled by a specialised department in the Foreign Ministry.

Switzerland had long believed that its neutrality made it an indispensable mediator in armed conflicts. But its role in this area has virtually disappeared in recent years. Small States with an active foreign policy, such as Sweden and Norway, stole a march on Switzerland a long time ago. The new peace and human rights endeavours are an attempt to play a more active international role once again. Hence, under the new law,

Switzerland

Switzerland is actively involving itself in the civil wars in Colombia and the Sudan, and has recently come to the fore as facilitator of the private peace plan between Israelis and Palestinians. As part of these new activities, it is also supporting a number of peace efforts by civil society organisations. The rising expenditure in this field is not at the expense of traditional development aid.

At the same time, Switzerland is trying to systematise human rights dialogues. There are dialogues on different levels with its developing country partners but not with *all* country partners. So-called 'full HR dialogues' — regular discussions on all levels — are only held with China and Iran (although Iran is not a partner country). These now include regular discussions between civil servants and exchanges of experts (such as prison governors and criminal law experts). But, as the case of China shows, the results are meagre. After 12 years of dialogue, the human rights situation remains practically unchanged. The Foreign Ministry argues that the dialogue has influenced reforms of the penal system. But it concedes that there is a big gap between the laws and their enforcement, as well as between Swiss and Chinese interpretation of the new norms. Finally, Swiss business is so eager to expand its presence in China that human rights questions are of minor importance in Swiss-Chinese relations.

The two state agencies for development aid, SDC and seco, have given added weight to good governance issues in recent years. Governance, including human rights, is one of SDC's five central guidelines. It is promoted on two levels. On the one hand, SDC wants to strengthen the capacities of public administrations; on the other, it tries to foster civil processes and to help civil society, for instance in influencing public administrations. Hence SDC supports local authorities, the improvement of public services, the training of police and prison officers, as well as decentralisation, local initiatives and local human rights NGOs. Special attention is given to the empowerment of marginalised groups.

According to SDC, the stronger focus on aspects of governance should not affect aid distribution, as it regards governance as a mainstreaming issue. An internal evaluation has nevertheless shown that the implementation of SDC's guidelines, and hence governance, must first be promoted among SDC staff and partner organisations in the South. Thus SDC's endeavour to move from a 'needs-based approach' to a 'rights-based approach' is only just beginning.

Despite 9/11, combating terrorism is not a major issue in Swiss foreign and aid policy. Switzerland does indeed consider the fight against terrorism an urgent task common to all nations but there is growing concern in the Foreign Ministry that fighting terrorism is becoming a licence to commit human rights violations. Not only is this tendency evident among the States belonging to the US alliance against terrorism but it is increasingly influencing the World Bank's donor coordination for PRSPs as well.

Forgiving one's allies for actions that conflict with one's own principles is nothing strange to Switzerland. To obtain a seat on the Executive Boards of the IMF and World Bank, Switzerland had to build a constituency that included, among others, almost all Central Asian countries. Although bad governance is in many respects the norm in these States, Switzerland has expanded its aid to them in recent years. Whatever Switzerland may demand in the way of human rights improvements is of little significance, for the governments involved know that Switzerland will not jeopardise

Switzerland

its seats on the Executive Boards of the Bretton Woods Institutions.

The Government has come under growing pressure to link ODA to the willingness of partner countries to take back 'illegal' migrants and refugees who have been refused asylum. Up to now, it has refused such conditionality, but there is no telling how long it may wish to hold out.

Notes

1 The Swiss Parliament consists of two Chambers. The Council of States (Senate) represents the Cantons; in each of the 26 Cantons (States), two members are elected. The National Council represents the people; its 200 seats are distributed among the Cantons according to the number of their inhabitants. All parliamentary decisions have to be accepted by both Chambers.

United Kingdom

Box 29. UNITED KINGDOM at a glance

How much aid does the UNITED KINGDOM give?

In 2002, the UNITED KINGDOM gave   US$4,924m or £3,282m

This means that, in 2002, each person
in the UK gave   US$84 or £56

In 2002, aid from the UK rose by   US$345m in cash terms. Because of inflation and exchange rate changes, the value of aid increased by only 0.04% in real terms

How generous is UNITED KINGDOM?

UNITED KINGDOM gave 0.31% of its national wealth in 2002. This compares with the average country effort of 0.41% and the UK's own previous highpoint of 0.51% in 1979.

UNITED KINGDOM was less generous than 10 other donors and less generous than in 2001 when aid was 0.32 of GNI.

How much of UNITED KINGDOM's aid goes to the poorest countries and people?

48% of total bilateral aid (US$1,684.0m) went to Least Developed and Low Income Countries where 3.5 billion people (60% of the global population) live and where average incomes are less than two dollars a day.

How much of UNITED KINGDOM's aid was spent on basic health, basic education, water supply and sanitation?

The UK spent

1.89% of its bilateral aid (US$68.36m) on basic education

3.11% of its bilateral aid (US$112.2m) on basic health

0.53% of its bilateral aid (US$19.2m) on water and sanitation.

Poverty focus stronger but 'war on terror' diverts funds

Audrey Gaughran, for BOND

Summary

- UK development assistance remains focused on poverty reduction and the Millennium Development Goals (MDGs). The 2002 International Development Act makes it illegal for UK aid to be spent on anything other than poverty reduction. The UK continues to emphasise working with the poorest countries: in 2001/02 78% of UK aid went to Least Developed Countries (LDCs). By 2005/6, this is expected to rise to 90%.
- However, the 'war on terror' has affected the allocation of UK development assistance; aid has been diverted from middle-income countries to fund post-war reconstruction in Iraq. Furthermore, aid to some countries that support the 'war on terror', such as Pakistan, has increased.[1] The UK government as a whole is increasingly interested in the issue of 'failed states'.

Aid volume

- The UK aid budget has continued to increase. In the 2002 Comprehensive Spending Review (reviews are held every two years) the aid budget increased by UK£1.5 billion; it will amount to UK£4.9 billion, or 0.4% of national wealth per year, by 2005/6. No timetable has yet been set for reaching the UN target of 0.7%. At the time of the 2002 Comprehensive Spending Review, the government, responding to NGO campaigning on 0.7%, suggested that if the rate of increase was maintained in subsequent Comprehensive Spending Reviews the UK would reach 0.7% by 2012. NGOs are campaigning for the rate of increase to be maintained but considering the 2004 Comprehensive Spending Review, which will set spending limits for the period 2005/6 to 2007/8, indications are that this may be difficult to achieve.
- While the increase in UK aid volume is welcome, a significant proportion of the increase to date has been absorbed by spending related to the 'war on terror'. In 2001/02, the aid budget was UK£3.25 billion. In this spending year, (2003/04) it is UK£3.7 billion. Much of the approximately UK£450 million increase since 2001/02 has, however, been spent in Afghanistan, Iraq and Pakistan. The UK announced its new package of aid to Pakistan on 18 October 2001.

298

United Kingdom

Table 11. Aid to Afghanistan, Pakistan and Iraq, pre- and post-11 September 2001, UK£ 000

Country	2000/01	2001/02	2003/04
Afghanistan	116	216	50,000
Pakistan	12,810	42,690	65,000
Iraq	8,929	7,554	5,900
Iraq Emergency Assistance	0	0	195,000
TOTALS	21,855	50,460	315,900

Source: DFID allocation by country. Source: DFID Departmental Report 2003, Table 4, pg 126 - 127

- The UK has made a total financial commitment towards Iraq's reconstruction of £544m (or about US$900m) over the three-year period from 2003-06. All UK assistance is in the form of grants.
- In October 2003, the UK announced that in order to fulfil its commitment to reconstruction in Iraq, it would have to reduce aid allocations to middle-income countries. Aid programmes in more than 20 countries — mainly in South America and Eastern Europe — are affected. Planned bilateral spending in middle-income countries in 2004/5 and 2005/6 is being reduced by approximately £100m. Bilateral aid to some countries, including Peru, Honduras, Anguilla, Romania, Bulgaria, Croatia and Macedonia, is being withdrawn completely. Spending in countries such as South Africa, Sri Lanka, Bolivia, and Jamaica will be reduced.
- The Secretary of State for International Development argues that the diversion of

funds from middle-income countries is in line with DFID's commitment to increase the share of bilateral aid going to low-income countries to 90% by 2005/6. However, civil society groups expressed serious concern about the government's actions, emphasising that those affected would be some of the poorest populations in middle-income countries.

Proposal for an International Finance Facility

- In January 2003, the UK launched a proposal for an International Finance Facility (IFF). The aim of the Facility is to frontload aid spending in the years prior to 2015, by issuing bonds on the international markets. The UK proposes that donors should make legally binding commitments to allocate the increases in aid they pledged at the Monterrey Financing for Development Conference in 2002 (US$15 billion a year from 2006) to

United Kingdom

the new IFF fund. Using these collective commitments as collateral, the IFF will raise money on the international financial markets. The IFF will use the money raised to increase aid disbursements to developing countries substantially over the period 2006 to 2015. This increased spending is intended to ensure that the MDGs are reached and global poverty is halved. Essentially, the IFF enables aid money promised for the future to be spent now.[2]

- In order for the IFF to become a workable reality, a significant number of donor countries (at least three) must sign up. While initial reaction to the proposal was lukewarm, the UK has strongly promoted the IFF internationally and it is now gaining in popularity, although important donors, such as the United States, remain indifferent. Moreover, donors who already meet the UN target may look somewhat sceptically at proposals to increase aid, coming from countries that have not yet fulfilled their 0.7% commitment. A decision on the IFF is expected in 2004. If the Facility goes ahead, it is likely to be less ambitious and involve fewer donor countries than originally envisaged. UK-based NGOs have given a cautious welcome to the proposal, although reservations have been expressed about repayment periods and about the type of conditionality that some donors may wish to attach to IFF funding.

Emphasis on 'failed states'

- The UK government is paying greater attention to the issue of 'failed states', particularly as breeding grounds for conflict and potential havens for international terrorists. In 2003, the Strategy Unit in the Cabinet Office began

a wide-ranging review of issues related to 'failed states'. Although DFID has always promoted continued engagement with difficult and failing states, it remains to be seen if and how this broader government attention to the issue will affect development policy and aid allocations.

- The relationship between 'failed states', poor governance and conflict, has been emphasised by DFID and the Prime Minister. The UK has continued to focus significant attention on conflict prevention, including through the activities of the Global Conflict Prevention Pool. Initiatives to tackle corruption include the Extractive Industries Transparency Initiative (EITI), launched by Prime Minister Tony Blair at the World Summit on Sustainable Development in 2002. The EITI is a voluntary initiative aimed at increasing accountability and transparency with respect to revenues obtained from oil, gas and other natural resource extraction. NGOs welcomed efforts to improve transparency under the Initiative, but questioned whether a voluntary approach would work.

DFID assistance directly linked to PRS

- In 2002/3, DFID changed the way its country plans were developed. Country Assistance Plans (CAPs) are now based on local Poverty Reduction Strategies (PRS). Each CAP starts from the basis of the recipient country's PRS. DFID country teams must report annually on progress against national poverty indicators and the related targets in DFID's Public Service Agreement.

DFID's new Public Service Agreement (2003-06) ties DFID performance to achievements in 16 countries in Sub-Saharan Africa, and four countries in Asia.

United Kingdom

Notes

[1] Clare Short announces 15 million for Pakistan. DFID Web site: www.dfid.gov.uk/News/PressReleases/files/pr18oct01.html

[2] The International Finance Facility Briefing Note prepared by Development Initiatives (Draft), September 2003.

United States

Box 30. UNITED STATES at a glance

How much aid does the UNITED STATES give?

In 2002, UNITED STATES gave   US$13,290m

That means that, in 2002, each person
in the USA gave   US$46

In 2002, aid from the USA rose by   US$1,861m in case terms or by 15% in real
terms

How generous is the UNITED STATES?

UNITED STATES gave 0.13% of its national wealth in 2002. This compares with the average country effort of 0.41% and UNITED STATES own previous highpoint of 0.58% in 1965.

The USA was the least generous of all donors — but a little more generous than in 2001, when aid was 0.11% of GNI.

How much of UNITED STATES aid goes to the poorest countries and people?

34.1% total bilateral aid (US$3,603.3m) went to Least Developed and Low Income Countries where 3.5 million people (60% of the global population) live and where average incomes are less than two dollars a day.

How much of US aid was spent on basic health, basic education, water supply and sanitation?

UNITED STATES spent

1.8% of its bilateral aid (US$218.2m) on basic education

5.55% of its bilateral aid (US$672.82m) on basic health

0.69% of its bilateral aid (US$83.42m) on water and sanitation

A year of new initiatives – at what cost?

Patricia MacWilliams, InterAction[1]

The Bush Administration is at the forefront of an unexpected re-emergence of US foreign assistance in the political discourse. The introduction of the National Security Strategy in September 2002, which unites diplomacy, defence, and development, placed US foreign assistance squarely in the foreign policy arena. Indeed, as the President noted in an earlier speech, 'the advancement of development is a central commitment of American foreign policy.'[2] With the introduction of the most significant new foreign assistance initiative in decades – the Millennium Challenge Account, 21 new presidential initiatives on foreign assistance, and a re-recognition of HIV/AIDS as a security risk – the door has begun to open for a debate and reconsideration of the foundations of the foreign assistance approach of the US government.

However, with this opportunity come challenges. US development assistance appears to be increasingly viewed through the lens of US security interests and the war on terror. Continuing engagement in Iraq and Afghanistan threatens to drain financial and human resources away from other priority areas and programmes. A focus on short-term results is distracting stakeholders from meaningful discussions on achieving long-term goals.

President Bush introduced the Millennium Challenge Account (MCA) on the eve of the Monterrey Financing for Development Conference. The initiative heralds a potential transformation in how the US provides development assistance. The proposal pledged US$5 billion in new foreign assistance funding annually by 2006 to reward countries promoting economic development, good governance, and social investment. The MCA has been allocated US$1 billion in the 2004 budget, its first year of operation. The authorising document calls for an independent entity governed by a board, chaired by the Secretary of State and including the Secretary of Treasury, the Administrator of the US Agency for International Development (USAID), the CEO of the Millennium Challenge Corporation, the US Trade Representative and four delegates of US civil society, to be appointed by the President from a list provided by Congress and confirmed by the Senate. The head of the Millennium Challenge Corporation, which will manage the MCA, will be appointed by the President and confirmed by the Senate, and will report to the Board. While the programme is expected to support a select group of 'top' countries committed to limiting corruption, investing in people, and enabling economic freedom, the final

United States

implementing regulations have yet to be issued.

Civil society groups and Members of Congress have expressed concern about creating a new foreign assistance entity to function alongside USAID, the US government's primary development agency. They have questioned the Bush Administration's failure to promote a more coherent development policy, by repeatedly relying on ad hoc initiatives without visible coordination. While US civil society organisations support the US government's decision to increase foreign assistance and recognise the potential for innovation, they caution that the MCA poses a risk of reducing funding for core development assistance programmes. The effect may be to limit US government attention to a select group of countries with the greatest chance of 'success.'

During the 2003 State of the Union Address, the Administration announced an additional major presidential initiative, to provide US$15 billion over five years for HIV/ AIDS. However, this proposal removes a major component of HIV/AIDS operations from its traditional home within USAID, creating a new office within the State Department and further fragmenting assistance mechanisms. Congress has provided US$2.4 billion in funding for HIV/AIDS in 2004, of which US$491 million will be managed by the new Global Aids Coordinator Office within the State Department as proposed by the Administration, US$561million to the Child Survival and Health budget for USAID, an additional US$500 million for the Global Fund, and US$654 million for programmes managed by the Department of Health and Human Services.

In total, Congress approved US$17.2 billion in regular appropriations for Foreign Operations for the fiscal year 2004, more than US$1.5 billion short of the President's

request of US$18.9 billion. Although there was increased funding for the HIV/AIDS initiative from the level requested by the Administration, funding for the MCA was scaled down and funding for other core humanitarian and development programmes remained unchanged. However, when one looks below the surface, country allocations show an increasing shift of resources away from traditional recipients in Africa and Latin America, towards countries that are seen to be key allies and on the front lines of the war on terrorism. This, combined with the increased resources in extra budgetary appropriations or supplementary appropriations for contingencies emanating from Iraq and Afghanistan, has prompted many to charge that traditional humanitarian and development priorities are being threatened by the emphasis on new initiatives and security priorities.

Development through a national security lens

In short, the national security lens has increasingly caused the US government to view foreign assistance as a tool for short-term goals and quick fixes. The current Administration has proposed presidential initiatives falling outside the traditional foreign assistance entities. US development assistance delivery mechanisms have become fragmented, with multiple agencies within the US government responsible for foreign assistance delivery and an increasing reliance on budget allocations for discrete special projects. A proliferation of implementing entities, many with little experience in providing foreign assistance, complicates decision making, resulting in a loss of coherence and coordination in the delivery of aid. This escalating incoherence in foreign policy implementation is exacerbated by the US government's continued focus on a largely unilateral approach, characterised by

United States

decreasing consultation with development partners, other donors, and recipient countries.

In this increasingly splintered foreign assistance arena, particularly in light of the establishment of the Millennium Challenge Corporation, USAID continues to search for its identity. One of its assigned new roles is to address 'fragile, failing, and failed' states. These states, including Nigeria, Zimbabwe, and Somalia, are often far from the front lines of the war on terror, but nonetheless are seen as posing a danger to security and stability. The necessary strategy for supporting these states is not straightforward, nor can it be based on a simple formula. Expectations of USAID are high, as it must work closely with governments and their citizens to craft appropriate and original approaches to further development at the national level.

USAID is currently drafting a new strategy, which is expected to detail how the agency will meet the challenges of providing development assistance in this new environment. Expected themes include preparing countries for MCA eligibility, strengthening fragile, failing, and failed states in order to construct a platform for transformation, continuing the provision of humanitarian aid, and supporting 'strategic states', as identified by the State Department and National Security Council. Without a larger review of, and comprehensive policy for, foreign assistance priorities and mechanisms, this and any other USAID strategy risks failure.

US policy and practice on governance and human rights

The US government has laid out its strategy towards governance and human rights in the in the first joint US State Department-USAID Strategic Plan, based on the earlier National Security Strategy. The US government defines governance as 'the development of

democratic institutions and processes to guarantee the rule of law; freedoms of speech, association, and worship; respect for women; and respect for private property'.[3] The promotion of democratic governance is seen as the best way to promote human rights, where these rights are prioritised for their ability to 'secure the peace, deter aggression, promote the rule of law, combat crime and corruption, strengthen democracies, and prevent humanitarian crises.'[4]

An example of this approach is the new presidential Middle East Program Initiative (MEPI), which was introduced by the Administration in May 2003. In his introductory speech, President Bush reiterated US commitment to advancing 'freedom and peace' in the Middle East as the best means of ensuring US security.[5] MEPI has been described as a 're-aligning of existing bilateral economic programs to champion democratic principles'. The programme prioritises economic and political development to ensure the strengthening of financial systems, electoral institutions and processes, legislative reforms, and trade education. Additional funding is provided for curriculum development, teacher training, and leadership training for women business and political leaders.

The promotion of democracy and the protection of national interests appear to have become synonymous in US government rhetoric. The US government frames the struggle for its national security in terms of the promotion of freedoms. But its own approach has not led to a transformation in foreign assistance that ensures the promotion, protection, and fulfilment of all the freedoms embodied in international human rights instruments. Neither has it resulted in greater transparency and accountability in governance by developing country recipients.

United States

Just as US organisations are raising concerns over the limited number of countries expected to be reached by the MCA, some groups have expressed reservations about the US government's narrow definition of governance, with its apparent emphasis on central government structures and the economic environment. By contrast, some US groups have introduced grassroots civil society development into their governance programming, in order to strengthen local capacity to fully participate in decision making. A few groups have begun to employ a human rights analysis when developing and implementing programming, enabling them to give more attention to political development and the roles and responsibilities of those having rights and obligations in society.

One of the legacies of the Bush presidency will be the heightened attention paid to foreign assistance. Indeed, the increasing consideration by the Administration and Congress of the priorities and intentions of foreign assistance has created an unprecedented opportunity to remake foreign assistance into an effective tool to eradicate poverty and bring about a safer and more equitable world. Realising this vision will require the creation and implementation of a comprehensive US foreign assistance strategy to ensure the fulfilment of these long-term development aims as well as these foundational national security interests.

Notes

[1] Parts of this analysis are drawn from an InterAction Policy Paper 'Emerging Trends', published in November 2003.

[2] President Bush remarks on Global Development at the Inter-American Development Bank, Washington, DC, March 14, 2002.

[3] 'Strategic Plan, 2004-2009' US Department of State and US Agency for International Development, August 2003, p. 19.

[4] Ibid. US Department of State, Bureau of Democracy, Human Rights, and Labor. www.state.gov/g/drl/hr/

[5] President Bush, 'Remarks in Commencement Address at the University of South Carolina', May 9, 2003. www.mepi.state.gov

Part VII
Reference Section

Boxes and Tables

Boxes

Tables

Boxes and Tables

Graphs

Figures

Glossary of Aid Terms

20/20 An Initiative proposed at the **Copenhagen Social Summit** (WSSD) for bilateral agreements between donor and recipient governments, whereby donors would agree to allocate 20% of their ODA to Basic Social Services (BSS) if recipients agreed to allocate 20% of public expenditure to enable universal access to Basic Social Services (BSS).

ACP African, Caribbean and Pacific States (see Lomé Convention).

ADB Asian Development Bank

AECI Spanish Agency for International Cooperation

AfDB African Development Bank

Aid see ODA Official Development Assistance

AIDS Acquired Immune Deficiency Syndrome

APEC Asia-Pacific Economic Cooperation, or APEC, is the premier forum for facilitating economic growth, cooperation, trade and investment in the Asia-Pacific region. APEC is the only inter governmental grouping in the world operating on the basis of non-binding commitments, open dialogue and equal respect for the views of all participants. Unlike the WTO or other multilateral trade bodies, APEC has no treaty obligations required of its participants. Decisions made within APEC are reached by consensus and commitments are undertaken on a voluntary basis. APEC has 21 members — referred to as 'Member Economies' — which account for more than 2.5 billion people, a combined GDP of 19 trillion US dollars and 47% of world trade.

APEC's 21 Member Economies are Australia; Brunei Darussalam; Canada; Chile; People's Republic of China; Hong Kong, China; Indonesia; Japan; Republic of Korea; Malaysia; Mexico; New Zealand; Papua New Guinea; Peru; The Republic of the Philippines; The Russian Federation; Singapore; Chinese Taipei; Thailand; United States of America; Vietnam.

ASEAN Association of South East Asian Nations

Associated Financing is the combination of Official Development Assistance, whether grants or loans, with any other funding to form finance packages. Associated Financing packages are subject to the same criteria of concessionality, developmental relevance and recipient country eligibility as *Tied Aid Credits*.

African Union (AU) Formed following the September 1999 Sirte Declaration by African Heads of State and Government, the AU succeeds the Organisation of African Unity (OAU) as the premier vehicle for accelerating integration in Africa, ensuring an appropriate role for Africa in the global economy, while addressing multifaceted social, economic and political problems compounded by certain negative aspects of globalisation. See http://www.africa-union.org

Bilateral Aid is provided to developing countries and countries on Part II of the DAC List on a country-to-country basis, and to institutions (normally in Britain), working in fields related to these countries.

Bilateral portfolio investment includes bank

311

Glossary of Aid Terms

lending, and the purchase of shares, bonds and real estate.

Bond Lending refers to net completed international bonds issued by countries on the DAC List of Aid Recipients.

BoP Balance of payments

BSS Basic Social Services (Basic Education, basic health and nutrition, safe water and sanitation) defined for the purposes of the 20/20 Initiative

Budgetary Aid is general financial assistance given in certain cases to dependent territories to cover a recurrent budget deficit.

CAP The Consolidated Appeal Process for complex humanitarian emergencies managed by UNOCHA

CAP Common Agricultural Policy (EU)

CDF Comprehensive Development Framework used by The World Bank

CEC Commission of the European Community

CEE/CA Countries of Central and Eastern Europe and Central Asia

CIS Commonwealth of Independent States

Commitment a firm obligation, expressed in writing and backed by the necessary funds, undertaken by an official donor to provide specified assistance to a recipient country or a multilateral organisation. Bilateral commitments are recorded in the full amount of expected transfer, irrespective of the time required for the completion of disbursements.

Concessionality Level is a measure of the 'softness' of a credit reflecting the benefit to the borrower compared to a loan at market rate (cf *Grant Element*).

Constant Prices Prices adjusted to take

inflation and exchange rates into account and so make a 'like with like' comparison over time.

Cotonou Partnership Agreement Signed in Cotonou, Benin, on 23 June 2000, the agreement replaces the Lomé Convention, as the framework for trade and cooperation between the EU and its Member States and African, Caribbean and Pacific (ACP) States. For more information, go to: http://europa.eu.int/comm/development/body/cotonou/index_en.htm

Current (cash) prices are prices not adjusted for inflation.

DAC Development Assistance Committee — the DAC of the Organisation for Economic Cooperation and Development (OECD) is a forum for consultation among 21 donor countries, together with the European Commission, on how to increase the level and effectiveness of aid flows to all aid recipient countries. The member countries are Australia, Austria, Belgium, Canada, Denmark, Finland, France, Germany, Ireland, Italy, Japan, Luxembourg, Netherlands, New Zealand, Norway, Portugal, Spain, Sweden, Switzerland, UK and USA. DAC sets the definitions and criteria for aid statistics internationally.

Debt Relief may take the form of cancellation, rescheduling, refinancing or re-organisation of debt.

a. Debt cancellation is relief from the burden of repaying both the principal and interest on past loans.

b. Debt rescheduling is a form of relief by which the dates on which

Glossary of Aid Terms

principal or interest payments are due are delayed or re-arranged.

c. *Debt refinancing* is a form of relief in which a new loan or grant is arranged to enable the debtor country to meet the service payments on an earlier loan.

d. *Official bilateral debts* are re-organised in the Paris club of official bilateral creditors. The Paris Club has devised the following arrangements for reducing and rescheduling the debt of the poorest, most indebted countries.

Toronto Terms agreed by the Paris Club in 1988 provided up to 33% debt relief on rescheduled official bilateral debt owed by the poorest, most indebted countries pursuing internationally agreed economic reform programmes.

Trinidad Terms agreed by the Paris Club in 1990 superseded Toronto Terms and provided up to 50% debt relief.

Naples Terms agreed by the Paris Club in 1994 superseded Trinidad Terms and provide up to 67% debt relief. They also introduced the option of a one-off reduction of 67% in the stock of official bilateral debt owed by the poorest, most indebted countries with an established track record of economic reform and debt servicing.

Enhanced Naples Terms Under the Heavily-Indebted Poor Countries (HIPC) debt initiative, Paris Club members have agreed to increase the amount of debt relief to eligible countries to up to 80%.

Developing Country The DAC defines a list of developing countries eligible to receive ODA. In 1996 a number of countries, including Israel, ceased to be eligible for ODA. A second group of countries, 'Countries and Territories in Transition' including Central and Eastern Europe are eligible for 'Official Aid' — not to be confused with 'Official Development Assistance'. OA has the same terms and conditions as ODA, but it does not count towards the 0.7% target, because it is not going to developing countries

Developing Countries Developing countries are all countries and territories in Africa; in America (except the United States, Canada, Bahamas, Bermuda, Cayman Islands and Falkland Islands); in Asia (except Japan, Brunei, Hong Kong, Israel, Kuwait, Qatar, Singapore, Taiwan and United Arab Emirates); in the Pacific (except Australia and New Zealand); and Albania, Armenia, Azerbaijan, Georgia, Gibraltar, Malta, Moldova, Turkey and the states of ex-Yugoslavia in Europe.

DFID Department for International Development (UK)

Disbursement Disbursements record the actual international transfer of financial resources, or of goods or services valued at the cost to the donor. In the case of activities carried out in donor countries, such as training, administration or public awareness programmes, disbursement is taken to have occurred when the funds have been transferred to the service provider or the recipient. They may be recorded *gross* (the total amount disbursed over a given accounting period) or *net* (less any repayments of loan principal during the same period).

Glossary of Aid Terms

EBRD European Bank for Reconstruction and Development

EC European Community

ECHO European Community Humanitarian Office

ECOSOC Economic and Social Council (UN)

ECOWAS Economic Community of West African States, described at: http://www.ecowas.int/

EDF European Development Fund – see Lomé Convention and Cotonou Partnership Agreement.

EFA Education for All

EIB European Investment Bank

EMU Economic and Monetary Union

ESAF (E/Sal/F) Enhanced Structural Adjustment (Loan)/Facility

Export Credits are loans for the purpose of trade extended by the official or the private sector. If extended by the private sector, they may be supported by official guarantees.

FAO Food and Agricultural Organisation (UN)

G24 Group of 24 developed nations meeting to coordinate assistance to Central and Eastern Europe

GATT General Agreement on Tariffs and Trade

GDP Gross Domestic Product

GEF Global Environment Facility

Gini coefficient is an indicator of income distribution, where 0 represents perfect equality and 1 perfect inequality.

GNI Gross National Income. Most OECD countries have introduced a new system of national accounts which has replaced Gross National Product (GNP) with GNI. As GNI has generally been higher than GNP, ODA/GNI ratios are slightly lower than previously reported ODA/GNP ratios.

GNP Gross National Product

Grant element reflects the *financial terms* of a commitment: interest rate, *maturity* and *grace period* (interval to first repayment of capital). It measures the concessionality of a loan, expressed as the percentage by which the present value of the expected stream of repayments falls short of the repayments that would have been generated at a given reference rate of interest. The reference rate is 10% in DAC statistics. Thus, the grant element is nil for a loan carrying an interest rate of 10%; it is 100 per cent for a grant; and it lies between these two limits for a loan at less than 10% interest. If the face value of a loan is multiplied by its grant element, the result is referred to as the *grant equivalent* of that loan (cf *concessionality level*) (Note: the grant element concept is not applied to the market-based non-concessional operations of the multilateral development banks.)

GSP General System of Preferences

HIC High Income Countries – those with an annual per capita income of more than US\$ 9385 in 1995.

HIPC Highly Indebted Poor Country (Debt Initiative)

HIV Human Immunodeficiency Virus

IADB InterAmerican Development Bank

IASC Inter-Agency Standing Committee (Committee responsible to ECOSOC for overseeing humanitarian affairs, the work of OCHA and the CAP).

IDA International Development Association (World Bank)

IDPs Internationally displaced persons

IDT International Development Targets

Glossary of Aid Terms

(for 2015) as outlined in the DAC document 'Shaping the 21st Century' also known as International Development Goals

IFAD International Fund for Agricultural Development

IFC International Finance Corporation

IFIs International Financial Institutions

IMF International Monetary Fund

Internal Bank Lending is net lending to countries on the List of Aid Recipients by commercial banks in the Bank of International Settlements reporting area, ie most OECD countries and most offshore financial centres (Bahamas, Bahrain, Cayman Islands, Hong Kong, Netherlands Antilles and Singapore), net of lending to banks in the same offshore financial centres. Loans from central monetary authorities are excluded. Guaranteed bank loans and bonds are included under *other private or bond lending.*

IsDB Islamic Development Bank

JANIC Japanese NGO Centre for International Cooperation

JICA Japan International Cooperation Agency

LIC Low Income Countries — those with an annual per capita income of less than US$765 in 1995

LDC (or sometimes LLDC) Least Developed Country — 48 poor and vulnerable countries are so defined by the United Nations, with an annual per capita income of less than US$765 in 1995

LMIC Lower Middle Income Countries — those with an annual per capita income of between US$766 and US$3035 in 1995

Lomé Convention Multi annual framework agreement covering development cooperation between the EU members and African, Caribbean and Pacific (ACP) States. Funding for Lomé came from the **EDF.** Lomé has now been replaced by the Cotonou Partnership Agreement.

MADCT More Advanced Developing Countries and Territories, comprising those that have been transferred to Part II of the DAC List of Aid Recipients. MDGs or Millennium Development Goals are the international goals for poverty reduction and development agreed by the United Nations in the year 2000. These include the IDTs.

Multilateral Agencies are international institutions with governmental membership, which conduct all or a significant part of their activities in favour of development and aid recipient countries. They include multilateral development banks (eg The World Bank, regional development banks), United Nations agencies, and regional groupings (eg certain European Union and Arab agencies). A contribution by a DAC Member to such an agency is deemed to be multilateral if it is pooled with other contributions and disbursed at the discretion of the agency. Unless otherwise indicated, capital subscriptions to multilateral development banks are recorded on a *deposit* basis, ie in the amount and as at the date of lodgement of the relevant letter of credit or other negotiable instrument. Limited data are available on an encashment basis, ie at the date and in the amount of each drawing made by the agency on letters or other instruments.

Multilateral aid is Aid channelled through international bodies for use in or on behalf of aid recipient countries.

Glossary of Aid Terms

Aid channelled through multilateral agencies is regarded as bilateral where the donor controls the use and destination of the funds.

Multilateral portfolio investment covers the transactions of the private non-bank and bank sector in the securities issued by multilateral institutions.

NEPAD New Partnership for Africa's Development. For information, go to http://www.nepad.org/ and see also African Union.

NGDO Non Governmental Development Organisation

NGO (PVO) Non-Governmental Organisations (Private Voluntary Organisations) also referred to as Voluntary Agencies. They are private non-profit-making bodies that are active in development work.

NIC Newly industrialised countries

NIPs National Indicative Programmes (EU)

NPV Net Present Value

OA Official Assistance (Aid) is government assistance with the same terms and conditions as ODA, but which goes to Countries and Territories in Transition which include former aid recipients and Central and Eastern European Countries and the Newly Independent States. It does not count towards the 0.7% target.

OAU Organisation of African Unity — now succeeded by African Union.

OCHA (See UNOCHA)

ODA Official Development Assistance (often referred to as 'aid') of which at least 25% must be a grant. The promotion of economic development or welfare must be the main objective. It must go to a developing country as defined by the DAC

ODF Official Development Finance is used in measuring the inflow of resources to recipient countries; includes [a]

bilateral ODA, [b] grants and concessional and non-concessional development lending by multilateral financial institutions, and [c] Other Official Flows that are considered developmental (including refinancing loans) which have too low a *grant element* to qualify as ODA.

OECD Organisation for Economic Cooperation and Development (see DAC)

OHCHR Office of the UN High Commissioner for Human Rights

OOF Other Official Flows — defined as flows to aid recipient countries by the official sector that do not satisfy both the criteria necessary for ODA or OA.

PARIS21 Partnership in Statistics for Development — capacity programme for statistical development

Partially Untied Aid is *Official Development Assistance* (or Official Aid) for which the associated goods and services must be procured in the donor country or a restricted group of other countries, which must however include substantially all recipient countries. Partially untied aid is subject to the same disciplines as *Tied Aid* and *Associated Financing*.

PRGF the Poverty Reduction and Growth Facility, which replaces the ESAF and is the name given to IMF Loan Facilities to developing countries. (See also *PRSP*).

Private Flows are long-term (more than one year) capital transactions by OECD residents (as defined for balance of payment purposes) with aid recipient countries, or through multilateral agencies for the benefit of such countries. They include all forms of investment, including *international bank lending* and *Export Credits*

Glossary of Aid Terms

where the original maturity exceeds one year. Private flows are reported to DAC separately for *Direct Investment*, *Export Credits* and *International Bank Lending, Bond Lending* and *Other Private* (lending).

Programme Aid is financial assistance specifically to fund (i) a range of general imports, or (ii) an integrated programme of support for a particular sector, or (iii) discrete elements of a recipient's budgetary expenditure. In each case, support is provided as part of a World Bank/ IMF coordinated structural adjustment programme.

PRSP   Poverty Reduction Strategy Papers

Real Terms A figure adjusted to take account of exchange rates and inflation, allowing a 'real' comparison over time — see *Constant Prices*

Recipient Countries and Territories is the current DAC list of Aid Recipients — see *LDC, LIC, LMIC, UMIC, HIC*.

Soft Loan A loan of which the terms are more favourable to the borrower than those currently attached to commercial market terms. It is described as concessional and the degree of concessionality is expressed as its grant element.

SPA   Special Programme of Assistance for Africa (World Bank)

SSA   Sub-Saharan Africa

SWA (SWAp) Sector Wide Approach

TA or TC Technical Assistance/Cooperation — includes both [a] grants to nationals of aid recipient countries receiving education or training at home or abroad, and [b] payments to consultants, advisers, and similar personnel as well as teachers and administrators serving in recipient countries (including the cost of associated equipment). Assistance of

this kind provided specifically to facilitate the implementation of a capital project is included indistinguishably among bilateral project and programme expenditures, and is omitted from technical cooperation in statistics of aggregate flows.

Tied Aid is Aid given on the condition that it can only be spent on goods and services from the donor country. Tied aid credits are subject to certain disciplines concerning their concessionality levels, the countries to which they may be directed, and their development relevance — designed to try to avoid using aid funds on projects that would be commercially viable with market finance, and to ensure that recipient countries receive good value.

TNC   Transnational Corporation

UMIC   Upper Middle Income Countries — those with an annual per capita income of between US$3036 and US$9385 in 1995

UN   United Nations

UNAIDS   Joint United Nations Programme on HIV/AIDS

UNCED   United Nations Conference on Environment and Development, Rio de Janeiro 1992

UNCHS   United Nations Centre for Human Settlements, Habitat

UNCTAD   United Nations Conference on Trade and Development

UNDCF   United Nations Capital Development Fund

UNDAC   United Nations Disaster Assessment and Coordination

UNDAF   United Nations Development Assistance Framework

UNDCP   United Nations Drugs Control Programmes

Glossary of Aid Terms

UNDP United Nations Development Programme

UNEP United Nations Environment Programme

UNESCO United Nations Educational, Scientific and Cultural Organisation

UNFPA United Nations Fund for Population Activities

UNHCR Office of the United Nations High Commissioner for Refugees

UNICEF United Nations Children's Fund

UNIDO United Nations Industrial Development Organisation

UNIFEM United Nations Development Fund for Women

UNITAR United Nations Institute for Training and Research

UNOCHA UN Office for the Coordination of Humanitarian Assistance

UNRISD United Nations Research Institute for Social Development

Untied Aid *Official Development Assistance* for which the associated goods and services may be fully and freely procured in substantially all countries.

UNV United Nations Volunteers

Uruguay Round Last round of multilateral trade negotiations under the GATT

WFP World Food Programme

WHO World Health Organisation

WID Women in Development

WSSD World Summit for Social Development, Copenhagen 1995. See 20/20 Initiative.

Sources consulted include: Reality of Aid, annual Development Cooperation Report of the DAC

WTO World Trade Organisation

Exchange Rates

Exchange rates of national currencies per US$
Updated January 2004
Average annualised US$ exchange rates for aid donors
Source: OECD DAC Statistics

	2001	2002	2003
Australia	1.94	1.84	1.54
Austria	15.37	1.06	0.89
Belgium	45.04	1.06	0.89
Canada	1.55	1.57	1.40
Denmark	8.32	7.88	6.58
Finland	6.64	1.06	0.89
France	7.32	1.06	0.89
Germany	2.18	1.06	0.89
Greece	380.49	1.06	0.89
Ireland	0.88	1.06	0.89
Italy	2.16	1.06	0.89
Japan (1)	121.50	125.20	115.90
Luxembourg	45.04	1.06	0.89
Netherlands	2.46	1.06	0.89
New Zealand	2.38	2.16	1.72
Norway	8.99	7.99	7.08
Portugal	223.86	1.06	0.89
Spain	185.79	1.06	0.89
Sweden	10.34	9.72	8.08
Switzerland	1.69	1.56	1.35
United Kingdom	0.69	0.67	0.61
United States	1.00	1.00	1.00
ECU/EURO	1.12	1.06	0.89

(1) Unit of national currency for 0.001US$